Markus Dahlweid, Uwe Schulze

High Level Transition Systems of CSP Specifications

Markus Dahlweid, Uwe Schulze

High Level Transition Systems of CSP Specifications

and their Application in Automated Testing

VDM Verlag Dr. Müller

Imprint

Bibliographic information by the German National Library: The German National Library lists this publication at the German National Bibliography; detailed bibliographic information is available on the Internet at http://dnb.d-nb.de.

Cover image: www.purestockx.com

Publisher:
VDM Verlag Dr. Müller Aktiengesellschaft & Co. KG , Dudweiler Landstr. 125 a, 66123 Saarbrücken, Germany,
Phone +49 681 9100-698, Fax +49 681 9100-988,
Email: info@vdm-verlag.de

Zugl.: Bremen, University, Diss., 2004

Produced in USA and UK by:
Lightning Source Inc., La Vergne, Tennessee, USA
Lightning Source UK Ltd., Milton Keynes, UK
BookSurge LLC, 5341 Dorchester Road, Suite 16, North Charleston, SC 29418, USA

ISBN: 978-3-639-00972-9

Abstract

State of the art quality assurance for safety critical software systems requires formal methods for verification and testing. The context of this thesis is the field of specification based testing of embedded reactive real-time systems. One of the drawbacks using formal methods to model large systems is the state explosion of transition systems generated from formal specifications. In this PhD-thesis the authors present an approach to reduce the problem of state explosions using a representation of the transition system of a CSP specification, that does not require the calculation of the complete state space.

The new representation consists of two parts: *high level transition graphs* to model sequential processes containing only low-level CSP operators and *synchronisation terms* that represent the high-level communication structure of sequential components expressed using high level transition graphs. High level transition graphs are an extension of conventional transition systems, which in addition to events also contain conditions and assignments of CSP specifications at the transitions. Those events and conditions can contain parameters and parametrised expressions. The value of a parameter is bound through assignments at transitions, which are created for those CSP operators like process references or prefixing that can introduce new variable bindings to a CSP specification. With this extension, a node in a high level transition graph can represent multiple states of the complete state space. The interpretation of a high level transition graph requires the evaluation of the conditions, events and assignments of a transition to perform a state change.

Specification based real-time testing requires an upper bound of time required for the calculation of the initial actions and refusals of a location. One way to achieve this is using normalised transition systems. Different stages of the normalisation of high level transition graphs and synchronisation terms have been developed, which can directly be used for real-time testing. To enable real-time testing with unnormalised graphs, an on-the-fly normalisation is introduced which imposes certain requirements on the CSP specification.

In some cases, the test evaluation needs not to be performed in real-time. Instead it is often sufficient to do the test evaluation with a slight delay of a few seconds. For those cases a new test algorithm for a delayed test evaluation is suggested, which can be used for testing purposes based on any type of transition systems, even unnormalised systems.

ii

Contents

List of Figures

List of Tables

Chapter 1

Introduction

The PhD-thesis *High Level Transition Systems of CSP Specifications and their Application in Automated Testing* is a joint work of the authors Markus Dahlweid and Uwe Schulze. The main focus of this thesis lies in the topic of specification based testing of embedded real-time reactive systems. During their research the two authors have been using the RT-Tester tool [ ] in several industrial projects. The RT-Tester – a product of the cooperation of University Bremen and Verified Systems International – is an automatic test system, that allows automatic test case generation and evaluation, based on formal specifications.

Test cases for the RT-Tester are usually developed using the formal event based specification language CSP[ ]. An introduction to CSP with its basic concepts and semantics is given in chapter 2. A process definition of such a test specification is parsed by a model checker and transformed into a normalised transition system. An overview of transition system concepts including their normalisation is provided in chapter 3.

The nodes of the generated transition system represent the internal states of the specified systems, and the transitions are labelled with events, which are used to model state changes. Transforming the generated transition system into its normal form, allows an interpretation of the simulated systems behaviour in hard real-time. This property of normalised transition systems has been proven in the normal form theorem in [ ].

Transition Systems

Especially when using large data-dependent or parallel specifications, the generation of the corresponding normalised transition system can lead to a state explosion. This is caused by the structure of the graphs, which are based on unfolding the complete state-space of the specification. A subsequent normalisation may even increase the size of the resulting graph.

One goal of this thesis is to develop a high level form of transition systems based on CSP specifications, that avoids many of the problems leading a to state explosion. The restriction remains, that those graphs still must be usable for the generation and evaluation of test cases in real-time.

The approach developed in chapter 5 of this thesis is based on the idea not to evaluate all variables, expressions, assignments and conditions existing in a CSP specification, but instead to keep these information labelled to the transitions in a new transition graph representation. In contrast to conventional transition systems, these types of transition systems model multiple events of one channel at a single transition instead of representing only one event at each transition. Each of these modelled events may contain variables and expressions that have to be evaluated using the current values of free variables, which values are determined by earlier assignments. Related to each of these events is a set of assignments, that are used to compute new variable *bindings* based on the values used to evaluate the expressions of the event. The labels at the transitions of the new type of transition system also contains conditions, which again may use variables in its boolean expressions. Those conditions must hold, before the corresponding transition may be taken.

These extended transition graphs are called *high level transition graphs*. With these extensions of conventional transition graphs, it is possible to model multiple states of the represented system in one single *location*. For the generation of those new transition systems, it is no longer necessary to compute all possible states of the simulated system, because the selected representation contains all variables and expressions of the CSP specification. It is in fact also possible to find a finite representation for certain types of infinite CSP specifications, since the complete state space is never unfolded. The generation of these transition systems is defined in chapter 7. In appendix A it is shown that the high level transition graphs of a CSP process in combination with the execution rules defined in chapter 5 is semantically equivalent to a conventional transition graph of the same process.

The results of the PhD-thesis of Oliver Meyer [ ] shows that it is possible to decompose Timed CSP specifications into an Untimed CSP specifications running in parallel with timer processes. The proven decomposition theorem allows to consider only Untimed CSP specification in this thesis, since a timed specification, which is used for testing, is assumed to be decomposed before the considerations of this thesis are applied. This allows the use of Untimed CSP specifications for timed testing purposes.

The authors additionally suggest to decompose an Untimed CSP specification into multiple sequential CSP processes, which are connected by high-level operators defining communication rule between the sub-processes. These communication rules are represented by *synchronisation terms*, which are introduced in section 5.2. Using these terms, it is no longer necessary to explicitly compute all combinations of states of parallel systems during the transition system generation process, which is another reason for state explosions of conventional transition systems derived from CSP specifications.

High level transition graphs are transition systems annotated with variable information and predicates. Similar approaches have been developed for other standard techniques like petri-nets and timed automata. Such related research is presented in chapter 9 and is compared to the results of this thesis. Additionally tools for generating different types of transition systems from formal specifications are discussed in this chapter.

Specification Based Testing

The evaluation of conventional transition systems in hard real-time forms the basis for an evaluation of the test results during a test run, as explained in chapter 10. In general only normalised transition systems allow an evaluation in real-time. Because each node represents exactly one state of the CSP process and each transition is labelled with exactly one event, an upper bound can be determined for each transition system, indicating how many transition have to be inspected at maximum, to determine the set of possible events in a state. This is possible since normalised graphs are always deterministic. Different normalisation algorithms for high level transition graphs and synchronisation terms are presented in chapter 8.

In general high level transition graphs cannot be evaluated in real-time, since they are not normalised and may be non-deterministic. Therefore it is not always possible to determine the exact current location after a given trace of events, since there may exist multiple possible locations. But the expressions in the events, assignments or conditions can be evaluated in hard real-time by using a representation technique like *Binary Decision Diagrams*, which are discussed in chapter 4.

One way to remove the non-determinism from transition systems is normalising them. But completely normalising the high level transition graphs would result in the same problems as with conventional transition systems, because the whole state space has to be calculated during the normalisation. Instead a normalisation of the synchronisation terms is suggested, which changes their structure into a standardised form. This can be done without effecting the semantics of the represented synchronisation term. This approach, which is explained in chapter 11, allows the evaluation of the represented transition system in hard real-time if certain design-patterns are used. Especially in the field of testing, those suggested design patterns typically impose no large restrictions on the test case design.

Testing with unnormalised high level transition graphs is discussed in chapter 12. It requires new concepts like an *on-the-fly* normalisation and an exploration of the state space, to evaluate the transition system in real-time. If a transition system is used to validate a test case, it is not always necessary to traverse the transition system in hard real-time, since a detection of errors of the system under test with a slight delay is often acceptable. Therefore a *delayed evaluation* algorithm is suggested, which allows to use any of the transition system types, that are considered in this thesis. Such algorithm can for example be used in an evaluator component of a test system.

Chapter 13 summarises the part about testing in this thesis. It compares the developed testing methods, and identifies appropriate applications and test designs for each method.

Implementation

The implementation of the CSP interpreter ClaO, which has been developed by the authors for their diploma thesis, has been extended by several components that constructs different types of transition systems as described above. Algorithms have been developed and implemented, that normalise synchronisation terms to completely unfolded transition systems, or ones that produces a normal form of synchronisation terms using normalised graphs for the sequential components.

The transition systems that are produced by this components are exported to a format, which can be processed by a specialised abstract machine of the RT-Tester tool, that has also been implemented for this purpose. Those implementations allow to use the new types of transition system representation directly in the RT-Tester tool together with conventional methods for testing purposes. The different tools of the ClaO system are introduced in chapter 14 while major concepts of the implementation are summarised in chapter 15.

Declaration of Authorship

Since this thesis is a joint work of the authors Markus Dahlweid and Uwe Schulze, the PhD examination regulations of the University Bremen requires a declaration of authorship, that shows the author of each chapter or section of this thesis. The following table assigns an author to each section. Sections or chapters, that have been written by both authors are declared as joint work. If a complete chapter was written by a single author, his name is not repeated for each section of the chapter.

Section	Title	Author
1	Introduction	Dahlweid, Schulze
2	CSP – Syntax and Semantics	
2.1	An Introduction to CSP	Dahlweid
2.2	CSP Syntax	Schulze
2.3	Semantics of CSP	Dahlweid
2.4	Operational Semantics of CSP	Dahlweid
2.5	Denotational Semantics of CSP	Dahlweid
3	Transition Systems and Graphs	Dahlweid
3.1	Introduction to Transition Systems	
3.2	Normalising a Labelled Transition System	
4	Binary Decision Diagrams	Schulze
4.1	An Introduction to BDDs	
4.2	Binary Decision Diagrams of General Expressions	
5	Definitions	Dahlweid, Schulze
5.1	Introduction to High Level Transition Graphs for Low Level CSP Operators	
5.2	Representing High-Level Operators	
6	Graphical Representation	Schulze
6.1	Locations	
6.2	Labels	
6.3	Graph Abbreviations	
6.4	Synchronisation Terms	
7	Generating HLTG and Synchronisation Terms	
7.1	Process Definitions	Schulze
7.2	Low level Operators	Schulze
7.3	High Level Operators	Dahlweid
8	Normalisation	Dahlweid
8.1	Normalising Sequential Graphs	
8.2	Parallel Normalisation Graphs	
8.3	Synchronised Normalisation Graphs	
8.4	Conclusion	
9	Related and Future Work	
9.1	FDR	Dahlweid
9.2	Timed Automata	Dahlweid
9.3	Hybrid Automata	Dahlweid
9.4	High-level Petri Nets	Dahlweid
9.5	SPIN	Schulze

Section	Title	Author
10	Specification based Testing	Dahlweid
10.1	Testing of Embedded Systems	
10.2	Test Theory for Untimed CSP	
10.3	Automated Test Systems	
11	Testing with normalised Transition Graphs	Dahlweid
11.1	Testing with Roscoe Style Graphs	
11.2	Testing with Synchronisation Terms	
12	Testing with High Level Transition Graphs	
12.1	Representation	Schulze
12.2	Exploring the State-Space	Schulze
12.3	Trace Generation	Schulze
12.4	Testing	Dahlweid, Schulze
12.5	Real-Time Capabilities	Dahlweid, Schulze
12.6	Delayed Evaluation	Dahlweid, Schulze
13	Implications for Test-Designs	Dahlweid, Schulze
13.1	Comparison of Transition Systems	
13.2	Test Case Design	
14	Applications	
14.1	Strict Alternation	Dahlweid
14.2	`csp_parser`	Schulze
14.3	ClaO	Schulze
14.4	XClaO	Dahlweid
14.5	`csp2rtt`	Dahlweid
14.6	`csp2alpha`	Schulze
14.7	`rttctgam`	Dahlweid
15	ClaO Implementation	
15.1	Abstract Syntax	Schulze
15.2	Classes of the Abstract Syntax	Dahlweid, Schulze
15.3	Supported Syntax	Dahlweid
15.4	Interpretation of CSP Specifications	Dahlweid
15.5	Compiling HLTGs	Schulze
15.6	High Level Transition Graph Classes	Dahlweid, Schulze
16	Conclusion	Dahlweid, Schulze
16.1	Summary	
16.2	Contributions	
16.3	Future Work	

Part I

Theoretical Background

Part 1

Theoretical Background

In the first part of this thesis the foundation of the theoretical background is presented, that is required for the results of the author's research work, which is going to be presented in later parts. The first chapter gives a brief introduction to CSP and its syntax. Beginning from section 2.3 the different semantics of CSP are described in more detail. Especially the operational and denotational semantics are required for the understanding of generating high level transition graphs in chapter 7 and normalising them as described in chapter 8.

An introduction to transition systems and graphs and normalisation of those graph structures are described in chapter 3. This topic is required as foundation of the chapters describing the structure of high level transition graphs (chapter 5) and the normalisation of high level transition graphs (chapter 8).

The final chapter in this part describes the structure of Binary Decision Diagrams (BDD) and their use in representing mathematical expressions. BDDs can be employed to represent expressions in high level transition graphs. This technique is used for testing purposes as explained in chapter 12.

12

Chapter 2

CSP – Syntax and Semantics

In 1985 Charles Antony Richard Hoare published a book about Communicating Sequential Processes [ ] in which he describes the formal language CSP that can be used to model "computer systems which continuously act and interact with their environment".

This chapter gives a brief introduction to the syntax and semantics of CSP and its machine readable form CSP$_M$. After a short introduction to the basic concepts of CSP, to give the reader an impression on the authors view on the application of the language, the formal syntax of CSP$_M$ will be introduced in section 2.2. Finally the semantical models of CSP are described in section 2.3.

2.1 An Introduction to CSP

As computer systems are steadily growing and getting more complex it is required that the development of those systems are done by large teams, who work on the same project, but often don't even know each other, since they are working on different parts of the system. The programmers often loose the view on the whole system, and only focus on those parts he is responsible for. But sometimes a small change, which was intended to have only a local effect, in fact results in a change to the whole systems behaviour. In case of safety critical systems, this may lead to catastrophic events.

Even if state of the art quality assurance methods are applied to the product cycle, such disasters cannot always be prevented, since the basis for most safety critical systems are requirement documents, which are written in natural languages. "Documents written in natural languages are always susceptible to misunderstanding, as it is generally impossible to write in a way that cannot be misinterpreted." [ ] Additionally there is no way to guarantee that such documents are a complete and correct description of the system, that is to be implemented. Even if this can be achieved it still has to be checked, whether there are requirements, that contradict each other.

There were a lot of different approaches to address these issues like CASE tools, which support the engineers during the development cycle, but most approaches are based on programming or natural languages. The problem of natural languages was already addressed in the previous paragraph, and the use of programming languages as specification language often tend to get to much into detail, which makes it difficult to understand the general systems behaviour.

A different approach is the use of formal specification languages, which allows an abstract specification of a systems behaviour, but still gives a clear and consistent way of interpreting the specification. With such languages techniques like model checking can be applied to check for inconsistencies of a specification. Additionally some languages can be employed to automatically derive test cases for the system from the formal systems specification as described in [ ].

The language CSP is one of such formal specification languages, that can be used, to model check two CSP specifications against each other, which is called *refinement* checking. The basic idea behind this concept is that not only the system specification, but also the implementation of the system can be abstracted in a CSP specification. A correct implementation should satisfy all requirements of the specification. If it can be assumed, that the abstraction from the system specification and the implementation to CSP specifications is correct, the refinement technique can be employed to find errors in the implementation or specification, if the implementation does not refine the specification. Model checking two CSP specifications against each other can be done automatically by model checking tools like FDR, which was developed by Formal Systems Ltd.

Even though CSP itself has no way of specifying timed system behaviour, which is required for most safety-critical systems, there is an extension of CSP, which addresses these issues: Timed CSP. In [ ] and [ ] Steve Schneider formally defines Timed CSP. The PhD-thesis of Oliver Meyer [ ] defines a structural decomposition of Timed CSP specifications into a system of parallel untimed CSP and timer processes. This structural decomposition of Timed CSP, which is explained in chapter 10.2, is especially important important to our work, since it enables us to consider only Untimed CSP even though out subject of interest is in real-time testing.

CSP was designed as a language, which helps to analyse parallel systems and their interactions between each other. Those interactions are represented as communication of *events* between the concurrent systems. An event, that can be communicated, is an element of the alphabet Σ, which contains all possible events in a context of a specification. Events can be used to mark situations, where the inner state of a system changes, therefore the production of an event always happens instantaneously and in no time. If a CSP specification is in a state P, $\alpha(P)$ denotes the possible actions of the specification in that state. Even though is it not possible to model time specificly in CSP, sequences of events, which are called *traces*, are used to specify the order of events as they occurred. An examplary trace of the events a, b and c, which are elements of the set Σ, can be denoted as follows: $\langle a, b, c \rangle$. The set of all possible sequences on events of the alphabet Σ is denoted Σ^*.

In parallel systems it is therefore not possible that two subsystems produce two events simultaneously. There is always one events that was produced before the other. Simultaneous production of events only occurs, if two systems are interacting with each other, by producing the same event. This is only possible, if all subsystems which are required for the communication are prepared to execute the common event. If one of the participants cannot emit the event, none of the systems may proceed with the production of it. This type of communication is often referred to as *handshake communication*.

A parallel communicating system specified in CSP is said to operate inside an *environment*, which always functions as a sink for all events, that can be produced by a specification. But the environment does not necessarily need to accept all events that can be produced by a specification. If fact it may select exactly one event at a time to be executed by the specification. This is why it is often said, that a specification *offers* certain events, from which only one is *selected* by the environment to be produced.

Concurrent systems tend to introduce *non-determinism*, even if the subsystems are completely deterministic. A system is called *deterministic*, if it always behaves identical after being given exactly the same inputs. For example a system consisting of three parallel processes can easily be non-determinstic, if two of the systems P and Q communicates on the same events with the system R. In a situation where all three systems offers the communication event, it is not specified, whether P and R or Q and R are engaging in the event.

Other problems of concurrent systems are *deadlocks* and *livelocks*. A system is called deadlocked, if it cannot produce any more events. Such situations can occur, if parallel systems compete for shared resources, which can only serve one system at any time. For example in a concurrent systems of two independent subsystems and two shared resources a situation may arise where both subsystems requires both resources to continue properly. If each subsystem already got hold of one resource and tries to get the other one for exclusive use, without releasing the one it already has, a deadlock occurs, since no subsystem will ever be able to continue its work.

If a system livelocks it seems similar to a deadlocked system, since the whole system never interacts with the environment anymore. But the behaviour is different, since a livelock results by infinite internal communication between subsystems. From a users point of view, who can observe the internal activity, it is not clear, whether the system will finally interact again with the environment. Another possibility for livelocks are *divergences*, which is characterised by an infinite unbroken sequence of internal events, called τ-events. Those internal events can neither be observed nor influenced by the environment. Since divergences can also occur in non concurrent systems, they are often handled separately from livelocks.

The termination of concurrent systems is specified in CSP as well. If a subsystem is able to terminate with a $\checkmark$-action, it cannot be stopped by the environment or the other parallel running systems. As soon as a subsystem has terminated, it stops producing as more events, since it is in a state called Ω, which offers no events and indicates a sucessfully terminates process. Only if all concurrent systems have terminated successfully, the whole system itself is able to terminate as well.

2.2   CSP Syntax

The basic concepts of CSP have already been explained in the previous section, but no information about the way of formalising those CSP specifications have been given yet. In this section the syntax of CSP_M, the machine readable form of CSP, will be introduced.

First the expression language of CSP_M will be explained in detail. Since the expressions are completely based on well known mathematical concepts, there will be no further explanation here. Later the type system of CSP_M and its effect on channel definitions will be described. Finally the CSP_M process operators are introduced. Their semantics will be explained in section 2.4.

2.2.1   Expressions

CSP_M supports a large number of different expressions. In the following certain variables stand for expressions of various types as stated here:

m, n numbers
s, t sequences
a, A sets, the capital A is a set of sets
b boolean
x general expression

Identifiers

Identifiers in CSP_M must start with a character followed by any number of characters, numbers or underscores. Finally an arbitrary number of primes may be appended to the identifier.

Syntax	Description
[a-zA-Z][a-zA-Z0-9_]*[']*	All Identifiers available in CSP_M.

Numbers

In general there is no range limitation for the values of numeral variables in CSP, but the internal representation of the integers in implementations of CSP_M

often uses the C type `long integer` to store the values. In this case only values between -2147483648 and 2147483647 are supported.

Syntax	Description
1, 2	integer literals
m+n	sum
m-n	difference
-m	unary minus
m*n	product
m/n	quotient
m%n	remainder

Booleans

Equality is defined for all expressions. It checks for structural equality which means that expressions containing operators or functions will be evaluated. If the expressions are not valid because a parameter or local identifier has no defined value, an error must occur. The ordering operators are defined for numbers only. Using them along with other types will result in an error.

Syntax	Description
`true`, `false`	boolean literals
b_1 `and` b_2	boolean and
b_1 `or` b_2	boolean or
`not` b	boolean not
x_1 == x_2, x_1 != x_2	equality operators
m < n, m <= n, m > n and m >= n	ordering operations
`if` b `then` x_1 `else` x_1	conditional expression

Sets

Sets in CSP$_M$ may contain elements of any type. Most functions operating on sets have a fixed number of arguments. Only the operators for set union and set intersection (`union` and `inter`) can have two or more arguments.

Syntax	Description
{}, {x_1, x_2, x_3}	set literals
{$x \mid x$ <- $a, b_1, ..., b_n$}	set comprehension
{m..n}, {m..}	closed and open intervals
#a, `card`(a)	cardinality of the set a
`diff`(a_1, a_2)	set difference
`union`($a_1, ..., a_n$)	set union
`inter`($a_1, ..., a_n$)	set intersection
`empty`(a)	checks whether $a = \emptyset$
`member`(x, a)	checks whether $x \in a$

Sequences

Sequences are similar to sets with the difference that equivalence of sequences requires the elements to be in the same order in the sequence. FDRs implementation of CSP$_M$ requires, that all elements in a sequence have the same type. This is in general not necessary for CSP$_M$.

Syntax	Description
`< >,< 1, 2, 3 >`	sequence literals
`< ` $m..n$ ` >`	closed range from integer m to integer n inclusive
`< ` $m..$ ` >`	open range, from integer m upward
$s\hat{}\,t$	sequence concatenation
`#`s	length of the sequence
`head(`s`)`	The first element of a non-empty sequence
`tail(`s`)`	All but the first element of a non-empty sequence
`null(`s`)`	checks whether the sequence s is empty

Tuples

Tuples are used to represent pairs of n-tuples of expressions. In CSP$_M$ their most important use can be found in process definitions.

Syntax	Description
$(x_1,\ x_2), (x_1,x_2,...,x_n)$	pair and n-tuple

Functions

A function in CSP$_M$ consists of a name, an optional tuple of parameters and a function body. The function body is an arbitrary expression of CSP$_M$.

Syntax	Description
$f(x_1,...,x_n)\ =\ y$	A function named f represents an expression y in with the functions parameters x_1 to x_n may occur as free variables.

2.2.2   Types

In CSP communication between concurrent systems can be achieved by synchronising on structures events, as they are going to be introduced below. To declare the structure of events channel-declarations are employed, which specify ranges of values, that may be communicated on the channels.

Those ranges can not only be specified directly in the channel declarations but also by *type* definitions. CSP$_M$ knows three different kinds of type definitions: *simple types*, *named types* and *datatypes*.

Simple Types

Simple types are explicit sets of atomic values such as {1, 2, 3} or {true, false}. They can occur as part of the definition of channels or other types. Type expressions as composite types are supported by the dot operation so that for example

{0,1}.{2,3}   denotes   {0.2, 0.3, 1.2, 1.3}

Product types are expressed by the tuple syntax, such that

({0,1}.{2,3})   denotes   {(0,2), (0,3), (1,2), (1,3)}

Named Types

The definition of a named type associates a name with a type expression, which can be expressed by the optional keyword `nametype`. Named types always have the following form:

[nametype] <identifier> = <type expression>

Examples for nametypes in CSP_M are:

```
Values = {0..199}
nametype Some = {1, 2, 3}
nametype Ranges = Some . Values
```

Datatypes

Datatypes definitions are used to model variant record types. This type can be employed to define a number of atomic constants as in

datatype T = A | B | C

which introduces the new constants A, B and C.

But also more complex type definitions are allowed:

```
nametype Powerset = {{}, {0}, {1}, {0,1}}
datatype T = A.{0..3} | B.Powerset | C
```

The newly created type T allows the use of constants like A.0, B.{1}, B.{0,1} or C for all occurrences of the type T in a CSP_M specification.

2.2.3   Channels

Channel declarations in a CSP_M specification define the ranges of the values, that may be communicated as events. CSP_M supports two types of channel definitions: *untyped* and *typed* channels.

Typed Channels

When defining a typed channel it is necessary to specify its type, using one of the three different type expressions described in 2.2.2. The type of a channel defines a set of values that can be used to communicate over this channel. The syntax for the definition of such a channel is:

```
channel <identifier>[, <identifier>] : <type>[.<type>. ...]
```

The specification `channel a:{1, 2, 3}` for example defines a channel a with the set $\{1, 2, 3\}$ as its type. This defines the possible events $a.1$, $a.2$ and $a.3$ that can be used in the specification. The type definition of a channel can consist of more that one type as defined above. In this case, the type of the channel is the Cartesian product of the single type sets.

Untyped Channels

Untyped channels are a special form of typed channels with no type set (equal to an empty set as type) and therefore cannot be used to send different values. They can only be used as single events in a specification. The syntax is:

```
channel <identifier>[, <identifier> ...]
```

Based on such channel definitions, a semantic function $type(c)$ can be defined, which requires the name of a channel c as argument and returns a set of all possible values, that can be communicated over the channel. In case of untyped channels, the value of this function returns an empty set, since no values can be communicated.

2.2.4   Events

Every channel definition defines a set of events. The definition `channel a` for example defines the single event a while `channel b : {1..3}` defines the events $\{b.1, b.2, b.3\}$. The set of all events of a CSP specification is called Σ. It is the alphabet of visible events. Σ^τ is the alphabet extended by the internal event τ, which is invisible to the environment. $\Sigma^\checkmark$ denotes the alphabet extended by the event $\checkmark$ which indicates successful termination. Finally $\Sigma^{\tau\checkmark}$ refers to the alphabet extended by τ and $\checkmark$. Both events $\checkmark$ and τ are not part of the alphabet ($\Sigma \cap \{\tau, \checkmark\} = \emptyset$).

The event notation in $\mathsf{CSP_M}$ allows to write definite events like in `a.3`, which represents exactly the event $a.3$. But also the use of variables and parameters is allowed in the event notation, such that it is required to apply the value a variable to an event like `a.x`.

Additionally $\mathsf{CSP_M}$ allows the distinction between input and output communication. A statement like $a!x$ in a $\mathsf{CSP_M}$ specification requires a value for the variable x to communicate the output event $a.\langle x \rangle$, where $\langle x \rangle$ denotes the value of x. Input events like a?x offers a variety of different events to the environment. Which events are offered depends on the definition of the channel a, which lays down the type (and thereby the possible values) for x. As soon as the environment selects one of the offered events the value x is set to the value, which is layed down by the event.

Below some examples for event expressions in CSP will be given. A function $comms(e)$ will be introduced, which denotes a set of all possible communication events of the prefix e.

- The prefix $d.3$ represents the set of all events generated by the prefix which is simple in this case: $comms(d.3) = \{d.3\}$.

- The element in the communications set of the prefix $d!(1-x)$ depends on the value of the variable x. If the value of x is an integer, the expression $(1-x)$ is evaluated and the result $r = 1-x$ is taken as the value of the expression: $comms(d!(1-x)) = \{d.r\}$

- It is possible to create new bindings of identifiers within the prefix operator: The prefix $c?x:A?y$ can represent a much bigger set than the previous examples: $comms(c?x:A?y) = \{c.a.b \mid a.b \in type(c), a \in A\}$. If the process $c?x:A?y \to P$ produces an event of the form $c.a.b$, the identifiers x and y carry the values a and b for the rest of their visibility in the process P. A detailed definition of visibility of variables will be given later in section 5.1.1.

- The last example is even more complicated since it is possible to produce events of different types by just one expression: $comms(a : \{x.1, y.2?b\}) = \{x.1\} \cup \{y.2.b \mid 2.b \in type(y)\}$

2.2.5 Processes

The behaviour of a CSP process is defined using process terms. They are constructed using process operators as described in table 2.1 and 2.2. Let T be a process term of CSP operators and let P denote an identifier with the name of the process. Then a process definition is the term $P = T$ assigning a *process term* to a *process name*. CSP processes can be parameterised, which is necessary to write generic process definitions. The process parameters can be used as free variables in the process term.

```
<identifier> [(x_1, ..., x_n)] = <process term>
```

Process Terms

CSP$_M$ allows a large number of different process operators, that can be found in the following tables. The semantics of each operator is defined in section 2.4. The operators are divided into *low level* and *high level* operators. Low level operators define sequential processes while high level operators describe parallel processes, hiding or renaming of events.

Syntax	Description
STOP	performs no actions
SKIP	successful termination with ✓ action
CHAOS(a)	chaotic process on the events in a
P	process reference
c -> P	prefix
c ?x .y: a !z -> p	complex prefix
P ; Q	sequential composition
P |~| Q	internal choice
P [] Q	external choice
if b then P else Q	condition
b & P	boolean guard
[] x:s @ P	replicated sequential composition
[] x:a @ P	replicated external choice
|~| x:a @ P	replicated internal choice

Table 2.1: The low level process operators of CSP.

Syntax	Description
P \ a	hiding
P [[c <- c']]	renaming
P ||| Q	interleaving
P [| a |] Q	parallel
P [a || a'] Q	alphabetised parallel
||| x:a @ P	replicated interleave
[| a' |] x:a @ P	replicated parallel
|| x:a @ [a'] P	replicated alphabetised parallel

Table 2.2: The high level process operators of CSP.

Process References

At the end of each valid process term there is always a process reference, naming either any predefined process like STOP, SKIP or CHAOS(a), or an identifier representing a process, which was defined as described above. With those references new values can be assigned to the parameters of the process definition.

Process Context

CSP specifications normally are a set of definitions, which include expressions, functions, channels and processes. They are commonly used to specify the behaviour of a single process defined in the specification. The process term can contain references to other processes defined in the specification. As suggested by Meyer in [ ] the set of these process definitions create the *process context* of the process. Consider a CSP specification defining for example the following processes:

```
1    channel a,b,c
2    P = a -> Q
3    Q = (b -> P) [] (c -> R)
4    R = a -> SKIP
5    S = SKIP
```

Considering the process term $a \to Q$, the corresponding process context $\mathcal{C}_{a \to Q}$ contains all process definitions of the specification that are required for it:

$$\mathcal{C}_{a \to Q} = \{ \ \begin{aligned} &P = a \to Q, \\ &Q = (b \to P) \square (c \to R), \\ &R = a \to SKIP \ \} \end{aligned}$$

To be able to evaluate the process term, this is only possible within its process context, which is denoted by the notation $(a \to Q, \mathcal{C}_{a \to Q})$.

Recursion

Recursion can be expressed by named recursion based on process references. Let $\mu X.P(X)$ denote a recursive process definition where $P(X)$ is a term including recursive calls of the process X. This process definition can be replaced by a definition using named recursion based on process references:

$$\mu X.P(X) \ \hat{=} \ (P(X), \{X = P(X)\})$$

The tuple on the right hand side consists of the current process term $P(X)$ and the process context of the CSP specification $\{X = P(X)\}$.

2.3   Semantics of CSP

In this thesis a new kind of transition system is introduced, that can be used for testing real time reactive systems, based on CSP specifications. An overview of the different semantics of CSP will be given in the following. Those semantics are required for the further considerations of this thesis. In [ ], Roscoe presents three different semantics of CSP namely an *operational*, an *denotational* and an *algebraic* semantics, from which only the first two are going to be explained in detail in later sections, since the algebraic semantics is not relevant in the context of this thesis.

The operational semantics describes the execution of processes by giving rules that apply for each operator. Each rule states which action must be performed to change the state of the program. This semantics explains how a CSP-specification is executed step by step, and is therefore the most direct approach to define a semantics of CSP. A detailed overview on the operational semantics can be found in section 2.4.

The denotational semantics in contrast to the operational semantics describes the behaviour of CSP processes on a more abstract level. It leaves the level of implementation and defines the meaning of processes based on traces, failures and divergencies. This semantics, which is described in more detail in section 2.5, is used to give an understanding of the inner meaning of a program.

The algebraic semantics defines the semantics of CSP using a set of algebraic laws which includes laws for each process operator. These laws about syntactic transformation are the basic axioms of the semantics which can be used to prove properties of processes. With these rules it is possible to transform one specification into another one that is still equivalent to the original. Some authors proposing process algebras have regarded algebraic semantics as the most basic means of defining process equality, in that they propose a given set of laws and investigate what equivalences they produce.

2.4   Operational Semantics of CSP

The operational semantics interprets CSP-specifications as transition systems with visible and invisible actions, which can be produced by the rules of the semantics. Each action leads to other states, which can be determined by the rules as well. The semantics which is going to be described on the following pages can be used to compute a labelled transition system, which consists of a set of nodes, and a relation $\xrightarrow{a}$ between nodes for all events a in the alphabet Σ.

Over the years the understanding of some CSP-processes changed a little, so there were a few changes in the operational semantics. These changes were made without affecting the other semantics at all. This fact is important, since, as we said before, all semantics are equivalent. At the time this thesis was written, a variety of publications are available, which give different semantics for recursion, the parallel operators and the CHAOS-operator.

The operational semantics A.W. Roscoe introduced in his book [ ] in chapter 7 was used as the basis of this section. Though his operational semantics is not complete, with regard to the operators relevant in this thesis, it is easy to fill the gaps with the help of other sources, for example the semantics Brian Scattergood introduces in his PhD-thesis [ ]. The decision is strongly influenced by the fact that Roscoe's book is one of the latest about CSP and its semantics. Even though this style used for the description of the operational semantics is not completely formal, it is used in this thesis, since it is the most common style of describing the operational semantics of CSP. For the description of the rules of the operational semantics some terms are going to be introduced:

Execution of CSP specifications is described here on the basis of transition rules. CSP specifications are transformed into others by application of a suitable instance of a rule. A specified process might try to communicate with another one in the same specification over channels which can be typed or untyped. Every time a process executes a rule where a signal is communicated over a channel, it is said that the system has produced an event. It is not necessary that another process must synchronise over that channel, since the whole system is interacting with the environment, which accepts all events.

But there are also internal events that are not visible to the environment, for example when some channels are hidden or when non-deterministic choices are made. In this case a τ-event is produced which is an invisible event, that cannot be influenced and observed by the environment. Another special event is the event $\checkmark$ which indicates that a process has terminated. A terminated process cannot be executed any further. For this reason terminated processes are represented by the special process Ω in the operational semantics, to differentiate them from simple states without any transitions.

The structure of this section is the following: For each operator a short description for which task the operator is the adequate modelling solution will be given. After that the number and the types of arguments the operator requires are described. Finally the set of transition rules for this operator is stated. Each transition rule follows the customary pattern that was suggested by Plotkin [ ] for structured operational semantics.

$$\frac{X}{Y \xrightarrow{e} Z}$$

X is a precondition that is required to hold for the rule to be applicable. If X is empty the rule is always applicable for a process of the form Y. The parameter Y always represents a pattern of a process, to which the rule is usable for. If at a given state of execution a process of the kind Y exists and the precondition X is valid, then the process may evolve to a process of the form Z, simultaneously producing the event e.

The operators themselves are sorted by means of complexity, starting with the basic processes SKIP, STOP followed by the inductive definitions for sequential processes and parallel composition. Finally special operators like guarded commands and CHAOS are introduced.

Basic Processes

There are two predefined processes which are interesting in CSP: The process
STOP has no actions at all, so no inference rules can be defined for this process.
Another predefined process is SKIP which can perform just one single event $\checkmark$.
After the event has been produced the process terminates and evolves to the
process Ω, where no further actions can be performed.

$$SKIP \ \stackrel{\checkmark}{\longrightarrow} \ \Omega \tag{2.1}$$

Prefix

The prefixing operator $e \to P$ is the only way of emitting signals from a process
to other processes or the environment. This operator can produce any kind of
event that can be specified in the prefix e, which can be a complex expression.

By producing an event $a \in comms(e)$, bindings for all free variables in the
term e are created. If for example e is the expression $c?x?y$ and the generated
event a is $c.1.2$, all further occurrences of x and y are representing the values
1 and 2 respectively. To express this in the rules of the operational semantics,
the function $subs(a, e, P)$ is introduced, which denotes the process P, where each
identifier bound by e is replaced by the corresponding value from a. If the event
from the example from above occurs in the process term $c?x?y \to d.x \to P(x, y)$,
this means:

$$subs(c.1.2, c?x?y, d.x \to P(x, y)) = d.1 \to P(1, 2)$$

The function $subs(a, e, P)$ does not just perform a textual replacement in the
process term P, but it also considers the scope of the variables introduced by e.
This is for example important, if the process term P contains another communication field, which creates new bindings for some of the variables bound by e.
$subs(a, e, P)$ is only introduced informally here, but an inductive definition could
easily be given for this function.

Based on this definition, the inference rule of the operational semantics for
the prefix operator looks as follows:

$$\frac{}{e \to P \ \stackrel{a}{\longrightarrow} \ subs(a, e, P)} \quad (a \in comms(e)) \tag{2.2}$$

Process References

Process references can be used to model infinite processes, by defining self referring process specifications. Some operational semantics for CSP use τ-events
to resolve process references. Later semantics, e.g. the one by Steve Schneider

[ ], omit the τ-events. This is a useful approach, since two processes describing the same behaviour would not be equivalent, if one representation uses recursion, which is resolved by a τ-event, where the other does not. On a semantical level the resolving of process references is just a *textual replacement* of the process reference with the actual definition of the process. But since there is no precise definition of the operational semantics of process references, the following rules have been defined by the authors of this thesis, to solve this remedy.

For the operational semantics of the prefix operator the function *subs* has already been introduced, which provides a textual replacement of variables bound by an expression in a process term. To reuse this functionality for process references, a function $\mathcal{C}(P(args))$ is going to be introduced in the following, which returns the triple of arguments, that can be used as arguments for the function $subs(a, e, P)$, which has been explained earlier in this section.

The argument of the function $\mathcal{C}$ is a process reference with all its corresponding arguments. The result of this function is a triple, where the first element is the original process reference, the second one is the left hand side of the process definition, that is going to be used to replace the process reference and the third element is the right hand side of the process definition. Lets take the following example:

```
P = a -> Q(1,2)
Q(x,y) = b.x -> c.y -> STOP
```

During the execution of the process P the process reference $Q(1, 2)$ is encountered, which has to be replaced by its definition. The function $\mathcal{C}(Q(1, 2))$ applies pattern matching to all available process definitions in the process context to determine, which process is used to replace the process reference. As a result this functions returns the triple $(Q(1, 2), Q(x, y), b.x \rightarrow c.y \rightarrow STOP)$, which are the required arguments for the function *subs*. Therefore *subs* can then be used to generate that instance of the process definition, which matches the process reference with it corresponding parameters.

$$subs(\mathcal{C}(Q(1,1))) = subs(Q(1,2), Q(x,y), b.x \rightarrow c.y \rightarrow STOP)$$
$$= b.1 \rightarrow c.2 \rightarrow STOP$$

This results in the following rule for the operational semantics of process references, where it is important to note, that replacing a process reference by its corresponding definition does not produce any events.

$$P(args) \quad \longrightarrow \quad subs(\mathcal{C}(P(args)))$$

(2.3)

Sequential Composition

Another important operator for sequential processes is the composition of two processes: $P; Q$. The first process P can produce events until it terminates and emits the $\checkmark$-event which is changed by the sequential composition operator into a τ-event. When this event is generated the process P terminates and is replaced by the process Q which can now continue to produce events, until it terminates. The whole process is described by two transition rules:

$$\frac{P \stackrel{a}{\longrightarrow} P'}{P; Q \stackrel{a}{\longrightarrow} P'; Q} \quad (a \neq \checkmark) \tag{2.4}$$

$$\frac{P \stackrel{\checkmark}{\longrightarrow} P'}{P; Q \stackrel{\tau}{\longrightarrow} Q} \tag{2.5}$$

Internal Choice

The internal choice operator is used to make non-deterministic choices. It needs two processes as arguments from which one is chosen to be executed in the future. There is no possibility for the environment to choose which process will be selected. When the operator makes its selection, a τ-event is produced.

$$\frac{}{P \sqcap Q \stackrel{\tau}{\longrightarrow} P} \tag{2.6}$$

$$\frac{}{P \sqcap Q \stackrel{\tau}{\longrightarrow} Q} \tag{2.7}$$

External Choice

The external choice operator allows the environment to choose from a number of alternative events to be produced. It is necessary to produce a visible event to make a selection. After the event is emitted, the process that produced that event can continue to produce events. If both processes can produce the same event, one of them is chosen non-deterministically.

$$\frac{P \stackrel{a}{\longrightarrow} P'}{P \square Q \stackrel{a}{\longrightarrow} P'} \quad (a \neq \tau) \tag{2.8}$$

$$\frac{Q \xrightarrow{a} Q'}{P \square Q \xrightarrow{a} Q'} \quad (a \neq \tau) \tag{2.9}$$

If one of the processes offers a τ-event, this can be selected, too. In this case the state of the corresponding process changes, but no decision is made which process will continue to produce events.

$$\frac{P \xrightarrow{\tau} P'}{P \square Q \xrightarrow{\tau} P' \square Q} \tag{2.10}$$

$$\frac{Q \xrightarrow{\tau} Q'}{P \square Q \xrightarrow{\tau} P \square Q'} \tag{2.11}$$

Hiding

The hiding operator leaves all events untouched that are produced by the subordinate process, as long as they are not in the set of events that are to be hidden.

$$\frac{P \xrightarrow{a} P'}{P \setminus B \xrightarrow{a} P' \setminus B} \quad (a \notin (B \cup \{\checkmark\})) \tag{2.12}$$

Events which are in the set of hidden events are changed into τ-events by this operator which makes them invisible for the environment.

$$\frac{P \xrightarrow{a} P'}{P \setminus B \xrightarrow{\tau} P' \setminus B} \quad (a \in B) \tag{2.13}$$

If the subordinate process offers to terminate, the whole process terminates and evolves to Ω.

$$\frac{P \xrightarrow{\checkmark} P'}{P \setminus B \xrightarrow{\checkmark} \Omega} \tag{2.14}$$

Renaming

The renaming operator itself produces no events, but transforms events from the subordinate process into other events. It is necessary to define a relation R which specifies which event should be changed into another event, to perform a transition. The default rule is the identity relation, where each event is in relation with itself. If $a, b \in \Sigma$ are in the relation R the following rule applies:

$$\frac{P \;\xrightarrow{a}\; P'}{P[\![R]\!] \;\xrightarrow{b}\; P'[\![R]\!]} \qquad (a \; R \; b) \tag{2.15}$$

The events $\checkmark$ and τ are not affected by this operator:

$$\frac{P \;\xrightarrow{\tau}\; P'}{P[\![R]\!] \;\xrightarrow{\tau}\; P'[\![R]\!]} \tag{2.16}$$

$$\frac{P \;\xrightarrow{\checkmark}\; P'}{P[\![R]\!] \;\xrightarrow{\checkmark}\; \Omega} \tag{2.17}$$

Interleaving

The interleaving operator is used to specify the behaviour of processes that can perform actions independent from each other. Bryan Scattergood demands in his PhD-Thesis [ ] a simultaneous termination of both subprocesses of the interleaving operator. This contradicts the paradigm of immediate termination, that cannot be refused by the environment. By using the following inference rules, that are suggested by A.W. Roscoe, an independent termination of the subprocesses of the interleaving operator is possible, which is closer to the intuitive modelling of terminating parallel processes.

The processes which are running un-synchronised in parallel can produce events independent from each other. The production of an event just has effect on the process which produced that event – the other process is unaffected:

$$\frac{P \;\xrightarrow{x}\; P'}{P \;|\!|\!|\; Q \;\xrightarrow{x}\; P' \;|\!|\!|\; Q} \qquad (x \neq \checkmark) \tag{2.18}$$

$$\frac{Q \;\xrightarrow{x}\; Q'}{P \;|\!|\!|\; Q \;\xrightarrow{x}\; P \;|\!|\!|\; Q'} \qquad (x \neq \checkmark) \tag{2.19}$$

If one of the processes can terminate, this can happen without changing the state of the other process. The produced $\checkmark$-event is changed into a τ-event.

$$\frac{P \xrightarrow{\checkmark} P'}{P \mathbin{|||} Q \xrightarrow{\tau} \Omega \mathbin{|||} Q} \tag{2.20}$$

$$\frac{Q \xrightarrow{\checkmark} Q'}{P \mathbin{|||} Q \xrightarrow{\tau} P \mathbin{|||} \Omega} \tag{2.21}$$

The whole process itself terminates if both subordinate processes have already terminated.

$$\frac{}{\Omega \mathbin{|||} \Omega \xrightarrow{\checkmark} \Omega} \tag{2.22}$$

It is important to understand that in the untimed semantics of CSP as we are using in this thesis, it is not possible that two events happen at exactly the same time. Even if some processes are running in parallel this cannot happen. Therefore it is not necessary to define rules for this special case.

Parallel

The basic intention in designing CSP was to model sequential processes that communicate with each other and the environment synchronously. With the interleaving operator it is just possible to model parallel processes with no communication at all. The parallel operator closes this gap.

This operator requires a set of events on which the two processes, connected by this operator, must synchronise with each other. Note that this set consists of elements of the alphabet Σ, "which contains all possible communications for processes in the universe under consideration" ([ ], page 8), but not the special events τ and $\checkmark$. Synchronisation means that both processes have to produce these events at the same time. The exact behaviour of this operator is defined by the following rules.

If one of the processes can produce a τ-event, this can be done by executing the corresponding process without effecting the state of the other one:

$$\frac{P \xrightarrow{\tau} P'}{P \mathbin{\underset{X}{\|}} Q \xrightarrow{\tau} P' \mathbin{\underset{X}{\|}} Q} \tag{2.23}$$

$$\frac{Q \;\xrightarrow{\;\tau\;}\; Q'}{P \parallel_X Q \;\xrightarrow{\;\tau\;}\; P \parallel_X Q'} \tag{2.24}$$

All events which are not in the set X of synchronisation events, can be produced without effecting the other process:

$$\frac{P \;\xrightarrow{\;a\;}\; P'}{P \parallel_X Q \;\xrightarrow{\;a\;}\; P' \parallel_X Q} \quad (a \in \Sigma \backslash X) \tag{2.25}$$

$$\frac{Q \;\xrightarrow{\;a\;}\; Q'}{P \parallel_X Q \;\xrightarrow{\;a\;}\; P \parallel_X Q'} \quad (a \in \Sigma \backslash X) \tag{2.26}$$

Any event that is in the event set X can only be produced by both processes simultaneously. For this reason a process willing to produce an event from X at a certain time can only do so, if the other process can engage in the same event at the same time, otherwise the process must wait. If both processes offer the same event, both can evolve under the production of that event. Note that only one event a is produced by this operator, even though both processes are evolving.

$$\frac{P \;\xrightarrow{\;a\;}\; P' \quad Q \;\xrightarrow{\;a\;}\; Q'}{P \parallel_X Q \;\xrightarrow{\;a\;}\; P' \parallel_X Q'} \quad (a \in X) \tag{2.27}$$

The other rules are analogous to the rules of the interleaving operator. If one of the processes can terminate, the operator will produce a τ-action and the process evolves to Ω.

$$\frac{P \;\xrightarrow{\;\checkmark\;}\; P'}{P \parallel_X Q \;\xrightarrow{\;\tau\;}\; \Omega \parallel_X Q} \tag{2.28}$$

$$\frac{Q \;\xrightarrow{\;\checkmark\;}\; Q'}{P \parallel_X Q \;\xrightarrow{\;\tau\;}\; P \parallel_X \Omega} \tag{2.29}$$

If both processes have already terminated independently of each other, the whole process terminates and evolves to Ω.

$$\frac{}{\Omega \parallel_X \Omega \;\xrightarrow{\;\checkmark\;}\; \Omega} \tag{2.30}$$

Alphabetised Parallel

The parallel operator, which has been introduced before, is a special variety of the alphabetised parallel operator. Instead of using just one event set for the synchronisation, the alphabetised parallel operator uses two event sets. If A and B are subsets of Σ, $P \parallel_{A \ B} Q$ is a parallel system, where P may only communicate on events in A and Q is only allowed to communicate events of B. The processes must synchronise on the intersection of the two sets $A \cap B$.

If one of the processes can produce a τ-event, this can be done by executing the corresponding process without effecting the state of the other one:

$$\frac{P \xrightarrow{\tau} P'}{P \parallel_{A \ B} Q \xrightarrow{\tau} P' \parallel_{A \ B} Q} \tag{2.31}$$

$$\frac{Q \xrightarrow{\tau} Q'}{P \parallel_{A \ B} Q \xrightarrow{\tau} P \parallel_{A \ B} Q'} \tag{2.32}$$

If one process can produce an event which is not in the intersection of A and B, then the corresponding process can evolve when it produces that event.

$$\frac{P \xrightarrow{a} P'}{P \parallel_{A \ B} Q \xrightarrow{a} P' \parallel_{A \ B} Q} \quad (a \in A \backslash B) \tag{2.33}$$

$$\frac{Q \xrightarrow{a} Q'}{P \parallel_{A \ B} Q \xrightarrow{a} P \parallel_{A \ B} Q'} \quad (a \in B \backslash A) \tag{2.34}$$

Events which are in both event sets can only be executed if both processes produce the same event simultaneously.

$$\frac{P \xrightarrow{a} P' \quad Q \xrightarrow{a} Q'}{P \parallel_{A \ B} Q \xrightarrow{a} P' \parallel_{A \ B} Q'} \quad (a \in A \cap B) \tag{2.35}$$

The rules for termination are identical to the rules of the interleaving and parallel operator.

$$\frac{P \xrightarrow{\checkmark} P'}{P \parallel_{A \ B} Q \xrightarrow{\tau} \Omega \parallel_{A \ B} Q} \tag{2.36}$$

$$\frac{Q \;\overset{\checkmark}{\longrightarrow}\; Q'}{P \underset{A}{\|}_{B} Q \;\overset{\tau}{\longrightarrow}\; P \underset{A}{\|}_{B} \Omega} \tag{2.37}$$

$$\frac{}{\Omega \underset{A}{\|}_{B} \Omega \;\overset{\checkmark}{\longrightarrow}\; \Omega} \tag{2.38}$$

The further considerations in this thesis will not deal with this operator any more, since the same behaviour can easily be expressed with the parallel operator, which has been indicated by Roscoe in [ ].

$$P \underset{A}{\|}_{B} Q = (P \underset{\Sigma\backslash A}{\|} STOP) \underset{A\cap B}{\|} (Q \underset{\Sigma\backslash B}{\|} STOP) \tag{2.39}$$

Conditions

Sometimes it is necessary to check some conditions in specifications and to act differently depending on the result of the condition. In CSP the *if-then-else* statement enables the developer to specify such conditions. If the condition in the statement evaluates to *true* the *then*-case, otherwise the *else*-case is executed.

In the following rules $C[\![b]\!]$ stands for the result of the evaluation of the boolean expression b. The resulting operational semantics for *if-then-else* statements is as follows:

$$\frac{C[\![b]\!] = true \qquad P \;\overset{a}{\longrightarrow}\; P'}{(if\ b\ then\ P\ else\ Q) \;\overset{a}{\longrightarrow}\; P'} \tag{2.40}$$

$$\frac{C[\![b]\!] = false \qquad Q \;\overset{a}{\longrightarrow}\; Q'}{(if\ b\ then\ P\ else\ Q) \;\overset{a}{\longrightarrow}\; Q'} \tag{2.41}$$

Guarded Commands

Guarded commands are a shortened form of if-then-else statements, since the definition of this operator is as follows:

$$b\&P = if\ b\ then\ P\ else\ STOP$$

According to this definition the operational semantics can easily be derived from 2.40 and 2.41: If the condition b evaluates to *true* the process P is processed as usual. If the condition evaluates to *false* instead, the process must stop producing events immediately.

$$\frac{C[\![b]\!] = true \qquad P \xrightarrow{a} P'}{b\&P \xrightarrow{a} P'} \tag{2.42}$$

$$\frac{C[\![b]\!] = false}{b\&P \longrightarrow STOP} \tag{2.43}$$

Replicated Functions

A useful shorthand for multiple occurrences of an operator over instances of the same process is provided by the replicated form of the operator. The following example results in eight interleaved processes:

$$|||\, x : \{1..8\} \bullet P(x)$$

This replicated interleaving process expresses exactly the same as the fully specified process:

$$P(1) \,|||\, P(2) \,|||\, P(3) \,|||\, P(4) \,|||\, P(5) \,|||\, P(6) \,|||\, P(7) \,|||\, P(8)$$

Such constructs are called "replicated" operators and are introduced for some of the operators we introduced before. The semantics of these operators is the natural extension of the semantics of the basic operators. At least the following replicated operators of previously defined operators exist, where a, $a' \subseteq \Sigma$ denotes a set of events and $s \in \Sigma^*$ is a sequence of events:

$;\, x : s \bullet P$	Replicated sequential composition
$\Box\, x : a \bullet P$	Replicated external choice
$\sqcap\, x : a \bullet P$	Replicated internal choice
$|||\, x : a \bullet P$	Replicated interleaving
$\|\, x : a \bullet P$	Replicated parallel
$\underset{a'}{\|}\, x : a \bullet [a']P$	Replicated alphabetised parallel

Chaos

The CHAOS process is the most non-deterministic process, that can be specified in CSP. There is nothing it might not do and furthermore there is nothing it might not refuse to do. CHAOS is defined as follows:

$$CHAOS(A) = STOP \sqcap SKIP \sqcap \square\, a : A \bullet a \rightarrow CHAOS(A)$$

As a result of this definition the process CHAOS can behave like each of the three processes. If CHAOS behaves like the STOP process, it stops without producing any further events.

$$\frac{}{CHAOS(A) \; \longrightarrow \; STOP} \quad (A \in \mathcal{P}(\Sigma)) \tag{2.44}$$

Or the process can behave like the SKIP-process and terminate after the production of a ✓-event.

$$\frac{}{CHAOS(A) \; \overset{\checkmark}{\longrightarrow} \; \Omega} \quad (A \in \mathcal{P}(\Sigma)) \tag{2.45}$$

Finally it can repeatedly produce any event from the event set the process gets as its parameter.

$$\frac{}{CHAOS(A) \; \overset{a}{\longrightarrow} \; CHAOS(A)} \quad (A \in \mathcal{P}(\Sigma),\ a \in A) \tag{2.46}$$

2.5   Denotational Semantics of CSP

The denotational semantics of CSP gives another way of describing the behaviour of a specification. The question, whether two different specifications are equivalent, can best be answered by the rules of the denotational semantics. If only *safety* conditions have to be checked, it is often sufficient to check whether certain conditions are true in the traces model of the specification. For model-checking purposes it is often interesting, whether two processes behave identically in the sense, that they do not only produce the same traces, but that both systems are refusing the same events after certain traces as well. This can best be investigated in the stable failures model. Finally it may be interesting, whether and when processes are diverging. Divergences and failures can be observed in the failures-divergences model of a specification. All three different views on CSP-processes are introduced in the following sections.

2.5.1   Traces Model

The traces model of the denotational semantics describes the sequences of events that a process can perform. As an introduction to this model we take a look at the following two processes:

$$P = (a \rightarrow P) \sqcap (b \rightarrow P)$$
$$R = (a \rightarrow R) \mathbin{\square} (b \rightarrow R)$$

The traces which these two processes can produce are identical. In each step of execution the processes can perform either an event a or an event b. The difference is that a process $P \mathbin{\square} Q$ can simultaneously offer all events to the environment that P and Q can produce. The process $P \sqcap Q$ on the contrary makes a non-deterministic choice which one of the two processes is allowed to produce an event. Consequently the traces of the two processes are identical, but the behaviour to the environment is completely different, but this is not handled in the traces model.

The traces model is defined by individual rules for the different CSP operators, which can be found on the following pages. As already defined earlier in this chapter, the term Σ^* describes a set of all finite sequences of the events in the alphabet Σ.

Basic Processes

The predefined CSP process STOP cannot produce any events, hence the set of possible traces of this process contains only the empty trace.

$$traces(STOP) \;=\; \{\langle\rangle\}$$

The process SKIP may terminate at any time under the production of the event $\checkmark$. Therefore the possible traces of this process contains the empty trace and the trace $\langle\checkmark\rangle$.

$$traces(SKIP) \;=\; \{\langle\rangle, \langle\checkmark\rangle\}$$

Prefix

A process like $a \rightarrow P$, which starts with the prefix operator, allows to produce an event a and then behaves like the remaining process P. The traces of this process contain the empty trace, which represents the fact, that the event a is still to be produced by the process. Additionally the traces of the process contains every trace, that the following process P can produce, prepended with the trace $\langle a \rangle$, since a must have been produced, before the process P may perform any actions.

$$traces(a \rightarrow P) \;=\; \{\langle\rangle\} \cup \{\langle a \rangle^\frown s \mid s \in traces(P)\}$$

Sequential Composition

Combining two processes with the sequential composition operator starts the execution of the first process until it terminates. The termination event $\checkmark$ is hidden from the environment and the second process continues producing events. Therefore the traces of $P; Q$ contain all traces of P, except those traces ending with $\checkmark$. The traces of P, which result in a successful termination of that processes are shortened by the $\checkmark$-event and prepended to all those traces that can be produced by the process Q.

$$
\begin{aligned}
traces(P;\, Q) \;=\; & (traces(P) \cap \Sigma^*) \\
& \cup \{ s\hat{\,}t \mid s\hat{\,}\langle \checkmark \rangle \in traces(P) \wedge t \in traces(Q) \}
\end{aligned}
$$

Internal and External Choice

The traces model does not allow to distinguish external and internal choice. For both operators the observed behaviour either corresponds to P or Q. Hence the traces of $P \sqcap Q$ and $P \,\square\, Q$ are the union of the traces of the subprocesses P and Q.

$$
\begin{aligned}
traces(P \sqcap Q) \;&=\; traces(P) \cup traces(Q) \\
traces(P \,\square\, Q) \;&=\; traces(P) \cup traces(Q)
\end{aligned}
$$

Hiding

In CSP, the hiding operator transforms visible events to τ-events, which are not observable in the traces model. Given a trace $s \in \Sigma^*$ and a set of events $X \subseteq \Sigma$ hiding on traces can be defined by restricting the elements of the trace to elements of the specified alphabet without those elements in X.

$$
s \setminus X \;=\; s \restriction (\Sigma \setminus X)
$$

In the resulting trace $s \setminus X$ all occurrences of events, which are in the set X are removed. Using this definition, the traces of the hiding operator can easily be defined based on the traces of the original process.

$$
traces(P \setminus X) \;=\; \{ s \setminus X \mid s \in traces(P) \}
$$

Renaming

The renaming operator requires a relation R, which maps certain events to other specified events. Implicitly this relation is an identity relation for all events that are not specified to be renamed. Like the hiding operator this operator can best be defined by describing the effects of the renaming on the traces of the original process. Therefore R^* is to be defined as an extension of R to traces, which maps traces of elements of $domain(R)$ to traces consisting of elements of $range(R)$.

$$\langle a_1, ..., a_n \rangle R^* \langle b_1, ..., b_m \rangle \quad \Leftrightarrow \quad n = m \wedge \forall i \leq n . a_i R b_i$$

The elements of the traces of $P[\![R]\!]$ can now be defined using the definition of R^*, since all occurrences of events of $domain(R)$ must be replaced by the specified events of $range(R)$.

$$traces(P[\![R]\!]) \quad = \quad \{t \mid \exists s \in traces(P) . s R^* t\}$$

Interleaving

Interleaving in CSP allows two processes to produce events independently from each other. Given two traces, all possible interleavings between those traces may occur as traces of the combined systems. If we specify two traces $s, t \in \Sigma^*$ and two arbitrary events $a, b \in \Sigma$ interleaving of traces can be defined as follows:

$$\langle \rangle \mathrel{|\!|\!|} s \;\; = \;\; \{s\}$$
$$s \mathrel{|\!|\!|} \langle \rangle \;\; = \;\; \{s\}$$
$$\langle a \rangle^\smallfrown s \mathrel{|\!|\!|} \langle b \rangle^\smallfrown t \;\; = \;\; \{\langle a \rangle^\smallfrown u \mid u \in (s \mathrel{|\!|\!|} \langle b \rangle^\smallfrown t)\} \cup \{\langle b \rangle^\smallfrown u \mid u \in (\langle a \rangle^\smallfrown s \mathrel{|\!|\!|} t(\}$$

Using this definition the traces of $P \mathrel{|\!|\!|} Q$ can be defined as the interleaved traces of all possible traces of the processes P and Q.

$$traces(P \mathrel{|\!|\!|} Q) \quad = \quad \bigcup \{s \mathrel{|\!|\!|} t \mid s \in traces(P) \wedge t \in traces(Q)\}$$

Even though interleaving is just a special case of the parallel operator, which set of synchronisation events is empty, this simple definition is much more distinct, since it must not deal with events in a synchronisation set. In the following sections on the other parts of the denotational semantics the interleaving operator is considered as a special case of the parallel operator, since the differences between both operators are not that significant in the other models.

Parallel

The parallel operator in CSP can be used to model parallel processes, which must synchronise over a specified set of events, which can only be performed simultaneously. All other events of the parallel processes may be produced independently from each other, like with the interleaving operator.

The following recursive definition can be used to compute all possible traces of two traces $s, t \in \Sigma^*$ of parallel processes. All occurrences of x and x' are representing events, which are in the synchronisation set X $(x, x' \in X)$, whereas $y, y' \in \Sigma \setminus X$ are events which are not in the synchronisation set.

$$s \underset{X}{\|} t = t \underset{X}{\|} s$$

$$\langle\rangle \underset{X}{\|} \langle\rangle = \{\langle\rangle\}$$

$$\langle\rangle \underset{X}{\|} \langle x\rangle = \{\}$$

$$\langle\rangle \underset{X}{\|} \langle y\rangle = \{\langle y\rangle\}$$

$$\langle x\rangle\hat{\ }s \underset{X}{\|} \langle y\rangle\hat{\ }t = \{\langle y\rangle\hat{\ }u \mid u \in \langle x\rangle\hat{\ }s \underset{X}{\|} t\}$$

$$\langle x\rangle\hat{\ }s \underset{X}{\|} \langle x\rangle\hat{\ }t = \{\langle x\rangle\hat{\ }u \mid u \in s \underset{X}{\|} t\}$$

$$\langle x\rangle\hat{\ }s \underset{X}{\|} \langle x'\rangle\hat{\ }t = \{\} \quad \text{if } x \neq x'$$

$$\langle y\rangle\hat{\ }s \underset{X}{\|} \langle y'\rangle\hat{\ }t = \{\langle y\rangle\hat{\ }u \mid u \in s \underset{X}{\|} \langle y'\rangle\hat{\ }t\} \cup \{\langle y'\rangle\hat{\ }u \mid u \in \langle y\rangle\hat{\ }s \underset{X}{\|} t\}$$

Applying these rules to two given traces express that events, which are in the synchronisation set, can only be produced, if both traces are starting with this event. On the contrary events of $\Sigma \setminus X$ can be produced independently of each other. Using this definition of parallel traces the definition of the traces of two parallel processes can be described by forming the union of all possible parallel traces of the subprocesses P and Q.

$$traces(P \underset{X}{\|} Q) = \bigcup \{s \underset{X}{\|} t \mid s \in traces(P) \wedge t \in traces(Q)\}$$

Conditions and Guarded Commands

The if-then-else operator chooses, depending on the value of a boolean expression b, whether the traces of the process P or Q must be evaluated for the computation of the traces of the process.

$$traces(if\ b\ then\ P\ else\ Q) = \begin{cases} traces(P) & \text{if } b \text{ evaluates to } true \\ traces(Q) & \text{if } b \text{ evaluates to } false \end{cases}$$

Guarded commands are defined analogous to the if-then-else operator, where the else-case refers to the process STOP.

$$traces(b\&P) = \begin{cases} traces(P) & \text{if } b \text{ evaluates to } true \\ traces(STOP) & \text{if } b \text{ evaluates to } false \end{cases}$$

2.5.2 Stable Failures Model

One of the biggest problems of the traces model is the incapability to describe whether it is possible to refuse an event at any time. This is indicated by the phenomenon, that the operators $\Box$ and $\sqcap$ are having the same semantics in the traces model. The ability to distinguish between offering all or only one alternative processes at a choice operator was introduced by another part of the family of denotational semantics: The stable failures model.

Each process in this model is represented by a set of failures. The failures of a process P (*failures*(P)) contain all pairs of the form (s, X), where s is a trace of the process P and X is a set of events that P can refuse after the trace s ($X = refusals(P \setminus s)$). A *stable failure* of a process P consists only of those pairs of traces s and refusals X, after which P is in a stable state, which means, that no τ-event can be produced after the trace s.

Since it is not inevitable, that some traces are leading to unstable states, e.g. those traces leading to τ-loops, it is necessary to state the traces in addition to the failures. Therefore each process P in the stable failures model is represented as the pair (*traces*(P), *failures*(P)), where *traces*(P) may also contain those traces of P, which lead to unstable states.

This model is especially useful, if a process is already checked for divergences. For testing purposes only non-divergent processes are useful and since the calculation of the refusal sets is already quite complex, there is no need to model additional divergences, if it can be assured, that the process is non-divergent.

Additionally it is sometimes useful to analyse a divergence-free process P by placing it in a context $C[P]$ in which it may diverge as the result of hiding some sets of actions. A refinement check using the failures-divergences model, as described in the next section, would fail in this case, whereas the stable failures model disregards the divergent parts of the specification.

The rules of the stable failures model introduced here will be required in the chapter 8 for the normalisation of high level transition graphs. Only the definition of the *failures*(P) will be given here, since the *traces*(P) have already been introduced in the previous section.

Basic Processes

The basic process STOP cannot perform any actions, hence the failures contains pairs with an empty trace and all subsets of the alphabet $\Sigma^{\checkmark}$. It is important to note, that the failures-set contains not only the pair $(\langle\rangle, \Sigma^{\checkmark})$, but also those pairs with empty traces and all possible subsets of $\Sigma^{\checkmark}$, which is often referred to by the term *subset closure*.

$$failures(STOP) = \{(\langle\rangle, X) \mid X \subseteq \Sigma^{\checkmark}\}$$

The SKIP-process behaves similar to the STOP-process, since it refuses all events but the $\checkmark$-event, if no event has been produced. Additionally it may refuse all events, after $\checkmark$ occurred in the trace of the process.

$$failures(SKIP) = \{(\langle\rangle, X) \mid X \subseteq \Sigma\} \cup \{(\langle\checkmark\rangle, X) \mid S \subseteq \Sigma^{\checkmark}\}$$

Prefix

The computation of the failures of the prefix operator in the process $a \rightarrow P$ consists of two failures sets. The first set contains all those pairs with an empty trace which contains those subsets of the alphabet $\Sigma^{\checkmark}$, where the event a is not in those sets. This set indicates, that the process can only perform an event a in the beginning, hence all other events must be refused. As soon as a has been produced, the process can refuse all those events, that can be refused by the process P. Therefore, those failures of P must be computed and the traces in the resulting pairs must be prepended with the trace $\langle a \rangle$, since the event a has already been produced.

$$\begin{aligned} failures(a \rightarrow P) \;=\; & \{(\langle\rangle, X) \mid a \notin X \wedge X \subseteq \Sigma^{\checkmark}\} \\ & \cup \{(\langle a \rangle\hat{\ }s, X) \mid (s, X) \in failures(P)\} \end{aligned}$$

Sequential Composition

The failures of a sequential composition $P; Q$ can be computed by calculating the failures of the two subprocesses P and Q. The failures of P remain unchanged in $failures(P; Q)$, except that all occurrences of $\checkmark$-events are removed from the refusals. Additionally the traces in the failures of Q must be appended to all possible traces of P that lead to a successful termination, since those events of Q may only occur, after P has terminated.

$$\begin{aligned} failures(P; Q) \;=\; & \{(s, X) \mid s \in \Sigma^* \wedge (s, X \cup \{\checkmark\}) \in failures(P)\} \\ & \cup \{(s\hat{\ }t, X) \mid s\hat{\ }\langle\checkmark\rangle \in traces(P) \wedge (t, X) \in failures(Q)\} \end{aligned}$$

Internal Choice

The internal choice operator chooses non-deterministically, whether those events of the first or the second process are accepted. Hence the failures are the union of the failures of the subprocesses.

$$failures(P \sqcap Q) = failures(P) \cup failures(Q)$$

External Choice

In contrast to the internal choice, the external choice allows the environment to choose, which events of the subprocesses should be produced, which means that only those events can be refused after an empty trace, which can be refused immediately in both subprocesses P and Q. After the initial event, which resolves the external choice, all those events may be refused, that can be refused either by P or by Q. Finally the process $P \,\square\, Q$ may refuse all events but the $\checkmark$-event, if either P or Q can terminate immediately.

$$failures(P \ \Box \ Q) =$$
$$\{(\langle\rangle, X) \mid (\langle\rangle, X) \in failures(P) \cap failures(Q)\}$$
$$\cup \{(s, X) \mid (s, X) \in failures(P) \cup failures(Q) \land s \neq \langle\rangle\}$$
$$\cup \{(\langle\rangle, X) \mid X \subseteq \Sigma \land \langle\checkmark\rangle \in traces(P) \cup traces(Q)\}$$

Hiding

The hiding operator in the stable failures model effects not only the visible traces, as already explained in the traces model on page 38, but it also has to be applied to the refusal set of the failure. Therefore all occurrences of events in the hiding set X must be removed from the trace, where only those refusal sets are contained in the failures, that contains all elements from the hiding set.

$$failures(P \setminus X) = \{(s \setminus X, Y) \mid (s, X \cup Y) \in failures(P)\}$$

Renaming

The relation R of the renaming operator describes, which events have to be replaced by which other events. All failures of the process $P[\![R]\!]$ are based on the failures of P, where the extension of the renaming relation R to traces is applied to all traces of the failures of P. Additionally all occurrences of events in the renaming relation have to be replaced in the refusals as well. This can be achieved by applying the inverse relation $R^{-1}(X) = \{a \mid \exists a' \in X . (a, a') \in R\}$ to all elements of the refusal sets of $failures(P)$.

$$failures(P[\![R]\!]) = \{(s', X) \mid \exists s . \ s \ R \ s' \land (s, R^{-1}(X)) \in failures(P)\}$$

Interleaving and Parallel

The failures of the interleaving and the parallel operator can be described by only one rule, since interleaving is just a special case of the parallel operator, where the set of synchronisation events is empty. To calculate the failures of a process $P \parallel_X Q$, it is first necessary to compute those failures of the subprocesses P and Q. The resulting failures of the parallel system consist of the parallel traces of both subprocesses and the corresponding refusals, which must not refuse any events not in the synchronisation set that are possible either in P or in Q. Additionally, the refusal must contain any event from the synchronisation set, unless it is offered by both subprocesses.

$$failures(P \parallel_X Q) \ = \ \{(u, Y \cup Z) \mid \ Y \setminus (X \cup \{\checkmark\}) = Z \setminus (X \cup \{\checkmark\})$$
$$\land \exists s, t.((s, Y) \in failures(P)$$
$$\land (t, Z) \in failures(Q) \land u \in s \parallel_X t)\}$$

Conditions and Guarded Commands

The if-then-else-operator chooses, depending on the value of a boolean expression b, whether the process P or Q must be evaluated for the computation of the failures of the process.

$$failures(if \ b \ then \ P \ else \ Q) \ = \ \begin{cases} failures(P) & \text{if } b \text{ evaluates to } true \\ failures(Q) & \text{if } b \text{ evaluates to } false \end{cases}$$

Since guarded commands are a shortened form of if-then-else statements the failures can be calculated as follows:

$$failures(b \ \& \ P) \ = \ \begin{cases} failures(P) & \text{if } b \text{ evaluates to } true \\ failures(STOP) & \text{if } b \text{ evaluates to } false \end{cases}$$

Summary

With this model it should be possible to distinguish the two processes P and R from the example on page 37. Assuming, that the alphabet Σ contains only the events a and b, let's take a look at the failures of the processes P and R. To do so, it is necessary to examine the failures of the processes $a \rightarrow P$ and $b \rightarrow P$:

$$failures(a \rightarrow P) \ = \ \{ \ (\langle\rangle, \{\}), \ (\langle\rangle, \{b\}), \ \}$$
$$\cup \{ \ (\langle a\rangle\hat{\ }s, X) \mid (s, X) \in failures(P) \ \}$$

and

$$failures(b \rightarrow P) \ = \ \{ \ (\langle\rangle, \{\}), \ (\langle\rangle, \{a\}), \ \}$$
$$\cup \{ \ (\langle b\rangle\hat{\ }s, X) \mid (s, X) \in failures(P) \ \}$$

According to the rule for the internal choice operator, the failures of the process P are the union of the failures of the subprocesses $a \rightarrow P$ and $b \rightarrow P$, so that the result is:

$$failures(P) \ = \ \{ \ (\langle\rangle, \{\}), \ (\langle\rangle, \{a\}), \ (\langle\rangle, \{b\}), \ \}$$
$$\cup \{ \ (\langle a\rangle\hat{\ }s, X) \mid (s, X) \in failures(P) \ \}$$
$$\cup \{ \ (\langle b\rangle\hat{\ }s, X) \mid (s, X) \in failures(P) \ \}$$

In contrast to this we take a look at the failures of the process R, which can be determined by applying the rule for the external choice operator.

$$failures(R) \ = \ \{ \ (\langle\rangle, \{\}) \ \}$$
$$\cup \{ \ (\langle a\rangle\hat{\ }s, X) \mid (s, X) \in failures(R) \ \}$$
$$\cup \{ \ (\langle b\rangle\hat{\ }s, X) \mid (s, X) \in failures(R) \ \}$$

The difference between these two failure sets is obvious and corresponds to the intuitive understanding of the operators, since the process R cannot refuse any event at all, while in contrast to that the process P may refuse any event at any time.

2.5.3 Failures-Divergences Model

Though the stable failures model is useful to express more properties of a given process as possible in the traces model, is it still not possible to check questions of *liveness*, since it cannot be expressed that a process will always continue producing new events. Two situations can arise, where this may not happen: deadlocks and livelocks. A *deadlock* analysis checks, whether a situation can occur, in which the process cannot produce any more events. Such situation can occur if parallel systems are trying to get hold of shared resources. Those deadlocks can easily be identified using the stable failures model of CSP.

A more severe problem are *livelock* situations. Even though they look identical to deadlocks from the outside, they are quite different, since livelocks occur if an infinite number of internal actions is produced by a system, that cannot be influenced by the environment. To solve this problem another model is required which is also a part of the family of denotational semantics: The *failures-divergences model*. Each process in this model is represented by a pair of failures and divergences.

Failures, as already introduced in the stable failures model, are pairs of traces and event sets. Since the failures of a process P in the failures-divergences model may be different than those in the stable failures model, a new term $failures_\perp(P)$ is introduced to discern these two notations. The divergences of a process P ($divergences(P)$) are the traces after which the process P can diverge, i.e. can perform an infinite, unbroken number of internal τ-actions which are not visible to the environment.

Basic Processes

The $failures_\perp$ of the basic processes STOP and SKIP are defined to be identical with the *failures* of those processes in the stable failures model. The divergence sets of those processes do not contain any elements, which is obvious, since neither process could diverge.

$$divergences(STOP) \;=\; \{\}$$
$$failures_\perp(STOP) \;=\; \{(\langle\rangle, X) \mid X \subseteq \Sigma^\checkmark\}$$

$$divergences(SKIP) \;=\; \{\}$$
$$failures_\perp(SKIP) \;=\; \{(\langle\rangle, X) \mid X \subseteq \Sigma\} \cup \{(\langle\checkmark\rangle, X) \mid S \subseteq \Sigma^\checkmark\}$$

Prefix

The definition of the prefixes $failures_\perp$ is identical to *failures* in the stable failures model as well. The process $a \rightarrow P$ cannot diverge immediately, since there is always the event a that can occur. Hence the set of divergent traces is only determined by the divergences of the following process P.

$$
\begin{aligned}
divergences(a \rightarrow P) &= \{\langle a \rangle \hat{\ } s \mid s \in divergences(P)\} \\
failures_\perp(a \rightarrow P) &= \{(\langle\rangle, X) \mid a \notin X \wedge X \subseteq \Sigma^\checkmark\} \\
&\quad \cup \{(\langle a \rangle \hat{\ } s, X) \mid (s, X) \in failures_\perp(P)\}
\end{aligned}
$$

Sequential Composition

A process $P; Q$ does always produce those failures and divergences of the process P, unless P has terminated successfully with the event $\checkmark$. The termination signal $\checkmark$ of P is hidden and transformed into a τ-event, since no $\checkmark$ may be emitted unless the process Q terminates after execution of P.

The divergences of $P; Q$ must of cause contain all divergent traces of the process P, additionally all possible traces of P on which the process terminates must be prepended to all divergent traces of Q. The set of $failures_\perp(P; Q)$ is once again based on $failures(P; Q)$, but extended by all pairs of divergent traces and any subset of Σ. These pairs are part of $failures_\perp$ since a process may perform and refuse any events after it has diverged.

$$
\begin{aligned}
divergences(P; Q) &= divergences(P) \cup \\
&\quad \{s\hat{\ }t \mid s\hat{\ }\langle\checkmark\rangle \in traces(P) \wedge t \in divergences(Q)\} \\
failures_\perp(P; Q) &= \{(s, X) \mid s \in \Sigma^* \wedge (s, X\cup\{\checkmark\}) \in failures_\perp(P)\} \\
&\quad \cup \{(s\hat{\ }t, X) \mid \ s\hat{\ }\langle\checkmark\rangle \in traces(P) \\
&\qquad\qquad\qquad \wedge (t, X) \in failures_\perp(Q)\} \\
&\quad \cup \{(s, X) \mid s \in divergences(P; Q) \wedge X \subseteq \Sigma\}
\end{aligned}
$$

Internal Choice

The internal choice $P \sqcap Q$ chooses non-deterministically whether either the process P or the process Q should be executed. If either of them may diverge the whole process may diverge as well. Hence $divergences(P \sqcap Q)$ is the union of the divergences of the subprocesses. The definition of the $failures$ remains unchanged from the stable failures model.

$$
\begin{aligned}
divergences(P \sqcap Q) &= divergences(P) \cup divergences(Q) \\
failures_\perp(P \sqcap Q) &= failures_\perp(P) \cup failures_\perp(Q)
\end{aligned}
$$

External Choice

Based on the $failures$ of the stable failures model for the external choice operator, $failures_\perp$ has to be expanded by those failures that occur, if either P or Q diverges immediately. In those cases all events from Σ may be refused immediately, even though the other process may offer an event.

If either of the processes P or Q can diverge, the whole process may diverge as well. Therefore the *divergences*$(P \mathbin{\square} Q)$ are the union of the divergences of the subprocesses.

$$divergences(P \mathbin{\square} Q) = divergences(P) \cup divergences(Q)$$

$$failures_\perp(P \mathbin{\square} Q) =$$
$$\{(\langle\rangle, X) \mid (\langle\rangle, X) \in failures_\perp(P) \cap failures_\perp(Q)\}$$
$$\cup \{(s, X) \mid (s, X) \in failures_\perp(P) \cup failures_\perp(Q) \wedge s \neq \langle\rangle\}$$
$$\cup \{(\langle\rangle, X) \mid X \subseteq \Sigma \wedge \langle\checkmark\rangle \in traces(P) \cup traces(Q)\}$$
$$\cup \{(\langle\rangle, X) \mid X \subseteq \Sigma \wedge \langle\rangle \in divergences(P) \cup divergences(Q)\}$$

Hiding

The hiding operator is the most complex operator in this semantics, since it introduces non-determinism to situations, which have been deterministic before. Additionally it may introduce divergences into a specification, if a set of events is hidden, such that infinite chains of τ-events occur in the specification.

A new notation on traces has to be introduced for the definition of the divergences: if s and t are traces, consisting of elements of Σ, $s < t$ is defined as follows:

$$s < t \;\equiv\; \exists\, u \in \Sigma^* . \, s\hat{\ }u = t \wedge u \neq \langle\rangle$$

The *failures*$_\perp(P \setminus X)$ are based on *failures*$(P \setminus X)$, but those situations, where divergences are introduced, have to be taken into account too. Therefore, all pairs of divergent traces of $P \setminus X$ may refuse all elements of X. Please note that this definition is consistent with the definition of Hoare in [ ], but differs from Roscoe's definition in [ ], page 199, which definition of the *failures*$_\perp$ seems to be inaccurate, since those rule could only refuse elements of the hiding set after diverging.

Σ^ω is a set of all infinite sequences over Σ.

$$divergences(P \setminus X) \;\subseteq\; \{(s \setminus X)\hat{\ }t \mid s \in divergences(P) \wedge t \in (\Sigma \backslash X)^*\}$$
$$\cup \{(u \setminus X)\hat{\ }t \mid \; u \in \Sigma^\omega \wedge (u \setminus X) \text{ is finite}$$
$$\wedge\, \forall\, s < u.s \in traces(P)\}$$
$$failures_\perp(P \setminus X) \;=\; \{(s \setminus X, Y) \mid (s, X \cup Y) \in failures_\perp(P)\}$$
$$\cup \{(s, Y) \mid s \in divergences(P \setminus X) \wedge Y \subseteq \Sigma\}$$

Renaming

The *failures*$_\perp$ for the renaming operator are identical to the *failures* in the stable failures model extended by all pairs of divergent traces and subsets of Σ for the subprocess the renaming operator is applied to. All occurrences of events in the $divergences(P)$ which have to be hidden, have to be removed.

$$
\begin{aligned}
divergences(P[\![R]\!]) &= \{s'^\frown t \mid t \in \Sigma^* \wedge \exists\, s \in divergences(P) \cap \Sigma^* \,.\, s\,R\,s'\} \\
failures_\perp(P[\![R]\!]) &= \{(s', X) \mid \exists\, s \,.\, s\,R\,s' \\
&\qquad \wedge (s, R^{-1}(X)) \in failures_\perp(P)\} \\
&\cup \{(s, X) \mid X \subseteq \Sigma \wedge s \in divergences(P[\![R]\!])\}
\end{aligned}
$$

Interleaving and Parallel

Since the interleaving and alphabetised parallel operators can directly be derived from the parallel operator, only the rules for the latter is specified here. The process $P \parallel_X Q$ may diverge on any trace that is created from a divergent trace of one process and an arbitrary trace of the other process. The $failures_\perp$ are an extension of $failures$ by all pairs of divergent traces and subsets of Σ for the parallel process.

$$
\begin{aligned}
divergences(P \parallel_X Q) &= \{u^\frown v \mid v \in \Sigma^* \wedge \exists\, s \in traces(P), t \in traces(Q) \,. \\
&\qquad u \in (s \parallel_X t) \cap \Sigma^* \\
&\qquad \wedge (s \in divergences(P) \vee t \in divergences(Q))\} \\
failures_\perp(P \parallel_X Q) &= \{(u, Y \cup Z) \mid Y \setminus (X \cup \{\checkmark\}) = Z \setminus (X \cup \{\checkmark\}) \\
&\qquad \wedge \exists\, s, t \,.\, (u \in s \parallel_X t \\
&\qquad \wedge (s, Y) \in failures_\perp(P) \\
&\qquad \wedge (t, Z) \in failures_\perp(Q))\} \\
&\cup \{(u, Y) \mid u \in divergences(P \parallel_X Q)\}
\end{aligned}
$$

Conditions and Guarded Commands

Depending on the value of the boolean expression of the if-then-else statement the failures and divergences are identical with the corresponding values of either the process in the *then*-case or in the *else*-case.

$$
divergences(\textit{if } b \textit{ then } P \textit{ else } Q) = \begin{cases} divergences(P) & \textit{if } b = true \\ divergences(Q) & \textit{if } b = false \end{cases}
$$

$$
failures_\perp(\textit{if } b \textit{ then } P \textit{ else } Q) = \begin{cases} failures_\perp(P) & \textit{if } b = true \\ failures_\perp(Q) & \textit{if } b = false \end{cases}
$$

Guarded commands are defined in an analogous way, where the process Q is replaced by $STOP$ in the definitions from above.

Summary

Once again lets take the example from the previous sections and modify it a little, by adding a hiding operator, which removes all occurrences of the event b.

$$P = P' \setminus \{b\}$$
$$P' = (a \to P') \sqcap (b \to P')$$

In the stable failures model, the calculation of the failures of this process would be problematic:

$$
\begin{aligned}
failures(P) &= failures(P' \setminus \{b\}) \\
&= \{(s \setminus \{b\}, Y) \mid (s, \{b\} \cup Y) \in failures(P')\} \\
&= \{ (\langle\rangle, \{\}), (\langle\rangle, \{a\}) \} \\
&\quad \cup\{ (\langle a\rangle\hat{\ }s, X) \mid (s, X) \in failures(P') \} \\
&\quad \cup\{ (s, X) \mid (s, X) \in failures(P') \}
\end{aligned}
$$

Obviously the term $\{ (s, X) \mid (s, X) \in failures(P') \}$ does not add new elements to the set of failures of the process P, but calls the function with unmodified arguments repeatedly. Even though a fixpoint of $failures(P)$ can be calculated, the problem becomes clearer: the hiding operator introduced a livelock to the specification, since it is possible, that the internal choice always selects the branch producing only τ-events. In the failures-divergences model those livelocks are easily identified by the divergences of P, which contain the empty trace and all traces with an arbitrary number of a-events, since the process may diverge at any time.

The biggest gain of this model, as can be observed by this example, is to recognise, if and where a process definition may diverge, which cannot be achieved with any other model of the denotational semantics. For testing purposes this model is not as important as the stable failures semantics, since safety critical systems must in general not be divergent.

2.5.4 Refinement

In this section the concept of refinement of CSP processes will be explained. Refinement can be used to check, whether an implementation of a system shows the same behaviour in one of the semantic models to a CSP specification describing the expected behaviour. The specification *SPEC* is an abstract CSP model which describes the properties of the desired behaviour of the implementation *IMP*, which is a CSP representation of an implementation of the problem.

A refinement check is successful, if the implementation *IMP* *refines* the specification *SPEC* which is denoted as $SPEC \sqsubseteq IMP$. There exists different kinds of refinement which are described as follows:

Traces refinement

In the traces model a process is described by all sequences of events a process can perform. A process *IMP* is refined in the traces model by another process *SPEC*, if all traces that *IMP* can produce can also be produced by the process *SPEC*:

$$SPEC \sqsubseteq_T IMP \equiv traces(IMP) \subseteq traces(SPEC)$$

Failures Refinement

In the failures model a process is described by all traces and all failures of the process. A process *IMP* is refined in the failures model by another process *SPEC* (*SPEC* $\sqsubseteq_F$ *IMP*), if all failures of IMP are included in the failures of the process *SPEC*. Hence all sets of events X, that can be refused by the process *IMP* after the trace s, can also be refused by *SPEC*.

$$SPEC \sqsubseteq_F IMP \equiv failures(IMP) \subseteq failures(SPEC)$$

Additionally this refinement check ensures, that the implementation *IMP* may only deadlock in those situations, where the specification *SPEC* also may.

Failures-Divergences Refinement

The failures model does not occupy with livelock situations, since it ignores the divergences of the implementation and the specification. Such checks are performed by the failures-divergence refinement, where the divergences are checked in addition to the failures. The failures-divergence refinement *SPEC* $\sqsubseteq_{FD}$ *IMP* is defined as follows:

$$\begin{aligned} SPEC \sqsubseteq_{FD} IMP \equiv\ & failures_\perp(IMP) \subseteq failures_\perp(SPEC) \wedge \\ & divergences(IMP) \subseteq divergences(SPEC) \end{aligned}$$

Failures-Divergences-Robustness Refinement

Finally it is sometimes required that every trace that is possible in the specification should also be performable in the implementation. Such property is checked in the failures-divergence-robustness refinement, which is defined as follows:

$$\begin{aligned} SPEC \sqsubseteq_{FDR} IMP \equiv\ & failures_\perp(IMP) \subseteq failures_\perp(SPEC) \wedge \\ & divergences(IMP) \subseteq divergences(SPEC) \\ & traces(SPEC) \subseteq traces(IMP) \end{aligned}$$

2.5.5 Normal Form of CSP Specifications

Equivalence between various CSP terms has already been described through out the semantics part of this chapter. It has been established that different CSP processes can express the same semantical behaviour. But it is possible to "isolate a particular subclass of terms, called *normal forms*, whose denotations in the model are reflected directly in their syntactic structure." [ ] Such normal forms of CSP processes, are described in theorem 2.1:

Theorem 2.1 *Normal Form Theorem:*
  Let P be a CSP *process, interpreted in the failures-divergence model.*

  1. If $\langle \rangle \notin divergences(P)$, then

$$P = \bigsqcap R : refusals(P) \bullet x : ([P]^0 \setminus R) \rightarrow P \setminus \langle x \rangle$$

  2. If $divergences(P) = \emptyset$, then $P \setminus s = P(s)$ with

$$P(s) = \bigsqcap R : refusals(P \setminus s) \bullet x : ([P \setminus s]^0 \setminus R) \rightarrow P(s^\smallfrown \langle x \rangle)$$

  3. For arbitrary P and $P_{NF} = P(\langle \rangle)$, $P \sqsubseteq_{FD} P_{NF}$ holds.

A normal form CSP process P_{NF} is structured in such a way, that for each execution step of the process after any trace s, one of the possible refusals R has to be selected first. All elements of the selected refusal R are removed from the set of initial events $[P \setminus s]^0$ of the process P after the trace s and the resulting set of events is offered to the external environment. As soon as some event e has been chosen, the evaluation continues in the state $P(s^\smallfrown \langle x \rangle)$.

Chapter 3

Transition Systems and Graphs

The theory of transition systems and transition graphs dates back to 1736, where Leonhard Euler tried to find a solution for the well known *Königsberger Brückenproblem*. This problem deals with the question, whether it is possible to find a way through the streets of the city Königsberg by passing each of the seven bridges, which connect parts of the city, only once.

Euler found out, that there is no solution to this problem, but proving this was much more difficult. His new proving technique abstracted from the actual map of Königsberg to a simpler mathematical model. The island, the north, south and east parts were abstracted to simple nodes, since Euler found out, that the ways in each part of the city are not related to the solution. Additionally he modelled the ways over the bridges as connections between the nodes.

This idea was sufficient to proof, that there can be no path in Königsberg, which only passes each bridge once. But the proving technique he used is still used for labelled transition systems, as they are going to be introduced in this chapter. As soon as the concepts of labelled transition systems and transition graphs are introduced, additional properties of and equivalences on transition systems are explained, leading to a definition of a normal form of transitions systems.

3.1 Introduction to Transition Systems

The transition systems we are talking about in this sections are *labelled transition systems* (LTS). The notation employed in the following definition is oriented at the widely-used CSP notation.

Definition 3.1 *Labelled Transition Systems ($\mathcal{L}_{LTS}$):*
An LTS is a 4-tuple $(S, s_0, \Sigma^{\tau\checkmark}, \rightarrow)$, where

1. *S is the set of states,*

2. *$s_0 \in S$ is the initial state,*

3. $\Sigma^{\tau\checkmark} = \Sigma \cup \{\tau, \checkmark\}$, where Σ is the set of observable actions. τ is an internal event, which cannot be observed, and $\checkmark$ indicates successful termination of a CSP process. Both events τ and $\checkmark$ are not elements of the alphabet Σ.

4. $\rightarrow \subseteq S \times \Sigma^{\tau\checkmark} \times S$, where $\rightarrow$ is a relation between states.

Since we are going to use this definition for the LTS in this chapter, we will introduce some notations, that will be required in the following sections:

Definition 3.2 *Some LTS notations. Let $\alpha \in \Sigma^{\tau\checkmark}$:*

$$s \xrightarrow{\alpha} s' \quad (s, \alpha, s') \in \rightarrow$$
$$s \xrightarrow{\alpha} \quad \exists\, s'.s \xrightarrow{\alpha} s'$$
$$s \xrightarrow{\sigma} s' \quad \exists\, s_1, s_2, \ldots, s_n.s \xrightarrow{\alpha_1} s_1 \xrightarrow{\alpha_2} s_2 \ldots \xrightarrow{\alpha_n} s_n$$
$$\qquad\quad with\ \sigma = \alpha_1 \cdot \alpha_2 \cdot \ldots \cdot \alpha_n \wedge s_n = s'$$
$$s \xrightarrow{\sigma} \quad \exists\, s'.s \xrightarrow{\sigma} s'$$
$$s \xrightarrow{\tau^*} s' \quad s \xrightarrow{\sigma} s'\ with\ \sigma = \alpha_1 \cdot \alpha_2 \cdot \ldots \cdot \alpha_n$$
$$\qquad\qquad\qquad \wedge \forall\, i \in \{1, \ldots, n\}.\alpha_i = \tau$$

Transition systems, that are displayed in a graphical representation, are also called *transition graphs*. Each state of a transition systems is represented by a node in the corresponding transition graphs. In the graphs the initial nodes are usually marked by distinguished nodes, which can be achieved by a thicker drawn border of the node. The relations between states are represented as transitions between nodes in the transition graphs, which are labelled with the events that have to be produced, if the transition is taken.

3.1.1   Properties of Transition Systems

The execution of an LTS begins at the special node s_0, which marks the starting point of the system. In order to proceed with the traversal of the graph, it is necessary to select one of the relations $l = (s, \alpha, s')$ with $l \in \rightarrow$, where s is the current state, α is a possible action and s' is the successor state. The set of initial actions of a state s will be denoted $[s]^0$ and is defined as follows:

Definition 3.3 *Initial actions of a state $s \in S$:*
$$[s]^0 = \{\, \alpha \in \Sigma^{\tau\checkmark} \mid \exists\, s' \in S\, .\, s \xrightarrow{\alpha} s'\}$$

As soon as an action $\alpha \in [s]^0$ is performed, the current state for the interpretation of the graph changes to s' and a new relation can be chosen by the environment. The *external environment* is a sink for all events that a CSP specification can produce. It selects one of the initial actions of the current state in the LTS and uses that event to change the current state to the target state of the selected transition.

In contrast to visible actions, which can only be performed in cooperation with the environment, τ-actions happen automatically without interaction. Therefore all states with relations that can perform a τ-action ($\tau \in [s]^0$) are called *unstable*, since some action (visible or τ) must occur any time. The other special action ✓ has properties of both visible and τ-actions: On the one hand it is visible to the environment, because it indicates successful termination of the whole system. On the other hand that action may not be blocked by the environment. Therefore all states containing a ✓-event in its initial actions must be considered unstable as well.

All other states are called *stable*, because it is not possible to leave that state without interaction from the environment. Internal events like τ and ✓ cannot be selected by the environment, since they happen automatically.

The external non-determinism of the environment is not to be mistaken with the internal *non-determinism* of an LTS, as illustrated in the figure 3.1. An LTS is deterministic, if the execution of an action in a given state leads to a unique successor state. In a non-deterministic LTS an action may lead to several other states. Additionally deterministic LTS must not contain any τ-events, since they cannot be observed by the environment and therefore it is not possible to predict in which state the LTS currently is. The graph on the left is deterministic, because the production of the action a does not lead to any decision, whether b or c must be taken in the next step, whereas the non-deterministic graph on the right hand side does.

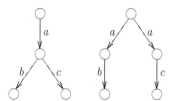

Figure 3.1: A deterministic *(left)* and a non-deterministic *(right)* labelled transition system

Definition 3.4 *Determinism:*
  An LTS is deterministic iff for any $s, s', s'' \in S$

1. $\not\exists s'.s \xrightarrow{\tau} s'$,

2. $s \xrightarrow{\alpha} s' \wedge s \xrightarrow{\alpha} s'' \implies s' = s''$

Another interesting question about CSP specifications represented as an LTS could be, whether they can guarantee, that it will always be possible to produce

a visible action. There are two different situations, in which this is not the case:
On the one hand the LTS could contain a state, which has no initial actions. In
that case it would never be possible to leave that state anymore. Whenever a
state has no initial actions it is called *deadlocked*. On the other hand the LTS
could contain a path through its structure consisting only of τ-transitions, which
lead back to the start state of the search. If this special path is chosen, it is
not guaranteed, that the system will ever interact with the environment again.
This situation is called *livelock*, since it is always possible to change the state of
the LTS although no actions can be observed. The following definition gives a
more formal understanding of deadlocks and livelocks in transition systems, but
expresses the same understanding of those two concepts as already introduced in
section 2.5.3.

Definition 3.5 *Deadlock and Livelock*
An LTS contains a deadlock, iff $\exists\, s.[s]^0 = \emptyset$
An LTS contains a livelock, iff $\exists\, s.s \xrightarrow{\tau^*} s$

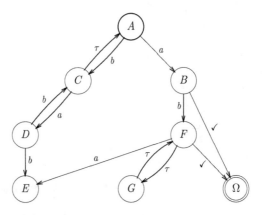

Figure 3.2: An example of a labelled transition system in its graph representation

Using the exemplary LTS in figure 3.2 the basic ideas introduced in the section
will be illustrated:

- The node labelled A is *stable*, since only transitions with actions of Σ are
  leaving this node. It is only possible to leave this node, if the environment
  selects any of the events a or b, which puts the process to the state B or
  state C, respectively.

- The state B is *unstable*, since if may perform two actions, where one of them cannot be blocked by the environment. The process may at any time decide non-deterministically to terminate successfully and move on to the state Ω, or allows the environment to select the event b.

- In node C it is possible to select one visible and one τ action, thus this state is *unstable*, too. If the environment chooses the action a as soon as it is possible, the transition to state D can be taken, otherwise the invisible τ-event will be selected at any time.

- D is a stable state once again, but it introduces the problem of *non-determinism* to this graph. The production of the event b can lead to the two different nodes C and E and it is not possible for the environment to determine the successor state.

- The set of relations $\rightarrow$ for the shown LTS does not contain any relations with the state E as source state. Therefore this state is stable, since it is not possible to leave this state anymore, but it also makes this LTS containing a deadlock.

- Node F has three different initial actions a, τ and $\checkmark$, which means that the environment can only select the a event to be produced, the other events cannot be influenced by the environment, which makes this state unstable. Therefore the system can terminate at any time, if it is in this state or move on to state G which does not offer the event a anymore.

- The system may choose to always select the τ-transition in state F, which leads to an infinite cycle, since G only has one τ-label. The system is continuously changing its state, but never produces an output to the environment anymore. This situation is called *livelock*.

- The state Ω represents a terminated system. Therefore, there are no transitions leaving this state.

Since CSP supports the employment of infinite types (like the natural numbers $\mathbb{N}$), it is easy to write specifications that could produce an infinite transition graph. The process $COUNT_0$, which is defined below, produces such an infinite transition graph, since it contains an infinite number of nodes. Such graph is depicted in figure 3.3.

$$
\begin{aligned}
COUNT_0 &= up \rightarrow COUNT_1 \\
COUNT_n &= up \rightarrow COUNT_{n+1} \\
&\quad \Box \\
&\quad down \rightarrow COUNT_{n-1}
\end{aligned}
$$

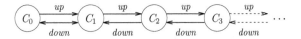

Figure 3.3: An example of an infinite LTS

The only possibility to transform such specification into *finite transition graphs* is to restrict the use of the parameters. In the example above an additional definition would make the transition graph starting at $COUNT_0$ finite.

$$
\begin{aligned}
COUNT_0 &= up \to COUNT_1 \\
COUNT_4 &= down \to COUNT_3 \\
COUNT_n &= up \to COUNT_{n+1} \\
&\quad \Box \\
&\quad down \to COUNT_{n-1}
\end{aligned}
$$

It is obvious, that the number of nodes, that can be reached from the state representing the process $COUNT_0$ is limited, since just the five states C_0 to C_4 representing the CSP processes $COUNT_0$ to $COUNT_4$ can be reached (as illustrated in Figure 3.4).

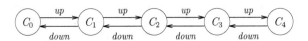

Figure 3.4: An example of a finite LTS

Definition 3.6 *Finite State LTS:*
An LTS is finite state, if the number of states reachable from the initial state s_0 via sequences of actions is finite.

The LTS we have introduced so far are well suited to represent the behaviour of a CSP process. But there is one problem left: the same behaviour can be represented in various different ways, as shown in Figure 3.5. All LTS depicted there are representing the same behaviour: the actions a and b are produced in arbitrary order. The small LTS on the left hand side of the figure is the smallest LTS that can be produced to represent this behaviour, the one is the middle is only slightly more complex, because it uses two states instead of one, where the state indicates, which event was taken last. Since the specified behaviour never terminates, it is also possible to specify an infinite graph, like the one on the right hand side, where for each possible sequence of actions a unique state exists in the graph.

3.1.2 Equivalence of Transition Systems

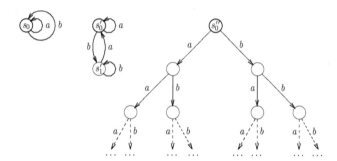

Figure 3.5: Different LTS describing the same behaviour

This leads to the question, how it is possible to determine, whether two LTS are representing the same behaviour. From the environments point of view it is only possible for each process state to view those actions that can be done immediately. Therefore all those states are equivalent, which have the same actions leaving, leading to states which are themselves equivalent, since those states cannot be distinguished by the environment.

In [ ] Milner introduces the term *strong bisimulation*, which describes an equivalency between transition systems, as follows: "*P* and *Q* are equivalent iff, for every action α, every α-derivative of *P* is equivalent to some α-derivative of *Q*, and conversely." This leads to the following more formal definition:

Definition 3.7 *Strong Bisimulation:*
A relation R on the set of states S of an LTS is said to be a strong bisimulation, iff both the following hold:

1. $\forall n_1, n_2, m_1 \in S . \forall x \in \Sigma^{\tau\checkmark}$.
   $n_1 \, R \, n_2 \wedge n_1 \xrightarrow{x} m_1 \implies \exists m_2 \in S . n_2 \xrightarrow{x} m_2 \wedge m_1 \, R \, m_2$

2. $\forall n_1, n_2, m_2 \in S . \forall x \in \Sigma^{\tau\checkmark}$.
   $n_1 \, R \, n_2 \wedge n_2 \xrightarrow{x} m_2 \implies \exists m_1 \in S . n_1 \xrightarrow{x} m_1 \wedge m_1 \, R \, m_2$

Two states of an LTS are said to be *bisimilar* if there is a bisimulation which relates them. It is possible to define a bisimulation of states between two different LTS which share the same set of actions $\Sigma^{\tau\checkmark}$, because the two systems can be embedded into one, where the two graphs are disjoint.

The two exemplary LTS in Figure 3.5 starting with the nodes s_0 and s_0' have two finite representations of the same behaviour, which can be proven, by finding a relation between the nodes, which is bisimilar. Since the simplest graph on the left hand side contains only one node, the obvious solution for the relation R is: $R = \{(s_0, s_0'), (s_0, s_1')\}$, where the node s_0 correlates to every node in the other graph.

Now the two conditions of Definition 3.7 have to be checked for all nodes and transitions:

1. $s_0 \; R \; s_0' \wedge s_0 \xrightarrow{a} s_0 \implies s_0' \xrightarrow{a} s_0' \wedge s_0 \; R \; s_0'$
   $s_0 \; R \; s_0' \wedge s_0 \xrightarrow{b} s_0 \implies s_0' \xrightarrow{b} s_1' \wedge s_0 \; R \; s_1'$
   $s_0 \; R \; s_1' \wedge s_0 \xrightarrow{a} s_0 \implies s_1' \xrightarrow{a} s_0' \wedge s_0 \; R \; s_0'$
   $s_0 \; R \; s_1' \wedge s_0 \xrightarrow{b} s_0 \implies s_1' \xrightarrow{b} s_1' \wedge s_0 \; R \; s_1'$

2. $s_0 \; R \; s_0' \wedge s_0' \xrightarrow{a} s_0' \implies s_0 \xrightarrow{a} s_0 \wedge s_0 \; R \; s_0'$
   $s_0 \; R \; s_0' \wedge s_0' \xrightarrow{b} s_1' \implies s_0 \xrightarrow{b} s_0 \wedge s_0 \; R \; s_1'$
   $s_0 \; R \; s_1' \wedge s_1' \xrightarrow{a} s_0' \implies s_0 \xrightarrow{a} s_0 \wedge s_0 \; R \; s_0'$
   $s_0 \; R \; s_1' \wedge s_1' \xrightarrow{b} s_1' \implies s_0 \xrightarrow{b} s_0 \wedge s_0 \; R \; s_1'$

Since both conditions holds for all nodes and transitions in both graphs, is has been shown, that R is a strong bisimulation between the states of the two graphs.

3.2   Normalising a Labelled Transition System

A.W. Roscoe described in the article "Model-checking CSP" [ ] the need for normalised transition graphs for model checking. The biggest problem for a model checker working on non-normalised graphs would be the non-determinism, which can be characterised by two properties of a transition system:

If the transition system contains τ-events at the transitions between states, it would not be possible to predict, in which state the system is at any specified time. The reason for this is, that τ-events cannot be observed by the environment, hence the specification could be in any state, that could be reached by a chain of τ-events. Another problem occurs, if a node has two identically-labelled actions. The environment can only observe the occurrence of that event, but it is not possible to predict, in which state the transition system is after the event has been produced.

Any transition system, which has τ-events or identically labelled actions leaving a node, must be considered non-deterministic. For model checking it is required to have exactly one state corresponding to each possible trace. This can be achieved by transforming the transition system into its *normal form*, which is semantically equivalent to the original form, as shown in [ ].

In analogy to theorem 2.5.5, any finite CSP term is equivalent to one in the following normal form:

- $\bot$ is a normal form

- all others take the form

$$\sqcap\{(x : A \to P(x)) \mid A \in \mathcal{A}\}$$

  for $\mathcal{A}$ a convex subset of Σ such that $\bigcup \mathcal{A} \in \mathcal{A}$, and each $P(x)$ a normal form which depends only on x, not an A.

It is important to note, that processes of such normal form can only produce visible events. Additionally this form branches uniquely on each visible event. As long as the process does not diverge, as indicated by the normal form $\bot$, such normal form provides a deterministic transition system. The non-determinism, which may have been modelled on purpose in the original CSP specification must not be dropped, if both forms ought to be semantically equivalent. Therefore each process is not only determined by the *initial actions* ($\bigcup \mathcal{A}$) and its behaviour after each initial action, but also by its *minimum acceptances*. Those minimal elements of $\mathcal{A}$ are in a direct correlation with the *maximum refusals*, which are used to model non-determinism in normal form transition systems.

The normalisation process requires two stages: The first stage generates a pre-normal form of any given transition system derived from a CSP specification. Such pre-normal form transition systems do not contain any non-determinism, but it is possible to create a potentially more dense graph, by identifying semantically identical nodes, which is done in the second stage of the algorithm.

3.2.1   Stage 1 – Generating the pre-normal form

Definition 3.8 *A labelled transition system* $\mathcal{L}_{LTS} = (S, s_0, \Sigma^{\tau\checkmark}, \to)$ *can be normalised in a graph* $\mathcal{P}_{\mathcal{L}}$ *whose nodes are members of* $\mathcal{P}(S)$ *as follows:*

- *The initial node of* $\mathcal{P}_{\mathcal{L}}$ *is* $\tau^*(s_0)$, *where* $\tau^*(s) = \{s\} \cup \{s' \mid s \xrightarrow{\tau^*} s'\}$.

- *For each node generated is is necessary to decide whether it is divergent. A newly created node* $n \in \mathcal{P}_{\mathcal{L}}$ *is divergent, if any of the contained nodes* $s \in \mathcal{L}$ *is divergent.*

- *For each non-divergent node n a set of non-τ-actions is determined. For each event e contained in this set, a new node is formed. The new node contains all those nodes of S, that can be reached by the event e and any number of τ-events from the members of n: $\bigcup \{\tau^*(s') \mid \exists\, s \in n.s \xrightarrow{e} s'\}$*

- *The pre-normalisation is completed, if all new nodes that have been generated have been previously expanded.*

The pre-normalisation technique described by the rules above can be demonstrated with a simple example. The following CSP specification can be used to generate an LTS as shown in the upper part of figure 3.6.

$$
\begin{aligned}
P_0 &= a \to P_1 \sqcap a \to \text{STOP} \\
P_1 &= a \to P_2 \,\square\, a \to \text{STOP} \\
P_2 &= a \to P_0 \,\square\, a \to P_1
\end{aligned}
$$

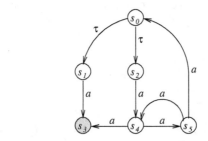

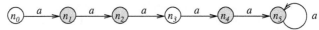

Figure 3.6: Pre-normalising a transition system

The process P_0 is represented by the transitions between the states s_0, s_1, s_2, s_3 and s_4, where the τ-transitions leaving s_0 are representing the non-determinism introduced by the internal choice operator. The state s_3 is a STOP-state, since no transitions are leaving this state. Process P_1 is modelled by the transitions from s_4 to the states s_5 and s_3; and process P_2 is represented by the transitions from s_5 to s_0 and s_4.

The pre-normalisation process starts with the generation of the initial node $n_0 = \tau^*(s_0)$, since s_0 is the start node of the LTS to be normalised: $\tau^*(s_0) = \{s_0, s_1, s_2\} = n_0$.

Since none of the nodes of the original LTS is divergent, the second rule of the pre-normalisation never applies. Therefore it is only required to determine the initial actions of the new node n_0. Since all transitions leaving the nodes s_1 and s_2 are labelled with the event a, it is possible to create a new node $n_1 = \bigcup \{\tau^*(s') \mid \exists s \in n_0.s \overset{a}{\rightarrow} s'\} = \{s_3, s_4\}$.

Now it is necessary to expand the new node n_1, which has just been created. s_3 is the STOP-state and can therefore not participate in the production of any events, but the state s_4 can produce two a-events leading to the states s_3 and s_5. Thus a new node can be created:
$$n_2 = \bigcup \{\tau^*(s') \mid \exists s \in n_1.s \overset{a}{\rightarrow} s'\} = \{s_3, s_5\}.$$

A node like n_2 has not been expanded by now, so the normalisation must continue with that node: $n_3 = \bigcup \{\tau^*(s') \mid \exists s \in n_2.s \overset{a}{\rightarrow} s'\} = \{s_0, s_1, s_2, s_4\}$, since s_5 has transitions labelled a that leads to the states s_0 and s_4. But the state s_0 has only τ-actions, that must be eliminated by this algorithm, therefore the targets of the τ-transitions must be in the resulting set representing node n_3 as well.

The algorithm continues producing the nodes $n_4 = \{s_3, s_4, s_5\}$ and $n_5 = \{s_0, s_1, s_2, s_3, s_4, s_5\}$. The calculation of $n_6 = \bigcup \{\tau^*(s') \mid \exists s \in n_5.s \overset{a}{\rightarrow} s'\}$ results once again in the set $\{s_0, s_1, s_2, s_3, s_4, s_5\}$. Both nodes n_5 and n_6 contain the same original states and can therefore be considered identical.

Finally the algorithm terminates, since node n_6 has been previously expanded and no other states have to be expanded as well. The resulting pre-normalised graph is shown in the lower part of figure 3.6.

3.2.2 Stage 2 – Generating the normal form

Figure 3.6 contains more information than only the names of the states and events, but also information about the refusals of the nodes. The original node s_3, which is filled in gray, is representing the STOP-state, i.e. no transition leaves this state. In the pre-normalised graph this information is not lost. States filled in gray are labelled with a maximum refusal set of $\{\Sigma, \Sigma \setminus \{a\}\}$, where no events may be produced, due to the refusal Σ. Unmarked states n_0 and n_3 are labelled with maximum refusal set $\{\Sigma \setminus \{a\}\}$ and can therefore not refuse to produce the event a.

A closer look at the graph represented by the states n_0 to n_5 raises the question, whether it would be possible to create a more dense representation of the graph. The idea would be to identify semantically identical states and create a normal form of the graph, where those identical states are represented by exactly one state. Such graphs would have exactly one representation for the same semantical behaviour.

To create a normal form from a pre-normal from graph, it is necessary to mark all nodes in the pre-normal graph with

- $\bot$, if the state is divergent,

- its initial actions and maximal refusals otherwise.

The first step to the answer of the question, which states should be identified equivalent, can be determined by the markings of the states. Only states with the same marking, i.e. either $\bot$ or the same initial actions and maximal refusals, can be taken under consideration. Then the fixed point $\sim$ of the following sequences of equivalence relations must be calculated.

Definition 3.9 *The fixed point $\sim$ of the sequences of equivalence relations can be computed as follows:*

- $n \sim_0 M$, *if, and only if, they have the same marking*

- $n \sim_{n+1} M \Leftrightarrow (n \sim_n M) \wedge$
  $$\forall n', M'.(n \xrightarrow{a} n' \wedge M \xrightarrow{a} M' \Rightarrow n' \sim_n M')$$

The fixed point computation for the example in figure 3.6 results in the following equivalence relations:

$$n_0 \sim n_0, \quad n_1 \sim n_1, \quad n_2 \sim n_2, \quad n_3 \sim n_3,$$
$$n_4 \sim n_4, \quad n_4 \sim n_5, \quad n_5 \sim n_5, \quad n_5 \sim n_4$$

This result shows, that each state is equivalent to itself, but it shows also that the states n_4 and n_5 are equivalent, therefore they can be identified in the resulting normalised graph, which is shown in figure 3.7.

"The normal form of the labelled transition system $\mathcal{L}_{LTS}$ is thus its pre-normal form under the equivalence relation $\sim$, where the initial node is the equivalence class of $\tau^*(s_0)$, the transition relation is the obvious one and the only detail we recode about each node is the marking as described above." [ ]

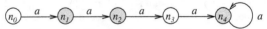

Figure 3.7: Normalising a transition system

3.2.3   Refusals and Acceptance Sets

The normalisation process for transition graphs make them deterministic, but there are operators in CSP which can be used to introduce non-determinism. Take the following CSP specification for example:

```
1   channel a, b
2
3   INT = a -> STOP |~| b -> STOP
4   EXT = a -> STOP [] b -> STOP
```

Two different process definitions are introduced in this specification. The process EXT offers both event a and b to the environment and the environment may select, which event shall be used to traverse the transition graph. In contrast to that the second process INT first selects internally, which τ-transition should be used. After that, the environment is offered either the event a or the event b, but never both events.

If the normalisation, as described in the previous section, is applied to both transition graphs, the resulting normalised form for both processes looks exactly the same, as shown in figure 3.8.

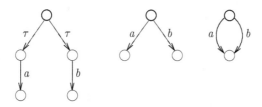

Figure 3.8: The transition graphs for INT (left), EXT (middle) and the resulting normal form (right)

The normal form of both processes is identical, if only the transition graph itself is taken under consideration. The information about the internal choice of the process INT seems to be lost, since there is no indication, that either the event a or the event b may be refused to be produced. On the other hand the normalised form of the process EXT must always accept both events a and b. Since this kind of information cannot be modelled in the transition graph, there needs to be additional information labelled to each node in the transition graph, which stores, which events must be accepted or may be refused.

The events to be accepted of refused in any given node of the transition system can be computed with the rules of the denotational semantics of CSP, which was already described in chapter 2.5. There are several models of the denotational semantics based on traces, failures and divergences from which we have to choose the one best suitable for the problem. In the traces model the choices made by internal events are not modelled properly. On the contrary the failures-divergences model, does not only carry information about *failures* (events that may be refused after a certain trace), but also about *divergences*.

Divergences are those traces of a specification, after which it can diverge, i.e. there can occur an infinite sequence of internal τ-events. For testing purposes the divergences are not that relevant, since it is only useful to test non-divergent systems, which implies, that the specifications to test those systems should be non-divergent as well. Therefore the best choice for the calculation of the events that may be refused in any node of the transition graph, would be the *stable failures model* described in detail in 2.5.2.

Based on these rules, it would be possible to calculate all failures for a given process. But the normalised graphs that are created by the pre-normalising process, do not require all failures of the process, since the transition graphs are modelling all possible traces of a process. Only the part of the failures, that represents the refusals, are required for the normalisation process, since those refusals are used to model for example the differences between internal and external choice in the normal form of transition graphs.

The failures of simple processes like $STOP$, defined as $failures(STOP) = \{(\langle\rangle, X) \mid X \subseteq \Sigma^{\checkmark}\}$, can already introduce, depending on the size of the alphabet, large sets of failures, since all possible subsets of Σ may be refused. To overcome this remedy the refusals of a process are defined to be *subset closed*, which means, that a failure (s, X) implies, that all pairs of s and the subsets of X are in the failures as well. With this definition the representation of the refusals labelled to nodes can be more efficient, since it is only necessary to specify the *maximum refusals*, from which all refusals can be derived.

Even though the maximum refusals can easily be used to reduce the number of sets, that have to be labelled to the nodes in the normalised graphs, the number of events contained in those sets are usually large. A CSP-specification, that is usually used for testing purposes, has large alphabets, but usually offers only a small subset of those at any time. Therefore it is more efficient to model not the refusals, but the *acceptances* a process offers, in the nodes of the transition systems. Those acceptance sets are defined to be the complements of the refusal sets, which means that they contain those events, that a process offers, instead of those events that a process can refuse. Analogous to the consideration about the maximum refusal sets of the failures, it is possible to define a set of *minimal acceptances*. These minimal acceptance sets are usually significantly smaller than the corresponding maximum refusal sets.

As stated before the pre-normalising process of the transition systems of the processes INT and EXT in figure 3.8 results in the same normal form. The different semantical behaviour can therefore only be modelled by adding refusals or acceptances to the nodes.

The failures of the internal choice operator in the stable failures semantics are the union of the subprocesses of the operator, which are $a \rightarrow STOP$ and $b \rightarrow STOP$ in this example. If the rules from the stable failures semantics are once again applied to these two processes, the following failures are computed:

$$
\begin{aligned}
\mathit{failures}(a \to STOP) \;=\; & \{(\langle\rangle, X) \mid a \notin X \land X \subseteq \Sigma^{\checkmark}\} \\
& \cup \{(\langle a\rangle, X) \mid X \subseteq \Sigma^{\checkmark}\} \\
\mathit{failures}(b \to STOP) \;=\; & \{(\langle\rangle, X) \mid b \notin X \land X \subseteq \Sigma^{\checkmark}\} \\
& \cup \{(\langle b\rangle, X) \mid X \subseteq \Sigma^{\checkmark}\}
\end{aligned}
$$

Hence the failures of the process INT are defined as follows:

$$
\begin{aligned}
\mathit{failures}(INT) \;=\; & \{(\langle\rangle, X) \mid a \notin X \land X \subseteq \Sigma^{\checkmark}\} \\
& \cup \{(\langle\rangle, X) \mid b \notin X \land X \subseteq \Sigma^{\checkmark}\} \\
& \cup \{(\langle a\rangle, X) \mid X \subseteq \Sigma^{\checkmark}\} \\
& \cup \{(\langle b\rangle, X) \mid X \subseteq \Sigma^{\checkmark}\}
\end{aligned}
$$

But, as stated before, only the refusal part of the failures is interesting for the transition graph, since the traces are modelled by the graph itself. Therefore only those refusals are selected to be labelled to the transition graph, which corresponding traces in the failures are empty. The resulting maximal refusal for the initial node of the normalised graph is $\{\Sigma^{\checkmark}\backslash\{a\}, \Sigma^{\checkmark}\backslash\{b\}\}$. The corresponding minimal acceptance set is $\{\{a\}, \{b\}\}$, which means that the environment is either offered the event a or b to be executed, but not both simultaneously.

The failures of the process EXT are looking different, since they contain all those failures with an empty trace which are in the conjunct of $\mathit{failures}(P)$ and $\mathit{failures}(Q)$. By definition, these are all those failures, which do not contain the events a and b in its refusals. Additionally the failures of the process EXT contain all those failures of the subprocesses, which traces are not empty.

$$
\begin{aligned}
\mathit{failures}(EXT) \;=\; & \{(\langle\rangle, X) \mid a, b \notin X \land \land X \subseteq \Sigma^{\checkmark}\} \\
& \cup \{(\langle a\rangle, X) \mid X \subseteq \Sigma^{\checkmark}\} \\
& \cup \{(\langle b\rangle, X) \mid X \subseteq \Sigma^{\checkmark}\}
\end{aligned}
$$

For the external choice operator the maximal refusals are different than from the internal choice operator, since they contain only one set of events: $\{\Sigma^{\checkmark} \backslash \{a, b\}\}$. The corresponding minimal acceptance set $\{\{a, b\}\}$ offers both events a and b simultaneously to the environment, which can now select, which one the execute.

Chapter 4

Binary Decision Diagrams

Binary Decision Diagrams (BDD) are a compact way of representing boolean functions, which have proven to be powerful tools in formal verification. The original publication of Randal E. Bryant can be found in [ ]. Since then, many research has been done in this area ([ ], [ ]) and a number of implementations have been developed which have been compared in [ ].

This chapter gives an introduction to BDDs and how they are used to represent boolean functions. After that, an extended use of BDDs to represent general expressions is developed. The representation of general expressions as BDDs can be used to represent expressions of CSP specifications in a compact way that still allows them to be evaluated in real-time. This becomes important in part III of this thesis.

4.1   An Introduction to BDDs

A BDD is a directed, acyclic graph (DAG) representation of a boolean function. Because equivalent sub-expressions are uniquely represented, a BDD can be exponentially more dense than the corresponding truth table. BDDs use *if-then-else* representations of boolean functions.

Definition 4.1

Let Ite be the three-place boolean if-then-else operator defined by

$$\mathit{Ite}(x, y_0, y_1) \;=\; (x \wedge y_0) \vee (\neg x \wedge y_1)$$

In this section the terms $\top$ and 1 are used as equivalent representations of the boolean value *true* and $\bot$ and 0 are used as representations of *false*. $\top$ and $\bot$ normally are used in the context of boolean expressions and terms while 1 and 0 are used in the graph representation.

As shown in [ ], all boolean operators can be expressed with Ite, $\top$ and $\bot$. Therefore it is possible to define an *If-then-else Normal Form* of a boolean expression containing only Ite operators, $\top$ or $\bot$.

Definition 4.2 If-then-else Normal Form *(INF)*:
The If-then-else Normal Form f_{INF} *of a boolean function f is a boolean expression that is equivalent to f and is built entirely from the* if-then-else *operator,* $\top$ *and* $\bot$.

Let $f[b/x]$ denote the boolean expression that is the result of replacing x in f with b being either $\top$ or $\bot$. For every boolean expression f with x as one of its free variables $(x \in vars(f))$, the following equivalence holds:

$$ f \quad \equiv \quad \textit{Ite}(x, f[\top/x], f[\bot/x]) $$

This is the so-called *Shannon expansion* of f with respect to x. It can be used to generate the INF from any boolean expression f. If f does not contain any variables, it is equivalent to $\top$ or $\bot$ which both are in INF. If f does contain variables, the Shannon expansion can be applied to it and recursively to its two sub-formulas $f[\top/x]$ and $f[\bot/x]$. Because each sub-formula has one less free variables than f, the recursion in a branch ends with a sub-formula $f_i[\top/x]$ or $f_i[\bot/x]$ having no free variables and therefore being equivalent to $\top$ or $\bot$.

In BDDs, $\top$ and $\bot$ are usually represented by 1 and 0. Every boolean expression f that is in INF is equivalent to a BDD where every $\textit{Ite}(x, f_1, f_2)$ sub-formula in f is represented as a node in the BDD with two outgoing labels to the BDDs of f_1 and f_2 labelled with 1 for the *then*-case and 0 for the *else*-case. The topmost *Ite* operator is represented by the root node of the BDD.

The variables of the expression can be ordered, so that the sequence in which they are replaced during the Shannon expansion is the same in every sub-formula. The result is an *ordered* INF that can be represented in an *ordered* BDD.

Definition 4.3 *Ordered BDD:*
An INF f_{INF} of a boolean expression f with a linear ordering $<$ on the free variables $x_1, ..., x_n$ of f is called ordered *(f_{OINF}), if for every sub-formula $\textit{Ite}(x_i, f_1, f_2)$ of f_{INF} and every sub-formula $\textit{Ite}(x_j, f_3, f_4)$ of f_1 or f_2, it holds that $x_i < x_j$ with $i, j \in 1, ..., n$. The BDD of an ordered INF is called* ordered BDD (OBDD).

Example: The *ordered* INF of the boolean expression $f = (x_1 \Leftrightarrow y_1) \wedge (x_2 \Leftrightarrow y_2)$ with the linear ordering $<$ of the variables being $x_1 < y_1 < x_2 < y_2$ can be created using the Shannon expansion. Figure 4.1 shows the truth table and the INF of this example and Figure 4.2 shows the OBDD.

Normally, there are redundant sub-formulas in the INF of an expression. Obviously, every sub-formula $\textit{Ite}(x, f_1, f_1)$ in the INF of f can be replaced by f_1. In the above example, every sub-formula $\textit{Ite}(y_2, \bot, \bot)$ can be replaced by $\bot$. This leads to the following INF of f:

$$ f'_{INF} \quad = \quad \textit{Ite}(x_1, \quad \textit{Ite}(y_1, \textit{Ite}(x_2, \textit{Ite}(y_2, \top, \bot), \textit{Ite}(y_2, \bot, \top)), \bot), $$
$$ \textit{Ite}(y_1, \bot, \textit{Ite}(x_2, \textit{Ite}(y_2, \top, \bot), \textit{Ite}(y_2, \bot, \top)))) $$

x_1	y_1	x_2	y_2	f
0	0	0	0	1
0	0	0	1	0
0	0	1	0	0
0	0	1	1	1
0	1	0	0	0
0	1	0	1	0
0	1	1	0	0
0	1	1	1	0
1	0	0	0	0
1	0	0	1	0
1	0	1	0	0
1	0	1	1	0
1	1	0	0	1
1	1	0	1	0
1	1	1	0	0
1	1	1	1	1

$$f_{INF} = Ite(x_1,$$
$$Ite(y_1,$$
$$Ite(x_2,$$
$$Ite(y_2, \top, \bot),$$
$$Ite(y_2, \bot, \top)),$$
$$Ite(x_2,$$
$$Ite(y_2, \bot, \bot),$$
$$Ite(y_2, \bot, \bot))),$$
$$Ite(y_1,$$
$$Ite(x_2,$$
$$Ite(y_2, \bot, \bot),$$
$$Ite(y_2, \bot, \bot)),$$
$$Ite(x_2,$$
$$Ite(y_2, \top, \bot),$$
$$Ite(y_2, \bot, \top))))$$

Figure 4.1: Truth table and INF of expression $f = (x_1 \Leftrightarrow y_1) \wedge (x_2 \Leftrightarrow y_2)$.

If names are introduced for identical sub-formulas in an INF, these can be replaced by their name. A INF that is *abbreviated* in this way is extended by a (nonrecursive) list of names for sub-formulas. A formula is *maximally abbreviated* if

1. no compound sub-formula $Ite(x, f_1, f_2)$ appears twice and

2. no two abbreviations have the same right hand side.

Replacing all redundant sub-formulas in an INF f_{INF} and maximally abbreviating it leads to a reduced form f_{RINF} of it. In the example, we replace the term $Ite(x_2, Ite(y_2, \top, \bot), Ite(y_2, \bot, \top))$ with the abbreviation β. The *reduced* INF of f now reads:

$$f_{RINF} = Ite(x_1, Ite(y_1, \beta, \bot), Ite(y_1, \bot, \beta))$$
$$\text{with } \beta = Ite(x_2, Ite(y_2, \top, \bot), Ite(y_2, \bot, \top))$$

There exist equivalent operations on the BDD of the INF for replacing redundant sub-formulas and introducing abbreviations in an INF. They are shown in figure 4.3. On the left side of the figure, it is shown how two nodes, that represent the same sub-formula, are joined together. This is equivalent to introducing an abbreviation for this sub-formula. On the right hand side of the figure, a redundant node is deleted. In this case, this is equivalent to replacing a redundant sub-formula $Ite(y_1, f_1, f_1)$ by f_1.

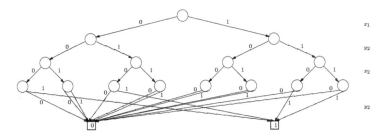

Figure 4.2: An OBDD of $f = (x_1 \Leftrightarrow y_1) \wedge (x_2 \Leftrightarrow y_2)$ with variable ordering $x_1 < y_1 < x_2 < y_2$.

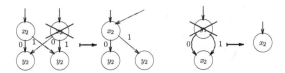

Figure 4.3: The reduction conditions of ROBDDs: nodes must be unique and only non redundant nodes should be present.

Definition 4.4 *Reduced OBDD:*
An ordered INF f_{OINF} of a boolean expression f is called reduced *(f_{ROINF}), if it does not contain any redundant sub-formulas and is maximally abbreviated. The OBDD of an* reduced *ordered INF is called* reduced OBDD (ROBDD).

As shown in [ ], for any boolean function $f : \{\top, \bot\}^n \to \{\top, \bot\}$, there exists exactly one ROBDD g with a variable ordering $<$, such that $f^g = f$. The left hand side of Figure 4.4 shows the ROBDD of the example with variable ordering $x_1 < y_1 < x_2 < y_2$. Changing the variable ordering leads to a different ROBDD. This can have a great impact on the size of the graph. The ROBDD on the left hand side of figure 4.4 consists of 6 nodes. If the variable ordering is changed to $x_1 < x_2 < y_1 < y_2$, the resulting ROBDD contains 9 nodes. This graph can be seen on the right hand side of figure 4.4.

4.2   Binary Decision Diagrams of General Expressions

BDD are representations of boolean functions but they can as well be used to represent general expressions. Each expression e with free variables $x_1, ..., x_n$ can

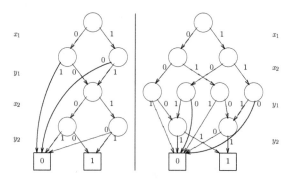

Figure 4.4: Two ROBDD of f with variable ordering $x_1 < y_1 < x_2 < y_2$ and $x_1 < x_2 < y_1 < y_2$.

be seen as a function $f : D_{x_1} \times ... \times D_{x_n} \rightarrow R_e$ from the domains of the variables of e into the range of e with $f(x_1, ..., x_n) = e$. There exists an equivalent function f^{bit} which uses only binary domains $D^{bit} = \{0,1\}^n$. For every domain D_{x_i} of a variable x_i of f, a new domain $D_{x_i}^{bit} = \{0,1\}^{n_i}$ is defined with $n_i = log_2(|\ D_{x_i}\ |)$. The range $R_e^{bit} = \{0,1\}^m$ of f^{bit} is a binary range with $m = log_2(|\ R_e\ |)$. An injective function $code_{x_i} : D_{x_i} \rightarrow D_{x_i}^{bit}$ is defined for every variable x_i of f, that maps the values of the domain of x_i to a unique binary encoded value in $D_{x_i}^{bit}$. The function $code_R : R \rightarrow R_e^{bit}$ is an analogous mapping for the range of f. $f^{bit} : D_{x_1}^{bit} \times D_{x_n}^{bit} \rightarrow R_e^{bit}$ can now be defined as

$$f^{bit}(x_{1\,1}, ..., x_{1\,log_2(|D_{x_1}|)}, ..., x_{n\,1}, ..., x_{n\,log_2(|D_{x_n}|)}) = code_R(f(x_1, ..., x_n))$$
$$\text{with } \forall\, i \in \{1, ..., n\}.code_{x_i}(x_i) = (x_{i\,1}, ..., x_{i\,log_2(|D_{x_i}|)})$$

Example

The expression $(x_1 + x_2)\%4$ for example can be interpreted as a function $f :$ $D_{x_1} \times D_{x_2} \rightarrow R_f$ with $f(x_1, x_2) = (x_1 + x_2)\%4$.Lets define $D_{x_1} = D_{x_2} = \{0,1,2,3\}$. The range of the function is $R_f = \{0,1,2,3\}$. Binary domains for the expression can be defined with $D_{x_1}^{bit} = D_{x_2}^{bit} = R_f^{bit} = \{0,1\}^2$. In this example, all functions that map the values of the domain to a unique binary encoded value in the binary encoded domain are defined as $code : \{0,1,2,3\} \rightarrow \{0,1\}^2$ with $code(0) = 00, code(1) = 01, code(2) = 10, code(3) = 11$. Now an equivalent function $f^{bit} :$ $D_{x_1}^{bit} \times D_{x_2}^{bit} \rightarrow R_f^{bit}$ can be defined with new variables x_{11}, x_{12}, x_{21} and x_{22} for the arguments of f^{bit} and y_1 and y_2 for the result. Table 4.1 gives the explicit definition of f^{bit}.

x_1	x_2	x_{11}	x_{12}	x_{21}	x_{22}	y_1	y_2	$f(x_1, x_2) = y$
0	0	0	0	0	0	0	0	0
0	1	0	0	0	1	0	1	1
0	2	0	0	1	0	1	0	2
0	3	0	0	1	1	1	1	3
1	0	0	1	0	0	0	1	1
1	1	0	1	0	1	1	0	2
1	2	0	1	1	0	1	1	3
1	3	0	1	1	1	0	0	0
2	0	1	0	0	0	1	0	2
2	1	1	0	0	1	1	1	3
2	2	1	0	1	0	0	0	0
2	3	1	0	1	1	0	1	1
3	0	1	1	0	0	1	1	3
3	1	1	1	0	1	0	0	0
3	2	1	1	1	0	0	1	1
3	3	1	1	1	1	1	0	2

Table 4.1: The function values of $f^{bit}(x_{11}, x_{12}, x_{21}, x_{22})$ coded in y_1, y_2.

The decision tree that can be created for f^{bit} is similar to a BDD except that the end nodes are not limited to 0 and 1. Every element $y^{bit} \in R^{bit}$ with $\exists y \in R.y^{bit} = code_R(y)$ is an end node in the decision tree. Similar to BDDs, redundant subtrees can be eliminated and identical subtrees can be joined. Unfortunately, the decision tree for injective functions f^{bit} is always as big as a table containing the whole function. Figure 4.5 shows the already reduced decision tree for the above example with the variable ordering $x_{11} < x_{12} < x_{21} < x_{22}$.

To be able to use the full power of BDDs, the function has to be represented as a boolean function. Therefore, a boolean function $f^{BDD} : D_{x_1}^{bit} \times ... \times D_{x_n}^{bit} \times R^{bit} \rightarrow \{0, 1\}$ is defined, that determines if an element of R^{bit} is the result of f^{bit} for given arguments $x_{11}, ..., x_{nm}$.

$$f^{BDD}(x_{11}, ..., x_{nm}, y_1, ..., y_k) = \begin{cases} 1 & if\ f^{bit}(x_{11}, ..., x_{nm}) = (y_1, ..., y_k) \\ 0 & otherwise \end{cases}$$
$$with\ (x_{11}, ..., x_{nm}) \in D_{x_1}^{bit} \times ... \times D_{x_n}^{bit}$$
$$\wedge (y_1, ..., y_k) \in R^{bit}$$

For the representation of e, it is not necessary to represent the values of the argument variables $x_{11}, ..., x_{nm}$ and the result variables $y_1, ..., y_k$ for that f^{BDD} is 0, because they are no solution of e. This leads to a further reduction of the ROBDD. Figure 4.6 shows the ROBDD of f^{bit} with variable order $x_{11} < x_{12} < x_{21} < x_{22} < y_1 < y_2$ without the end node 0 and without all paths leading to it.

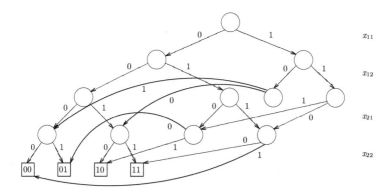

Figure 4.5: The decision tree of f^{bit} with variable order $x_{11} < x_{12} < x_{21} < x_{22}$.

4.2.1   Variable Order and Evaluation

For a variable ordering $x_{11} < ... < x_{nm} < y_1 < ... < y_k$, the evaluation of e for the variables $x_1, ..., x_n$ can be done using the functions $code_{x_i}$ to get the binary representation of the variables. According to the variable order, there exists exactly one path in the BDD for $x_{11}, ..., x_{nm}$ being the binary representation of the chosen variable values for $x_1, ..., x_n$. Because there is only one solution of e for a chosen set of variable values and all paths that lead to 0 end nodes are eliminated, the solution of e for the chosen variable values is represented as a single path of nodes for the variables $y_1, ..., y_k$ at the end of the path for $x_{11}, ..., x_{nm}$. $y_1, ..., y_k$ is the binary encoded solution of e for the chosen variable values $(code_R(e(x_1, ..., x_n)) = y_1, ..., y_k)$.

The most compact representation normally can be achieved by changing the variable ordering. In this case, the evaluation can become more complex, because the solution variables $y_1, ..., y_n$ and the argument variables $x_{11}, ..., x_{nm}$ are mixed. An exemplary ROBDD of f^{BDD} with variable ordering $x_{12} < x_{22} < y_2 < x_{11} < x_{21} < y_1$ can be seen in figure 4.7. Compared with the ROBDD in figure 4.6, it is more dense, because it identifies similar subtrees for the values of the variables x_{12} and x_{11}.

Independent of the variable ordering, there exists only a single path in the BDD for a given set of values for $x_{11}, ..., x_{nm}$, but finding this path can involve backtracking, since at a node with two labels depending on the values of one of the result variables y_i, it is not known which one to choose. This situation does not occur in the ROBDDs of the example because for the chosen variable ordering, the value of the result variables are always definite. Consider a variable ordering in which all result variables y_i being less than the argument variables

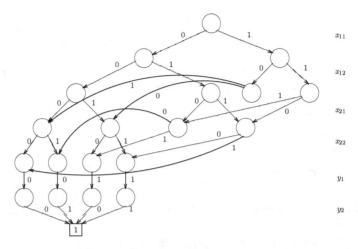

Figure 4.6: The ROBDD of f^{bit} with variable order $x_{11} < x_{12} < x_{21} < x_{22} < y_1 < y_2$ without the end node 0.

x_i: $\forall\, y_i, x_i.y_i < x_i$. In this case, the values of the argument variables can not be used to compute the value of the result variables. If the represented function is bijective, all possible combinations of the values of the result variables will be present in the ROBDD because there are no values for the argument and result variables for that f^{bit} is 0. Finding the path for a set of given values for the argument variables can make it necessary to check all paths of the ROBDD. Since the function is injective, there is a single path of values for the argument variables at the end of every path of result variables. For n result variables and m argument variables, these are 2^n paths of the length $n + m$. If the function is surjective but not injective, the paths of argument variables are not unique. If all values that can be represented with the result variables can be reached, the maximum of paths that have to be searched in the worst case for a function with n result variables and m argument variables is the grater of 2^n or 2^m.

When representing expressions as ROBDDs, it is necessary to decide which variable ordering should be used. The resulting BDD can be the minimal ROBDD but includes backtracking when it is evaluated or it can have more nodes and labels but does not include backtracking. The decision has to be made according to the purpose, the BDD is created for: fast evaluation or minimal representation.

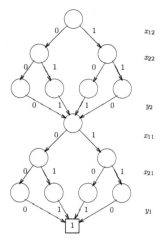

Figure 4.7: The ROBDD of f^{bit} with variable order $x_{12} < x_{22} < y_2 < x_{11} < x_{21} < y_1$ without the end node 0.

Part II

Highlevel Transition Graphs

Model-checking and testing based on CSP specifications suffers from one drawback, that is inherent to the way how transition systems are created from CSP specifications: state explosions. Even for relatively small specifications, which behaviour is strongly data dependant, the corresponding transition system may contain too many states and transitions to be completely represented in a computers memory. The standard way of solving such problem is decomposing the original CSP specification into several specifications, which only model a part of the behaviour of the system.

Another way to solve this issue is suggested in this part of this thesis: high level transition graphs. Instead of unfolding the complete state space of the specification, an implicit modelling of the state space is introduced, which is achieved by annotating labelled transition system, that are generated from a CSP specification, with additional conditions and assignments at the transitions. Those conditions and assignments are applied to variables, that are directly derived from the original CSP specification. Using this idea for transition systems, reduces the size of the generated graph structures significantly. Instead of creating one state in a transition system for each internal system state, the new approach summarises several similar states into one and parametrises that state over the possible values of the variables.

This concept, which is introduced in detail in section 5.1, only applies to the sequential parts of CSP without the high-level operators like parallel, interleaving and hiding. For those operators section 5.2 introduces another concept, which models the hiding and synchronisation structure of parallel high level transition graphs: the synchronisation terms. In contract to high level transition graphs, synchronisation terms do not carry any state information, but only synchronisation and hiding information, which is sufficient, to compute at any time the behaviour of the parallel system.

Chapter 6 introduces the notations, that are used throughout this thesis to represent high level transition graphs and synchronisation terms in a graphical way. These notations are especially employed in chapter 7, which gives a detailed description, on how those new transition systems can be generated from a CSP specification.

Especially for the third part of this thesis, which explains how to use the new types of transition systems for testing purposes, a normalisation of the high level transition graphs and synchronisation terms is introduced in chapter 8. First a normalisation algorithm is presented, which can be applied to high level transition graphs, that results in a completely normalised transition system. In an additional step a partial normalisation of synchronisation terms is suggested, that uses the previous results to describe a parallel system in such a way, that it is represented more efficient than with conventional methods, but still allows an evaluation of the structure in real-time. This real-time capability of an evaluation algorithm will be a required property of transition systems in part III.

A conclusion of this part is given in chapter 9, where the results of the author's research is compared to other formalisms, which are also used for testing or model checking purposes. This comparison includes the tools FDR and SPIN, which are both model checkers, and the specification formalism Timed Automata, which is widely used in the area of specification based testing. The similarities and differences between high level transition graphs, synchronisation terms and the different approaches are discusses in that chapter.

Chapter 5

Definitions

In "Theory and Practice of Concurrency" [ ] A.W. Roscoe describes in detail the relationship between CSP and transition graphs. Based on his work, a definition of the special type of transition graphs will be given in this chapter, that is used to generate a compact representation of CSP specifications. This type of transition system is used as a basis for other transformations, which are described later in chapter 8.

This chapter defines the structure and semantics of the high level transition graphs in section 5.1 and synchronisation terms in section 5.2.3. High level transition graphs can be used to model CSP specifications containing only low-level CSP operators. Synchronisation terms represent interacting high level transition graphs and therefore can be used to model the CSP high level operators. Definitions describing how high level transition graphs and synchronisation terms can be generated for CSP specifications are introduced later in chapter 7.

5.1   Introduction to High Level Transition Graphs for Low Level CSP Operators

In section 3.1 we introduced a general approach to labelled transition systems. The transition system introduced in this section is an extended kind of LTS, with the intention to generate a compressed representation of the specified systems.

Using CSP specifications to generate transition systems can results in a very large system, even though the CSP specification itself is rather small. There are several reasons for such *state explosions*:

Specifications of parallel processes produce a graph, which in the case of no synchronisation models all possible interleavings of the subgraphs. In this case the resulting number of nodes in the interleaved graph is the product of the number of nodes of the subgraphs. Another problem leading to a large transition graph is the use of variables in CSP specifications. If a new variable is introduced e.g. by the event $a?x$, the transition system contains as many transitions as values are possible for the variable x, which is determined by the definition of the channel a. Depending on the process definition it is possible that each transition leads to different nodes. It is obvious that such transition systems can get large.

The main idea behind the approach of high level transition graphs is based on the latter observation. In high level transition graphs special states and transitions are created that concentrate different states and transitions of a classical LTS into one without affecting the semantics. This is achieved by keeping the variables and parameters of a specification and attaching assignments and conditions to the transitions. Instead of creating transitions for each possible value of a variable, the high level transition graphs contain only one transition, in which the events are not unfolded explicitly. The definition of high level transition graphs will only apply to CSP specifications built from low level CSP operators, which do not include parallelism and hiding. Those high level operators are considered later in section 5.2.

5.1.1   Definition of High Level Transition Graphs

Before an exact definition of high level transition graphs can be given, it is necessary to introduce some new terms, that will be required later in this section:

Definition 5.1 *Locations and High-level Tranistions:*
Nodes in high level transition graphs are called locations. *This new term is introduced, since locations may carry additional properties that are going to be defined in the following chapters.*

High-level transitions in high level transition graphs lead from a source location to a target location and are marked with conditions, events and assignments. They are represented as tuples (l_S, c, E, l_T) of source and target location l_S, l_T and the label (c, E), where c is a condition and E is a set of tuples (α_i, a_i) of an event α_i and a corresponding set of assignments a_i.

Each transition (l_S, c, E, l_T) in a high level transition graph always contains at least one element (α, a) in the set E of event-assignment pairs. The set a of assignments in those pairs may be empty, but there must always exist one event α. Each assignment at a transition is created either by the low level CSP operator *prefix* or *process reference*. These are the only operators with defining occurrences of variables. The assignments of these defining occurrence are expressed in the operational semantics using the function *subs*, see section 2.4. The function *subs* is used in the operational semantics to define a replacement of applied occurrences of variables by the values that have been assigned to them at their defining occurrence. When creating a high level transition graph, a different approach to handle assignments was chosen: instead of replacing all applied occurrences of bound variables in a process term, an assignment is created and added to the high level transition, which is equal to the assignment of the defining occurrence of the variables. In this way, the variables and assignments are represented in the high level transition graph, which allows to use parameterised graphs or subgraphs.

In section 2.4, two different ways of defining the operational semantics of process references where mentioned: one approach uses τ-events and the other one simply considers resolving process references as textual replacement which can be done without producing any events. In the approach presented here, no τ-events are produced for process references. As process references can lead to assignments, these have to be represented in the resulting transition graph. Labels with a special event π are used to do this. Like a τ-event, the π-event can not be observed. Unlike τ-events, they do not lead to a selection of states. This is described in more details in section 5.1.3.

Since the π-event is not covered by the semantics of CSP they must not interfere with any other rules of the semantics. Its purpose is to connect several locations with different values for variables, which are representing one state of the specified system. Each action, that is possible for a location l', that can be reached from a location l by a π-event, is possible for l, as well.

Definition 5.2 π-*Events:*
Transitions marked with π-events are representing a process reference of the original CSP *specification in a created high level transition graph. The event π is not an event of the semantics of* CSP *and does only exist only in the represented graph structure.*

For the following definitions, it is necessary to introduce some general sets which will be used in range and domain definitions. These sets are:

Definition 5.3

Expressions	:	*The set of all* CSP$_M$ *expressions as introduced in 2.2.1*
Conditions	:	*The set of all boolean* CSP$_M$ *expressions*
		Conditions $\subset$ Expressions
Identifier	:	*The set of all identifiers*
		Identifier $\subset$ Expressions
Variables	:	*The set of all variables*
		Variables $\subset$ Identifier

Assignments	:	*The set of all assignments. Assignments are tuples of variables and an assigned expression.*
		Assignments = Variables × Expressions
Events	:	*The set of all* CSP$_M$ *events except* $\checkmark$ *and* τ.
		Events are part of the expressions of CSP *and can include parameters, expressions and input-fields (see def. 5.5).*
		Events $\subset$ Expressions,
		Events$^{\tau\checkmark}$ = $\{\tau, \checkmark\} \cup$ Events,
		Events$^{\pi\tau\checkmark}$ = $\{\pi\} \cup$ Events$^{\tau\checkmark}$,
		$\Sigma \subset$ *Events*
Locations	:	*The set of all locations that can occur in HLTGs.*
Transitions	:	*The set of all possible high-level transitions of HLTGs*
		Transitions = Locations×Conditions×
		$\mathcal{P}$*(Events,$\mathcal{P}$(Assignments))×Locations*

In high level transition graphs there exists transitions, that may represent multiple events instead of just one, as in classical transition graphs. Therefore it is necessary to make some considerations about the structure of the represented events.

When talking about events, the channels defining the possible events of a specification have to be defined more formally. A channel definition consists of the name of the channel followed by the type definition of the channel. For untyped channels, no type definition is given. The type definition is a Cartesian product of the sets of values possible for the communication fields of the events defined by the channel.

Definition 5.4 *A channel is defined by a unique identifier and a type definition*

CSP *channel* : $(c, t_1 \times ... \times t_n)$

with the unique name c of the channel and the sets $t_1, ..., t_n$ of CSP *types.*

The alphabet of a CSP$_M$ specification is defined through channel definitions. Events as introduced in section 2.2.4 consist of a channel or a channel together with a field expression. A field expression is a sequence of communication fields. Field expressions define the data that is communicated when the event occurs. With this, any event e can be written as $e = cf = cf_1...f_n$ with c being the channel of the event and $f = f_1...f_n$ being a field expression consisting of the communication fields $f_1, ..., f_n$.

Definition 5.5 *Valid communication fields of a* CSP *event*
Let set, expression $\in$ Expressions, variable $\in$ Variables.

$$f_i = \begin{cases} !\,expression & \textit{output field: the value of expression.} \\ ?variable & \textit{input field: any valid value according to the channel} \\ & \textit{definition.} \\ ?variable:set & \textit{input field: any value that is an element of set. All} \\ & \textit{elements must be in the type of that input field.} \\ .\,expression & \textit{either an input or an output field depending on the} \\ & \textit{previous communication field. If used as the first} \\ & \textit{communication field of a field expression, it is an} \\ & \textit{output field.} \end{cases}$$

The *. expression* communication fields are interpreted as input or output fields depending on the previous communication field of the field expression, they are used in. This is just a syntactic speciality and *. expression* communication fields can be replaced by the appropriate unambiguous *! expression* or *?variable* field. For the following definitions, it is assumed that all *. variable* communication fields that are interpreted as input fields are replaced by *?variable* communication field so that *. expression* fields are always output fields. Any event $a?x.y$ is automatically turned into the event $a?x?y$ without changing the semantics.

To be able to calculate all events that are possible according to a channel definition $(c, t_1 \times ... \times t_n)$, a function *sigma* is defined here. Because every channel c can only occur in exact one channel definition, the function only gets the channel as argument. This has the advantage, that it can be used with the channel of an event later.

Definition 5.6 *The function sigma : Identifier $\rightarrow \mathcal{P}(Events)$ calculates the set of all possible events of a channel.*

$$sigma(c) = \{cf_1...f_n \mid \forall i \in \{1...n\} . (f_i = .\,expr_i \wedge \\ \exists \, channel \; definition \; (c, t_1 \times ... \times t_n) . expr_i \in t_i)\}$$

The alphabet Σ of a specification contains all possible events that are untyped or only consist of field expressions created of *. expression* output fields. For every event $e = cf_1...f_n$ with $\forall i \in \{1...n\}.f_i = .\,expr_i$ in the alphabet Σ of a CSP_M specification, there must exist a channel definition $(c, t_1 \times ... \times t_n)$ so that the expression of the communication field is an element of the type of that field $expr_i \in t_i$.

Definition 5.7 *The Alphabet Σ of a* CSP_M *specification can be defined as:*

$$\Sigma = \bigcup \{sigma(c) \mid \exists \, channel \; definition \; (c, t_1 \times ... \times t_n)\}$$

In some cases it is necessary to get the name of the channel from an event. With the previous definitions, a function *channel* can be defined that does exactly this extraction. This function is not defined for the special events τ and $\checkmark$ because they do not have a channel definition.

Definition 5.8 *The function channel* : *Events$\rightarrow$ Identifier extracts the name of the channel out of an event.*

$\qquad$ *channel*$(e) = c$ *with* $e = cf, f$ *is field expression of* e.

As stated above, events can represent a set of events like for example the event $a?x$ with the channel definition $(a, \{1, 2, 3\})$ represents the set $\{a.1,\ a.2,\ a.3\}$ of events. The function *comms* can be used to calculate this set of events, a $\mathsf{CSP_M}$ event represents.

Definition 5.9 *The function comms* : *Events$^{\pi\tau\checkmark} \rightarrow \mathcal{P}(Events)$ calculates the set of events that are represented by an event*

$\qquad comms(e) =$
$\qquad\qquad \{e \mid e \in \{\pi, \tau, \checkmark\}\} \cup$
$\qquad\qquad \{cf_1'...f_n' \mid\ \exists\ channel\ definition(c, t_1 \times ... \times t_n)\ .$
$\qquad\qquad\qquad e = cf_1...f_n \wedge$
$\qquad\qquad\qquad \forall\, i \in \{1...n\}.\ \ f_i =!expr \wedge expr \in t_i \Rightarrow f_i' = .expr \wedge$
$\qquad\qquad\qquad\qquad\qquad\qquad\quad f_i = .expr \wedge expr \in t_i \Rightarrow f_i' = .expr \wedge$
$\qquad\qquad\qquad\qquad\qquad\qquad\quad f_i =?var, var \in Variables$
$\qquad\qquad\qquad\qquad\qquad\qquad\quad \Rightarrow f_i' = .expr \wedge expr \in t_i\}$

If an event e does contain variables in the expressions of an output field, the resulting events $\alpha_i \in comms(e)$ do contain these parameters, as well. Therefore they cannot be elements of Σ, because all elements of the alphabet are concrete values without free variables.

Another extension of the high level transition graphs is the concept of conditions and assignments at transitions. The conditions, assignments and events may consist of expressions containing variables and parameters, which are directly related to the ones in the CSP specification, the high level transition graph is created from.

CSP does not support the concept of declared variables. They are introduced implicitly in the specification using parameters for processes and functions or input fields. Parameters of processes or functions are visible in the whole scope of the definition. The scope of variables introduced by other input fields starts at the point where they are introduced and ends at the end of the process definition or at the next sequential composition operator. They can overload other previously defined variables. The values of such variables can be observed till the end of the subprocess, where they are introduced. But the *visibility* of a variable in fact ends at the last *applied occurrence*.[1] After that point the value is no longer needed. Applied occurrences of the variables can be found in events, expressions or process references. It is not possible to have an applied occurrence of a variable without either a previous *defining occurrence*, or outside its scope. Assignments are created only by defining occurrences of variables. An assignment is a tuple of a variable and an assigned expression.

To distinguish overloaded variables in the transition graph, it is possible to create unique names for all variables without changing the semantics of the specified process. For each variable v that overloads another variable v, a new variable v' is created. The defining occurrence of the overloading variable v is replaced by v' and each applied occurrence of v is replaced by v' as long as the overloading instance of v is visible. This transformation can be done on the syntax tree of the specification, without changing its semantics. For the rest of this thesis it will be assumed, that the identifiers for all variables and parameters are unique and that all overloaded instances have been removed as described here.

Expressions containing variables can only be evaluated if the value of each free variable is known. Therefore it is necessary to obtain the set of free variables of an expression:

Definition 5.10 *Free Variables:*
The function vars(e) denotes the set of all variables of the expression e with an applying occurrence, where vars : Expressions → Variables.

The following definition formally defines High Level Transition Graphs (HLTG). They are an extension of $\mathcal{L}_{LTS}$, as introduced in definition 3.1. This extension allows to use variables, conditions and assignments in the graph.

Definition 5.11 *High level transition graphs ($\mathcal{L}_{HLTG}$):*
A high level transition graph is a 5-tuple $(L, l_0, \Sigma^{\pi\tau\checkmark}, \mathcal{E}^{\pi\tau\checkmark}, \rightarrow_{CA})$, where:

1. *L is a set of all locations.*

2. *$l_0 \in L$ is the initial location.*

3. *$\Sigma^{\pi\tau\checkmark} = \Sigma \cup \{\pi, \tau, \checkmark\}$ is a set of observable actions and the events $\pi, \tau, \checkmark$.*

4. *$\mathcal{E}^{\pi\tau\checkmark}$ is a set of tuples of events and assignment sets.*
   $\forall (\alpha, a) \in \mathcal{E}^{\pi\tau\checkmark}.\big(\alpha \in Events^{\pi\tau\checkmark} \wedge a \subseteq Assignments \wedge$
   $\forall (x_1, y_1), (x_2, y_2) \in a . x_1 \neq x_2\big)$

5. *$\rightarrow_{CA} \subseteq L \times Conditions \times \mathcal{P}(\mathcal{E}^{\pi\tau\checkmark}) \times L$ is a relation between locations with*
   $\forall (l_S, c, E, l_T) \in \rightarrow_{CA} .$
   $\big(\forall (\alpha_1, a_1), (\alpha_2, a_2) \in E .((\alpha_1, \alpha_2 \in \{\pi, \tau, \checkmark\} \wedge \alpha_1 = \alpha_2)$
   $\vee channel(\alpha_1) = channel(\alpha_2)))$

---

[1] The terms *applied* and *defining occurrence* are used according to Loeckx and Sieber [ ].

For the following definitions, it is in some cases necessary to be able to know the set of all variables, conditions or assignments of a high level transition graph. Variables can occur in conditions of labels, in events and in assignments. A function $vars_{HLTG}$ which collects all these variables, a function $conds_{HLTG}$ which collects all conditions and a function $assigns_{HLTG}$ that collects all assignments of a high level transition graph can be defined as follows:

Definition 5.12 *The function* $conds_{HLTG} : \mathcal{L}_{LTS} \rightarrow \mathcal{P}(Conditions)$ *calculates the set of all conditions that occur in a high level transition graph. It can be defined as:*

$$conds_{HLTG}(HLTG) = \{c \in Conditions \mid \exists (l, c, E, l') \in \rightarrow_{CA}\}$$

Definition 5.13 *The function* $assigns_{HLTG} : \mathcal{L}_{LTS} \rightarrow \mathcal{P}(Assignments)$ *calculates the set of all assignments that occur in a high level transition graph. It can be defined as:*

$$assigns_{HLTG}(HLTG) = \{a \in Assignments \mid \exists (l, c, E, l') \in \rightarrow_{CA} .$$
$$(\exists(\alpha, a) \in E . v \in vars(\alpha))\}$$

Definition 5.14 *The function* $vars_{HLTG} : \mathcal{L}_{LTS} \rightarrow \mathcal{P}(Variables)$ *calculates the set of all variables that occur in a high level transition graph. It can be defined as:*

$$vars_{HLTG}(HLTG) =$$
$$\{v \in Variables \mid \exists (l, c, E, l') \in \rightarrow_{CA} .$$
$$v \in vars(c) \vee$$
$$\exists(\alpha, a) \in E . (v \in vars(\alpha) \vee$$
$$\exists(v, e) \in a, e \in Expressions)\}$$

5.1.2   Environments for Locations

During the execution of a high level transition graph $HLTG = (L, l_0, \Sigma^{\pi\tau\checkmark}, \mathcal{E}^{\pi\tau\checkmark}, \rightarrow_{CA})$ it is necessary to be able to determine the current values of variables. This can be achieved by holding a set of variable bindings for each execution step. This set is called an *environment* and is defined as follows:

Definition 5.15 *Environment of a high level transition graph:*
A set of tuples $(var, value)$ *is an environment* ε *of a high level transition graph HLTG, iff both of the following constraints hold:*

1. $\varepsilon = \{(var, value) \mid var \in vars_{HLTG}(HLTG), vars(value) = \emptyset\}$

2. $\forall v_1, v_2 \in Variables, w_1, w_2 \in Expressions.(v_1, w_1) \in \varepsilon \wedge (v_2, w_2) \in \varepsilon$
   $\implies (v_1 \neq v_2) \vee (v_1 = v_2 \wedge w_1 = w_2)$

Note that this environment is different to the environment introduced in section 3.1. To distinguish between these two, we will call the environment defined in section 3.1 the *external* environment. The following definition introduces the set *Env* containing all possible environments.

Definition 5.16 *All possible environments:*
The set of all possible environments can be defined as:

$$Env = \mathcal{P}(Variables \times Expressions)$$
$$with \ \forall(v, e) \in Env \ . \ vars(e) = \emptyset$$

When expressions are evaluated, it is necessary to provide an environment, in which the values of their free variables are defined. Because the types *Variables* and *Events* are subsets of *Expressions*, they can also be evaluated. For events containing defining occurrences of variables, these variables are unaffected by the evaluation.

Definition 5.17 *Evaluation of expressions:*
The function eval : Expressions × Env → Expressions is used to evaluate expressions. eval(e, ε) calculates the value of the expression e, using the bindings of the environment ε for each variable in vars(e).

The evaluation of expressions is only possible, if the environment contains valid values for the free variables of the expression. Therefore it is necessary to check whether a variable is visible in a certain location of the transition graph.

Definition 5.18 *Visible parameters of a location:*
The functions visible : L → $\mathcal{P}$(Variables) retrieves the visible parameters of a location. Thus visible(l) denotes the set of those variables, which are visible in a location l ∈ L.

In section 5.1.3 assignments must be applied to an environment. The result is a new environment containing the old bindings of those variables, which are not affected by the assignments, and new variable bindings of those which are affected.

Definition 5.19 *Applying an assignment to an environment.*
Let ε, ε′ ∈ Env an environment and a ∈ Assignments an assignment. The application of a to ε resulting in ε′ is denoted by $\varepsilon \overset{a}{\leadsto} \varepsilon'$ and defined as

$$\varepsilon \overset{a}{\leadsto} \varepsilon' \ \equiv \ \varepsilon' \ = \ \{(x, y) \in \varepsilon \mid \forall(v, w) \in a \ . \ v \neq x\}$$
$$\cup$$
$$\{(x, y) \mid y \in Expressions \wedge \exists(x, z) \in a \ . \ y = eval(z, \varepsilon)\}$$

As shown by this definition the order of the execution of the assignments is not important, since all values for free variables in the expressions are taken from the environment ε. Therefore a representation of assignment as pairs of variables and expressions is sufficient for high level transition graphs.

5.1.3   Interpretation of High Level Transition Graphs

This section will introduce a way of interpreting high level transition graphs, defining a stepwise execution of those graphs. In order to increase clearness of the following definitions, a few notations will be introduced here:

Definition 5.20 *Notations for high level transition graphs.*
Let $l, l' \in L$, $\varepsilon, \varepsilon' \in Env$, $c \in Conditions$ and $E \in \mathcal{P}(\mathcal{E}^{\pi\tau\checkmark})$.

$$
\begin{aligned}
l \xrightarrow{c,E} l' \quad &\equiv \quad (l, c, E, l') \in \rightarrow_{CA} \\
l \xrightarrow{c,(\alpha,a)} l' \quad &\equiv \quad \exists\, E \in \mathcal{P}(\mathcal{E}^{\pi\tau\checkmark}) \,.\, l \xrightarrow{c,E} l' \wedge (\alpha, a) \in E \\
l, \varepsilon \rightarrowtail^{c,(\alpha,a)} l', \varepsilon' \quad &\equiv \quad l \xrightarrow{c,(\alpha,a)} l' \wedge \; vars(c) \subseteq visible(l) \\
&\qquad\quad \wedge\; eval(c, \varepsilon) = true \wedge \; \varepsilon \overset{a}{\rightsquigarrow} \varepsilon' \\
l, \varepsilon \overset{\alpha}{\mapsto} l', \varepsilon' \quad &\equiv \quad \exists\, l'' \in L, \varepsilon'' \in Env, c \in Conditions, a \in Assignments \,. \\
&\qquad\quad (l, \varepsilon \overset{\pi}{\mapsto} l'', \varepsilon'' \vee (l = l'' \wedge \varepsilon = \varepsilon'')) \wedge\; l'', \varepsilon'' \rightarrowtail^{c,(\alpha,a)} l', \varepsilon' \\
l, \varepsilon \overset{\sigma}{\mapsto} l', \varepsilon' \quad &\equiv \quad \exists\, l_1, ..., l_n \in L, \varepsilon_1, ..., \varepsilon_n \in Env \,. \\
&\qquad\quad l, \varepsilon \overset{\alpha_1}{\mapsto} l_1, \varepsilon_1 ... l_n, \varepsilon_n \overset{\alpha_n}{\mapsto} l', \varepsilon', \; with\; \sigma = \alpha_1 \cdot ... \cdot \alpha_n \\
l, \varepsilon \overset{\tau^*}{\mapsto} l', \varepsilon' \quad &\equiv \quad l, \varepsilon \overset{\sigma}{\mapsto} l', \varepsilon' \; with\; \sigma = \tau \cdot ... \cdot \tau
\end{aligned}
$$

Since these notations are used throughout this thesis, they are going to be explained in more detail in the following:

- The first notation $l \xrightarrow{c,E} l'$ states, that in the HLTG under investigation, there exists a transition leading from location l to l'. This transition is marked with the label (c, E).

- The second notation $l \xrightarrow{c,(\alpha,a)} l'$ is an extension of the first one, specifying that there exists an event-assignment pair (α, a), which is element of the set E of the transitions label (c, E).

Where the first two notations can only be used to statically describe the structure of a HLTG, the following rules all apply to environments, which provide bindings for those variables, that are valid is a location.

- The third notation $l, \varepsilon \rightarrowtail^{c,(\alpha,a)} l', \varepsilon'$ describes a single atomic step of the interpretation of a HLTG. It denotes, that there is a transition in the HLTG, which leads from l to l' and carries a label (c, E), where $(\alpha, a) \in E$. Additionally it is required, that all variables of the condition c must be in the set of visible variables of the location l, since before any variable can be used in an expression, a binding occurrence of those variable must have filled the corresponding value in the environment. Furthermore the condition c must hold under the variables bindings defined in ε. Finally all assignments from a applied to the environment ε must yield in the new environment ε'.

- The fourth notation $l, \varepsilon \overset{\alpha}{\longmapsto} l', \varepsilon'$ describes a rule to produce a single event α in a HLTG, by performing several atomic steps simultaniously. If there already exists an atomic step from l, ε to l', ε' producing α this notation describes the same atomic step. Otherwise a recursive definition specifies a chain of automic steps leading from l, ε to l', ε'. The last element of this chain is a transition (l'', e, E, l'), with $l'', \varepsilon'' \overset{c,(\alpha,a)}{\succ\!\!\longrightarrow} l', \varepsilon'$. All other atomic steps leading to the last but one location l'' must contain π-actions.

- The two remaining notations just provide a simple shorthand describing chains of transitions producing traces of events, which are denoted by σ, or chains of τ-events denoted by τ^*.

The following definition provides a function *trans*, that calculates the set of all transitions leaving a location:

Definition 5.21
Let $HLTG = (L, l_0, \Sigma^{\pi\tau\checkmark}, \mathcal{E}^{\pi\tau\checkmark}, \rightarrow)$, $l, l' \in L$, $\varepsilon \in Env$, $c \in Conditions$, $E \in \mathcal{E}^{\pi\tau\checkmark}$. The function trans : Locations $\rightarrow \mathcal{P}(Transitions)$ can be defined as:

$$trans(l) = \{(l, c, E, l') \mid (l, c, E, l') \in \rightarrow\}$$

The definition of the interpretation of a high level transition graph requires two subordinate definitions: rules for starting the interpretation and conditions for changing states of the high level transition graph.

Starting the Interpretation

The start condition consists of the initial location (defined in definition 5.11) and an initial environment. Because of the scope of variables and parameters in the syntax tree, they can not occur at arbitrary points in the HLTG. Every variable, that is visible for a location can occur in the expressions of all outgoing transitions of this location. The values that are given in an environment are defined only for variables that are visible in the location.

High level transition graphs that are not part of a synchronisation term, as defined in section 5.2.3, are only created for processes that do not have any visible variables at their start location l_0, thus the start environment ε_0 of high level transition graphs can be any element of Env: $\varepsilon_0 \in Env$. If high level transition graphs are part of a synchronisation term, they can be created for processes with visible parameters at the start location. In this case, the start environment is calculated during the construction of the synchronisation term, as defined later in section 7.3.

Changing States

As stated before, the interpretation of a HLTG begins at the special location l_0, which marks the starting point of the system with the environment ε_0. To traverse the graph, it is necessary to select one element (l, c, E, l') of the relation $\rightarrow_{CA}$, where l is the current location, c holds in the current environment ($eval(c, \varepsilon) = true$), E is a set of possible actions and their corresponding assignments and l' is the target location. The actions α in the elements of E of all transitions leaving l are called initial actions of l. Additionally the initial actions contain all those events of (l'', c, E, l'), where l'' can be reached from the location l via chains of π-events. This is the required behaviour, since the π-labels represent resolved process references. According to the operational semantics of the process reference, resolving a process reference does not cause a state change of the process. Therefore locations connected by π-labels must be considered as one location. The set of all initial actions of a location l in an environment ε will be denoted $[l]_\varepsilon^0$ and is defined as follows:

Definition 5.22 *Initial actions of a location $l \in L$ in an environment $\varepsilon \in Env$:*
$[l]_\varepsilon^0 = \{\alpha \in \Sigma^{\tau\checkmark} \mid l, \varepsilon \overset{\alpha}{\mapsto} l', \varepsilon' \wedge l' \in L \wedge \varepsilon' \in Env\}.$

To make progress, one of the initial actions $[l]_\varepsilon^0$ of a location l in an environment ε must be chosen for execution. According to the definition of $l, \varepsilon \overset{\alpha}{\mapsto} l', \varepsilon'$, the evaluated event $eval(\alpha, \varepsilon)$ of the chosen action α can be offered directly by the current location or by one of the locations that can be reached by π-transitions[2].

If the action is possible directly at the location, there must be at least on element $(l, c, E, l') \in \rightarrow_{CA}$ which contains the chosen action α ($\exists (\alpha, a) \in E$) and for which its condition c holds in the environment ε. If there exists more then one such element (l, c, E, l'), one of them must be chosen. Execution proceeds by producing the evaluated action $\alpha' = eval(\alpha, \varepsilon)$ and applying its corresponding assignments a to the environment ε. This leads to the location l' with a new environment ε'.

If the action is not possible directly at the location, the notation $l, \varepsilon \overset{\alpha}{\mapsto} l', \varepsilon'$ implies that there exists a location l'' with an environment ε'' that can be reached by π-events and that the action α is possible for this location l''. In this case the execution proceeds by following the transitions marked with π-labels to the location l'' and always applying the assignments of the labels to ε. Having reached l'', the resulting environment is ε''. Now the behaviour is nearly the same as if the action was possible for l itself. Due to definition 5.22 there must be at least on element $(l'', c'', E, l') \in \rightarrow_{CA}$ which contains the chosen action α ($\exists (\alpha, a'') \in E$) and for which its condition c'' holds in the environment ε''. If there exist more then one such element (l'', c'', E, l'), one of them must be

---

[2]If the event is possible at a location l'', that can be reached by π-transitions, the current environment ε'' of the respective location has to be used for the evaluation of the event α.

chosen. Execution proceeds by producing the evaluated action $\alpha' = eval(\alpha, \varepsilon'')$ and applying its corresponding assignments a'' to the environment ε''. This leads to the location l' with a new environment ε'.

If a chosen action is possible in a location itself and in one of its π-reachable locations, it is chosen non-deterministically which transition will be taken.

Reachable Environments

With these definitions, it is now easy to define the set of all possible environments that can be reached during an interpretation of a HLTG.

Definition 5.23
The set of all reachable environments of a HLTG can be defined as:
$$Env_{reach} = \{\varepsilon \in Env \mid \forall\, l \in L\, .\, l_0, \varepsilon_0 \overset{\sigma}{\longmapsto} l, \varepsilon\}$$

Sometimes it is necessary to know the set of all environments that can occur in a given location l during the interpretation of a HLTG. This is specified in the following definition:

Definition 5.24
The set of all reachable environments of a location $l \in L$ can be defined as:
$$Env_l = \{\varepsilon \in Env \mid l_0, \varepsilon_0 \overset{\sigma}{\longmapsto} l, \varepsilon\}$$

5.1.4 Properties of High Level Transition Graphs

All properties for LTS as introduced in section 3.1 can as well be defined for high level transition graphs.

A high level transition graph is deterministic if there is no location $l \in L$ and environment $\varepsilon \in Env_l$ with a τ-event in its initial actions $[l]_\varepsilon^0$. Additionally there must not exist two different transitions, leading from any location $l \in L$ and its environment $\varepsilon \in Env_l$, to different locations or the same location with a different environment. This is expressed in the following definition.

Definition 5.25 *Determinism of high level transition graphs:*
A HLTG is deterministic, iff for all possible environments ε

1. $\nexists\, l, l' \in L, \varepsilon \in Env_l\, .\, l, \varepsilon \overset{\tau}{\longmapsto} l', \varepsilon'$

2. $\forall\, l, l', l'' \in L, \varepsilon, \varepsilon', \varepsilon'' \in Env_l\, .\; l, \varepsilon \overset{\alpha_1)}{\longrightarrow} l', \varepsilon' \wedge l, \varepsilon \overset{(\alpha_2)}{\longrightarrow} l'', \varepsilon''$
$$\wedge\; eval(\alpha_1, \varepsilon) = eval(\alpha_2, \varepsilon)$$
$$\implies l' = l'' \wedge \varepsilon' = \varepsilon''$$

The definitions of deadlock and livelock situations in HLTG are similar to those of LTS. A HLTG contains a deadlock, if there is any location, that has no initial actions in one of its possible environments. A HLTG contains a livelock, if there is any location that can reach itself by a trace only containing τ-events.

Definition 5.26 *Deadlock and Livelock of high level transition graphs:*
A HLTG contains a deadlock, iff $\exists\, l \in L, \varepsilon \in Env_l \,.\, [l]^0_\varepsilon = \emptyset$
A HLTG contains a livelock, iff $\exists\, l \in L, \varepsilon \in Env_l \,.\, l, \varepsilon \xmapsto{\tau^*} l, \varepsilon$

The term *finite state* does no longer correspond to the number of locations the HLTG has, but to the combination of locations and environments. Thus a HLTG is *finite*, iff only a finite set of pairs (l, ε) exists with $l \in L$ and $\varepsilon \in Env_l$. Those requirements lead to the deduction that the domain of all variables must be finite if a HLTG is finite state.

Definition 5.27 *Finite state:*
A HLTG is finite state, iff
$\{(l, \varepsilon) \mid l \in L \wedge \varepsilon \in Env_l \subseteq Env_{reach}\}$ *is a finite set.*

Note by this definition, there may exist a HLTG that is infinite state but which only has a finite set of locations. This means that the representation of these infinite state graphs is finite as shown in the following example.

The transition graph of the the specification $COUNT_0$, which was defined on page 57, was infinite. But the representation of this process as a HLTG only consists of four nodes, which are shown in figure 5.1. The transformation of a CSP specification into a high level transition graph is described in detail in chapter 7.

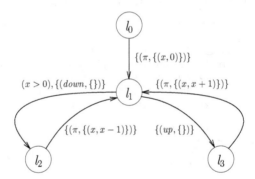

Figure 5.1: A finite representation of an infinite state HLTG

The resulting HLTG contains two cycles starting at node l_1: one labelled with the *down*-event, and one labelled with the event *up* both followed by a π-event, which leads back to node l_1. This internal event is required to assign new values to the variable x. The event *down* must not always be available, since the specification states, that it is forbidden to have more *down*- than *up*-events in any trace (i.e. the value of x must always be larger than 0, before a *down*-event can be performed).

It is obvious that this type of specification is infinite, since it is possible to perform an infinite number of *up*-events as indicated in figure 3.3. In contrast to this observation the HLTG itself has a finite representation, since it only consists of four locations and five transitions.

A HLTG representing the finite version the the specification $COUNT_0$, which was described on page 58, is basically identical to the one in Figure 5.1, where only an additional condition ($x < 4$) is added to the transition $(l_1, true, \{(up, \{\})\}, l_3)$.

5.2 Representing High-Level Operators

One of the issues not addressed in the last section is the problem of parallelism. A common objective is to model two or more different processes and their behaviour interacting with each other and the external environment. In this section a new way of representing parallel transition graphs of CSP specifications will be introduced: the synchronisation terms. Before that the conventional way of modelling parallelism will be explained.

5.2.1 Parallelism in Transition Graphs

The conventional way to model parallel systems as a transition system would be to compute a *product graph* of the transition graphs of the subordinate processes. These graphs model the behaviour of two or more parallel transition systems by calculating all possible interactions of those systems. Each state in the resulting transition system represents a tuple of states, where each element of this tuple represents a state in one of the original graphs. The total number of states in the product graph is determined by the product of the number of states of the original graphs.

This last statement is only true if there is no synchronous communication between the different systems and each system uses a unique alphabet. Communication between different systems via synchronisation points or shared alphabets result in smaller product graphs, which model all relevant behaviour of the parallel system. Due to the synchronisation of systems not all combinations of states are reachable in such product graph, since the interaction may prevent some events to occur.

If two transition systems represented by LTS_1 and LTS_2 do not synchronise over any events the type of parallelism is called *interleaving*. A definition for the product graph of two interleaved transitionsystems is given in definition 5.28.

Definition 5.28 *Interleaving (|||):*
A product graph of two interleaved LTS can be defined as follows:
Let $LTS_1 = (S, s_0, \Sigma^{\tau\checkmark}, \to)$ and $LTS_2 = (S', s_0', \Sigma^{\tau\checkmark'}, \to')$ be two transition systems, with a disjoint set of nodes, i.e. $S \cap S' = \emptyset$. A product graph of LTS_1 and LTS_2 is an LTS $(S^*, s_0^*, \Sigma^{\tau\checkmark*}, \to^*)$, such that:

1. $S^* = \{ \Upsilon(s, s') \mid s \in S \land s' \in S' \}$ *is the set of states of the LTS, and Υ is an bijective function* $\Upsilon : S \times S' \to S^*$

2. $s_0^* = \Upsilon(s_0, s_0')$,

3. $\Sigma^{\tau\checkmark*} = \Sigma^{\tau\checkmark} \cup \Sigma^{\tau\checkmark'}$,

4. $\to^* = \{ \Upsilon(P, R) \xrightarrow{\alpha}^* \Upsilon(P', R) \mid P \xrightarrow{\alpha} P' \land P, P' \in S \land R \in S' \}$
   $\cup \{ \Upsilon(R, Q) \xrightarrow{\beta}^* \Upsilon(R, Q') \mid Q \xrightarrow{\beta}' Q' \land R \in S \land Q, Q' \in S' \}$.

It is also possible that both LTS share some common events $A \in \Sigma^{\tau\checkmark*}$ which both can only produce simultaneously. Such parallel graphs usually contains less elements in the relation $\to^*$, as can be observed by the following definition:

Definition 5.29 *Parallelism ($\parallel_A$):*
A product graph of two parallel LTS synchronising over events in A, where $\checkmark \notin A \land \tau \notin A$, can be defined as follows:
Let $LTS_1 = (S, s_0, \Sigma^{\tau\checkmark}, \to)$ and $LTS_2 = (S', s_0', \Sigma^{\tau\checkmark'}, \to')$ be two transition systems, with a disjoint set of nodes, i.e. $S \cap S' = \emptyset$. A product graph of LTS_1 and LTS_2 is an LTS $(S^*, s_0^*, \Sigma^{\tau\checkmark*}, \to^*)$, such that:

1. $S^* = \{ \Upsilon(s, s') \mid s \in S \land s' \in S' \}$ *is the set of states of the LTS, and Υ is an bijective function* $\Upsilon : S \times S' \to S^*$

2. $s_0^* = \Upsilon(s_0, s_0')$,

3. $\Sigma^{\tau\checkmark*} = \Sigma^{\tau\checkmark} \cup \Sigma^{\tau\checkmark'}$,

4. $\to^* = \{ \Upsilon(P, R) \xrightarrow{\alpha}^* \Upsilon(P', R) \mid P \xrightarrow{\alpha} P' \land \alpha \notin A \land P, P' \in S \land R \in S' \}$
   $\cup \{ \Upsilon(R, Q) \xrightarrow{\beta}^* \Upsilon(R, Q') \mid Q \xrightarrow{\beta}' Q' \land \beta \notin A \land$
   $\qquad\qquad\qquad\qquad Q, Q' \in S' \land R \in S \}$
   $\cup \{ \Upsilon(P, Q) \xrightarrow{\gamma}^* \Upsilon(P', Q') \mid P \xrightarrow{\gamma} P' \land Q \xrightarrow{\gamma}' Q' \land \gamma \in A \land$
   $\qquad\qquad\qquad\qquad P, P' \in S \land Q, Q' \in S' \}$.

This simple definition of product graphs for synchronised parallel graphs may contain too many elements in its relation $\to^*$, since some transitions cannot be reached from the initial state of the graph. Those elements of the relation can easily be identified by well known algorithms on transition graphs, e.g. breadth-first search, depth-first search or even by minimum spanning trees. Such algorithms as described in detail in [ ], part *VI - Graph Algorithms*. As soon as these elements which can be reached from the initial state are identified, all relations leading from or to states that cannot be reached can be disregarded.

Both definitions apply not only for two but for an arbitrary number of parallel LTS, since it is always possible to calculate the resulting LTS of two original ones and then apply the rules repeatedly on the resulting LTS and the remaining original LTS:

$$LTS_1 \parallel LTS_2 \parallel LTS_3 = (LTS_1 \parallel LTS_2) \parallel LTS_3$$

One major problem of this approach is the rapidly increasing number of states in the product graphs introduced by interleaving or parallelism.

5.2.2 Hiding on Transition Graphs

Modelling parallel systems in CSP introduces the problem of internal communication in the different subsystems. Internal communication of subsystems is often necessary for specifying the behaviour of parallel systems. The communication should not always be visible to the environment, since the implementation of the subsystem may not be relevant for the behaviour of the whole system. On the other hand a system, parallel to the subsystem using internal communication, may prevent some events to occur, if there is synchronisation on the internal communication events. To prevent both situations, the CSP hiding operator can be used, which makes events invisible and uncontrollable by the environment.

The hiding operator can best be understood by observing the effects on a transition system. If hiding is applied to a transition graph, the structure of the graph is not changed, but only the events. All actions on the transitions, which are in the set of hiding events are replaced by the τ-event. The effect of the hiding operator on transition systems is illustrated in figure 5.2.

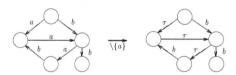

Figure 5.2: Hiding on a transition graph

It is important to note that the hiding operator is often used in combination with the parallel operator in CSP. There are a number of laws that can be found in [, p. 78-82], that apply to this unary operator, which will become important in the next section.

Theorem 5.1 *Null-hiding law:*

$$P \setminus \emptyset = P$$

Theorem 5.2 *Hiding-combine law:*

$$(P \setminus Y) \setminus X = P \setminus (X \cup Y)$$

Theorem 5.3 *Hiding-$\underset{X}{\|}$-distributive law:*

$$(P \underset{X}{\|} Q) \setminus Z = (P \setminus Z) \underset{X}{\|} (Q \setminus Z), \text{ if } X \cap Z = \emptyset$$

5.2.3   Synchronisation Terms

The high level transition graphs introduced previously can directly be derived from the CSP operators, which do not model parallelism. All high level operators, which are parallel, interleaving or hiding, will not be modelled as high level transition graphs directly, since the synchronisation on sets of events would make the creation of parallel high level transition graphs very complex. An alternative approach is the computation of the product graphs, as described before. But this has all disadvantages of labelled transition systems, that should be avoided with the high level transition graph approach.

A different approach to the creation of product graphs are the *Synchronisation Terms* that are going to be introduced in this section. Those terms store information about the structure of parallel systems without unfolding all possible interactions between the parallel systems.

Synchronisation terms can best be represented as a tree, which stores hiding and synchronisation information in its nodes and has complete high level transition graph with environments as its leafs. Hence the structure of a synchronisation term can best be described as follows:

Definition 5.30 *A synchronisation term Λ can be used to describe the synchronisation between different high level transition graphs and hiding on single high level transition graphs. Let there be n different high level transition graphs $HLTG_i = (L_i, l_{0i}, \Sigma_i^{\pi\tau\checkmark}, \mathcal{E}_i^{\pi\tau\checkmark}, \rightarrow_{CAi})$, with $i \in \{1..n\}$. The set of all events Σ of this synchronisation term is the union of all $\Sigma_i^{\pi\tau\checkmark}$ for $i \in \{1..n\}$.*

$$
\begin{aligned}
\Lambda \quad := \quad & (HLTG_i, l_i, \varepsilon_i) && \text{where } l_i \in L_i \text{ is a location of } HLTG_i \\
& && \text{and } \varepsilon_i \in Env \text{ is an environment for } HLTG_i. \\
\mid \quad & (\Lambda, h) && \text{where } h \subseteq \Sigma \text{ denotes a hiding set.} \\
\mid \quad & (\Lambda, s, \Lambda) && \text{where } s \subseteq \Sigma \text{ denotes a synchronisation set.} \\
\mid \quad & (\Lambda, s, h, \Lambda) && \text{as an abbreviation for } ((\Lambda, s, \Lambda), h).
\end{aligned}
$$

Figure 5.3 illustrates this definition with an example. The shown graph is representing a synchronisation term that can be produced by a CSP specification like $(P_1 \parallel_s P_2) \setminus h$, where P_1 and P_2 are arbitrary sequential CSP processes. For the processes P_1 and P_2 the high level transition graph can be computed by the rules introduced in chapter 7, if both sub-processes do not contain any hiding, parallel or interleaving operator. The resulting start locations of both graphs are named l_1 and l_2.

Since the sequential processes P_1 and P_2 can be represented by the synchronisation terms $\lambda_{P_1} = (HLTG_{P_1}, l_1, \varepsilon_1)$ and $\lambda_{P_2} = (HLTG_{P_2}, l_2, \varepsilon_2)$, the parallel process $P_1 \parallel_s P_2$ can than be represented by the synchronisation term $\lambda = (\lambda_{P_1}, s, \lambda_{P_2})$, which means that the high level transition graphs of P_1 and P_2 starting with the initial locations l_1 and l_2 have to run in parallel, only synchronising on the events in s. ε_1 and ε_2 denotes the environments of $HLTG_{P_1}$ and $HLTG_{P_2}$, under which all expressions, conditions and assignments are evaluated.

The hiding set h in the synchronisation term (λ, h) denotes those events, which must be hidden in the synchronisation term λ. Therefore the synchronisation graph $((\lambda_{P_1}, s, \lambda_{P_2}), h)$ represents the CSP specification $(P_1 \parallel_s P_2) \setminus h$. Since it is a frequently used pattern that events are hidden after the evaluation of a parallel or interleaving operator, an abbreviation is introduced, which allows to write this term as $(\lambda_{P_1}, s, h, \lambda_{P_2})$.

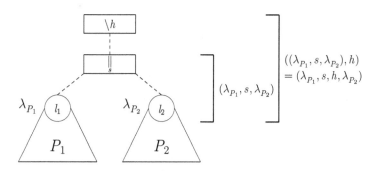

Figure 5.3: The graphical representation of a synchronisation term.

The interpretation of synchronisation terms is based on the definitions for high level transition graphs in section 5.1.3. It always starts with the initial term λ_0. Each term is representing one state in the product graph, that could be computed by the rules in section 5.2.1. The production of an event $\alpha \in \Sigma^{\tau\checkmark}$ based on a synchronisation term λ results in a new term λ', which represents the target state in the product graph.

Based on the notations introduced in definition 3.2, the notation $\lambda \xrightarrow{\alpha} \lambda'$ expresses, that the synchronisation term λ can produce the event α resulting in a new synchronisation term λ'.

Definition 5.31 *Interpretation of synchronisation terms*
$\lambda \xrightarrow{\alpha} \lambda'$ *evaluates to true, if one of the following does:*

1. *The synchronisation term contains only a high level transition graph HLTG with a current location l and a current environment ε: $\lambda = (HLTG, l, \varepsilon)$.*

$$l, \varepsilon \xmapsto{\alpha'} l', \varepsilon' \;\wedge\; \alpha = eval(\alpha', \varepsilon) \;\wedge\; \lambda' = (HLTG, l', \varepsilon')$$

2. *The synchronisation term contains a hiding pattern as the outmost term: $\lambda = (\lambda_h, h)$.*

   (a) $\lambda_h \xrightarrow{\alpha} \lambda'_h \wedge \alpha \notin h \;\wedge\; \lambda' = (\lambda'_h, h)$

   (b) $\lambda_h \xrightarrow{\alpha'} \lambda'_h \wedge \alpha' \in h \;\wedge\; \lambda' = (\lambda'_h, h) \wedge \alpha = \tau$

3. *The synchronisation term contains a parallel pattern as the outmost term: $\lambda = (\lambda_1, s, \lambda_2)$.*

   (a) $\lambda_1 \xrightarrow{\alpha} \lambda'_1 \wedge \alpha \notin s \;\wedge\; \lambda' = (\lambda'_1, s, \lambda_2)$

   (b) $\lambda_2 \xrightarrow{\alpha} \lambda'_2 \wedge \alpha \notin s \;\wedge\; \lambda' = (\lambda_1, s, \lambda'_2)$

   (c) $\lambda_1 \xrightarrow{\alpha} \lambda'_1 \wedge \lambda_2 \xrightarrow{\alpha} \lambda'_2 \wedge \alpha \in s \;\wedge\; \lambda' = (\lambda'_1, s, \lambda'_2)$

The interpretation shows, that the synchronisation terms changes with each execution step. Since understanding this definition is vital for chapter 8, we are going to give some more explanations to this definition.

1. The event α can only be produced, if there exists a transition in the location l of the high level transition graph $HLTG$, which condition c evaluates to *true* in the current environment ε. As a result of the application of the assignment a to the environment ε, a new environment ε' is created. If the transition is taken, the new configuration λ' contains the target location l' of the transition and the newly created environment ε'.

2. If the event α is not in the hiding set h, all those transitions possible with the term λ_h and labelled with the event α are also possible in (λ_h, h). If on the other hand, there are events $\alpha' \in h$ in the synchronisation term λ_h, those events must be renamed to τ-events by the synchronisation term λ.

   The synchronisation term representing the target state, contains those synchronisation terms λ'_h, which result from the synchronisation term $\lambda_h \xrightarrow{\alpha} \lambda'_h$, where all events from h are hidden.

3. If one synchronisation term can produce the event α and the event is not in the synchronisation set s, the structure of the other synchronisation term remains unchanged in the target term.

   Only if both sub terms of a synchronisation pattern can produce an event α that is in the synchronisation set s, λ can produce the event as well. The target term λ' contains both target terms of the subordinate synchronisation terms, since both terms need to produce the event simultaneously.

Since now the structure and a way of interpreting the synchronisation terms has been introduced, it is possible to find out, which actions can be performed immediately by a synchronisation term.

Definition 5.32 *Initial Actions*
The initial actions $[\lambda]^0$ *of a synchronisation term* λ *are defined as follows:*

$$[\lambda]^0 = \{\alpha \mid \exists\,\lambda'.\,\lambda \xrightarrow{\alpha} \lambda'\}$$

The following CSP processes define a parallel system, that can be used as an example, on how to interprete synchronisation terms.

$$SYS = (P \underset{\{|in,out|\}}{\|} VAR(0)) \setminus \{intern\}$$

P	$=$	$intern \to P$	$VAR(x)$	$=$	$in?y \to VAR(y)$
		$\sqcap$			$\square$
		$out?x \to P$			$out.x \to VAR(x)$

The synchronisation term, that can be derived from the process SYS contains two high level transition graph definitions $HLTG_P$ and $HLTG_V$ with its corresponding initial locations l_0^P and l_0^V. The initial environments for both high level transition graphs are empty. Hence the initial synchronisation term, that is also shown in it graphical representation in figure 5.4, looks as follows:

$$\lambda_0 = (((HLTG_P, l_0^P, \varepsilon_P), \{|\ in, out\ |\}, (HLTG_V, l_0^V, \varepsilon_V)), \{intern\})$$

The initial synchronisation terms is the starting point for the interpretation of the transition system represented by the term. To find out, what events can be produced on the initial step, first the high level transition graphs are examined to find their initial actions:

$$[l_0^P]_{\varepsilon_P}^0 = \{intern, out.0, out.1\}$$
$$[l_0^V]_{\varepsilon_P}^0 = \{out.0, in.0, in.1\}$$

As soon as the initial actions of the high level transition graphs are determined, the initial actions of the nested synchronisation terms can be computed. The

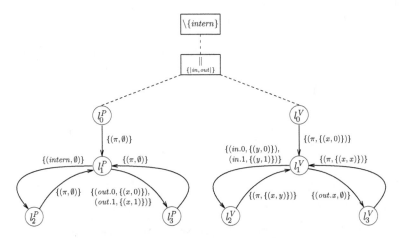

Figure 5.4: Synchronisation term of SYS

synchronisation term representing the synchronisation on all events of the channels in and out, allow only the events $intern$ and $out.0$, since $out.1$, $in.0$ and $in.1$ are only offered by one of the two sub-terms – each represented by a high level transition graph. Finally a hiding pattern is applied to the synchronisation term, which removes all occurrences of the event $intern$ and renames them to τ. Therefore the initial actions of the synchronisation term are:

$$[\lambda_0]^0 = \{\tau, out.0\}$$

The environment may now select the event $out.0$ to be executed. In this case the execution begins at the level of the sequential high level transition graphs. The sub-term $(HLTG_P, l_0^P, \varepsilon_P)$ leads to the execution of the rule $l_0^P, \varepsilon_P \xrightarrow{out.0} l_3^P, \varepsilon'_P$ consisting of the atomic steps $l_0^P, \varepsilon_P \overset{true,(\pi,\emptyset)}{\succ\!\!\longrightarrow} l_1^P, \varepsilon''_P$ and $l_1^P, \varepsilon''_P \overset{true,(out.0,\{(x,0)\})}{\succ\!\!\longrightarrow} l_3^P, \varepsilon'_P$, which creates a new synchronisation term $(HLTG_P, l_3^P, \varepsilon'_P)$. The other high level transition graph can also participate in the production of the event $out.0$, since $l_0^V, \varepsilon_V \xrightarrow{out.0} l_3^V, \varepsilon'_V$ is valid. As described in definition 5.31 the resulting synchronisation term is $(HLTG_V, l_3^V, \varepsilon'_V)$. Now the rules for the synchronisation and hiding patterns can be applied, which results in a new synchronisation term λ_1. This term is representing the following state of the transition system, after the event $out.0$ has been produced using the synchronisation term λ_0. The described behaviour is expressed by the term $\lambda_0 \xrightarrow{out.0} \lambda_1$, where

$$\lambda_1 = (((HLTG_P, l_3^P, \varepsilon'_P), \{| \ in, out \ |\}, (HLTG_V, l_3^V, \varepsilon'_V)), \{intern\})$$

If on the other hand in the synchronisation term λ_0 the internal τ-event is executed without interaction of the environment, it is only necessary, that the high level transition graph representing the process P evolves by applying the rule $l_0^P, \varepsilon_P \xmapsto{internal} l_3^P, \varepsilon_P'$. The synchronisation pattern allows only the one HLTG to evolve, since *internal* is not in its set of synchronisation events. Finally the hiding pattern replaces the *internal* event by a τ-event. Therefore the synchronisation term λ_0 can produce a τ-event, changing to a new synchronisation term λ_2. This behaviour is described by the term $\lambda_0 \xrightarrow{\tau} \lambda_2$, where λ_2 looks as follows:

$$\lambda_2 = (((HLTG_P, l_2^P, \varepsilon_P'), \{|\ in, out\ |\}, (HLTG_V, l_0^V, \varepsilon_V')), \{intern\})$$

Starting with the synchronisation term λ_1, a new configuration can be reached, by producing a τ-event. If the high level transition graph of P produces a *intern* event starting at location l_1^P with the environment ε_P', its state changes to l_2^P with the environment ε_P'', which can be expressed by $l_2^P, \varepsilon_P' \xmapsto{internal} l_3^P, \varepsilon_P''$. The state of the high level transition graph representing VAR does not change, since the parallel pattern of the synchronisation term allows only one high level transition graph to change, if the produced event is not in its synchronisation set. Finally the event *internal* is once again hidden by the hiding pattern, so the internal τ-event can be produced. This leads to the new transition if the modelled transition system $\lambda_1 \xrightarrow{\tau} \lambda_3$, where λ_3 is defined as follows:

$$\lambda_3 = (((HLTG_P, l_2^P, \varepsilon_P'), \{|\ in, out\ |\}, (HLTG_V, l_3^V, \varepsilon_V')), \{intern\})$$

There are many more transitions, that are modelled by the initial and its reachable synchronisation term:

$$\lambda_0 \xrightarrow{out.0} \lambda_1 \quad \lambda_0 \xrightarrow{\tau} \lambda_2 \quad \lambda_1 \xrightarrow{out.0} \lambda_1 \quad \lambda_1 \xrightarrow{\tau} \lambda_3$$
$$\lambda_2 \xrightarrow{out.0} \lambda_1 \quad \lambda_2 \xrightarrow{\tau} \lambda_2 \quad \lambda_3 \xrightarrow{out.0} \lambda_1 \quad \lambda_3 \xrightarrow{\tau} \lambda_3$$

These interpretations can also be represented in the graphical representation already introduced for labelled transition systems, as can be observed in the figure 5.5. This example shows, that with synchronisation terms it is possible to model labelled transition systems, without the need to unfold the whole transition system. On the contrary each reachable synchronisation term, that can be derived via chains of productions of events beginning at the initial synchronisation term, represents exactly one state in a transition system modelling the same system.

For complex CSP-specifications those synchronisation terms with the underlying high level transition graphs can get large. Therefore it is useful to create a normal form of those graphs, which makes use of the abbreviation introduced in definition 5.30. Such normalisation will be introduced in detail in section 8.3, but some basic properties of the normal form of synchronisation terms, are best described here.

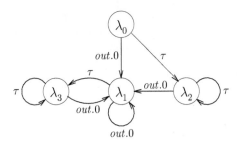

Figure 5.5: Interpreting the synchronisation term of SYS

Theorem 5.4 *If the synchronisation term* $\lambda = (\lambda_h, h)$ *is as a hiding pattern with no elements in the hiding set* h, *the sub-term* λ_h *can produce the same events as the term* λ. *This can be directly derived from the null hiding law in theorem 5.1.*

$$(\lambda, \emptyset) = \lambda$$

Theorem 5.5 *The previous theorem 5.4 can be used to show, that it is always allowed to use the abbreviated form of the synchronisation terms, even if there is no hiding above a parallel pattern:*

$$\begin{aligned}(\lambda_1, s, \lambda_2) &= ((\lambda_1, s, \lambda_2), \emptyset) \\ &= (\lambda_1, s, \emptyset, \lambda_2)\end{aligned}$$

Theorem 5.6 *Multiple nested hiding patterns can be combined into one hiding term containing the union of the hiding sets, as defined in hiding-combine law 5.2:*

$$((\lambda, h_2), h_1) = (\lambda, h_1 \cup h_2)$$

Theorem 5.7 *The hiding-* $\|_X$ *-distributive law in theorem 5.3 allows us to change the nesting of the hiding and parallel terms in the synchronisation terms:*

$$\begin{aligned}(\lambda_1, s, h, \lambda_2) &= ((\lambda_1, s, h \setminus s, \lambda_2), h \cap s) \\ &= (((\lambda_1, h \setminus s), s, \emptyset, (\lambda_2, h \setminus s)), h \cap s) \\ &= ((\lambda_1, h \setminus s), s, h \cap s, (\lambda_2, h \setminus s))\end{aligned}$$

Even though definition 5.7 seems to create a more complex synchronisation term, it uses a benefit of sequential high level transition graphs: Since high level transition graphs allows using hiding directly on the transitions of the graph, any hidden event, that is not in a synchronisation set of any parallel operator of the specification, can directly be hidden in the sequential graph. Therefore it is not necessary to consider those events in the evaluation of the synchronisation terms, because they have been removed from the underlying high level transition graph.

Chapter 6

Graphical Representation of High Level Transition Graphs

The theoretical foundation of high level transition graphs, defined in the previous chapter, can be used to generate transition graphs of CSP specifications. In this chapter, a graphical representation of high level transition graphs is presented. The representation that is introduced here is similar to the one used by the tool csp2rtt, which can generate high level transition graphs from CSP specification.

The main difference between classical transition graphs and high level transition graphs are the conditions and assignments at the transitions. Another difference is that the events at the transitions can use forms of pattern matching like question marks (e. g. a?x). Because of these differences, high level transition graphs can contain transitions that in fact represent a family of transitions with explicit events. These transitions are called *implicit transitions*. The high level transition graphs may also contain transitions that can only be used if a specified condition evaluates to true under the environment of the current state.

6.1 Locations

Like all transition graphs, the representation of high level transition graph consists of nodes and transitions. The nodes represent the locations. Each node in a high level transition graph is identified by a unique name, for example a serial number, which would be the easiest way of creating unique names. These names are assigned during the generation of the graph. To make the transition graphs more readable to humans, the name of the node can be extended by a string which is automatically derived from the CSP specification. This string can be ambiguous, since it usually consists of the CSP operator, which was responsible for the creation of that node.

The graphical representation of locations consists of a node with a unique name. Figure 6.1 shows three different nodes: *0:P*, *1:P* and Ω. The starting

Figure 6.1: Different types of nodes

node of a high level transition graph is always marked by a thicker circle around it like in node *0:P*. Another special state is represented by the 'Ω' node, which represents a successful termination of the process represented by the graph, since the only rule in the operational semantics, which allows to get to an Ω-node is a successful termination. The Ω-node are not numbered like the other nodes, since all nodes marked Ω are end nodes of the transition graph. In fact all nodes labelled Ω are semantically equivalent and can be identified as one.

6.2   Labels

Transitions in high level transition graphs are displayed as arrows pointing from one node to another. This is the obvious representation normally used in transition graphs. The markings at the transitions represent the labels of a HLTG. They must contain a condition and pairs of events and assignments.

Figure 6.2 shows a simple transition from the node *0:P* to the node Ω. The transition contains an event ✓, which indicates the successful termination of the process, and no corresponding assignments. In this case the boolean expression *true* is used as the condition of the label, which means that the transition can always be taken. For simplicity reasons a condition *true* may be omitted in the graphs.

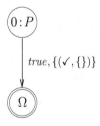

Figure 6.2: A simple transition

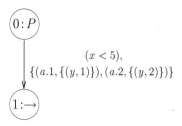

Figure 6.3: A transition with a condition and an assignment.

A little more complex example is given in figure 6.3, which shows a transition with conditions, multiple events and assignments. This figure shows a part of a transition graph for the process

```
P(x) = (x<5) & a?y -> SKIP
```

where the channel a is defined as $(a, \{1..2\})$.

The condition at the transition is $x < 5$, i.e. it may only be taken, if the value of x in the current environment is smaller then 5. The set at the transition states all events and their corresponding assignments, that may be taken. If the external environment chooses for example the event $a.2$ to be produced, the corresponding assignment $(y, 2)$, which represents the assignment of the value 2 to the variable y, must be applied to the current environment, which results in a new binding for the variable y.

Conditions

Conditions are an essential part of the high level transition graphs. Without them it would not be possible to create these small transition graphs. The evaluation of the conditions must be done during the execution of the graph. Therefore a tool evaluating those types of graphs must implement the whole expression language CSP supports or the expressions must be represented in a standardised format like BDDs.

Before a transition in the high level transition graphs can be taken, the condition must be checked first, whether it holds in the current environment. If it does, the transition may be taken. Conditions are always written before the set of possible event/assignment pairs. If there is no condition in the graph, this implies the condition *true*, which means, that the transition may always be taken.

The conditions at the labels can automatically be generated from the CSP specification. The following CSP specification can be transformed into a transition graph containing two conditions, as shown in figure 6.4.

```
1    channel out : { 1..10 }
2
3    P = OUTPUT(1)
4
5    OUTPUT(x) = if (x > 10)
6                then SKIP
7                else out.x -> OUTPUT(x+1)
```

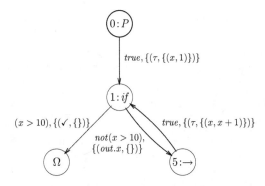

Figure 6.4: High level transition graph with conditions

The high level transition graph generated by this CSP specification consists of four nodes and transitions, where two of these transitions have labels with non trivial conditions attached. The transition from node *1:if* to node Ω represents the *then*-case of the CSP specification and therefore is labelled with the condition $(x > 10)$. The *else*-case of the specification is represented by the transition from node *1:if* to the node *5:→*. The condition of the *else*-case must be the negation of the condition of the *then*-case. Therefore the condition at this label is $not(x > 10)$.

Events and Assignments

As shown before events and assignments always exists as pairs. For each event there is a set of assignments, which are binding new values to those variables, which are affected by the production of the event. On each label exists a set of pairs of events and assignments. Each pair represents one event, that can be produced by that rule.

The simplest kind of pairs are shown in figure 6.2: $\{(\checkmark, \{\})\}$. The set of possible events contains only one pair. This pair consists of one event and no assignments. Instead of ✓ any other event would also be possible in this situation. The selection of this transition leads to the production of the given event. Additionally all assignments must be applied to the environment, which is simple in this case, since there are no assignments.

Another possibility of pairs is shown in figure 6.3, where several pairs exists in the set of possible events: $\{(a.1, \{(y, 1)\}), (a.2, \{(y, 2)\}), (a.3, \{(y, 3)\})\}$. Such sets with a cardinality larger than one are representing a choice, which is introduced by the ?-operator. The environment may choose any of the events from the pairs, to be produced. After the production of that event the corresponding assignments must be applied to the environment. That means, that if the environment chooses to produce event $a.2$, the corresponding assignment $\{(y, 2)\}$ changes the value of the variable y in the current environment to 2.

The third possible type of pairs is introduced in figure 6.4 by the transition from node $1{:}if$ to the node $5{:}{\rightarrow} - \{(out.x, \{\})\}$. In this case the identifier x of the event $out.x$ must be replaced by the current binding of the variable x, which is stored in the environment. This transition can produce only one event at any time, since there is always a binding for each variable, that can occur, but which event is produced depends on the value of the variable.

Finally a combination of the last two types may occur. If a channel can communicate at least two different parameters it is possible to write processes like

```
P(y) = inout?x!y -> SKIP
```

with channel *inout* defined as

```
channel inout : {1..3}.{1..3}
```

In this case a new binding for the variable x is introduced by the event statement, whereas the binding of the variable y is used from the process definition. Therefore the resulting set of pairs looks as follows:
$\{(a.1.y, \{(x, 1)\}), (a.2.y, \{(x, 2)\}), (a.3.y, \{(x, 3)\})\}$.

6.3 Graph Abbreviations

When illustrating the structure of a high level transition graph, it is not always necessary to know the internal structure of the subgraphs. In these cases, graphical abbreviations can be used to describe a subgraph. In this section, some of these abbreviations are introduced which will be used in the following chapters:

- Figure 6.5 displays the subgraph of a process P with its start node l, representing the initial location of P. The internal structure of the process is not depicted.

Figure 6.5: The subgraph of a process P with its initial node l.

- Figure 6.6 again shows the subgraph of a process P with a start node l, but in this case the initial transition with the labels c_1, E_1 to c_n, E_n of the subgraph are shown explicitly. For some rules e. g. the *if-then-else* operator, it is important to know all initial transitions of a subgraph.

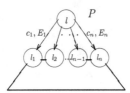

Figure 6.6: The subgraph of a process P with its initial transitions $(l_0, c_1, E_1, l1)$ to (l_0, c_n, E_n, l_n)

- Figure 6.7 shown the subgraph of P with some special transitions, labelled with c_1, E_1 to c_n, E_n, leading to end nodes of P. These end nodes and the transitions leading to them will become important in some rules like the ones of the *sequential composition*.

6.4   Synchronisation Terms

Synchronisation terms have been introduced in 5.2.3 as a way to model parallelism and hiding in high level transition graphs. Synchronisation terms can be displayed as trees. The graphical representation of the synchronisation term nodes is different to those of nodes representing low level locations in several ways: the high level nodes are shown as boxes instead of ellipses. The operator, which is responsible for the creation of the synchronisation term node, is displayed inside the box, to make the structure easier to read. Depending on whether the operator is an unary operator like hiding, or a binary operator, like parallel or interleaving, one or two dashed lines are leading to other nodes, which

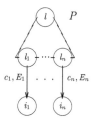

Figure 6.7: The subgraph of a process P with special transitions (l_0, c_1, E_1, l_1) to (l_0, c_n, E_n, l_n)

must be a synchronisation sub term. If the sub term is a HLTG with a current location l_i and a current environment ε_i, defined by the tuple $(HLTG_i, l_i, \varepsilon_i)$ (see definition 5.30, section 5.2.3), it is represented by a dashed line leading to the given location of the HLTG.

This graphical representation directly reflects the structure of the synchronisation term. Figure 6.8 for example illustrates the synchronisation term $(\lambda_1, S, \lambda_2)$, where λ_1 and λ_2 are representing the nodes $1{:}Q$ and $2{:}R$.

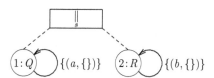

Figure 6.8: A synchronisation term.

Chapter 7

Generating High Level Transition Graphs and Synchronisation terms from CSP Specifications

High level transition graphs can be generated from the abstract syntax tree of CSP processes. This chapter describes how high level transition graphs for low level and high level processes can be created. A strict hierarchy of high and low level operators is required for CSP processes. A CSP process containing high level and low level operators must be build of sequential subprocesses containing the low level operators and a high level part referencing the low level subprocesses. Such CSP specifications are called *process nets*. A low level process results in a high level transition graph as defined in section 5.1. The rules specified in section 7.2 define the subgraphs created for each low-level CSP operator. The high level part of a CSP specification results in a synchronisation term as defined in Section 5.2.3 with the low level part as its leafs.

The HLTG of a CSP process is combined from the subgraphs of the process operators of the process term. The top level process operator in the process term creates its subgraph using the subgraphs of the process terms of its arguments if it has process terms as arguments. In this way, the HLTG is created bottom up from the subgraphs of all process operators. In the following sections, a definition of the subgraphs of each process operator is given. A proof of these concepts is given in appendix A.

7.1 Process Definitions

Unlike all CSP operators, the process definition creates its start location immediately before creating the subgraph of its process term. This is necessary to be able to create high level transition graphs of recursive process definitions as described in 7.2.1. When the subgraph of the process term is complete, the process definition replaces the start location of the subgraph with the previously created start location of the process definition.

Definition 7.1

The subgraph $HLTG_{procdef}$ of the process definition $P = T$ *where T is a* CSP *process term with the subgraph of T being $HLTG_T = (L_T, l_{T0}, \Sigma_T^{\pi\tau\checkmark}, \mathcal{E}_T^{\pi\tau\checkmark}, \rightarrow_T)$ can be defined as:*

$$HLTG_{procdef} = (L_{procdef}, l_0, \Sigma_{procdef}^{\pi\tau\checkmark}, \mathcal{E}_{procdef}^{\pi\tau\checkmark}, \rightarrow_{procdef})$$

with

$$
\begin{aligned}
L_{procdef} &= (L_T \setminus l_{T0}) \cup \{l_0\} \\
\Sigma_{procdef}^{\pi\tau\checkmark} &= \Sigma_T^{\pi\tau\checkmark} \\
\mathcal{E}_{procdef}^{\pi\tau\checkmark} &= \mathcal{E}_T^{\pi\tau\checkmark} \\
\rightarrow_{procdef} &= (\rightarrow_T \setminus (\ \{(l_{T0}, c, e, l) \mid c \in Conditions, e \in \mathcal{E}_T^{\pi\tau\checkmark}, l \in L_T\} \\
&\qquad\qquad \cup \{(l, c, e, l_{T0}) \mid c \in Conditions, e \in \mathcal{E}_T^{\pi\tau\checkmark}, l \in L_T\})) \\
&\quad \cup \{(l_0, c, e, l) \mid \exists (l_{T0}, c, e, l) \in \rightarrow_T \wedge l \in L_T \setminus l_{T0}\} \\
&\quad \cup \{(l, c, e, l_0) \mid \exists (l, c, e, l_{T0}) \in \rightarrow_T \wedge l \in L_T \setminus l_{T0}\}
\end{aligned}
$$

7.2 Low level Operators

The rules for creating the subgraphs of the different process operators are derived directly from its operational semantics. This section presents the definitions of the subgraphs of the CSP operator and how to connect them. The definitions of the high level transition graphs are also illustrated in a graphical notation that uses variations of the constructs shown in section 6.3, figure 6.5, 6.6 and 6.7.

7.2.1 Basic Processes

Stop

The basic process STOP has no actions at all, so its subgraph consists of a start location without any transitions and the alphabet Σ does not contain any events. The subgraph of the *STOP* process is defined in definition 7.2 and figure 7.1 shows this simple subgraph.

Definition 7.2 *The subgraph of the STOP process ($HLTG_{STOP}$):*

$$HLTG_{STOP} = (\{l_0\}, l_0, \{\pi, \tau, \checkmark\}, \{(\pi, \emptyset), (\tau, \emptyset), (\checkmark, \emptyset)\}, \emptyset)$$

Figure 7.1: The subgraph of *STOP*.

Skip

The basic process SKIP can perform just one single event ✓. After the event has been produced, the process terminates and evolves to the process Ω, where no further actions can be performed. When generating the high level transition graph, the SKIP process returns a location with a ✓-transition leading to a location named Ω. The label at the transition does not contain any conditions or assignments. Figure 7.2 shows the subgraph of the SKIP operator and the high level transition graph is defined in definition 7.3.

Definition 7.3
The subgraph of the SKIP process (HLTG$_{SKIP}$):

$$HLTG_{SKIP} = (\{l_0, \Omega\}, l_0, \{\pi, \tau, \checkmark\}, \{(\pi, \emptyset), (\tau, \emptyset), (\checkmark, \emptyset)\},$$
$$\{(l_o, true, \{(\checkmark, \emptyset)\}, \Omega)\})$$

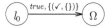

Figure 7.2: The subgraph of *SKIP*.

Process References

Process references can be used to model infinite processes, by defining process specifications, which calls itself repeatedly. In contrast to earlier semantics, the operational semantics for process references as described in 2.4 does not use τ-events[1]. In high level transition graphs, a transition labelled with the special event π is used for process *references*, leading to the start location of the subgraph of the referenced *process*. This special transitions label is used to carry the assignments of the process reference, for processes can be called with a tuple of arguments. The concept of π-events has been introduced and discussed in section 5.1.3 in detail. The assignments of the π-labels can be computed using the following definitions.

---

[1]For details about the benefit of this variant see section 2.4.

The function *arguments* returns the tuple of expressions which a are the arguments of a *function-* or *process reference*. It can as well be used to calculate the tuple of variables for a *function-* or *process definition*. Process definitions in ClaO can have only variables as parameters because no pattern matching is supported, so far. Since variables are also expressions, the function *arguments* can be used for both, function- or process *references* and function- or process *definitions*.

Definition 7.4
The function arguments : Expressions → Expressions denotes the tuple of arguments of a process or function reference or definition. It can be defined as:

$$arguments(e) = \begin{cases} () & \text{where } e \text{ is no function or process} \\ & \text{reference or definition} \\ & \text{or } e = f() \text{ has no arguments.} \\ (a_1, ..., a_n) & \text{where } e = f(a_1, ..., a_n) \end{cases}$$

The function *assigns* calculates the set of assignment that is needed to follow a process or function reference. These assignments are pairs of a variable and an expression, assigning every variable of the function- or process definition the expression that is used in the function- or process reference for this variable.

Definition 7.5
The function assigns : Expressions × Expressions → $\mathcal{P}$(Variables × Expressions) denotes the set of assignments required for evaluating a function or executing a process with the arguments of a function- or process reference. It can be defined as:

$$assigns(func\_ref, func\_def) =$$
$$\{(var_i, e_i) \mid i \in \{1, ..., n\} \wedge (e_1, ..., e_n) = arguments(func\_ref) \wedge$$
$$(var_1, ..., var_n) = arguments(func\_def)\}$$

The subgraph of a process reference consists of the subgraph for the referenced process and a π-transition, together with the assignments of the process invocation. This transition leads from a new and unnamed location to the start location of the subgraph representing the corresponding process term. The subgraph of a process reference $P(arg_1, ..., arg_n)$ can be seen in figure 7.3.

The subgraph of the corresponding process may not be complete when calculating the subgraph of the process reference, e.g. if a process references itself. In this case, at least the start location of the process must exist or must have been created as defined in section 7.1. If the subgraph of the referenced process is created later, it must use this start location.

Definition 7.6

The subgraph $HLTG_{procref}$ of the process reference $P_{ref} = P(arg_1, ..., arg_n)$ *to a process* $P_{def} = P(var_1, ..., var_n)$ *with the subgraph of P being* $HLTG_P = (L_P, l_{P0}, \Sigma_P^{\pi\tau\checkmark}, \mathcal{E}_P^{\pi\tau\checkmark}, \rightarrow_P)$ *can be defined as:*

$$HLTG_{procref} = (L_{procref}, l_0, \Sigma_{procref}^{\pi\tau\checkmark}, \mathcal{E}_{procref}^{\pi\tau\checkmark}, \rightarrow_{procref})$$

with

$$
\begin{aligned}
L_{procref} &= L_P \cup \{l_0\} \\
\Sigma_{procref}^{\pi\tau\checkmark} &= \Sigma_P^{\pi\tau\checkmark} \\
\mathcal{E}_{procref}^{\pi\tau\checkmark} &= \mathcal{E}_P^{\pi\tau\checkmark} \\
\rightarrow_{procref} &= \rightarrow_P \cup \{(l_0, true, \{(\pi, assigns(P_{ref}, P_{def}))\}, l_{P0})\}
\end{aligned}
$$

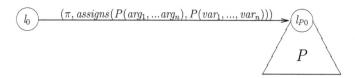

Figure 7.3: The subgraph of a process reference $P(arg_1, ..., arg_n)$.

The process that a process reference refers to must exist in the context of the specification[2]. The subgraph of the referenced process is created before the subgraph of the process reference is created if the process reference is not part of a recursive process. If the process reference does refer to itself or results in a recursion like the reference to P at the end of process Q in the following example, the subgraph of the referred process has not been completely created. In this case it must be assured that the start location exists and that it remains the start location after the subgraph of the process has been built completely. This is done by the rules for the *process definition*.

$$
\begin{aligned}
P &= a \rightarrow Q \\
Q &= b \rightarrow P
\end{aligned}
$$

---

[2]The context of a specification is the set of all its process definitions. It is described in section 2.2.5.

7.2.2 Sequential Process Operators

Prefixing

The prefixing operator $e \rightarrow P$ can produce any kind of event that can be specified in the prefix e. The process $e \rightarrow P$ can evolve to the process P, when the event α, being one of the events represented by e, is emitted. This event α must be an element of $comms(e)$, evaluated under the current environment – $\alpha \in comms(eval(e, \varepsilon))$. The set $comms(e)$ contains all possible communication events of the event e. It is defined in section 5.1.1, definition 5.9.

As stated in section 5.1, events consist of a channel and a possibly empty field expression. The field expressions can introduce new variables when containing input-fields. To maintain the correct environment, it is necessary to create the correct assignments for an event α that can be produced by an event e. Because this is not necessary for untyped events, as they cannot introduce variables, the following definitions assume typed events.

For the labels of a high level transition graph, it is necessary to know for each element of $comms(e)$ the set a of assignments that are necessary to transform e into the element of $comms(e)$. The set a_i for an event $\alpha_i \in comms(e)$ therefore must contain an assignment for each variable with a defining occurrence in e. The values assigned to these variables must match the values used for α_i so that evaluating e with the assignments of a_i must result in α_i. For the event $a?x!y$ with the channel definition $(a, \{1, 2, 3\} \times \{4, 5, 6\})$ for example, the set of assignments of the event of $comms(a?x!y)$ are $\{(x, 1)\}$ for the event $a.1!y$, $\{(x, 2)\}$ for the event $a.2!y$ and $\{(x, 3)\}$ for the event $a.3!y$.

Definition 7.7

The function $assigns_{event} : Events \times Events \rightarrow \mathcal{P}(Assignments)$ denotes the set of assignments that are necessary for the variables with defining occurrences of an event e to evaluate to an event $\alpha \in comms(e)$. It can be defined as:

$$assigns_{event}(e, \alpha) = \{(p, v) \mid e = cf_1...f_n \land \alpha = cf_1'...f_n' \land \alpha \in comms(e) \land$$
$$\exists i \in \{1, ..., n\}.(f_i =?p \land f_i' = .v\}$$

If the event argument of a prefix operator introduces new variables, all possible assignments of these variables together with their corresponding event must be assigned to the new label. The function *events* returns all pairs (α_i, a_i) of an event and a set of assignments that are represented by a CSP event e. This function is designed for typed and untyped channels, because it will be used to compute the events of the HLTG of prefixing.

Definition 7.8

The function $events : Events \rightarrow \mathcal{P}(Events \times \mathcal{P}(Assignments))$ denotes the set of tuples (α_i, a_i) of events and assignment sets with α_i being an element of comms *of the event and a_i being the set of corresponding assignments for all defining occurrences of variables in that event. It can be defined as:*

$$events(e) \quad = \quad \begin{cases} \{(e, \emptyset)\} & \textit{if } comms(e) = \{e\} \\ \{(\alpha, a) \mid \ \alpha \in comms(e) \ \wedge & \textit{if } comms(e) \neq \{e\} \\ \qquad a = assigns_{event}(e, \alpha) \end{cases}$$

Note that the events α still can contain applying occurrences of variables and have to be evaluated under the current environment. So they can still represent multiple elements of the alphabet Σ.

The prefix operator creates a new location and a new transition leading from the new location to the start location of the process argument of the prefix. The result of events(e) is added to this label of the transition. If the event argument does not introduce new variables, $comms(e) = e$, the event is unambiguous and the function $events(e)$ returns the event itself without any assignment $\{(e, \emptyset)\}$. If $comms(e)$ contains more than one element, $events(e)$ returns all possible events together with their assignments. This set is added to the label. Figure 7.4 gives an illustration of the subgraph of $e \rightarrow P$, which can be defined as:

Definition 7.9
The subgraph $HLTG_{prefix}$ of the process $e \rightarrow P$ with the subgraph of P being $HLTG_P = (L_P, l_{P0}, \Sigma_P^{\pi\tau\checkmark}, \mathcal{E}_P^{\pi\tau\checkmark}, \rightarrow_P)$ can be defined as:

$$HLTG_{prefix} \quad = \quad (L_{prefix}, l_0, \Sigma_{prefix}^{\pi\tau\checkmark}, \mathcal{E}_{prefix}^{\pi\tau\checkmark}, \rightarrow_{prefix})$$

with

$$
\begin{aligned}
L_{prefix} &= L_P \cup \{l_0\} \\
\Sigma_{prefix}^{\pi\tau\checkmark} &= \Sigma_P^{\pi\tau\checkmark} \cup sigma(c) \text{ with } e = cf_1...f_n \\
\mathcal{E}_{prefix}^{\pi\tau\checkmark} &= \mathcal{E}_P^{\pi\tau\checkmark} \cup events(e) \\
\rightarrow_{prefix} &= \rightarrow_P \cup \{(l_0, true, events(e), l_{P0})\}
\end{aligned}
$$

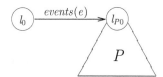

Figure 7.4: The subgraph of $e \rightarrow P$.

Sequential Composition

According to the operational semantics of the sequential composition of two processes $P;Q$, the first process P can produce events until it terminates and emits the $\checkmark$-event which is changed by the sequential composition operator into a τ-event. When this event is generated, the process P terminates and is replaced by the process Q which can now continue to produce events, until it terminates. Any conditions of the label of the $\checkmark$-transition will stay unchanged and have to be valid for the τ-transition before they can be taken. Figure 7.5 shows the subgraph of the subprocesses P and Q before applying the rules for the sequential composition.

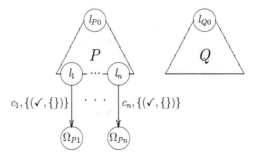

Figure 7.5: The subgraphs of the subprocesses P and Q.

When creating the high level transition graph of $P;Q$, all $\checkmark$-events in P are turned into τ-events and the transitions of the former $\checkmark$-events are changed so that they lead to the start location of Q instead of Ω. Figure 7.6 shows the resulting subgraph of $P;Q$.

This approach imposes one restriction on the format of the process definition using the sequential composition operator: It must never occur, that a process reference before a sequential composition operator references the same process, or a process which references back to the same process. This restriction is necessary, since the referenced process must by generated completely, otherwise the generation would produce an infinite high level transition graph.

Definition 7.10

The subgraph $HLTG_{seqcomp}$ of the process $P;Q$ with the subgraphs of P and Q being $HLTG_P = (L_P, l_{P0}, \Sigma_P^{\pi\tau\checkmark}, \mathcal{E}_P^{\pi\tau\checkmark}, \rightarrow_P)$ and $HLTG_Q = (L_Q, l_{Q0}, \Sigma_Q^{\pi\tau\checkmark}, \mathcal{E}_Q^{\pi\tau\checkmark}, \rightarrow_Q)$ can be defined as:

$$HLTG_{seqcomp} \;=\; (L_{seqcomp}, l_0, \Sigma_{seqcomp}^{\pi\tau\checkmark}, \mathcal{E}_{seqcomp}^{\pi\tau\checkmark}, \rightarrow_{seqcomp})$$

with

$$
\begin{aligned}
L_{seqcomp} &= L_Q \cup (L_P \setminus \{\Omega\}) \\
l_0 &= l_{P0} \\
\Sigma_{seqcomp}^{\pi\tau\checkmark} &= \Sigma_P^{\pi\tau\checkmark} \cup \Sigma_Q^{\pi\tau\checkmark} \\
\mathcal{E}_{seqcomp}^{\pi\tau\checkmark} &= \mathcal{E}_P^{\pi\tau\checkmark} \cup \mathcal{E}_Q^{\pi\tau\checkmark} \\
\rightarrow_{seqcomp} &= (\rightarrow_P \setminus \{(l, c, \{(\checkmark, \emptyset)\}, \Omega) \in \rightarrow_P | \ c \in Conditions, l \in L_P\}) \\
&\quad \cup \rightarrow_Q \\
&\quad \cup \{(l, c, \{(\tau, \emptyset)\}, l_{Q0}) \mid \exists \ (l, c, \{(\checkmark, \emptyset)\}, \Omega) \in \rightarrow_P, \\
&\qquad\qquad\qquad\qquad\qquad c \in Conditions, l \in L_P\}
\end{aligned}
$$

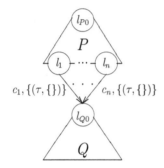

Figure 7.6: The subgraph of $P;Q$.

7.2.3 Choices

Conditions

The *if-then-else* statement in CSP enables the programmer to use conditions. If the condition in the statement evaluates to *true* the *then*-case, otherwise the *else*-case is selected.

When creating the high level transition graph of a process *if b then P else Q*, the condition b is added to all labels of the subgraph of Ps initial transitions, and the negation of b is added to all labels of the initial transitions of the subgraph of Q. Finally a new common start locations replaces both start locations of P and Q. This is demonstrated in figure 7.7. The subgraph that is created for an *if-then-else process* can be defined as:

Definition 7.11

The subgraph $HLTG_{cond}$ of the process if b then P else Q with the subgraphs of P and Q being $HLTG_P = (L_P, l_{P0}, \Sigma_P^{\pi\tau\checkmark}, \mathcal{E}_P^{\pi\tau\checkmark}, \rightarrow_P)$ and $HLTG_Q = (L_Q, l_{Q0}, \Sigma_Q^{\pi\tau\checkmark}, \mathcal{E}_Q^{\pi\tau\checkmark}, \rightarrow_Q)$ can be defined as:

$$HLTG_{cond} = (L_{cond}, l_0, \Sigma_{cond}^{\pi\tau\checkmark}, \mathcal{E}_{cond}^{\pi\tau\checkmark}, \rightarrow_{cond})$$

with

$$
\begin{aligned}
L_{cond} &= (L_P \setminus \{l_{P0}\}) \cup (L_Q \setminus \{l_{Q0}\}) \cup \{l_0\} \\
\Sigma_{cond}^{\pi\tau\checkmark} &= \Sigma_P^{\pi\tau\checkmark} \cup \Sigma_Q^{\pi\tau\checkmark} \\
\mathcal{E}_{cond}^{\pi\tau\checkmark} &= \mathcal{E}_P^{\pi\tau\checkmark} \cup \mathcal{E}_Q^{\pi\tau\checkmark} \\
\rightarrow_{cond} &= \quad \rightarrow_P \setminus (\ \{(l, c_i, E_i, l_i) \in \rightarrow_P | \ l = l_{P0}\} \\
&\qquad\qquad \cup \{(l_i, c_i, E_i, l) \in \rightarrow_P | \ l = l_{P0}\}) \\
&\cup \rightarrow_Q \setminus (\ \{(l, c_i, E_i, l_i) \in \rightarrow_Q | \ l = l_{Q0}\} \\
&\qquad\qquad \cup \{(l_i, c_i, E_i, l) \in \rightarrow_Q | \ l = l_{Q0}\}) \\
&\cup \{(l_0, (c_i \wedge b), e, l) \mid \exists (l_{P0}, c_i, e, l) \in \rightarrow_P \wedge l \in L_P \setminus l_{P0}\} \\
&\cup \{(l, c_i, e, l_0) \mid \exists (l, c_i, e, l_{P0}) \in \rightarrow_P \wedge l \in L_P \setminus l_{P0}\} \\
&\cup \{(l_0, (c_i \wedge \neg b), e, l) \mid \exists (l_{Q0}, c_i, e, l) \in \rightarrow_Q \wedge l \in L_Q \setminus l_{Q0}\} \\
&\cup \{(l, c_i, e, l_0) \mid \exists (l, c_i, e, l_{Q0}) \in \rightarrow_Q \wedge l \in L_Q \setminus l_{Q0}\}
\end{aligned}
$$

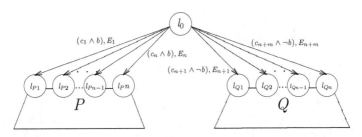

Figure 7.7: The subgraph of *if* b *then* P *else* Q.

Guarded commands are a shortened form of *if-then-else* statements where the else-case is the $STOP$ process. The high level transition graph of a *guarded command* can be calculated in the same way as the graph of an *if-then-else* statement, for which the *else-case* is the $STOP$ process. Because the subgraph of the $STOP$ process contains only a start location and no transitions, the above definition 7.11 can directly be used for the guarded command, as well.

Internal Choice

The internal choice operator is used to model non-deterministic choices. It needs two processes as arguments from which one is chosen to be executed. There is no possibility for the environment to choose which process will be selected. When the operator makes its selection, a τ-event is produced.

When creating the high level transition graph of a process $P \sqcap Q$, a new location is created, with two τ-transitions leading to the start locations of the subgraphs of the processes P and Q. This can be seen in figure 7.8. The subgraph of $P \sqcap Q$ can be defined as:

Definition 7.12
The subgraph $HLTG_{intchoice}$ of the process $P \sqcap Q$ with the subgraphs of P and Q being $HLTG_P = (L_P, l_{P0}, \Sigma_P^{\pi\tau\checkmark}, \mathcal{E}_P^{\pi\tau\checkmark}, \rightarrow_P)$ and $HLTG_Q = (L_Q, l_{Q0}, \Sigma_Q^{\pi\tau\checkmark}, \mathcal{E}_Q^{\pi\tau\checkmark}, \rightarrow_Q)$ can be defined as:

$$HLTG_{intchoice} = (L_{intchoice}, l_0, \Sigma_{intchoice}^{\pi\tau\checkmark}, \mathcal{E}_{intchoice}^{\pi\tau\checkmark}, \rightarrow_{intchoice})$$

with

$$
\begin{aligned}
L_{intchoice} &= L_P \cup L_Q \cup \{l_0\} \\
\Sigma_{intchoice}^{\pi\tau\checkmark} &= \Sigma_P^{\pi\tau\checkmark} \cup \Sigma_Q^{\pi\tau\checkmark} \\
\mathcal{E}_{intchoice}^{\pi\tau\checkmark} &= \mathcal{E}_P^{\pi\tau\checkmark} \cup \mathcal{E}_Q^{\pi\tau\checkmark} \\
\rightarrow_{intchoice} &= \rightarrow_P \cup \rightarrow_Q \\
&\quad \cup \{(l_0, true, \{(\tau, \emptyset)\}, l_{P0}), (l_0, true, \{(\tau, \emptyset)\}, l_{Q0})\}
\end{aligned}
$$

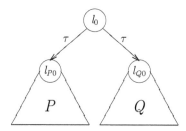

Figure 7.8: The subgraph of $P \sqcap Q$.

External Choice

The external choice operator allows the environment to choose one process from a number of alternatives. It is necessary to produce a *visible* event to make the selection. After the event is emitted, only the process which produced that event is further executed, the other one is not. If more than one process offer the same event, one process is chosen non-deterministically. If a subprocess can perform invisible events before the first visible event occurs, these events can be performed without effecting the choice.

The high level transition graph of a process $P \square Q$ contains three subgraphs, $P_{remainder}$, $Q_{remainder}$ and $\tau_P \times \tau_{Q'}$. $P_{remainder}$ is that part of the high level transition graph of P, that represents the actions of the process after the selection by one of the initial visible events of P. Analogously to $P_{remainder}$, the subgraph $Q_{remainder}$ is that part of the high level transition graph of Q, that represents the actions of this process after the selection is done by one of the initial visible events of Q. The possible combinations of invisible actions of both processes P and Q are covered by the subgraph $\tau_P \times \tau_{Q'}$. The only connection between these three subgraphs are transitions representing the initial visible actions of P and Q, where the transitions representing actions of P always lead from $\tau_P \times \tau_{Q'}$ to P and the transitions representing actions of Q always lead from $\tau_P \times \tau_{Q'}$ to Q. The start location of the whole high level transition graph is the start location of $\tau_P \times \tau_{Q'}$.

For external choices between two processes that contain no invisible events in their initial actions, the subgraph $\tau_P \times \tau_{Q'}$ contains no transitions but only a start location. For these simple forms of external choices, the subgraph is created by joining the start locations of the subgraphs of the two processes into the start location of $\tau_P \times \tau_{Q'}$. This can be seen in figure 7.9. Because the definition of the high level transition graph for the general case of external choices does cover this special case, no separate definition needs to be given here.

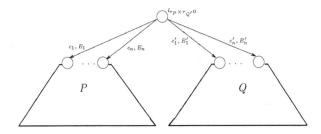

Figure 7.9: The subgraph of $P \square Q$ without initial τ- or π-events.

If one or both of the subgraphs contain τ- or π-events in their initial actions, the subgraph $\tau_P \times \tau_{Q'}$ becomes more complex. The subgraph is calculated by generating all traces of τ- or π-events that are possible when interleaving the respective parts of the processes P and Q, before a visible event occurs.

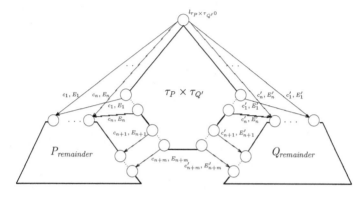

Figure 7.10: The subgraph of $P \,\square\, Q$.

For the generation of the subgraph $\tau_P \times \tau_{Q'}$, it is necessary to check if one of the arguments of the external choice operator can produce invisible events before the selection is made and to retrieve the set of these actions. The function *initialInvisibles* denotes this set of transitions of a high level transition graph that represent the *invisible* actions of the process that can be produced before any visible action.

Definition 7.13
The function initialInvisibles : $\mathcal{L}_{HLTG} \rightarrow \mathcal{P}(Transitions)$ denotes the set of transitions of a HLTG containing only invisible events and having a source location that can be reached from the starting location using only transitions labelled with invisible events.

$$initialInvisibles(HLTG) =$$
$$\big\{ (l_n, c_n, e_n, l'_n) \mid \ \exists\ (l_1, c_1, e_1, l'_1), ..., (l_n, c_n, e_n, l'_n) \in \rightarrow_{CA} \ .\, l_1 = l_0$$
$$\wedge \forall\, i \in \{1, ..., n-1\} \ . \ l'_i = l_{i+1}$$
$$\wedge \forall (\alpha, a) \in e_i \ . \ \alpha \in \{\pi, \tau\} \ \big\}$$

As already mentioned, the choice is done by the first visible action of one of the processes. Therefore it is necessary to know the set of all actions of a process, that can be used to make the choice. The function *initialVisibles* denotes the set of all transitions of a high level transition graph that represent the initial *visible* actions of the process.

Definition 7.14
The function initialVisibles : $\mathcal{L}_{HLTG} \rightarrow \mathcal{P}(\textit{Transitions})$ *denotes the set of transitions of a HLTG containing visible events and that can be taken directly from the start location or from a location that can be reached using only transitions labelled with invisible events.*

$$initialVisibles(HLTG) =$$
$$\{(l_0, c, e, l') \in \rightarrow_{CA} |\ \ c \in \textit{Conditions}, e \in \mathcal{E}^{\pi\tau\checkmark}, l' \in L$$
$$\wedge \forall (\alpha, a) \in e.\alpha \notin \{\pi, \tau\}\}$$

The high level transition graph τ_P is the part of the high level transition graph of P that does only cover the initial invisible actions of P. This subgraph is necessary to calculate the subgraph $\tau_P \times \tau_{Q'}$, that is part of the high level transition graph of $P \square Q$. It can be defined as:

Definition 7.15
The subgraph $HLTG_{\tau_P}$ of the process P with the subgraph of P being $HLTG_P = (L_P, l_{P0}, \Sigma_P^{\pi\tau\checkmark}, \mathcal{E}_P^{\pi\tau\checkmark}, \rightarrow_P)$ can be defined as:

$$HLTG_{\tau_P} \ = \ (L_{\tau_P}, l_0, \Sigma_{\tau_P}^{\pi\tau\checkmark}, \mathcal{E}_{\tau_P}^{\pi\tau\checkmark}, \rightarrow_{\tau_P})$$

with

$$L_{\tau_P} \ = \ \{l \in L_P \mid \ \exists(l, c, e, l') \in initialInvisibles(HLTG_P)$$
$$\vee \exists(l', c, e, l) \in initialInvisibles(HLTG_P)\}$$
$$l_0 \ = \ l_{P0}$$
$$\Sigma_{\tau_P}^{\pi\tau\checkmark} \ = \ \{\pi, \tau\}$$
$$\mathcal{E}_{\tau_P}^{\pi\tau\checkmark} \ = \ \{e \in \mathcal{E}_P^{\pi\tau\checkmark} \mid \exists(l, c, e, l') \in initialInvisibles(HLTG_P)\}$$
$$\rightarrow_{\tau_P} \ = \ initialInvisibles(HLTG_P)$$

The π-labels, that holds the assignments of process parameters of process references, need a special handling for the external choice operator. If the processes P and Q both contain initial π-events, it is possible, that the assignments of the corresponding π-labels assign different values to the same variable. This problem becomes clear when looking at the following example:

```
1    channel a,b : {1,2}
2    E = P(1) [] P(2)
3    P(x) = a.x -> b.x -> STOP
```

The process E consists of an external choice between the subprocesses $P(1)$ and $P(2)$ which both are process references. Their subgraphs are beginning with a π-transition containing a label that assigns either 1 or 2 to the parameter x.

Because the π-labels are not visible to the environment, the subgraph $\tau_{P(1)} \times \tau_{P(2)}$ contains a path of π-transitions where the value 1 is assigned to x and after this, the value 2 is assigned to x. The problem is, that at the end of this trace, it is possible to take a transition with the event $a.x$ leading into the subgraph $P(1)_{remainder}$ and a transition containing the event $a.x$ leading into the subgraph $P(2)_{remainder}$. The first label obviously is incorrect, because the event would be $a.2$ which is not possible for P(1). This situation can be seen in node $l_\times$ figure 7.11.

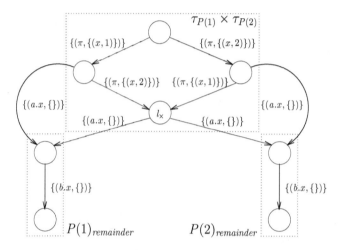

Figure 7.11: The subgraph of $P(1) \,\square\, P(2)$ *without* variable substitution.

The solution is to rename the parameters so that they are unique and insert extra re-assignments. Only the parameters in $\tau_{P(2)}$ that occur in $\tau_{P(1)}$ have to be replaced. Every transition with a visible event in the subgraph of $P(2)$, that does the choice, must get a reassignment, so that the values of the newly introduced variables are assigned to the original variables. In this example, a new variable x' is created in the subgraph of $P(2)$. In the subgraph $\tau_{P(1)} \times \tau_{P(2)}$, the π-labels of $P(1)$ only contain assignments of the value 1 to the variable x and the π-labels of $P(2)$ only contain assignments of the value 2 to the variable x'. The choice is done by the transitions with the visible event $a.x$ or $a.x'$. The $a.x'$ transitions lead into $P(2)_{remainder}$. In this subgraph, x was not replaced by x'. Therefore, the value of the new variable x' has to be reassigned to the original variable x. This reassignment is added to the label of the transition, that does the choice $(a.x')$. Figure 7.12 shows the graph with unique variables and re-assignments.

The subgraph $\tau_{P(1)} \times \tau_{P(2)}$ is renamed to $\tau_{P(1)} \times \tau_{P(2)'}$ to show that it contains the new variables and assignments.

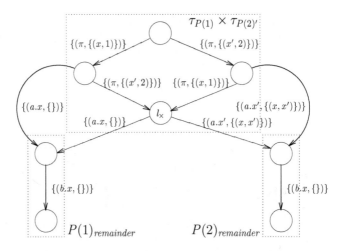

Figure 7.12: The subgraph of $P(1) \; \Box \; P(2)$ *with* variable substitution and re-assignments.

The new assignments have to be created for the variables that occur in assignments in both subgraph $HLTG_{\tau_P}$ and in $HLTG_{\tau_Q}$. For every variable, which has values assigned to in both subgraphs, a new assignment has to be created in the subgraph $HLTG_{\tau_{Q'}}$. Instead of creating new assignments only for those variables that occur in both subgraphs, new assignments can be created for all assignments in $HLTG_{\tau_Q}$. In this case it is not necessary to check if a variable occurs in both graphs. The first step is to calculate the set of pairs (v, v') of new variables v that do not occur in $HLTG_{\tau_P}$ or $HLTG_{\tau_Q}$ and a that should replace the variable v' in $HLTG_{\tau_Q}$. This is done by the function *newVars* which is defined as follows:

Definition 7.16
Let $\mathcal{V}_{spec}$ be the set of all variables of a given CSP *specification that defines P and Q. The function newVars : $\mathcal{L}_{HLTG} \times \mathcal{L}_{HLTG} \rightarrow \mathcal{P}(Variables \times Variables)$ denotes a set of tuples (v, v') of new variables v' with a unique variable v in $vars_{HLTG}(HLTG_Q)$. It can be defined as:*

$$newVars(HLTG_P, HLTG_Q) =$$
$$\{(v, v') \mid \exists\, e \in Expressions \,.\, (v, e) \in assigns_{HLTG}(HLTG_Q) \wedge v' = \gamma(v)\}$$

with $\gamma : vars_{HLTG}(HLTG_Q) \rightarrow Variables \setminus \mathcal{V}_{spec}$ being bijective.

Every defining and applied occurrence of the old variables v in $HLTG_Q$ has to be replaced by the new variable v'. This can be done in the canonical way as described in the following function $subst_{HLTG}$ does this substitution.

Definition 7.17 *The function* $subst_{HLTG} : \mathcal{L}_{HLTG} \times \mathcal{P}(\text{Variables} \times \text{Variables}) \rightarrow \mathcal{L}_{HLTG}$ *replaces variables in a high level transition graph. It is defined as:*

$subst_{HLTG}(HLTG, V) = HLTG'$
with $HLTG' = HLTG$ *where for each pair* (v, v'), *that is an elements of* V,
every occurrence of v *has been replaced by* v'.

The high level transition graph $HLTG_{\tau_{Q'}}$ is a new subgraph that is created by introducing the new variables for the subgraph $HLTG_{\tau_Q}$.

Definition 7.18 *The subgraph* $HLTG_{\tau_{Q'}}$ *being the subgraph* $HLTG_{\tau_Q}$ *with new variables* v' *for all variables* v *occurring in assignments of* $HLTG_{\tau_Q}$ *with* $HLTG_{\tau_Q} = (L_{\tau_Q}, l_{\tau_{Q0}}, \Sigma_{\tau_Q}^{\pi\tau\checkmark}, \mathcal{E}_{\tau_Q}^{\pi\tau\checkmark}, \rightarrow_{\tau_Q})$ *and* $HLTG_{\tau_P} = (L_{\tau_P}, l_{\tau_{P0}}, \Sigma_{\tau_P}^{\pi\tau\checkmark}, \mathcal{E}_{\tau_P}^{\pi\tau\checkmark}, \rightarrow_{\tau_P})$ *can be defined as:*

$$HLTG_{\tau_{Q'}} = subst_{HLTG\tau_Q}(HLTG, newVars(HLTG_{\tau_P}, HLTG_{\tau_Q}))$$

The high level transition graph $HLTG_{\tau_P \times \tau_{Q'}}$ contains all possible combinations of the invisible actions, both processes can produce before the choice is made. It is the product graph of $HLTG_{\tau_P}$ and $HLTG_{\tau_{Q'}}$.

Definition 7.19 *The subgraph* $HLTG_{\tau_P \times \tau_{Q'}}$ *being the product graph of the subgraphs of* $HLTG_{\tau_P}$ *and* $HLTG_{\tau_{Q'}}$ *with* $HLTG_{\tau_P} = (L_{\tau_P}, l_{\tau_{P0}}, \Sigma_{\tau_P}^{\pi\tau\checkmark}, \mathcal{E}_{\tau_P}^{\pi\tau\checkmark}, \rightarrow_{\tau_P})$ *and* $HLTG_{\tau_{Q'}} = (L_{\tau_{Q'}}, l_{\tau_{Q'0}}, \Sigma_{\tau_{Q'}}^{\pi\tau\checkmark}, \mathcal{E}_{\tau_{Q'}}^{\pi\tau\checkmark}, \rightarrow_{\tau_{Q'}})$ *can be defined as:*

$$HLTG_{\tau_P \times \tau_{Q'}} = (L_{\tau_P \times \tau_{Q'}}, l_0, \Sigma_{\tau_P \times \tau_{Q'}}^{\pi\tau\checkmark}, \mathcal{E}_{\tau_P \times \tau_{Q'}}^{\pi\tau\checkmark}, \rightarrow_{\tau_P \times \tau_{Q'}})$$

with

$$L_{\tau_P \times \tau_{Q'}} = L_{\tau_P} \times L_{\tau_{Q'}}$$
$$l_0 = (l_{\tau_{P0}}, l_{\tau_{Q'0}})$$
$$\Sigma_{\tau_P \times \tau_{Q'}}^{\pi\tau\checkmark} = \Sigma_{\tau_P}^{\pi\tau\checkmark} \cup \Sigma_{\tau_{Q'}}^{\pi\tau\checkmark}$$
$$\mathcal{E}_{\tau_P \times \tau_{Q'}}^{\pi\tau\checkmark} = \mathcal{E}_{\tau_P}^{\pi\tau\checkmark} \cup \mathcal{E}_{\tau_{Q'}}^{\pi\tau\checkmark}$$
$$\rightarrow_{\tau_P \times \tau_{Q'}} = \{((l_1, l_2), c, e, (l_1', l_2))) \mid \exists (l_1, c, e, l_1') \in \rightarrow_{\tau_P} \wedge l_2 \in L_{\tau_{Q'}}\}$$
$$\cup \{((l_1, l_2), c, e, (l_1, l_2'))) \mid \exists (l_2, c, e, l_2') \in \rightarrow_{\tau_{Q'}} \wedge l_1 \in L_{\tau_P}\}$$

Because the new variables are introduced only for the invisible part of Q, the visible events of Q, that can make the choice must get special re-assignments. They assign the value of every new variable to the appropriate old variable of Q. The old variable can now be used for the rest of the process. In the conditions and events of these initial visible labels, the new variables must still replace the old variables as in $HLTG_{\tau_Q}$, because the re-assignments only take effect after the respective transition has been chosen. The function $subst_{expr}$ does the same substitution, $subst_{HLTG}$ does on high level transition graphs, on expressions.

Definition 7.20
The function $subst_{expr}$: Expressions $\times$ $\mathcal{P}$(Variables $\times$ Variables) $\to$ Expressions replaces variables in an expression. It is defined as:

$subst_{expr}(e,\, V) = e'$
with $e' = e$ where for each pair (v, v'), that is an element of V,
    every occurrence of v has been replaced by v'.

The function *reassignEvents* of an event $e \in \mathcal{E}$ denotes a new event e', which is the event e with the re-assignments added to every pair $(\alpha, a) \in e'$ and all variables in α have been replaced by the appropriate new variable, if it exists. The replacement of the variables in α is necessary, since the selection is made by these events. Until the selection has not been made, the problem with the different assignments to the same variable still exists.

Definition 7.21
The function reassignEvents : Events $\times$ $\mathcal{L}_{HLTG}$ $\times$ $\mathcal{L}_{HLTG}$ $\to$ $\mathcal{P}$(Events) denotes the re-assignment event. It can be defined as:

$reassignEvents(e, HLTG_P, HLTG_Q) =$
    $\{(\alpha', a') \mid\ \exists(\alpha, a) \in e\,.\,(a' = a \cup newVars(HLTG_P, HLTG_Q)$
        $\land\ \alpha' = subst_{expr}(\alpha, newVars(HLTG_P, HLTG_Q)))\}$

The function *reassignTrans* calculates the set of that can be used to make the choice for process Q. These transitions already contain the re-assignment events.

Definition 7.22
The function reassignTrans : $\mathcal{L}_{HLTG}$ $\times$ $\mathcal{L}_{HLTG}$ $\to$ $\mathcal{P}$(Transitions) denotes the set of transitions of a high level transition graph that contain the appropriate reassignments. It can be defined as:

$reassignTrans(HLTG_P, HLTG_Q) =$
    $\{(l, c', e', l') \mid\ \exists(l, c, e, l') \in initialVisibles(HLTG_Q)\,.$
        $(e' = reassignEvents(HLTG_P, HLTG_Q, e)$
        $\land\ c' = subst_{expr}(c, newVars(HLTG_P, HLTG_Q)))\}$

Finally, the high level transition graph $HLTG_{extchoice}$ of the external choice of two processes P and Q can be defined.

Definition 7.23 *The subgraph $HLTG_{extchoice}$ of the processes P and Q with the subgraph of P being $HLTG_P = (L_P, l_{P0}, \Sigma_P^{\pi\tau\checkmark}, \mathcal{E}_P^{\pi\tau\checkmark}, \rightarrow_P)$ and the subgraph of Q being $HLTG_Q = (L_Q, l_{Q0}, \Sigma_Q^{\pi\tau\checkmark}, \mathcal{E}_Q^{\pi\tau\checkmark}, \rightarrow_Q)$ can be defined as:*

$$HLTG_{extchoice} = (L_{extchoice}, l_0, \Sigma_{extchoice}^{\pi\tau\checkmark}, \mathcal{E}_{extchoice}^{\pi\tau\checkmark}, \rightarrow_{extchoice})$$

with

$$
\begin{aligned}
L_{extchoice} &= (L_P \setminus L_{\tau_P}) \cup (L_Q \setminus L_{\tau_Q}) \cup L_{\tau_P \times \tau_{Q'}} \\
l_0 &= l_{\tau_P \times \tau_{Q'} 0} \\
\Sigma_{extchoice}^{\pi\tau\checkmark} &= \Sigma_P^{\pi\tau\checkmark} \cup \Sigma_Q^{\pi\tau\checkmark} \\
\mathcal{E}_{extchoice}^{\pi\tau\checkmark} &= \mathcal{E}_P^{\pi\tau\checkmark} \cup \mathcal{E}_Q^{\pi\tau\checkmark} \\
\rightarrow_{extchoice} &= \quad \rightarrow_P \setminus (\quad initialInvisibles(HLTG_P) \cup initialVisibles(HLTG_P)) \\
&\qquad \cup \{(l, c_i, E_i, l_i) \in \rightarrow_P | \; l = l_{P0}\} \\
&\qquad \cup \{(l_i, c_i, E_i, l) \in \rightarrow_P | \; l = l_{P0}\}) \\
&\quad \cup \rightarrow_Q \setminus (\quad initialInvisibles(HLTG_Q) \cup initialVisibles(HLTG_Q)) \\
&\qquad \cup \{(l, c_i, E_i, l_i) \in \rightarrow_Q | \; l = l_{Q0}\} \\
&\qquad \cup \{(l_i, c_i, E_i, l) \in \rightarrow_Q | \; l = l_{Q0}\}) \\
&\quad \cup \{(l, c, e, l_0) \; | \; \exists (l, c, e, l_{P0}) \in \rightarrow_P \wedge l \in L_P \setminus l_{P0}\} \\
&\quad \cup \{(l, c, e, l_0) \; | \; \exists (l, c, e, l_{Q0}) \in \rightarrow_Q \wedge l \in L_Q \setminus l_{Q0}\} \\
&\quad \cup \rightarrow_{\tau_P \times \tau_{Q'}} \\
&\quad \cup \{((l_1, l_2), c, e, l') \; | \; \exists (l_1, c, e, l') \in initialVisibles(HLTG_P) \\
&\qquad\qquad\qquad \wedge (l_1, l_2) \in L_{\tau_P \times \tau_{Q'}}\} \\
&\quad \cup \{((l_1, l_2), c, e, l') \; | \; \exists (l_2, c, e, l') \in \\
&\qquad\qquad\qquad reassignTrans(HLTG_P, HLTG_Q) \\
&\qquad\qquad\qquad \wedge (l_1, l_2) \in L_{\tau_P \times \tau_{Q'}}\}
\end{aligned}
$$

7.2.4 Replicated Functions

The replicated forms of CSP operators are special syntactic constructs that express that the operator is used several times. The semantics of these operators is the natural extension of the semantics of the basic operators. ClaO currently implements the generation of the high level transition graphs of the *replicated external choice* operator, the *replicated internal choice* operator and the *replicated interleaving* operator. The high level transition graphs can be compiled by creating the explicit form for the operators and then calculate the high level transition graph as described before.

The replicated variants of the operators always have the from `<operator>` `<variable>` : `<set>` @ `<process>`. The just described approach carries the restriction, that the replicated operator may not be parametrised in the set of values that are possible for the variable, as the high level transition graph is created before parameters can be evaluated. Another disadvantage is that creating the explicit form of the operator can result in a very large syntax tree.

Replicated Internal Choice

The only replicated operator that is not build using the explicit syntax tree is the *replicated internal choice* operator. The high level transition graph of $\sqcap x : A \bullet P$ simply consists of a τ transition leading to the start location of P. The label at the transition actually contains a set of pairs (τ, a) of a τ-event and a set of assignments. For each element of A, this set contains an element (τ, a) where a contains only one assignment, assigning the element of A to the variable x. The set of assignments of x and elements of A can be calculated using the following definition of $assign_{rep}(x, A)$. The high level transition graph is defined in definition 7.25 and illustrated in figure 7.13.

Definition 7.24
The function $assign_{rep} : Variables \times \mathcal{P}(Expressions) \rightarrow \mathcal{P}(Assignments)$ denotes the set of assignments, that for each element of a set contain an assignment, assigning the element to the variable argument. It can be defined as:

$$assign_{rep}(x, A) \quad = \quad \{(x, e) \mid e \in A\}$$

Definition 7.25
The subgraph $HLTG_{repint}$ of the process $\sqcap x : A \bullet P$ with the subgraph of P being $HLTG_P = (L_P, l_{P0}, \Sigma_P^{\pi\tau\checkmark}, \mathcal{E}_P^{\pi\tau\checkmark}, \rightarrow_P)$ can be defined as:

$$HLTG_{repint} \quad = \quad (L_{repint}, l_0, \Sigma_{repint}^{\pi\tau\checkmark}, \mathcal{E}_{repint}^{\pi\tau\checkmark}, \rightarrow_{repint})$$

with

$$
\begin{aligned}
L_{repint} &= L_P \cup \{l_0\} \\
\Sigma_{repint}^{\pi\tau\checkmark} &= \Sigma_P^{\pi\tau\checkmark} \\
\mathcal{E}_{repint}^{\pi\tau\checkmark} &= \mathcal{E}_P^{\pi\tau\checkmark} \cup \{(\tau, a) \mid \exists a_i \in assign_{rep}(x, A) . a = \{a_i\}\} \\
\rightarrow_{repint} &= \rightarrow_P \\
&\quad \cup \{(l_0, true, \{(\tau, a) \mid \exists a_i \in assign_{rep}(x, A) . a = \{a_i\}\}, l_{P0})\}
\end{aligned}
$$

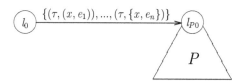

Figure 7.13: The subgraph of $\sqcap\; x : A \bullet P$ with $A = \{e_1, ..., e_n\}$.

7.3 High Level Operators

Synchronisation terms as defined in section 5.2.3 are defined for the high level operators *hiding*, *parallel* and *interleaving*, with the high level transition graphs of the sequential part of the process as leafs. They store meta-information about the structure of combined high level transition graph systems. Synchronisation terms can be used to represent hiding on processes and to model parallel and interleaved processes without creating the complete product graph of the process.

Hiding

The only meta information, that has to be stored for the synchronisation terms of the hiding operator $P \setminus h$ is the hiding set h and the process P it applies to. The synchronisation term of P can be the result of another high level operator or the HLTG of a low level process together with its start location and the start environment. Figure 7.14 shows the synchronisation term of $P \setminus h$. In the figure, it is assumed, that P is a low level process.

Definition 7.26
The synchronisation term $\lambda_{P \setminus h}$ of the high level process $P \setminus h$ with an existing synchronisation term λ_P of P can be defined as:

$$\lambda_{P \setminus h} \;\; = \;\; (\lambda_P, h)$$

Parallel and Interleaving

The meta information, that has to be stored in the synchronisation term of the parallel operator are the two processes that should run in parallel and the set of events, they ought to synchronise over. In case of the interleaving operator, the synchronisation set is empty.

The synchronisation term for $P \parallel_s Q$ contains the two sub terms of P and Q and the synchronisation set s. Again, the synchronisation terms of P and Q can either be the result of another high level operator or the HLTG of a low level process

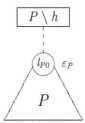

Figure 7.14: The subgraph of $P \setminus h$.

together with its start location and start environment. The synchronisation term of $P \parallel_s Q$ is shown in figure 7.15. In the figure, it is assumed, that P is a low level process and Q is starting with a high level process operator.

Definition 7.27

The synchronisation term $\lambda_{P \parallel_s Q}$ of the high level process $P \parallel_s Q$ with the existing synchronisation terms λ_P and λ_Q of P and Q can be defined as:

$$\lambda_{P \parallel_s Q} = (\lambda_P, s, \lambda_Q)$$

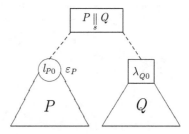

Figure 7.15: The subgraph of $P \parallel Q$.

Because interleaving is a special case of synchronised parallel with an empty synchronisation set, the above definition can be used for interleaving, as well.

Process reference

Process references are extremely useful to create complex processes out of sub processes. That is why the process reference is the only low level operator that is allowed in the high level part of a CSP process. If process references occur between high level operators, no subgraph is created as defined in section 7.2.1. Instead, the assignments for the process parameters that are defined by the process reference are used to adjust the start environment of the high level transition graph(s) $HLTG_i$ of the synchronisation term created by the high level operator after the process reference. This can be expressed through a recursive definition of $\lambda[a]$ which stands for *adding the assignments of a to the environment and set of Variables for all HLTG in λ*.

Definition 7.28 *Let $a = \{(p_1, v_1), ..., (p_n, v_n)\}$ be a set of assignments, . $\lambda[a]$ is defined as*

$$
\begin{array}{llll}
\lambda[a] = & (\lambda_1[a], h) & \text{if } \lambda = (\lambda_1, h) \\
 & | & (\lambda_1[a], s, \lambda_2[a]) & \text{if } \lambda = (\lambda_1, s, \lambda_2) \\
 & | & (\lambda_1[a], s, h, \lambda_2[a]) & \text{if } \lambda = (\lambda_1, s, h, \lambda_2) \\
 & | & (HLTG_i, l_i, \varepsilon_i') & \text{if } \lambda = (HLTG_i, l_i, \varepsilon_i)
\end{array}
$$

with

$$
\varepsilon_i' = a \cup (\varepsilon_i \setminus \{(p, v) \mid \exists (p', v') \in a.p = p'\})
$$

Definition 7.29
The synchronisation term $\lambda_{P_{ref}}$ of the process reference $P(v_1, ..., v_n)$ with the existing synchronisation term λ_P of the process $P(p_1, ..., p_n)$ starting with a high level operator, can be defined as:

$$
\lambda_{P_{ref}} = \lambda_P[assigns(P_{ref}(v_1, ..., v_n), P_{def}(p_1, ..., p_n))]
$$

The process reference does not effect the structure of the synchronisation term but the start environments. Synchronisation terms are trees with tuples $(HLTG_i, l_i, \varepsilon_i)$ of a high level transition graph, a current location in that graph and a current environment for that graph as leaves. During the execution of a synchronisation term, the current location and the current environment are changed. Initially, the current location is the start location of the high level transition graph and the current environment is the start environment of the graph. Normally, the start environment of a high level transition graph can be any environment that is valid for the graph, because no initial parameter bindings exist. If process references are mixed with high level operators, they define bindings in that start environment. Lets take for example the following process definition:

```
1   channel a, b : {0..3}
2
3   P = Q(0) ||| Q(2)
4   Q(x) = R(x) ||| S(x+1)
5   R(y) = a.y -> R(y)
6   S(z) = b.z -> S(z)
```

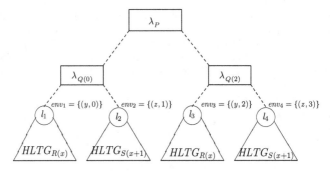

Figure 7.16: The synchronisation term of P.

Figure 7.16 shows the synchronisation term λ_P for P, with $\lambda_{Q(0)}$ and $\lambda_{Q(2)}$ being the synchronisation terms of $Q(0)$ and $Q(2)$ and $HLTG_{R(x)}$ and $HLTG_{S(x+1)}$ being the high level transition graphs of $R(x)$ and $S(x+1)$ with appropriate start locations $l_1, ..., l_4$. In this example, the synchronisation term λ_P can be calculated as:

$$
\begin{aligned}
\lambda_P &= (\lambda_{Q(0)[\{(x,0)\}]}, \emptyset, \lambda_{Q(2)}[\{(x,2)\}]) \\
&= (((\lambda_{R(x)}[(y,x)])[(x,0)], \emptyset, (\lambda_{S(x+1)}[(z,x+1)])[(x,0)]), \\
&\quad \emptyset, \\
&\quad ((\lambda_{R(x)}[(y,x)])[(x,2)], \emptyset, (\lambda_{S(x+1)}[(z,x+1)])[(x,2)])) \\
&= (((((HLTG_{R(x)}, l_1, \emptyset)[y,x])[(x,2)], \emptyset, ((HLTG_{S(x+1)}, l_1, \emptyset)[z,x+1])[(x,2)]), \\
&\quad \emptyset, \\
&\quad (((HLTG_{R(x)}, l_1, \emptyset)[y,x])[(x,2)], \emptyset, ((HLTG_{S(x+1)}, l_1, \emptyset)[z,x+1])[(x,2)])) \\
&= (((HLTG_{R(x)}, l_1, \{(y,x)\})[(x,2)], \emptyset, (HLTG_{S(x+1)}, l_1, \{(z,x+1)\})[(x,2)]), \\
&\quad \emptyset, \\
&\quad ((HLTG_{R(x)}, l_1, \{(y,x)\})[(x,2)], \emptyset, (HLTG_{S(x+1)}, l_1, \{(z,x+1)\})[(x,2)])) \\
&= (((HLTG_{R(x)}, l_1, \{(x,0),(y,x)\}), \emptyset, (HLTG_{S(x+1)}, l_1, \{(x,0),(z,x+1)\})), \\
&\quad \emptyset, \\
&\quad ((HLTG_{R(x)}, l_1, \{(x,2),(y,x)\}), \emptyset, (HLTG_{S(x+1)}, l_1, \{(x,2),(z,x+1)\}))) \\
&= (((HLTG_{R(x)}, l_1, \{(x,0),(y,0)\}), \emptyset, (HLTG_{S(x+1)}, l_1, \{(x,0),(z,1)\})), \\
&\quad \emptyset, \\
&\quad ((HLTG_{R(x)}, l_1, \{(x,2),(y,2)\}), \emptyset, (HLTG_{S(x+1)}, l_1, \{(x,2),(z,3)\})))
\end{aligned}
$$

Note, that the the notation of the environments used here only lists the defined parameters. Environments as defined in section 5.1.2 always contain tuples (*variable, value*) for all variables of the HLTG but only the bindings for the currently visible parameters of a node have to be correct. In figure 7.16, only the assignments for the visible parameters are shown.

In the environments calculated for the example, there occurs the variable x in the values assigned to y or z. This is necessary, because the synchronisation terms are constructed bottom up from the high level transition graphs. Therefore parameters of higher-ranking process references can not be bond to any values. The environments of the HLTGs must be evaluated after the complete synchronisation term is generated.

Note that recursion is not allowed in the high level part of a CSP process when using synchronisation terms. This is only a minimal restriction, because every such process is divergent. Without recursion, it is ensured, that the parameters of each process reference on a path to a HLTG of a synchronisation term are disjoint. Because of this, there is exactly one assignment for each process reference parameter to be applied to the environment of the HLTG. For a valid CSP process, there must be a defining occurrence before every applied occurrence of a parameter and therefore it must exist an assignment for every parameter occurring in the expression of any other assignment in the environment.

Chapter 8

Normalisation

The high level transition graphs as introduced in chapter 5 are not well suited for real time testing, since they are not deterministic. Therefore it is not possible to determine, which transition to take during test execution. Traversing such non-deterministic graphs on runtime during test execution requires backtracking, to check, whether a given trace is possible in the transition graph. This approach has the disadvantage, that the evaluation of test results is no longer possible in real time.

One remedy to solve such problem is the *normalisation* of transition systems. Normalisation is a process, during which all kinds of non-determinism is removed from a transition graph, while it is necessary to keep the semantics of the process. Since the normalisation of conventional transition systems has already been explained in detail in section 3.2, in this chapter we will describe different kinds of normalisation based on the high level transition graphs and synchronisation terms.

In this chapter three different types of normalisations are going to be introduced. Section 8.1 defines the Roscoe-style normalisation for high level transition graphs, which results in a graph similar to the ones FDR produces, containing neither conditions nor assignments. But this normalisation is only defined for sequential graphs without synchronisation terms. The types of normalisation, which are going to be explained in sections 8.2 and 8.2, are utilising the structure of the synchronisation terms and the results of the former approach to generate normal forms for parallel transition systems.

8.1 Normalising Sequential Graphs

This chapter describes a normalisation of high level transition graphs (HLTG), which results in a normalised graph, which no longer contains τ- or π-events at its transitions, and which branches uniquely on each visible event. We call this normalisation of a high level transition graph the Roscoe-style normalisation.

The resulting graph is called the Roscoe-style normalisation graph.

First a formal definition and an example of the Roscoe-style normalisation will be given, to emphasise the differences to Roscoes definitions introduced earlier. Additional considerations about refusals and acceptance sets are required, before finally an algorithm for the normalisation of high level transition graphs will be described.

8.1.1 Normal Form of High Level Transition Graphs

A normalisation algorithm for high level transition graphs, which is going to be introduced in this section, can be based in the considerations in section 3.2. The following definitions are providing a 2-stage algorithm to transform a HLTG into it normal form, without any assignments and conditions. This implies, that the normal form HLTG can just have exactly one event labelled to each transition.

High level transition graphs in normal form share the same properties of normal form LTS: they can only produce visible events and they ensure unique branching. Hence the normal form of a high level transition graph provides a deterministic transition system. Divergences are not considered in this model, since it is not useful to define divergent system specifications for real time testing, which is our application domain.

The first stage of the process generates a pre-normal form, which does not contain any non-determinism, like the pre-normal form of an LTS. During the second stage of the algorithm all semantically identical nodes are identified and joint together, which usually reduces the size of the graph.

Bindings

Essential to the algorithm which is going to be introduced next is the use of bindings, which store information on the current values of variables in a certain node.

Definition 8.1 *Bindings:*
A binding β is that part of the current environment ε, in which only the visible parameters of the current location l are contained:

$$\beta(l, \varepsilon) = \{(x, y) \in \varepsilon \mid x \in visible(l), y \in Expressions\}$$

Bindings consists of pairs of identifiers and values, which represents the binding of a value to a certain variable. Each binding may contain at maximum one pair for each visible parameter of a node. Therefore a binding is representing not only one, but all those environments, that can occur, if the execution of the transition system reaches the location. Common to all those environments are the same values for the visible parameters.

Stage 1 – Generating the Pre-Normal Form

Definition 8.2 *Pre-normal form of high level transition graphs:*
A high level transition graph $HLTG = (L, l_0, \Sigma^{\pi\tau\checkmark}, \mathcal{E}^{\pi\tau\checkmark}, \rightarrow_{CA})$ can be normalised in a pre-normal form graph $HLTG_{PNF} = (L_{PNF}, l_{PNF0}, \Sigma^{\checkmark}_{PNF}, \mathcal{E}^{\checkmark}_{PNF}, \rightarrow_{PNF})$ whose nodes are represented by a set of pairs of locations and corresponding bindings:

- *The initial node $l_{PNF0} \in L_{PNF}$ of $HLTG_{PNF}$ is $\tau^*(l_0, \varepsilon_0)$, where:*

$$\tau^*(l, \varrho) = \{(l, \varrho)\} \cup \{(l', \varrho') \mid \exists \varepsilon, \varepsilon' \in Env \; . \; l, \varepsilon \xrightarrow{\tau^*} l', \varepsilon' \wedge \varrho = \beta(l, \varepsilon) \\ \wedge \varrho' = \beta(l', \varepsilon')\}$$

  ε_0 is an arbitrary environment, since having no visible parameters in the initial state (visible(l_0) = $\emptyset$) implies that $\beta(l_0, \varepsilon_0) = \emptyset$.

- *For each newly created location $n \in L_{PNF}$ the set of non-τ-actions for all nodes $(l, \varrho) \in n$ must be determined. For each event α in this set a new node n' is formed, which contains all those pairs of locations of L and their corresponding bindings, that can be reached by the event α and any number of τ- or π-events. Additionally all assignments on the path must be evaluated and all conditions are required to hold.*

  For each such visible event $\alpha \in \Sigma^{\checkmark}_{PNF}$ a new transition $n \xrightarrow{true,(\alpha,\emptyset)} n'$ is added to the relation $\rightarrow_{PNF}$ of normalised graph $HLTG_{PNF}$, where
  $$n' = \bigcup \{\tau^*(l', \varrho') \mid \exists \varepsilon, \varepsilon' \in Env, (l, \varrho) \in n \; . \; l, \varepsilon \xrightarrow{\alpha} l', \varepsilon' \wedge \\ \varrho = \beta(l, \varepsilon) \wedge \varrho' = \beta(l', \varepsilon')\}$$

  The generation algorithm ensures, that the transitions in the resulting pre-normal form graph are only labelled with the condition true, completely evaluated events and no assignments. The alphabet $\Sigma^{\checkmark}_{PNF}$ of the pre-normal form is basically unchanged from the original alphabet, only the events τ and π are not contained in it, since they are eliminated by the pre-normalisation algorithm.

- *The pre-normalisation is completed, if all new nodes that have been generated have been previously expanded, using the second rule of this definition.*

This pre-normal form of a high level transition graph is completely deterministic and contains neither conditions (other than *true*) nor assignments at the transitions of the graph. But the result of this normalisation step does not identify semantically equivalent nodes. This task is performed in the second step of the algorithm.

Stage 2 – Generating the Normal Form

Stage 2 of the normalisation process is basically identical to the one described in section 3.2.2, since the result of the first stage is a Roscoe-style transition graph. As described there, it is only necessary to mark all normalised nodes with its initial actions and maximal refusals. The computation of the refusals of a transition system is described in detail later in section 8.1.3.

The labelling process does not need any information about the original nodes and bindings, which are contained in the normalised nodes of the pre-normal form graph. Therefore the rules for the stage-2 normalising process of labelled transition systems can be applied on this kind of graphs as well.

The initial step of the stage-2 normalising process, marks all locations with the initial actions and its minimal acceptances. It is not necessary to deal with divergent locations, because we can assume, that the results of the pre-normalisation are non-divergent, since the original transition system was non-divergent as well. The considerations in section 3.2.3 allows the use of minimal acceptances instead of maximal refusals for the normalisation algorithm, since they can easily be transformed into each other.

After the initial step the fixed point $\sim$ as described in definition 3.9 can be computed to determine which nodes of the pre-normal form graph are semantically equivalent. In the normal form of the high level transition graph, the equivalent locations are identified as one, such that the size of the normal form graph is as small as possible.

The resulting high level transition graph of the stage-2 normalisation in the worst case consists of the same number of locations like the pre-normal form graph, if no locations can be identified. Before the rules for the stage-2 normalisation can be stated specifically, a function has to be introduced, which maps locations of the pre-normal form graph ($l \in L_{PNF}$) to locations in the stage-2 graph:

Definition 8.3 *Locations of the normal form graph:*
Each location of the normal form graph represents at least one location from the pre-normal form graph. $\Upsilon_L(l)$ *describes the set of all nodes of L equivalent to l via the relation $\sim$.*

$$\Upsilon_L(l) \;=\; \{l' \in L \mid l \sim l'\}$$

With this simple projection each location of the pre-normal form graph can be mapped to exactly one location in the normal form. Using a pre-normal form high level transition graph its normal form high level transition graph can be defined as follows:

Definition 8.4 *Normal form of high level transition graphs:*
The normal form of a pre-normal form high level transition graph $HLTG_{PNF} = (L_{PNF}, l_{PNF0}, \Sigma^{\checkmark}_{PNF}, \mathcal{E}^{\checkmark}_{PNF}, \rightarrow_{PNF})$ *is a* $HLTG_{NF} = (L_{NF}, l_{NF0}, \Sigma^{\checkmark}_{NF}, \mathcal{E}^{\checkmark}_{NF}, \rightarrow_{NF})$, *where:*

$$L_{NF} \;=\; \{\Upsilon_{L_{PNF}}(l) \mid l \in L_{PNF}\}$$
$$l_{NF0} \;=\; \Upsilon_{L_{PNF}}(l_{PNF0})$$

$$\Sigma_{NF}^{\checkmark} = \Sigma_{PNF}^{\checkmark}$$
$$\mathcal{E}_{NF}^{\checkmark} = \mathcal{E}_{PNF}^{\checkmark}$$
$$\rightarrow_{NF} = \{(\Upsilon_{L_{PNF}}(l), true, (\alpha, \emptyset), \Upsilon_{L_{PNF}}(l')) \mid l \xrightarrow{true,(\alpha,\emptyset)}_{PNF} l'\}$$

Such normal form high level transition graphs have all the advantages and disadvantages of conventional normalised transition systems, since they do not contain any expressions or assignments at the transitions, but only single events. All conditions are *true*, so every transition can always be taken. Therefore it is possible to transform the resulting graphs in an *LTS*, by removing all conditions and assignments from the transitions. As a result the graphs can easily be evaluated and interpreted in real-time for testing purposes. But a big difference is that such normal form of high level transition graphs do not have the problem of state explosion, since this is usually introduced by using parallelism to compose more complex systems. The high level transition graphs as introduced in this thesis do not model either of those CSP operators. This problem will be addressed in detail in section 8.2 of this chapter.

8.1.2 An Example of the Normalising Process

To explain the normalisation of high level transition graphs a little further, a simple example will be given, on how a normalised graph can be derived.

```
1    channel out : {0..2}
2
3    NORM = NORM'(1)
4    NORM'(x) = out.x -> NORM'((x+1) % 3)
```

The specification for the process NORM is simple, since it only produces the events *out.1, out.2, out.0, out.1* and so on. This is done by increasing the value of the parameter x in the tail recursion of the process NORM' by 1 and use the modulo operator on the result to keep the result in the range from 0 to 2. The resulting HLTG is shown on the left hand side of figure 8.1.

Generating the pre-normal form of a HLTG starts at the initial location l_0 of the original HLTG. At the beginning of the generation process, there is no binding for any variable at all, therefore the binding of the initial node is an empty set. The initial node of the pre-normalisation is determined by the calculation of $\tau^*(l_0, \emptyset) = \{ (l_0, \emptyset), (l_1, \{(x, 1)\}) \} = n_0$, which is marked as the starting node of the the pre-normal form graph in figure 8.1. The only visible event, that can be produced from any of the original locations and their corresponding bindings in n_0 is the event *out*.1 in location l_1 with its binding $\{(x, 1)\}$.

After the production of the event *out*.1 the interpreted HLTG is in the state l_2 and the assigned value of x is still 1, which is represented by the pair $(l_2, \{(x, 1)\})$. The normalised location n_1 consists of all original locations of the HLTG, that

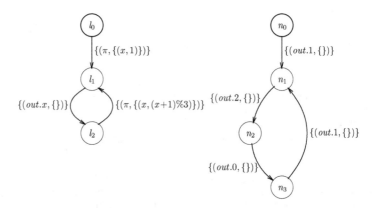

Figure 8.1: HLTG of the process NORM (left) and its pre-normal form (right).

can be reached from any of the locations contained in the current location of the pre-normal form HLTG by τ- or π-events and therefore contains the following pairs: $n_1 = \tau^*(l_2, \{(x,1)\}) = \{ (l_2, \{(x,1)\}), (l_1, \{(x,2)\}) \}$

Starting from the collected original nodes in n_1, the event $out.2$ may be produced by a transition from l_1 to l_2 using the current binding $\{(x,2)\}$. This results in the production of the event and a new normalised location $n_2 = \tau^*(l_2, \{(x,2)\}) = \{(l_2, \{(x,2)\}), (l_1, \{(x,0)\})\}$. As soon as the following transition labelled with the event $out.0$ and its corresponding location $n_3 = \tau^*(l_2, \{(x,0)\}) = \{ (l_2, \{(x,0)\}), (l_1, \{(x,1)\}) \}$ has been produced in the pre-normal form graph, it is once again possible to produce the event $out.1$. The target of the transition labelled with $out.1$ in the normal form graph is a new node $n_4 = \tau^*(l_2, \{(x,1)\}) = \{(l_2, \{(x,1)\}), (l_1, \{(x,2)\})\}$. This node is identical to the already processed node n_1, since they consists of the same pairs of original locations and corresponding bindings, and both therefore can be identified. The result of this process is a transition in the pre-normal form graph leading from n_3 to n_1 labelled with the event $out.1$. This completes the computation of the pre-normal form of the HLTG, since all newly generated nodes have been previously expanded.

The generation of the pre-normal form of the transition graph for the process NORM results in a transition system with four nodes and four transitions. As described in the previous section it is necessary for creating the normal form of the graph, to determine semantically identical nodes in the pre-normal form and identify those. For computing the fixed point, all nodes must be found, that are labelled with the same initial actions and maximal refusals or minimal acceptances respectively. The required markings are shown in the table 8.1.

Node	Initial actions	Maximum refusals	Minimal acceptances
n_0	$out.1$	$\Sigma \setminus \{out.1\}$	$\{out.1\}$
n_1	$out.2$	$\Sigma \setminus \{out.2\}$	$\{out.2\}$
n_2	$out.0$	$\Sigma \setminus \{out.0\}$	$\{out.0\}$
n_3	$out.1$	$\Sigma \setminus \{out.1\}$	$\{out.1\}$

Table 8.1: Initial actions and maximum refusals in the pre-normal form graph

These results are the basis for the fixed point computation of the semantically identical nodes. Since the locations n_0 and n_3 share the same initial actions and minimal acceptance sets, the following equivalence relations are valid for the initial step:

$$n_0 \sim_0 n_0, \quad n_1 \sim_0 n_1, \quad n_2 \sim_0 n_2, \quad n_3 \sim_0 n_3, \quad n_0 \sim_0 n_3, \quad n_3 \sim_0 n_0$$

The computation of the next step of the fixed point results in the following set of equivalence relations:

$$n_0 \sim_1 n_0, \quad n_1 \sim_1 n_1, \quad n_2 \sim_1 n_2, \quad n_3 \sim_1 n_3, \quad n_0 \sim_1 n_3, \quad n_3 \sim_1 n_0$$

Since the set of equivalent nodes does not change from the initial step to the first one, the fixed point is reached immediately. The following nodes are semantical identical and can therefore be identified.

$$n_0 \sim n_0, \quad n_1 \sim n_1, \quad n_2 \sim n_2, \quad n_3 \sim n_3, \quad n_0 \sim n_3, \quad n_3 \sim n_0$$

Of cause each node is semantically identical to itself, but also the nodes n_0 and n_3 represent the same behaviour and are therefore identified in the normal form graph. The resulting normal form transition graph of the process NORM consists therefore only of three nodes and three transitions, which are shown in figure 8.2.

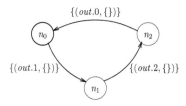

Figure 8.2: HLTG of the process NORM in its normal form

8.1.3   Calculation of Refusal and Acceptance Sets

The concept of acceptance sets was already explained in section 3.2.3, where it was necessary to use the definitions of the failures-semantics of CSP to compute the refusal set of a process. Based on the unnormalised graph, it is possible to derive the same refusals during the pre-normalisation process, which will be described in this section. This approach does not require for an implementation to compute all failures of a process, but just evaluating the structure of the original transition graph.

A refusal set is a set of events, that a process can refuse to produce for an infinite time. It is not sufficient, that the events can only be refused for a finite time. Therefore only those locations of a transition graph can be used to calculate the set of refusals, which do not contain any τ-events leaving this location. Such locations are according to the definitions in section 3.1.1 called *stable locations*, since they can only be left by taking a transition with a visible event, which can be observed by the environment. Locations with τ-transitions are considered *unstable*, since the τ-event may be used at any time to leave the location.

The stable locations can only produce those events, that are in its initial actions, all other events from the alphabet Σ must be refused indefinitely. Starting with a location in the unnormalised graph, all transitions carrying τ-labels must be followed, to get to the stable locations, which contains refusal information. This can be observed in the examples in figures 8.3 and 8.4.

The two unnormalised graphs, which can be seen in the upper part of figure 8.3 show the computation of the refusal sets for the normal form graphs, which are shown in the lower part of the figure. The graph on the left hand side of the figure, could have been created by a process like $a \rightarrow a \rightarrow STOP \,\square\, b \rightarrow b \rightarrow STOP$. The refusal in location l_0 shows, that only the events of $\Sigma = \{a, b, c\}$, that are not in the initial events of the location, can be refused: $\Sigma \setminus \{a, b\} = \{c\}$. This consideration also applies for the stable locations l_1 to l_4 as well, since none of the locations has a transition carrying a τ-label leaving the node. In the normal form of this process only the ending states l_3 and l_4 are joint, since both carry the same refusal set and cannot perform any further events. This transition system is completely deterministic, which can be recognised by having only one refusal in each refusal set in the normal form graph.

The second example on the right hand side of the figure, is a non-deterministic transition system, since there are two transitions leaving the location l_0' with the same event. In this case the environment cannot determine, which transition has been taken, after the event c has been produced. Therefore the normal form of the graph contains only one location n_1' representing both original locations l_1' and l_2'. The refusal set of n_1' contains all refusals of the original locations resulting in a refusal set $\{\{b, c\}, \{a, c\}\}$, which indicates a non-deterministic transition system. As in the previous example the locations l_3' and l_4' are identified in the normal form graph sharing their common refusal set.

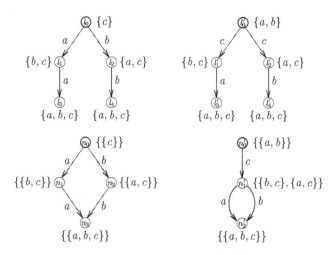

Figure 8.3: The refusal sets of some transition systems with stable states and their normal form

In figure 8.4 two examples can be found, which show the effect of unstable states in the computation of the refusal sets of a process. The first example on the left hand side of the figure contains two unstable locations l_0 and l_2, which both have a τ-transition leaving the location. Such locations do not have refusals, since it is not possible to stay there for an infinite amount of time. In the normal form of the graph the original locations l_0 and l_1 are identified by the normalised location n_0 and the locations l_2, l_3 and l_4 are represented by the location n_1. Since l_0 does not have any refusals only l_1 is used to determine the refusal set of n_0. This is why there is only the refusal $\{b, c\}$ in the refusal set of n_0. As stated before, the acceptances of a process are the inverse set of the refusals. This illustrates the difference between the initial events and the acceptances of a process: based on the refusal the location n_0 has the acceptances set $\{\{a\}\}$, which does not contain the event b, even though it is in the initial events of n_0.

The fourth example could have been created from a simple process like $a \rightarrow STOP \sqcap b \rightarrow STOP$. Since l'_0 is unstable and l'_1 and l'_2 can be reached by chains of τ-events from l_0, these three nodes are represented in the normal form by only one location n'_0. Both refusals of the locations l'_1 and l'_2 are contained in the refusal set of n'_0.

It is obvious, that those locations, that carry refusals, are exactly those, which are reached from the current location by chains of τ-events during the pre-normalisation process. Each of the locations in the unnormalised form graph

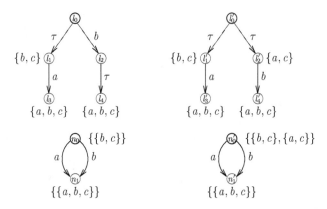

Figure 8.4: The refusal sets of some transition systems with unstable states and their normal form

carries exactly one set of events, that may be refused. The location in the pre-normal form graph is representing all those locations in the unnormalised graph, that can be reached from the location under consideration by chains of τ-events. Therefore a set of all refusals of those locations is used to describe the refusals of the pre-normal form node. This representation as sets of refusals is most intuitive, since the failures model allows multiple failures for each state a process may be in as well.

The calculation of the refusal sets of a normal form high level transition graph is done during the pre-normalisation process. The addition of the refusal set to this algorithm requires just a few extensions to the pre-normalisation algorithm:

First of all it is required to find out, whether a given location is stable or unstable. For high level transition graph it is not sufficient to check, whether there are transitions carrying τ-labels leaving a location, to deduce that the locations is unstable, since there may be conditions on those labels, that may not hold. Therefore it is necessary to check each location under the current binding during the normalisation process. Only those labels, which conditions evaluate to *true*, have to be checked, whether a possible event is a τ-event. Only if the condition holds and the event is τ, the location has to be considered unstable.

Definition 8.5 *Stable locations of a high level transition graph:*
The function stable(l, ε) evaluates to true, iff no transition of l carries a label, which condition c holds under the current environment ε, contains a τ-event.

$$stable(l, \varepsilon) \quad = \quad \forall \, l, \varepsilon \xmapsto{\alpha} l', \varepsilon' \, . \, \alpha \neq \tau$$

Stable locations of unnormalised high level transition graphs are marked with their acceptances, which are defined to be the initial actions (see definition 5.22) of that location. On the contrary the refusals are all those elements that are not in the initial actions of that location.

Definition 8.6 *Refusals and acceptances in unnormalised high level transition graphs:*
The refusals and acceptances of a stable location l under a current environment ε can be defined as follows:

$$
\begin{aligned}
refusal(l, \varepsilon) &= \Sigma^{\checkmark} \setminus [l]_{\varepsilon}^{0} & \text{if } stable(l, \varepsilon) = true \\
accept(l, \varepsilon) &= [l]_{\varepsilon}^{0} & \text{if } stable(l, \varepsilon) = true
\end{aligned}
$$

The refusal sets of the locations in the normal form graph of the high level transition graph contains all the refusals of the stable locations in the unnormalised graph represented by the normalised location. Based on the definition of $\tau^{*}(l, \varrho)$ on page 143, it is possible to define a function, which collects all refusals of the stable nodes, that can be reached by τ-events from a given location in the unnormalised graph.

Definition 8.7 *Refusal sets of normal form high level transition graphs:*
During the creation of new locations by the normalisation algorithm it is possible to derive the refusal set of each newly created node n'. n' is represented by pairs of locations and bindings (l, ϱ). The refusals of those pairs, where l is a stable location, are elements of the refusal set of n'.

$$refusals(n') = \{ refusal(l, \varepsilon) \mid \exists (l, \varrho) \in n' \, . \, stable(l, \varepsilon) \wedge \varrho = \beta(l, \varepsilon) \}$$

The elements of the refusal set *refusals(n')* can be subsets of each other. As stated before the preferred representation are the maximum refusals, from which all other possible subsets can be derived. Therefore only those maximum refusals are required to be in the refusal set of n.

Definition 8.8 *Maximum refusal sets of normal form HLTG:*
refusals$_{max}(n')$ contains only those elements of refusals(n'), that is not a subset of any other element of this set.

$$refusals_{max}(n') = \{ r \in refusals(n') \mid \nexists \, r' \in refusals(n') \, . \, r \subset r' \}$$

The acceptances of a normalised location can be defined analogous to the definition of $refusals(n')$. The only difference is that $acceptances(n')$ contains the acceptances of the locations in the original graph instead of the refusals.

Definition 8.9 *Acceptance sets of normal form HLTG:*

$$acceptances(n') = \{accept(l,\varepsilon) \mid \exists (l,\varrho) \in n' \,.\, stable(l,\varepsilon) \wedge \varrho = \beta(l,\varepsilon)\}$$

The most efficient representation for the acceptance sets are the minimal acceptance sets, from with all possible acceptances can be derived by the super-set closure. Therefore the super-set closed set of acceptances can be defined as follows:

Definition 8.10 *Minimal acceptance sets of normal form HLTG:*

$$acceptances_{min}(n') = \{r \in acceptances(n') \mid \not\exists\, r' \in acceptances(n') \,.\, r' \subset r\}$$

8.1.4   The Algorithm

The normalisation algorithm described in this section, uses a stack of items representing locations of the high level transition graph where the next normalisation step should start. With this technique it is possible to implement the whole normalisation using an iterative loop which first takes the top stack item and then calls functions to do the normalisation step. During each normalisation step new stack items can be created. Each item, which is put onto the stack, contains a *normalisation node*. A normalisation node is an extension of a location, which has additional attributes: a set of pairs of bindings and original locations of the high level transition graph. The algorithm has to stop, as soon as there are no unprocessed items on the stack.

The *initial step* of the algorithm, as indicated in Listing 8.1, takes the target node of the start transition of the high level transition graph and puts it into a new normalisation node. Since it is not possible to have initialised variables or parameters at the beginning of a process, no bindings may be added as an attribute. A new start transition points to this normalisation node, which will be the root of the Roscoe-style normalisation graph. Finally the newly created node is put onto the stack. The stack contains all those normalisation nodes, that still have to be processed for normalisation.

The following *normalisation step* does not need to process the original high level transition graph sequentially. It is sufficient to process only small parts of the original graphs, which is the reason for using a stack of nodes for the normalisation. The algorithm has to check in each step, if the stack is empty. In this case the normalisation algorithm terminates successfully, otherwise the top element is taken from the stack. This behaviour matches the termination condition of the pre-normalisation as stated in definition 8.2.

```
tg_normalise_roscoe(hltg)
BEGIN
   hltg, norm ∈ HLTG; hltgloc, normloc ∈ LOCATION; tra ∈ HLTRANS
   stack ∈ STACK; bind ∈ BINDING; processed ∈ SET

   (* Create a new initial location for the normalised HLTG with a  *)
   (* pairof the initial location of the HLTG and no bindings as *)
   (* attributes *)
   normloc = {(l_0(hltg), ∅)}
   L(norm) = L(norm) ∪ {normloc}
   l_0(norm) = normloc
   (* Put the new location on the normalisation stack *)
   push(stack, normloc)

   (* Iterate until all newly created locations have been processed *)
   WHILE size(stack) > 0 DO
      (* Get the top item from the stack *)
      normloc = top(stack), pop(stack)

      (* Check, whether normloc already has been processed *)
      IF normloc ∉ processed THEN
         (* Repeat for all pairs of original locations and *)
         (* bindings of the normalised location.  *)
         FORALL (hltgloc, bind) ∈ normloc DO
            (* Use the τ-elimination algorithm to build *)
            (* the next step of the graph *)
            eliminateTaus(normloc, norm, hltgloc, hltg, stack, bind, ∅, false)
         OD
         processed = processed ∪ {normloc}
      FI
   OD
   RETURN norm
END
```

Listing 8.1: The initial step of the Roscoe style normalisation

```
eliminateTaus(nloc, norm, hltgloc, hltg, stack, bind, acc, viapi)
BEGIN
    hltg, norm ∈ HLTG; hltgloc, nloc, nloc' ∈ LOCATION
    stack ∈ STACK; bind, bind' ∈ BINDING; acc, acc' ∈ ACCEPTANCE
    tra, tra' ∈ HLTRANS; ev, ev' ∈ EVENT; assign ∈ ASSIGNMENT; viapi ∈ BOOL

    (* If hltgloc is stable a new acceptance set is created *)
    IF stable(hltgloc, hltg, bind) ∧ viapi THEN acc' = acc
    ELSE acc' = ∅   FI

    (* Perform the following loop for all transitions of hltgloc *)
    FORALL tra ∈ {(l_S, c, E, l_T) ∈→_CA (hltg) | l_S = hltgloc} DO
        (* Does the binding hold under the condition of the transition? *)
        IF eval(c(tra), bind) THEN
            FORALL (ev, assign) ∈ E(tra) DO
                (* Calculate event and bindings for the target state *)
                ev' = eval(ev, bind)
                bind' = apply(assign, bind)
                CASE ev'
                τ) eliminateTaus(nloc, norm, l_T(tra), hltg, stack, bind', ∅, false)
                π) eliminateTaus(nloc, norm, l_T(tra), hltg, stack, bind', acc', true)
                *) (* Create normalized location and corresponding transition *)
                    nloc' = {(l_T(tra), bind')}
                    tra' = (nloc, true, {(ev', ∅)}, nloc')
                    IF stable(hltgloc, hltg, bind) THEN   acc' = acc' ∪ {ev'}   FI

                    (* Check whether a transition with the same event *)
                    (* already exists in the normalised location *)
                    IF ∃ tra'' ∈→_CA (norm)•(ev', ∅) ∈ E(tra'') ∧ l_S(tra'') = nloc ∧ l_T(tra'') ≠ nloc'
                    THEN
                        (* Extend existing location *)
                        l_T(tra'') = l_T(tra'') ∪ nloc'
                    ELSE
                        (* Add the new location to the normalised HLTG *)
                        (* and push it on the normalisation stack *)
                        L(norm) = L(norm) ∪ {nloc'}
                        →_CA(norm) = →_CA(norm) ∪ {tra'}
                        push(stack, nloc')
                    FI
                ESAC
            OD
        FI

        (* Add acceptance to nloc if hltgloc was not reached by a π-event *)
        IF stable(hltgloc, hltg, bind) ∧ not(viapi) THEN
            acceptances(nloc) = acceptances(nloc) ∪ {acc'}
        FI
    OD
END
```

Listing 8.2: The τ-elimination algorithm

If the location contained in the item from the stack is not an element of the normalised transition graph, the *τ-elimination process*, which is going to be described later, must be started. The elimination function, which is indicated in listing 9.2, can be called recursively, since it has to eliminate chains of τ-events stepwisely. The arguments required for the process are the location to be normalised and its complete corresponding normalised high level transition graph, the original location of the high level transition graph, its complete corresponding normalised graph, the stack of unprocessed items, the current bindings for the original location. Further arguments are a currently used acceptance set, and a boolean value, indicating whether the current location was reached by a π-transition. Both parameters are required for the calculation of the acceptance sets of the normalised location and are set to an empty set respectively false.

If the location from the stack item is already contained in the set of previously processed events, it is not necessary to call the τ-elimination process. Since normalised locations of high level transition graphs are defined to be identical, if they contain the same pairs of original nodes of the HLTG and their corresponding bindings, this abstraction guarantees, that all transitions to this location lead to the previously existing one. Therefore it is not necessary to process this location again.

At the beginning of each τ-elimination step, which is indicated in Listing 9.2, it has to be checked, whether the original location of the high level transition graph, which is represented by the functions argument hltgloc, is stable under the current binding. If the location is stable and was not reached via a π-transition – indicated by the value *false* of the parameter viapi – a new acceptance set is used as initial value for the acceptance created by this location. The only exception to this rule is if the functions parameter acc already references a non-empty acceptance set and viapi has the value *true*. This is only the case, if the *eliminateTaus*-function was recursively called while following a π-transition, since a transition with a π-label must not interfere in the calculation of the refusals/acceptances of a process, because of the special semantics of π-transitions explained in 5.1.3

For all transitions of the high level transition graph, which originate in the current location hltgloc, the τ-elimination process needs to check the conditions under the current binding. Only those transitions may be taken into further consideration, for which the condition holds. If the condition holds under a certain binding, the pairs of events and assignments, attached to the labels must be considered. First the event at the label has to be evaluated, to derive the precise event for the current bindings. Additionally the result of applying the assignments to the bindings is used as the initial bindings of the next node, that should be normalised. Then the behaviour of the normalisation step depends on the event labelled at the transition under consideration. If the event is a τ- or a π-event it is necessary to make another normalisation step for the same normalisation node. Some of the parameters for this functions are changed for the recursion: the normalisation node is not changed, since it is still the same

location to be normalised, but the new original location is changed to the target of
the current transition, and the binding is set to the calculated value as described
previously. The behaviour for τ- and π-events differs only for the acceptances and
values for the parameter viapi passed for the recursion. While τ-events represent
an internal decision, which introduces new refusals to a refusal set, the π-events
are not allowed to do so. Therefore they pass the current acceptances to the
recursive function and set viapi to *true*, whereas for τ-events viapi is set to *false*,
which makes the algorithm ignore the value for the acceptances.

If the event labelled to the transition is neither τ nor π, it is necessary to create
new transitions in the normalised transition graph. In the HLTG it is possible
to have multiple events labelled to a transition, but in the normalised form, it is
necessary to write only one event at each one. Therefore it is necessary to create
a new transition and a new normalisation node for each single event. Before the
new locations are added to the stack, it has to be checked, whether there is already
a transition leaving from the normalised locations labelled with the same event.
If that is the case, no new normalised location must be created, but the old one
has to be expanded: the pair of HLTG location and corresponding binding must
be added to the already existing normalised location. If no transition leaving
from the normalised locations having the same event exists, the newly created
location is added to the stack, so the location may be used for the normalisation
process later on.

Finally it has to be checked, whether the currently calculated acceptances
can be added as an attribute to the normalised node. This is only allowed, if
the acceptance was created in the same run of the recursive function, i.e. the
current location must not been reached by π-transitions, since otherwise, not all
transitions of the original locations have been processed.

8.2   Parallel Roscoe Style Normalisation Graphs

In section 8.1 the normalisation of Roscoe-style normalisation graphs was introduced, but there were no statements, how to handle parallelism and hiding. One
way to handle those CSP high level operators, is to create a transition graph,
which already contains all possible combinations of events, that are created by
those operators. Such product graphs have been described in 5.2.1. This type
of handling for the high level operators is implemented in tools like FDR, which
create one transition graph for a parallel process system, where the parallelism
is completely unfolded.

Another way of representing parallelism and hiding for high level transition
graphs has already been introduced in section 5.2.3. Synchronisation terms can
be used to represent a system consisting of several parallel or interleaved high level
transition graphs. The synchronisation terms can be used to create a Roscoe-style
normalisation graph, where all interactions of parallel systems are modelled in

one deterministic transition graph, which is semantically identical to the results FDR produces.

A simple way to create the normal form graph from a synchronisation term is based on the *interpretation of synchronsation terms* in definition 5.31 and Roscoe's normalisation algorithm as described in section 3.2. The interpretation of synchronsation terms allows an abstraction of synchronsation terms as labelled transition systems, on which Roscoe's algorithm can be executed directly. The advantage of this approach is that it is not required to explicitly create the compltly unfolded unnormalised graph, but instead the more efficient representation as synchronisation term can be used. Therefore it is possible to derive the normal form of graphs, that are larger than those other approached would allow. A disadvantage of this approach is the more complex evaluation of the synchronisation terms and its underlying high level transition graphs, which is more time consuming, since more computations are required to determine a possible transition and its following state.

8.3 Synchronised Normalisation Graphs

Instead of implicit modelling the high level CSP operators, which has been described in the previous section, another approach was already described in section 5.2: all synchronisation information for the parallel operators and the hiding information for the hiding operator are stored in synchronisation terms. The normalisation algorithm which will be introduced in this section normalises the synchronisation and hiding information, but preserves the basic idea of the synchronisation terms for the high level operators of CSP. For the sequential parts of the high level transition graph the algorithm described in section 8.1.1 has to be slightly expanded, to deal with hiding on the low level graph structures.

This approach seems to be practical, since it is possible to create a graph representation of a process, which is smaller than the graph of the same process, where the parallel operator is used to create an unfolded product graph. Either the parallel or interleaving operator is often responsible if a *state explosion* occurs during the generation of a transition graph in tools like FDR. *Synchronisation terms* do not have this disadvantage, since parallel processes are not combined in one transition graph. For special purposes like software testing the Roscoe-style normalisation graphs in combination with synchronisation terms provides a compressed representation for parallel systems, which might otherwise be too large for testing. For this approach it is necessary to use the synchronisation and hiding information on the sequential Roscoe-style graphs to compute all events, that are possible in any state of the combined system. The testing algorithm for Roscoe-style normalisation graphs with synchronisation terms will be described in detail in section 11.2. On the following pages the normalisation of the synchronisation terms and their related high level transition graphs is described. The aim is to define a compressed representation of a specification, which has eliminated all non-determinism from the graphs as far as it is possible without unfolding the whole product graph.

8.3.1   Pre-Normalising Synchronisation Terms

Synchronisation terms, as introduced in detail in section 5.2, carry information about the structure of parallel processes. Two systems running in parallel synchronising over a set of events, are represented by a synchronisation term which references both sequential high level transition graphs and carries additional synchronisation and hiding information. The synchronisation information specifies, which events must be performed simultaneously by both high level transition graphs to make them happen. Additionally the hiding information indicates, which events of a system should be hidden from the environment. Processes represented by such synchronisation terms cannot be completely normalised, since the synchronisation terms may always introduce non-determinism, e.g. by hiding certain events. The pre-normal form of the synchronisation terms introduced in this section eliminates the non-determinism as far as it is possible.

Lets imagine a simple CSP process, which consists of two interleaved subprocesses, which may produce any event from the alphabet of the specification at any time. Additionally all but one event, that can be produced by the interleaving of those two processes are hidden by a hiding operator. The resulting trace of such process can only contain that event, that was not hidden.

The straight forward modelling solution of this problem using synchronisation terms would create a synchronisation term for such process, that contains no synchronisation information, but almost the whole alphabet in its hiding set. The sequential high level transition graphs could be huge depending on the size of the specification of the sequential subprocesses. Executing this structure for testing purposes would be inefficient, since it would have to cope with hiding on the synchronisation term level. This requires a lot of transitions to be processed, which must not be shown to the outside.

A more efficient way of representing such specification using synchronisation terms was already introduced in definition 5.7: only those hiding events, that are contained inside a synchronisation set are hidden by a high level hiding operator. Events, that are not contained in the synchronisation set, need not to be hidden above a parallel operator, but it is sufficient to hide all occurrences of those events in the corresponding subgraphs. This improvement does not change the behaviour of the specified system in the failures semantics as shown on page 106.

In the example above, the synchronisation term contains no synchronisation set and hence no set of hiding events. Instead the events are hidden in each subgraph. The hiding of the events in the subgraphs results in smaller graphs for each subgraph, since the the pre-normalisation algorithm uses the introduced non-determinism to generate the refusals of the system.

Figure 8.5 shows the general approach for the pre-normalisation of the synchronisation term. The terms for hiding and parallel operators are joined in a single term, which carries both: hiding and synchronisation information. The hiding set of the newly created node contains only those events, which are in the original hiding set h and in the synchronisation set s, and can therefore be calculated as $h \cap s$. The synchronisation set remains unchanged. In the case of an interleaving operator this set is empty, since the interleaving operator is semantically identical to the parallel operator, which synchronisation set is empty. Those events, which are to be hidden, but are not in the hiding set $h \cap s$ have to be hidden in the subterms of the synchronisation term representing the parallel operator, which may again be synchronisation terms or a term referencing a high level transition graph.

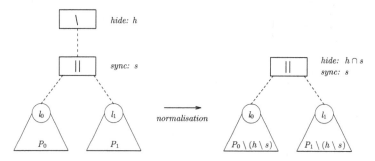

Figure 8.5: A Pattern for Pre-Normalising Synchronisation Terms

The pre-normalisation of the synchronisation terms creates a more compressed representation of the specified system, which uses only the abbreviation (Λ,s,h,Λ), which has been introduced in definition 5.30. The aim of the algorithm, which is going to be introduced in the following, is to create a pre-normal form of the synchronisation terms which has the following properties:

1. All terms in the synchronisation term are of the form $(\lambda_1, s, h, \lambda_2)$, except for those subterms $(hltg, l_0, \varepsilon)$, which directly references a high level transition graph.

2. The hiding set contains only those elements, which are also contained in the synchronisation set. All other events, which should have been hidden, are directly hidden in both subterms λ_1 and λ_2.

3. All high level transition graphs are normalised according to the algorithm already described in section 8.1.1, where additionally all those events are

hidden, which have been element of any hiding set in the original synchronisation term but which are not in any synchronisation set. The result
is a synchronisation term of the form $(hltg', l'_0, \emptyset)$, where $hltg'$ is the normalised high level transition graph, l'_0 its corresponding initial location and
the environment contains any elements, since the graphs are completely
normalised.

The algorithm to create such pre-normal form of synchronisation terms are
shown in listings 8.3 and 8.4 and explained in the following.

```
normalise_syncterm(λ, hiding)
BEGIN
    λ, λ₁, λ₂, λ', λ₁', λ₂' ∈ SYNCTERM
    hiding, hide, hide', hide", sync ∈ SET
    hltg ∈ HLTG;  l ∈ LOCATION;  bind ∈ BINDING

    (* Check the pattern of the outmost synchronisation term *)
    CASE λ
    (λ₁, sync, λ₂))
            hide' = hiding ∩ sync
            hide" = hiding \ hide'
            λ₁' = normalise_syncterm(λ₁, hide")
            λ₂' = normalise_syncterm(λ₂, hide")
            λ' = (λ₁', sync, hide', λ₂')
    (λ₁, hide))
            λ' = normalise_syncterm(λ₁, hiding ∪ hide)
    (λ₁, sync, hide, λ₂))
            hide' = (hiding ∪ hide) ∩ sync
            hide" = (hiding ∪ hide) \ hide'
            λ₁' = normalise_syncterm(λ₁, hide")
            λ₂' = normalise_syncterm(λ₂, hide")
            λ' = (λ₁', sync, hide', λ₂')
    (hltg, l, bind))
            λ' = normalise_hltg(hltg, l, bind, hiding)
    ESAC
    RETURN λ'
END
```
Listing 8.3: Normalising a synchronisation term

The pre-normalisation algorithm for synchronisation terms described in listing
8.3 is a recursive process, which requires two arguments: the synchronisation term
itself and a set of events to hide. In the initial step of the algorithm, which is
applied to the initial synchronisation term λ, the set of events to hide is empty.
The result of the algorithm is again a synchronisation term λ', which contains
the pre-normal form of the term: $\lambda' = \text{normalise\_syncterm}(\lambda, \emptyset)$

Starting with the outmost term of the synchronisation term the algorithm
checks each subterm, whether it is representing a high level or a low level operator.

If the term represents a high level operator, the algorithm checks, whether it is a hiding or parallel operator. Synchronisation terms representing a hiding operator do not participate in the creation of new synchronisation terms during pre-normalisation, but adds the events of the hiding set to the algorithms current set of hiding events and continues with the subterm of the current synchronisation term, which is also returned as the result of this normalisation step.

If the term is representing a parallel or interleaving operator, a synchronisation term is created for its pre-normal form. The newly created term contains the set of events sync, on which the two subprocesses must synchronise. This set is empty in the case of an interleaving operator. Additionally the new term must contain information, which events must be hidden in this node. The considerations in the example above show, that it is sufficient to keep only those elements in the hiding set hide', which are also contained in the synchronisation set, since the other events can be hidden on both subterms: hide' = hiding ∩ sync.

The remaining hiding events hide" = hiding \ hide' must be hidden in the subprocesses of the current synchronisation term. Therefore the synchronisation term pre-normalisation algorithm is called recursively for each subterm with hide" as its hiding set. The resulting terms λ_1' and λ_2', which are already pre-normalised according to this algorithm, are combined with the already derived synchronisation and hiding set to a new pre-normalised synchronisation term $(\lambda_1',\ \text{sync},\ \text{hide}',\ \lambda_2')$, which is returned as the result of the algorithm.

Descending through the structure of the nested synchronisation terms finally leads to the leafs of the term, referencing the sequential high level transition graphs. Due to the pre-normalisation algorithm of the synchronisation terms, it is possible, that it is necessary to hide certain events on the high level transition graphs. Those hiding event sets are introduced by the hiding operator in a synchronisation term and are passed through the synchronisation structure, since they are in any synchronisation set. Those events must be hidden directly on the sequential subgraphs to ensure the pre-normalised transition graph is as small as possible.

The pre-normalisation algorithm described in listing 8.4 for the sequential subgraphs is basically the same as described in section 8.1.1. The only difference is the handling of the hiding set and the initial bindings, which have to be used during the pre-normalisation of the subgraph. In contrast to the first version of the algorithm in listing 8.1, the initial pre-normalised location now gets the pair of the current location and the initial binding, which are both stored in the synchronisation term, as attributes.

Additionally the τ-elimination algorithm has to be slightly expanded, since the one described in listing 8.2 is not sufficient to handle hiding. Therefore the interface definition has to be expanded with a set of events, which are to be hidden, looking as follows:

```
eliminateTaus'(nloc, nhltg, cloc, hltg, stack, bind, acc, hide, viapi)
```

As soon as the elimination algorithm has calculated a new event, which must be added to a new transition in the pre-normalised graph, the extended algorithm checks, whether this event is in the set of events to hide. If this is the case the algorithm should exactly behave, as if the original transition in the high level transition graph would have been a τ-event. Hence the τ-elimination function has to be called recursively with the target of the transition, which is to be hidden, as new parameter for the current location in the original high level transition graph. The rest of the algorithm remains unchanged and therfore is not described here again in detail.

```
normalise_hltg(hltg, I, bind, hide)
BEGIN
    hltg, norm ∈ HLTG; hltgloc, normloc ∈ LOCATION
    stack ∈ STACK; bind ∈ BINDING; processed ∈ SET

    (* Create new initial location for the normalised HLTG with a pair *)
    (* of the specified initial location and bindings as attributes *)
    normloc = {(I, bind)}
    L(norm) = L(norm) ∪ {normloc}
    l₀(norm) = normloc
    (* Put the new location on the normalisation stack *)
    push(stack, normloc)

    (* Iterate until all newly created locations have been processed *)
    WHILE size(stack) > 0 DO
        (* Get the top item from the stack *)
        normloc = top(stack), pop(stack)

        (* Check, whether normloc already has been processed *)
        IF normloc ∉ processed THEN
            (* Repeat for all pairs of original locations and *)
            (* bindings of the normalised location.   *)
            FORALL (hltgloc, bind) ∈ normloc DO
                (* Use the τ-elimination algorithm to build *)
                (* the next step of the graph *)
                eliminateTaus'(normloc,norm,hltgloc,hltg,stack,bind,∅,hide,false)
            OD
            processed = processed ∪ {normloc}
        FI
    OD
    RETURN norm
END
```
Listing 8.4: Normalising a high level transition graph

8.3.2   Normalising Synchronisation Terms

The combination of the two pre-normalisation algorithms described above leads to the representation of transition graphs as synchronisation terms with Roscoe-style normalisation graphs. All sequential parts of a CSP specification are modelled by deterministic Roscoe-style normalisation graphs. Additionally the combination of parallel or interleaved system parts in the specification are modelled by the synchronisation terms.

This type of representation is especially practical for parallel systems, which can be modelled in CSP by the interleaving operator. Interleaved systems often tend to produce large transition graphs due to the creation of the Cartesian product. The synchronisation terms prevents the computation of those product graphs, since all required information is contained in the term itself.

Each leaf of the pre-normalised synchronisation term representing a parallel CSP specification contains exactly one Roscoe-style normalisation graph. A fairly often used feature of CSP_M is the use of process patterns, which are instanciated with different values, which run in parallel. This is for example useful to model the behaviour of several variables simultainously in CSP. Since those different processes often show similar behaviour, it seems reasonable to check, whether it is possible to reuse the transition graphs of those processes. Lets take the following process for example:

```
1    channel out : {0..2}
2
3    NORM = NORM'(0) ||| NORM'(1)
4    NORM'(x) = out.x -> NORM'((x+1) % 3)
```

Each of the two processes, which are referred by the interleaving operator behaves basically the same: the process $NORM(0)$ produces a trace of events $\langle out.0, out.1, out.2, out.0, out.1, ...\rangle$. The only difference to $NORM(1)$ is that the trace starts at $out.1$ instead of $out.0$. Hence both processes could in principal share the same transition graph, since only the start transition into the transition graph differs, as indicated by the dashed lines on the left hand side of figure 8.6.

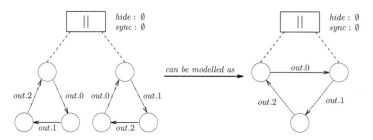

Figure 8.6: Normalising Synchronisation Terms

Such shared transition systems can easily be produced by generating the normal form of the synchronisation terms. This idea is based once again on the normalisation of transition systems as described earlier in section 3.2.2. Generating a normal form synchronisation term starts with a process, during which all locations and transitions of the different Roscoe-style normalisation graphs in the pre-normalised synchronisation term are joined together in a single transition system, where each original graph uses each own unique subset of locations. The structure of the synchronisation term itself remains unchanged, except, that all references to high level transition graphs are referencing the same one and the initial location l_0 is replaced by $\Upsilon_L(l_0)$, as introduced on page 144.

Based on this single transition system, all those nodes can easily be identified, which share the same initial actions and maximal refusals. During the generation of the normal form of this transition system, it does not matter whether those identical locations are originally from different graphs. According to definition 3.9 a fixed point can now be computed, which identifies all nodes, which are semantically identified, leading to the normal form of the constructed transition system.

The result of this process is a normal form transition system, where all semantically identical nodes are identified. Those subterms of the synchronisation term which referenced to the pre-normal form transition graph now references the normal from graph with their corresponding initial locations.

8.4   Conclusion

In this chapter the standard technique for normalising a transition system has been adapted for high level transition graphs. The resulting normalised transition systems can easily be used for testing purposes in the RT-Tester tool, since the result is identical to the one tools like FDR would produce for the same CSP specification.

A more efficient approach for real time testing has been introduced in section 8.3. For most specifications, that are derived from design patters for test applications, the resulting synchronisation terms are smaller then the transition graphs produced by the standard normalisation algorithm, since the interleaving and parallel operators are not unfolded. The normal form of such graphs is as deterministic as possible, but it is still possible to have non-determinism introduced by evaluating the synchronisation terms. An evaluation algorithm for normal form synchronisation terms, will be introduced later in chapter 11.2. Based on this algorithm some design patterns for CSP specifications will be given, on how non-determinism in synchronisation terms can be avoided. With such knowledge it will be possible to execute synchronisation terms in real-time for testing applications.

This approach works well for heavily interleaved systems, but has its weakness in parallel systems, which synchronise over many events of the alphabet. High level transition graphs model each sequential subgraph and stores the synchronisation information in the synchronisation terms. Completely unfolded transition graphs are likely to be significantly smaller, since the synchronisation information is evaluated during the computation of the transition graph, which reduces the size of the resulting graph, because branches in the sequential graphs, which can never be reached due to the synchronisation, can be removed from the resulting graph. But it is important to note, that during the computation of the Roscoe-style normalisation graph, all sequential subgraphs have to be computed, so only the resulting graph may be smaller, but it takes the same amount of memory during the computation of the graph. Hence a transition graph of the specification may not be computed, since the temporary graphs are too big to fit into the computers memory, even though the resulting graph would be small enough.

Chapter 9

Related Work

The concept of generating transition graphs or automata out of formal specifications is well known and often used for testing and model checking. One of the main problems of testing or model checking complex or parallel systems is the state explosion of the resulting graphs. High level transition graphs and synchronisation terms have been developed to avoid state explosions. This chapter concludes our discussion about the advantages and weaknesses of these approaches. Therefore we are going to reference other research and tools, which deals with similar objectives and discuss their results. During this discussion, ideas and aspects of possible future work are presented.

The model checker FDR generates traditional transition graphs of CSP specifications and is capable of normalising them. These Roscoe-style normalisation graphs can be used as input to the RT-Tester. Normalised high level transition graphs and synchronisation terms together with normalised graphs can as well be used to define Abstract Machines of the RT-Tester. Section 9.1 gives a short introduction to FDR2 and explains how this software can be used to check refinement conditions on two CSP specifications.

Timed automata are another mechanism of defining the behaviour of processes. The concepts of timers and conditions are added to traditional transition graphs. They are mentioned here because of the aspect of conditions and assignments labelled to transitions in HLTGs and their relation to realtime testing. An extension of timed automata that can be used to model mixed discrete-continuous systems are hybrid automata, which are explained in section 9.3.

Section 9.4 describes the formalism of High-level Petri Nets and High-level Petri Net Graphs, which concepts of describing parallelism are similar to synchronisation terms. They also provide means of specifying conditions and expressions at transitions, which have to be evaluated, if a transition occurs. This approach is similar to the concepts of conditions and assignments labelled to transitions in a HLTGs.

Finally the model checker SPIN is examined and put in context to testing and transition graphs. The methods of compressing automata and their memory management are investigated and related to synchronisation terms and future enhancements of high level transition graphs.

9.1   FDR

In this section the model-checking tool FDR is going to be described. FDR takes a CSP specifications and generates transition systems of it to perform model checking on process level. In contrast to the high level transition graphs FDR strictly uses labelled transition systems as already introduced in 3.1. Of cause FDR therefore has the problems of state explosion with large parallel systems, which have been described throughout this thesis, but it is still a powerful model checker for CSP. Therefore after a short introduction to the key features of FDR, the model checking algorithm is going to be described in more detail and it will be discussed on how this algorithm can be extended to perform model checking on high level transition graphs.

The model-checking tool FDR (Failures-Divergence Refinement), which has been developed by Formal Systems Ltd., is based on the theory of Untimed CSP as C.A.R. Hoare suggested in [ ]. FDR employs well known techniques as described in detail in [ ] and [ ] to generate a labelled transition system from a CSP specification. On these transition systems FDR can perform a deadlock or livelock analysis, by analysing the structure of the graph and identifying states with no transition or states which can be reached by a loop of τ-labelled transitions. Additionally FDR allows to check, if a specification meets certain properties, by performing refinement checks on the transition system of the specification.

The foundation for the implementation of FDR2, which is the current version of the implementation, was the development of a parser for CSP by B. Scattergood [ ], which has been funded by the U.S. Office of Naval Research. This is the reason, that the grammar is available to the public and can be used in any software project using CSP. In later publications [,] Scattergood describes the concepts used in FDR to derive a labelled transition system from the abstract syntax tree generated by the parser.

The operational semantics of CSP can be used to generate a labelled transition system from a CSP specification. For all sequential subprocesses a transition system representing its behaviour can easily be determined by applying the rules of the semantics for each operator. The parallel operators generate a synchronisation tree referencing the sequential graphs, which allows to completely compute the product graph of the specified system. As soon as the labelled transition system is completely generated, standard techniques like normalisation (see section 3.2) can be applied to create a smaller graph representation.

Refinement checks are performed by comparing the transition systems of two processes. FDR can perform checks for all different types of refinement as explained in section 2.5.4. Depending on the kind of refinement to be done, the corresponding set inclusion checks can directly be performed on both transition systems modelling the particular behaviour.

It is not necessary to generate a completely normalised transition system with refusals and divergences for each refinement check. For trace refinement checks, which are employed to check safety properties of systems, it is sufficient to check the trace spaces of the processes under consideration. Therefore it is just necessary to perform this refinement check on a transition system without any refusal or divergence information. On the contrary a failures/divergence refinement check, which are used for safety, deadlock and livelock properties, requires fully computed labelled transition systems annotated with refusals and divergences for each state. FDR only computes those graphs, that are required to achieve a desired task.

The task of determining whether an implementation *IMP* refines a specification *SPEC* in the failures/divergences model, which is expressed by *SPEC* $\sqsubseteq_{FD}$ *IMP*, first requires the graph of the specification to be normalised as explained in section 3.2. Then it is necessary to identify all states in the transition system of the implementation, which are divergent and marking them accordingly. For failures- or trace-refinement this step is not necessary. Finally the implementation has to be model checked against the normal form of the specification.

An algorithm for this model checking task is indicated in listing 9.1. This algorithm has been introduced and explained in detail in [ ], and is implemented in the FDR2 model checker. It is going to be described on a rather detailed level, since the question is going to be addressed later, if and how this algorithm can be adopted for high level transition graphs. The function `check_refinement` requires the normal form transition system of the implementation and another transition system representing the specification as arguments. The algorithm works on sets of pairs, representing two states related under the refinement order. A set *checked* contains all those pairs, which have already been checked, while *pending* is a set to which pairs are added, that still have to be checked. Initially *pending* contains only the pair of the initial nodes of both transition systems. The algorithm stops, as soon as pending contains no more elements.

Each pending pair of states (s, i) is checked whether all of the following holds:

1. It must never occur, that the state s is non-divergent, when the state i of the unnormalised graph is divergent simultaneously.

2. The initial actions if the implementation's state i is a subset of those of the specifications state s.

3. Either i is an unstable state, or the events i refuses are a subset of one of the maximal refusals of s.

If any of those conditions fails the corresponding pair is one for which the refinement does not hold. On the contrary if all conditions are holding, all pairs, that are reachable from (s, i) have to be added to the *pending* set.

```
check_refinement(impl, spec)
BEGIN
   impl, spec ∈ TG,  i,i',s,s' ∈ STATE,  checked, pending ∈ SET

   (* Create an initial pair from the initial states *)
   pending = {(s₀(spec),  s₀(impl))}
   checked = ∅

   (* Loop until pending is empty *)
   FORALL  (s,i) ∈ pending DO
      checked = checked ∪ {(s,i)}
      pending = pending \ {(s,i)}
      IF  (   divergent(s) ∨ ¬divergent(i)
          ∧   [i]⁰ ⊆ [s]⁰
          ∧   ¬stable(i, impl) ∨ ∃ ref ∈ refusals_max(s) . Σ \ [i]⁰ ⊆ ref   )
      THEN
         FORALL  (s',i') ∈ reachable(s,i) DO
            IF (s',i') ∉ checked THEN
               pending = pending ∪ {(s',i')}
            FI
         OD
      ELSE
            RETURN false
      FI
   OD
   RETURN true
END
```

Listing 9.1: Refinement checking algorithm

Definition 9.1 *Reachable Pairs:*
A pair (s', i') is reachable from a pair (s, i), if either

- $i \xrightarrow{\tau} i' \land s = s'$, or

- $i \xrightarrow{\alpha} i' \land s \xrightarrow{\alpha} s'$, with $\alpha \neq \tau$.

The function reachable(s, i) if the listing 9.1 returns a set of all those pairs, that are reachable from the pair (s, i).

Especially this algorithm could be interesting for future work on high level transition graphs. FDR requires the transition system of the specification to be normalised, while the one of the implementation needs not to be. This algorithm adopted for high level transition graphs could in principal function on synchronisation terms, where only the one representing the specification has to be normalised according to the algorithm described in 8.3, while the other one needs not to be. This would allow to model check large systems, since it is not necessary to completely compute the unfolded transition system. Instead only the required parts can be derived from the synchronisation terms on the fly, which requires just the on-the-fly computation of the refusals, as described in 11.2.

9.2 Timed Automata

Another approach of extending transition systems are the Timed Automata as explained in detail by Rajeev Alur and David L. Dill in [ ], and summarised later with recent developments in [ ]. Timed automata are used to model the behaviour of real-time systems. Therefore a state-transition system is annotated with timing constraints using finitely many real-value clock variables.

The states of the transition system modelling a timed automata are called *locations*, and the transitions are called *switches*. The flow of time is modelled by continuously increasing the values of the clock variables while being in a location, which is in contrast to the traversion of a switch, which happen instantaneously. A switch can be used to reset clocks to zero, which is expressed by the term $z := 0$ in the graphical representation of a timed automata, as for example in figure 9.1. Additionally switches may carry timing constraints. A switch can only be taken, if the current value of the timer satisfies the timing constraint. Also locations may carry timing constraints as well, which are called invariants, since they express, that a location can no longer be visited, if the constraint no longer holds. In this case the location must be left immediately via any switch, which timing constraint holds.

Some ideas of timed automata are similar to the ones of high level transition graphs, since there are conditions guarding the transitions and assignments to variables, which are used in the case of timed automata to reset timers. Timed automata are additionally interesting to the topic of this thesis, since they allow testing of system in a timed model. Such testing algorithm for timed automata was suggested by Rachel Cardell-Oliver in [,   ].

Lets consider as an example parts of the timed automaton *TRAIN* in figure 9.1, which will be required later for further considerations. The start location is s_0, which is marked by an arrow pointing to it. Initially all timers are reset and start running as soon as the interpretation of the timed automaton begins in location s_0. Since there is no invariant in s_0 the system may remain an arbitrary amount of time in this state before the *approach*-labelled switch is taken, resulting in a reset of the timer x. Now time has to pass in location s_1, since the timing constraint at the switch requires the timer x to have a value larger than 2, before engaging in *in*. But since there is no maximum progress rule in timed automata, the system may still remain in location s_1, even though the constraint holds. The invariant $x \leqslant 5$ of location s_1 ensures, that the location is left, when the clock x finally reaches the value 5. More complex examples may use several different timers or more switches leaving a location.

To give a formal definition of the timed automata, it is necessary to formally specify the format of the clock constraints, which may appear at the switches or as invariants in the locations. The clock constraints $\varphi \in \Phi(X)$, where X is the

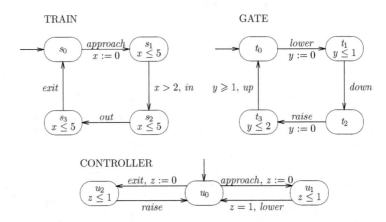

Figure 9.1: Timed Automata for a Train-Gate Controller

set of all clocks, are defined by the following grammar:

$$\varphi := x \leqslant c \mid c \leqslant x \mid x < c \mid c < x \mid \varphi_1 \wedge \varphi_2$$

where $x \in X$ is an element of the set of all clocks X and c is any constant in $\mathbb{N}_0$. A *clock interpretation* $\nu(x)$ provides a mapping from any clock $x \in X$ to a value in $\mathbb{R}$.

Definition 9.2 *A timed automaton A is a tuple $(L, l_0, \Sigma, X, I, E)$, where*

- L *is a finite set of locations.*

- l_0 *is the start location.*

- Σ *denotes the alphabet of events.*

- X *is a finite set of clocks.*

- I *is a mapping, that assigns a set of clock constraints of $\Phi(X)$ to a location.*

- $E \subseteq L \times \Sigma \times \mathcal{P}X, \Phi(X) \times L$ *denotes the set of all switches. A switch $(s, a, \varphi, \lambda, s')$ is a transition from location s to the location s' producing a. The switch may only be taken, if the timing constraints φ are true for the current timer values. The set λ contains all those clocks, that are reset by taking the transition.*

Interpreting a timed automaton requires state changes when time elapses. There are two possible reasons, why state changes via one of the active switches of the current state may occur:

Elapse of time: the constant incrementing of the timers can lead to a timer value, which no longer satisfies the clock constraint $I(s)$, which results in an immediate state change via a switch as described below.

Traversing a switch: a switch $(s, a, \varphi, \lambda, s') \in E$ may be taken, resulting in a new current location s'. To take the switch, it is necessary that the clock constraint φ enables the switch under the current clock values. While traversing the switch, the signal a is produced and all clocks from λ are reset to the value 0.

Checking a trace of a SUT against a timed automata with the interpretation as specified above, is still not possible in real time, since it cannot be guaranteed, that the timed automaton is deterministic. The following definition provides the means to determine whether or not a given timed automata is deterministic.

Definition 9.3 *A timed automaton $(L, l_0, \Sigma, X, I, E)$ is called deterministic iff for all locationss $s \in S$ and $a \in \Sigma$ there do not exist two distinct switches $(s, a, \varphi_1, \lambda_1, s_1)$ and $(s, a, \varphi_2, \lambda_2, s_2)$, such that the clock constraints φ_1 and φ_2 can be true at the same time.*

The example in figure 9.1 consists of three deterministic timed automata, which semantics are explained by the definitions given above. But still the semantics of the parallel system consisting of the three interacting timed automata has not been introduced yet.

Composing two timed automata P and Q via the parallel operator $\parallel$ requires them to synchronise on all common events, all other events may be produced independently. Taking two timed automata with disjunct locations $A_1 = (L_1, l_{01}, \Sigma_1, X_1, I_1, E_1)$ and $A_2 = (L_2, l_{02}, \Sigma_2, X_2, I_2, E_2)$ a parallel construction of those two is a timed automaton $(A_1 \parallel A_2) = (L_1 \times L_2, l_0, \Sigma_1 \cup \Sigma_2, X_1 \cup X_2, I, E)$, where $l_0 = (l_{01}, l_{02})$ and $I(s_1, s_2) = I(s_1) \wedge I(s_2)$. The switches E are composed as follows:

1. $\forall\, a \in \Sigma_1 \cap \Sigma_2.\ (s_1, a, \varphi_1, \lambda_1, s_1') \in E_1 \wedge (s_2, a, \varphi_2, \lambda_2, s_2') \in E_2$
   $\Rightarrow ((s_1, s_2), a, \varphi_1 \wedge \varphi_2, \lambda_1 \cup \lambda_2, (s_1', s_2')) \in E$

2. $\forall\, a \in \Sigma_1 \setminus \Sigma_2, (s, a, \varphi, \lambda, s') \in E_1, t \in L_2\ .\ ((s, t), a, \varphi, \lambda, (s', t)) \in E$

3. $\forall\, a \in \Sigma_2 \setminus \Sigma_1, (s, a, \varphi, \lambda, s') \in E_2, t \in L_1\ .\ ((t, s), a, \varphi, \lambda, (t, s')) \in E$

Figure 9.2 shows such a composed timed automata for the train-gate controller example from figure 9.1. All locations are represented as triplets of the locations of

TRAIN ‖ CONTROLLER ‖ GATE

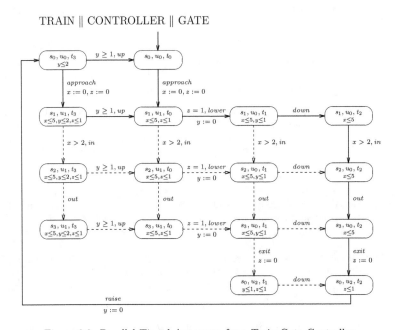

Figure 9.2: Parallel Timed Automata for a Train-Gate Controller

the three original timed automata. The switches have been determined in the way as described above. But only those locations and switches are shown, that can be reached by any number of switches starting at the initial location (s_0, u_0, t_0). The locations and switches, that are not connected to the reachable graph are not displayed, even though they exist in the timed automata by definition.

The generation algorithm for the composed timed automaton does not consider any order of the clocks, that are contained in the product graph. Lets take e.g. the location (s_1, u_1, t_0) of the product timed automata, which can be reached starting at (s_0, u_0, t_0) via a switch that resets both clocks x and z. The invariant $x \leq 5, z \leq 1$ guarantees, that the switch leading to (s_1, u_0, t_1) must always be taken, since the timers x and z are increasing at the same rate. Therefore it is never possible to take the switch leading to (s_2, u_1, t_0), which invariant is $x > 2$. All switches, which cannot ever be taken due to timing considerations are marked with dashed lines in figure 9.2. The reachable timed automata modelling the train-gate controller therefore consists only of 9 locations and 10 switches.

In this simple example it is easy to reckon, that certain locations cannot be reached from the initial location due to timing considerations, but in larger applications this usually is more difficult. Therefore a reachability analysis is required, which determines, depending on the possible clock value ranges, what locations can be reached from the initial location.

Definition 9.4 *Extended states:*
For a timed automaton $(L, l_0, \Sigma, X, I, E)$ the term $\langle l, \nu \rangle$ denotes an extended state, where $l \in L$ and ν is a clock interpretation for X.

Even though there in an uncountable number of such extended states in each timed automata, since the interpretation of clocks can yield to any real numbered value, there are extended state who behave similar. Consider two different extended states $\langle l_1, \nu_1 \rangle$ and $\langle l_2, \nu_2 \rangle$, which depend on the two clocks $x_1, x_2 \in X$. Obviously those two state can only behave similarly, if the locations l_1 and l_2 are identical, but additionally their similarity depends also on the values of the clocks. Since clock constraints contain only natural numbers two similar interpretations of the clocks must agree on the same integral part of the clocks. Additionally they must agree on the same order of the fractional parts of the clock interpretations as well, since this guarantees, that in both clock interpretations the same clock changes its integral part first.

For a timed automata $(L, l_0, \Sigma, X, I, E)$ and each clock $x \in X$ there is a clock constraint $\varphi \in I$ such that c_x is the largest integer constant in any constraint for the clock x. $\lfloor t \rfloor$ denotes the integral part of any value $t \in \mathbb{R}$ and $fract(t)$ denotes the fractional part, such that $t = \lfloor t \rfloor + fract(t)$.

Definition 9.5 *Clock regions*
Two clock interpretations ν and ν' are considered to be equivalent under the relation $\sim$, if all of the following hold:

1. *$\forall\, x \in X.(\lfloor \nu(x) \rfloor = \lfloor \nu'(x) \rfloor) \vee (\nu(x) > c_x \wedge \nu'(x) > c_x)$*

2. *$\forall\, x, y \in X.fract(\nu(x)) \leq fract(\nu(y)) \Leftrightarrow fract(\nu'(x)) \leq fract(\nu'(y))$, with $\nu(x) \leq c_x$ and $\nu(y) \leq c_y$*

3. *$\forall\, x \in X.fract(\nu(x)) = 0 \Leftrightarrow fract(\nu'(x)) = 0$, with $\nu(x) \leq c_x$*

All those clock interpretations being equivalent under the relation $\sim$ are considered to form a clock region.

Clock regions are denoted as $[\varphi]$, where φ uniquely characterises the region by a set of clock constraints. Since all clocks are steadily increasing simultaneously it is always possible to find a *time successor* α' of a clock region α, such that $\forall \nu \in \alpha \,.\, \exists\, t \in \mathbb{R}^+ \,.\, \nu + t \in \alpha'$.

Based on these considerations it is possible to define a transition system abstraction, which only has events at its transitions and contains clock regions in its states.

Definition 9.6 *Region Automaton*
For a timed automaton $A = (L, l_0, \Sigma, X, I, E)$ a labelled transition system $\mathcal{R}(A) = (R, r_0, \Sigma, \rightarrow)$ can be derived as region automaton:

- $R = \{\langle l, \alpha \rangle \mid l \in L \wedge \alpha \text{ is a clock region of } A\}$

- $r_0 = \langle l_0, [\nu_0] \rangle$, *where* $\forall x \in X . \nu_0(x) = 0$

- $\langle s, \alpha \rangle \xrightarrow{a} \langle s', \alpha' \rangle$, *iff there is a switch* $(s, a, \varphi, \lambda, s') \in E$ *and a clock region* α'' *such that*

    1. *α'' is a time-successor of α*

    2. *α'' satisfies φ*

    3. *α' equals α'', where all clocks in λ are reset.*

The computation of such region automaton for a timed automata identifies all combinations of locations and clock regions, that can be reached from the initial location of the timed automata and the clock region, where all clocks are reset to 0.

The structure of the timed automata as explained in this section do not differ that much to the one of the high level transition graphs. Even though timed automata do not use any model of variables at all, the timers have similar functions that the variables in high level transition graphs. The clock constraints at the switches have basically the same functionality as the conditions on high level transition graph transitions: both prevent a transition to be taken, if the condition evaluates to false in the current location. Additionally the assignments of high level transition graphs and the clock resets of timed automata serves similar functions: both are used to change the values of variables or timers respectively. Therefore it could be interesting to investigate, whether i.e. the region automaton of a timed automata can be adapted for high level transition graphs. Even though transitions of high level transition graphs may contain conditions, it is not necessary that those are mutually exclusive. An interesting approach would be to generate a region automaton from a high level transition graph, which contains no more nondeterminism introduced by conflicting guards at transitions labelled with the same event.

9.3   Hybrid Automata

Hybrid automata are an extension of timed automata and can be used to model mixed discrete-continuous systems, like an engine controller, which consists of discrete components like digital controllers and of continuous components like analog sensors, which values can change over time.

Discrete components of a system are modelled in a similar way than with timed automata: discrete states are modelled as control modes, which relate to the locations of timed automata, and discrete state changes are represented by control switches, which have a similar semantics than the switches in timed automata. The continuous components of a system are modelled as values from $\mathbb{R}^n$, where the change of those values can be represented by differential equations.

The state of a modelled system is therefore determined by the control mode of the hybrid automata; state changes occur, when a control switch is taken. Labelled at each control switch is a jump condition, which can cause discrete changes of the system by changing values of the systems variables, if additional conditions evaluate to true under the current variable values. Additionally in each control mode the continuous values are monitored and checked against invariant conditions of the state. A violation of an invariant will trigger a control switch to another control mode of the system.

The following definition for hybrid automata has been given by T. Henzinger in his article "The Theory of Hybrid Automata" [ ].

Definition 9.7 *Hybrid automata*
A hybrid automaton H consists of the following components.

Variables. A finite set $X = \{x_1, ..., x_n\}$ of real-numbered variables. The number n is called the *dimension* of H. We write $\dot{X}$ for the set $\{\dot{x}_1, ..., \dot{x}_n\}$ of dotted variables (which represent first derivatives during continuous change), and we write X' for the set $\{x'_0, ..., x'_n\}$ of primed variables (which represent values at the conclusion of discrete change).

Control graph. A finite directed multigraph (V, E). The vertices in V are called *control modes*. The edges in E are called *control switches*.

Initial, invariant, and flow conditions. Three vertex labelling functions *init*, *inv*, and *flow* that assign to each control mode $v \in V$ three predicates. Each initial condition $init(v)$ is a predicate whose free variables are from X. Each invariant condition $inv(v)$ is a predicate whose free variables are from X. Each flow condition $flow(v)$ is a predicate whose free variables are from $X \cup \dot{X}$.

Jump conditions. An edge labelling function *jump* that assigns to each control switch $e \in E$ a predicate. Each jump condition $jump(e)$ is a predicate whose free variables are from $X \cup X'$.

Events. A finite set Σ of events, and an edge labelling function $event : E \rightarrow \Sigma$ that assigns to each control switch an event.

Figure shows an exemplary hybrid automata for the gate of the train-gate controller, which as already been introduced in section 9.2. But in hybrid automata this gate can be modelled without timeouts, as has been necessary for timed automata. Instead the angle of the gate is being computed and the variable y stores the current angle at any time. An angle of 90° stands for open and 0° means closed. During lowering and raising the angle $y \in \mathbb{R}$ may take an arbitrary value in the interval $]0, 90[$.

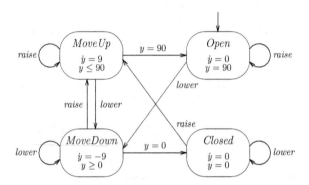

Figure 9.3: Hybrid Automata for a Train-Gate Controller

The initial state of this hybrid automata is the control mode *Open*. On entering this state the global variable y is initialised with the value 90. The only control switch to leave this mode is the only marked with the event *lower*, which causes a state change to the mode *MoveDown*. During the hybrid automaton resides in this state, the value of y is reduced by the value 9 in each time interval, which represents the closing of the gate. This states invariant specifies, that the system may only stay in this state, as long as $y \geq 0$. If this invariant is violated, any control switch must be taken to leave this control mode. Therefore this mode can be left by two different ways. Either the event *raise* can be produced, which causes a state change of the system to *MoveUp*, or the gate reaches the angle 0, which enables the condition at the control switch to the state *Closed*. As soon as this switch is enabled it is accepted and the state changes to *Closed*, since otherwise the invariant of *MoveDown* would have been violated. In the state *Closed* the gate is stopped, represented by $\dot{y} = 0$, and the invariant ensures, that $y = 0$, which represents a closed gate.

The event *raise* starts a similar process on the hybrid automata passing through the control modes *MoveUp* until the angle of the gate reaches the value 90 indicating the gate has opened completely. The control switch to the state *Open* stops the movement of the gate at the angle of 90.

In contrast to the gate timed automata from the previous chapter, the behaviour of the gate can be modelled without the need for explicit timers. Instead a differential equation on a global variable specifies the behaviour of the system on the flow of time. In this case the movement of the gate is specified by the three differential equations $\dot{y} = 0$, $\dot{y} = 9$ and $\dot{y} = -9$.

High level transition graphs as specified in this part of this theses have similar properties than the hybrid automata described by T. Henzinger. Both approaches have in common that they use variables to reduce the number of discrete states and transitions. In contrast to hybrid automata, where variables are global and can carry real values, CSP has local variables that can carry higher order values like integers, sets, sequences or even processes or functions, but no number values from $\mathbb{R}$. Another difference is that hybrid automata allow to specify changes of the variables values, either by differential equations or by assigning new values. In high level transition graphs on the other hand local variables can only be initialised in a process once and can be used throughout the process definition. Assignments of new values can only occur at process references or at the prefix operator, but it exists no explicit assignment operator then in hybrid automata.

The control modes and control switches relate directly to the locations and transitions of high level transition graphs. Since CSP has no way of specifying continuous behaviour, there is no analogy to the $init(v)$, $inv(v)$ and $flow(v)$ functions of control modes in CSP. But the jump conditions are very simular to the transitions of high level transition graphs, since both formalisms allow to label conditions, events and assignments to the transitions.

9.4 High-level Petri Nets

This section gives a short overview about High-level Petri Nets and High-level Petri Net Graphs, as they are defined in the final draft of the International Standard ISO/IEC 15909 [ ]. The defined formalisms are based on Predicate-Transition Nets [ ] and Coloured Petri Nets [ ], which have been introduced and developed in the 1980s. It also uses some of the notations developed for Algebraic Petri Nets. This approach can be "used directly to specify systems or to define the semantics of other less formal languages. It may also serve to integrate techniques currently used independently such as state transition diagrams and data flow diagrams. The technique is particularly suited to parallel and distributed systems development as it supports concurrency" [ ].

Definition 9.8 *High-level Petri Nets (HLPN)*
A HLPN is a structure $HLPN = (P, T, D, Type, Pre, Post, M_0)$, where

- *P is a finite set of elements called Places.*

- *T is a finite set of elements called Transitions disjoint from P ($P \cap T = \emptyset$).*

- *D is a non-empty finite set of non-empty domains were each element of D is called a type.*

- *Type* : $P \cup T \rightarrow D$ *is a function used to assign types to places and to determine transition modes.*

- *Pre, Post* : $TRANS \rightarrow \mu PLACE$ *are the pre and post mappings with*

$$TRANS = \{(t, m) \mid t \in T, m \in Type(t)\}$$
$$PLACE = \{(p, g) \mid p \in P, g \in Type(p)\}$$

- $M_0 \in \mu PLACE$ *is a multiset called the initial marking of the net.*

The term $\mu PLACE$ denotes the sets of multisets over the set PLACE. A multiset B over a non-empty basis set A is a function $B : A \rightarrow \mathbb{N}$, which associates a multiplicity, possible zero, with each of the basis elements. The term $B(a)$ denotes the multiplicity of $a \in A$ in the multiset B.

The marking M of a HLPN is a multiset $M \in \mu PLACE$. A transition mode $tr \in TRANS$ is enabled, if $Pre(tr) \leq M$. This expression states, that all elements of the pre mapping of a transition mode, which is a set of multisets over $PLACE$, must also be contained in the marking M of the $HLPN$. This is similar to the concept of conditions in high level transition graphs, where a condition guards each transition, which must evaluate to *true* under the current environment, before that transition can be taken.

It is also possible, that multiple transition modes can be enabled simultaneously. A finite multiset of transition modes $T_\mu \in \mu TRANS$ is enables at a marking M, if $Pre(T_\mu) \leq M$, where $Pre(T_\mu)$ is the linear extension of Pre and is defined as:

$$Pre(T_\mu) = \sum_{tr \in TRANS} T_\mu(tr) Pre(tr)$$

In this definition $T_\mu(tr)$ denotes the multiplicity of the transition mode tr in the multiset T_μ, and $Pre(tr)$ is the pre mapping of that transition mode. The linear extension of Pre is therefore the sum of the products of the multiplicity and the pre mapping of each transition mode in T_μ. All transition modes in T_μ are concurrently enabled, if $Pre(T_\mu) \leq M$, which means, that the current marking contains enough tokens to satisfy all pre mappings of T_μ.

The transition rule requires a finite multiset of transition modes T_μ to be enabled concurrently in a marking M. A transition *step* results in a new marking M', which is defined as follows:

$$M' = M - Pre(T_\mu) + Post(T_\mu)$$

where $Post(T_\mu)$ is the linear extension of $Post$ applied to the multiset T_μ. Such step is denoted by $M \xrightarrow{T_\mu} M'$.

The addition and subtraction operators on multisets $B_1, B_2 \in \mu A$, which are used in the previous definition, are defined as follows:

$$B = B_1 + B_2 \quad \Leftrightarrow \quad \forall\, a \in A \,.\, B(a) = B_1(a) + B_2(a)$$
$$B = B_1 - B_2 \quad \Leftrightarrow \quad \forall\, a \in A \,.\, (B_1(a) \geq B_2(a)) \wedge (B(a) = B_1(a) + B_2(a))$$

The concurrent enabling of transition modes has simular aspects to the synchronisation terms of high level transition graphs. With synchronisation terms multiple steps in a high level transition graph can also be performed simultaneously, even though those steps usually are performed in different processes of a CSP specification. Simultaneous execution of transitions in synchronisation terms with high level transition graphs, are only possible for the synchronised parallel operators of CSP. The interleaving operator of CSP only performs a step in one of its sub-processes at a time. In high-level petri nets it is on the contrary possible, that a step even uses a transition mode multiple times in a step.

The high-level petri net definition contains no variable model at all, but the ISO standard 15909 also defines high-level petri net graphs, which are a graphical form of high-level petri net: *High-level Petri Net Graphs*. Those high-level petri net graphs provides a graphical notation for places, transitions and their relationships. They consist of the following components:

A *Net Graph* describes the transition system represented by the HLPNG. It consists of two different types of nodes: places and transitions, and arcs connecting places to transitions and transitions to places. Each place is marked with a corresponding *type*, which is a non-empty set of elements the place may carry as *markings*.

The arcs of the net graph are labelled with *arc annotations*, which may consist of constants, types variables and functions. Expressions in those annotations are evaluated by assigning values to each of the variables. The result of such evaluation of an expression is a collection of items taken from the type of the arc's place. Each transition in the net graph is labelled with a *transition condition*, which is a boolean expression, which may use variables, which are used at the arcs of the transition.

Finally a High-level Petri Net Graph must contain *declarations* of the place types, types of variables, function definitions and initial markings of the net graph.

A simple High-level Petri Net Graph is shown in figure 9.4. It consists of the places p_1 and p_2 and the transition t_1, which has a condition $x < y$. There are two arcs from p_1 to t_1 and t_1 to p_2, which is each labelled with an arc annotation. The place p_1 contains tokens of the type A, and the place p_2 of the type B. The initial markings of the HLPNG are $M_0(p_1) = 1'1 + 2'3$ and $M_0(p_2) = \emptyset$. The notation $1'1 + 2'3$ describes a multiset, which contains the element 1 once and the element 3 twice.

The execution of such high-level petri net graphs again requires, that transitions are enables based on the markings of the places in the net graph, which

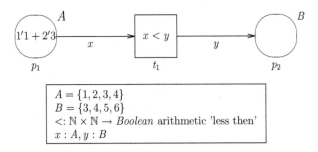

Figure 9.4: HLPNG with a Transition Condition

is called *net marking*. A transition is enabled in a transition mode, where an assignment of values to the transition's variables satisfies the condition of the transition. If a transition is enabled, tokens are removed from the input places of the transition's input arc. As a result of such occurrence of a transition new tokens are added to the place of the output arc of the transition.

Executing the example from figure 9.4 first requires to identify the modes, in which the condition of the transition t_1 evaluates to *true*. In the initial marking of p_1 the transition t_1 is enabled in the following modes $\{(1,3),(1,4),(1,5),(1,6),(3,4),(3,5),(3,6)\}$, where the first element of the pair represents a value bound to the variable x and the second represents a binding for y, under which the condition $x < y$ evaluates to *true*.

Using the initial markings of p_1 several different multisets of modes are enabled: for example $1'(1,4) + 2'(3,6)$, or $1'(1,3) + 1'(3,4) + 1'(3,5)$, or $1'(1,6)$ and many more combinations. If the transition t_1 for example occurs in the mode $1'(1,6)$, the resulting marking is:

$$M(p_1) = 2'3$$
$$M(p_2) = 1'6$$

Or if it occurs in mode $1'(1,3) + 1'(3,4) + 1'(3,5)$ the resulting marking would be:

$$M(p_1) = \emptyset$$
$$M(p_2) = 1'3 + 1'4 + 1'5$$

The model of variables used in this context significantly differs from the use of variables in HLTGs, since each variable in a HLPNG is only visible on the arcs of a single transition and the transition itself. These variables are not used to store values, which is completely different to the variables model in HLTGs, but only used to modify the markings of places connected by the arcs of a transition. The values of computations can be stored as markings of a place instead. Therefore high-level petri net graphs do not need any concept like the environments of high level transition graphs, since all computed values are represented as markings of the HLPNG.

9.5 SPIN

During the design of complex or safety critical software systems, it is necessary to specify the design choices in a way, that the implementation can be tested or verified against them later. If there is an error in the design specification, this error will also occur in the implementation if it is a correct implementation of the specification. Therefore design choices normally are specified on a high level of abstraction to assist the developers making less mistakes. Of course, that does not guarantee that the specification is correct.

The verification of the design of a system is vital to testing the implementation later. As stated before, every error in the specification of the system can not be found when testing the behaviour of the implementation against it, because the specification is assumed to be correct.

The model checker SPIN is a generic verification system for models of asynchronous process systems. It can be used to verify the requirements and behaviour of a design or prototype before refining[1] it to the real implementation. It provides a notation for unambiguously specifying the design choices and a notation to express general correctness requirements. After the design choices and correctness requirements are specified, SPIN can verify, that they are logically consistent.

SPIN represents the system and correctness claims using finite automata. This is related to the creation of a transition graph of the CSP specification of a system. Like all tools creating automata for process systems, SPIN has the problem of state explosion. Various methods have been developed to reduce or compress the automata.

The design choices have to be specified in the verification language PROMELA (Process Meta Language). Models that can be specified in PROMELA are always required to be bounded and have only countably many distinct behaviours. Process interaction can be specified using rendevouz primitives, asynchronous message passing (buffered channels) and shared variables. The correctness claims are specified in LTL (Linear Temporal Logic).

Having specified a process system and a set of requirement claims, the system can be interactively simulated to see if the design is basically as intended. After this, an optimised model checker can be generated for the specified system and a requirement claim. This model checker can be used to find counterexamples to

---

[1]Note that the term refinement here does not necessarily equals one of the CSP refinements defined in section 10.2.

the correctness claims, that afterwards can be executed in the interactive simulation of the system. Thus SPIN can be used to formalise the potential violation of correct system behaviour and check for occurrences of these violations. If counterexamples can be found during the verification, the design must be revised as long as it is correct. Verifying the design before implementing a system can only find the errors in the design that violate a given set of requirements. Guaranteeing the correctness of the design requires the completeness and correctness of the requirements.

Processes and Correctness Claims

To understand the mechanism of SPIN it is necessary to inspect how processes and correctness claims are represented. Processes are instantiations of process templates where a process template describes a class of processes with the same type of behaviour. As stated before, all processes defined in PROMELA are bounded and have only countably many distinct behaviours. SPIN generates a finite automaton for each specified process. The global system is represented as an interleaving product automaton of the process automata of all its sub processes. This global system automaton is also called the state space or the reachability graph of the system.

The correctness claims are represented using LTL formulas which can be used to express both safety and liveness conditions. Vardi and Wolper showed in 1983 that any LTL formula can be translated into a Büchi automaton. SPIN uses Büchi automata to represent the correctness claims. The generated automata formally accept only those system executions that satisfy the corresponding LTL formula.

Perform Verification

To perform the verification, SPIN computes the synchronous product of the Büchi automaton of the correctness claim and the global system automaton. The result again is a Büchi automaton. If the language accepted by this automaton is empty, the LTL formula representing the correctness claim can not be satisfied by the specified system. Otherwise every accepted word describes a behaviour of the system that does satisfy the correctness claim. Because the correctness claims are used to specify erroneous behaviour, every behaviour satisfying the correctness claim is a counterexample to the desired system behaviour. SPIN uses a nested depth first algorithm that does not guarantee to find every system behaviour that satisfies the LTL formula but it can be proven that if there exist any, at least one of them will be found.

Partial Order Reduction

Like other formal verification and testing tools, SPIN has the problem, that the specified system can result in a state space that is too large to be useful. In the worst case the state space has the size of the Cartesian product of the automata of all sub processes. A partial order reduction method was developed to reduce the complexity. It is based on the fact that an LTL formula often is insensitive to the order in which concurrent and independently events are interleaved. A reduced automaton represents only classes of execution sequences that are indistinguishable for a given correctness property. In the best case, this reduces the complexity from exponential growth in the number of participating processes to linear growth. In more typical cases, this is not reached but still the reduction is considerable.

The concept of calculating classes of indistinguishable execution sequences can not be used to reduce the size of the transitions graphs as long as they are used for testing. As stated above, these classes are always valid for a special correctness property. Testing with transition graphs as described in chapter 10 does not use correctness claims. So every execution sequence that is legal for the system under test must be represented in the transition system.

For transition graphs it would instead be interesting to find classes of equivalent test values (events), to reduce the size of a transition graph. It is possible to calculate all possible variable values for every location of a high level transition graph. With this it has to be examined if it is possible to generate a normalised transition graph that contains locations for equivalent events and transitions with sets of events but no conditions or assignments anymore. This could tremendously decrease the size of the transition graph, while it could still be executed in realtime.

Memory Management

Even a reduced reachability graph can be too large to fit in the memory of a target machine. For this reason a special memory management was developed to represent these graphs in SPIN which reduces the uses of memory, as well. Greater reduction of memory usage normally leads to greater run time penalties. SPIN provides a state compression algorithm that provides a remarkable reduction of memory usage together with an acceptable growth of the runtime. The method is based on representing the states of the reachability graph as a vector of references to the states of the sub processes. This has the effect, that every state of the sub processes is represented only once but can be referred to as often as it is necessary for the combined system. Together with the fact, that more memory is needed for the representation of a state than for a reference, this leads to a considerable reduction of the memory usage.

Though this compression does not reduce the number of states but only the amount of memory used to represent them, it has a relation to the synchronisation terms as defined in section 5.2.3. In both cases, the states of the subprocesses are used to model the behaviour of the parallel system. A synchronisation term can be seen as a vector of a current state for each sub process together with meta information about the synchronisation. Executing a parallel system using synchronisation terms with normalised high level transition graphs, is similar to on-the-fly creation of only that part of the state space that is used for a special run. This is different to SPIN where still the whole state space of the system is built.

Part III

Testing with Transition Systems

Software systems, that are currently developed, are usually so large, that it is almost impossible to perform manual tests to cover the complete functionality of the system. One remedy is using automated test systems, which perform any number of tests on the system under test (SUT) automatically. But the problem of designing each test case individually is still a manual task. This is where formal methods fill the gap. The test designer just specifies the behaviour of the system in a formal way and the test software derives all relevant test cases from that specification. With this method it is possible to use non-terminating test specifications instead of simple test scripts, to continuously engage different test cases on the SUT.

This part of the thesis is about specification based testing using the CSP approach. In chapter 10 the advantages and methods of this approach are described in detail. After a general introduction to the topic a test theory for Untimed CSP will be presented, which describes how CSP specifications can be used to test embedded systems. The chapter closes with a description of automated test systems in general and the RT-Tester test system in particular.

In part II different representations for transition systems and corresponding normalisation algorithms have been explained. Based on these different transition system representations test algorithms for normalised (chapter 11) and unnormalised transition systems (chapter 12) are introduced. Of special importance for these algorithms is the real-time capability. If it is not possible to calculate the initial events and the refusals of a state in the transition system within a bounded amount of time, it cannot be guaranteed, that the test system detects errors or responds to system outputs on time.

Chapter 13 summarises the results of this parts and identifies different purposes, that testing machines are used for in a test case. Each of this purposes has different requirements to the real-time capability of the evaluation algorithms for the transition system representations. This results in a matrix which states what transition system representations can be used for what testing purposes.

The most common of this test purposes is the checking of the correct behaviour of the SUT. Those test machines only processes the outputs of the SUT and checks, whether the observed behaviour matches the expected results. The checking itself must consider timing constraints of the SUT, but the test results need not be available in hard real-time. This finding resulted in the design of a delayed checking test algorithm in section 12.6, which operates on any transition system representation. This algorithm allows to use synchronisation terms with unnormalised high level transition graphs for checking purposes in automatic test systems like the RT-Tester.

190

Chapter 10

Specification based Testing

The lifecycle of software systems usually starts with a document by the customer, in which the required properties of the system are described in detail: the *requirements document*. During the subsequent phases of development a piece of software is implemented, which shall meet those specified requirements.

There are several techniques to ensure, that the implemented system fulfils the specified requirements. Since the requirements specification is usually an informal or semiformal document, there is no way to formally prove that the implementation is correct according to the requirements. But *validation* as defined in the DO-178 B standard [ ] can determine by informal techniques like simulation or testing a prototype system, whether or not the system satisfies the customers needs.

> **Validation** is the process of determining that the requirements are the right requirements and that they are complete.

During the different development phases subsequently new products like system specification, design documents or an implementation are created, which can be used, to verify the results of the next phase. If the result of one phase is a *formal specification* of the system, this result can be used for a *formal verification*, to show that the implementation is correct. But in the context of testing the term *verification* is not that strictly used, as shown by Storey's definition [ ]:

> **Verification** is the process of determining whether the output of a lifecycle phase fulfils the requirements specified by the previous phase.

While *validation* and *verification* can be performed on specification documents which are results of certain lifecycle phases, finally it is necessary to verify or validate the implemented system (or some of its components) against the specifications. These *testing* activities are done by executing the implemented system components and providing input data to the systems interfaces while observing the systems behaviour and verify it against the specifications.

Testing is the process used to verify or validate a system or its components.

In this thesis a new type of transition systems for CSP specifications has been introduced in chapter 5, which can be used for automated testing with the testing system RT-Tester. This chapter tries to give a basic introduction to *automated testing* (10.1) and corresponding automated test systems like the RT-Tester (10.3). The theoretical background for testing applications with the new type of transition systems, that are going to be introduced in this thesis, can be found in section 10.2, where the *test theory for untimed CSP* is described in detail.

10.1   Testing of Embedded Systems

Testing in the context of this thesis occupies with embedded systems, which interact with their operational environment. The communication between the operational environment and the embedded controller happens over the input and output interfaces of the controller. Those interfaces can provide digital or analog data, depending on the needs of the embedded application. Executing the implemented system components for testing purposes, requires, that specific data is provided to the input interfaces, while the systems behaviour is observed. The compliance of the behaviour with the specified requirements has to be established, otherwise a test fails.

In many testing scenarios the real operational environment is not available for the tests, since it may be too expensive to provide (e.g. aircrafts) or it may even be not available at the development location (e.g. for satellites). Therefore a simulation of the environment often is the only solution to properly test the controller.

Especially for controller tests, the operational environment is replaced by a test system, which simulates the environment. Such tests are called *hardware-in-the-loop* tests. The test system provides the controller with required input data and receives the outputs of the *system under test* (SUT). The general test configuration for embedded controllers is shown in figure 10.1.

In the case of a non-deterministic controller it is not sufficient to monitor the outputs and check them against the expected results. Additional internal monitoring channels may be required to the SUT, to get the internal state of the controller. With these additional data from the system, statements about internal SUT states can be made, that would not be possible otherwise.

The same approach is also possible for software systems or software components. An *environment simulator* stimulates the software interfaces and allows access to the global data of the software system. Often the simulators consist of hard- and software components, to create the environment the system requires to function properly. Since such simulator can be used to force the system into

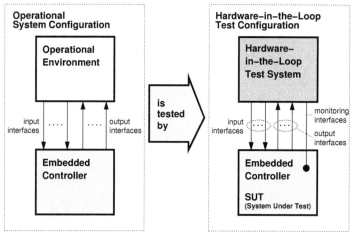

Figure 10.1: General Test Configuration

desired situations that have to be tested, it is called *test driver*. The results produced by the tested software modules can be compared to the expected results leading to a failed or passed test. Following the naming convention of the hardware testing approach this type of testing is called *software-in-the-loop* testing.

A decision whether a test has failed or passed can only be made, if a previously defined *test case* exists, which states a "set of inputs, execution conditions and expected results for a particular objective" [ ]. The expected results usually can be directly derived from the system specification, so it can be determined, whether or not the behaviour of the SUT is correct. In contrast to a test case, a *test procedure* also describes the set-up of the test system, which set of test cases is relevant for the test and how the test results shall be evaluated to determine whether or not the test was successful.

As already indicated before, tests are not only exercised on the complete system. Usually a testing scenario starts on the level of the isolated components of the system, which is called *unit testing*. During these tests most errors can be found, that occur in the single components. As soon as those errors has been eliminated, several components can be tested in combination with each other. During these so called *integration test*, successively more single units are combined, until the system is completely constructed. Testing the complete system, being is usually a combination of hardware and software, is called *system testing*.

System testing requires an environment simulator to stimulate the inputs of the SUT and to observe the corresponding outputs. During *black box tests*, there is – except from the data of the interfaces – no additional information about the internal state of the SUT available. Therefore it is not possible to check, whether the SUT reached certain internal states, which could be important to code coverage issues. This is only possible in *white box testing*, where additional monitoring channels are used to inspect the internal state of the SUT. Additionally it may also be possible to use the knowledge on the actual implementation, to force the system into states, that cannot be tested otherwise.

10.2   Test Theory for Untimed CSP

Testing reactive embedded real-time systems with Untimed CSP seems to contradict each other, since Untimed CSP itself provides no means to model time at all. But there exists several extensions of CSP, which provide the means to specify timed behaviour (Timed CSP) or even model continuous changes of variables by differential equations (Hybrid CSP).

Since there exists no model checker for any of those extensions of CSP, specifying tests directly in Hybrid CSP or Timed CSP is not supported by the RT-Tester. Also FDR only provides support for Untimed CSP. Therefore Amthor and Meyer proposed a structural decomposition of Hybrid CSP (HCSP) [ ] and Timed CSP (TCSP) [ ] in their PhD-theses. The structure of these structural decompositions is presented in figure 10.2.

A HCSP specification can be decomposed into a TCSP specification, which models the timed behaviour of the original specification, running in parallel with HCSP pattern processes synchronising over an auxiliary set of events. Additionally the resulting Timed CSP specification can again be decomposed into an Untimed CSP specification and several parallel TCSP patterns for timer processes synchronising over internal events, which are used to mark the setting and elapsing of a timer. Finally the Untimed CSP specification may also be decomposed into several Untimed CSP specifications, which do not contain any CSP high level operators like interleaving, parallel and hiding, and a CSP communication skeleton, describing the concurrent structure of the sequential processes. This third decomposition is a part of this thesis and will be described in chapter 5 in more detail.

These three steps of decomposing Hybrid CSP specifications into semantically identical Untimed CSP specifications allows to formulate a test theory based only on Untimed CSP, with just a few extensions for each of the decomposition steps. Therefore it is completely sufficient to describe a test theory for Untimed CSP, which was introduced in detail in [ ].

Even though this thesis in the following will consider only Untimed CSP, the decomposition of Timed CSP allows to apply the results presented in this part to timed testing as well.

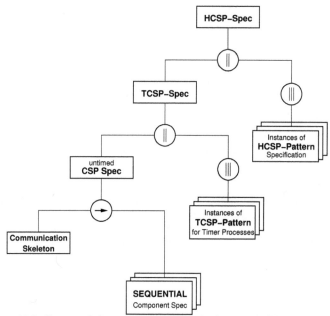

Figure 10.2: Structural decomposition hierarchy for Hybrid CSP specifications

10.2.1 Correctness Requirements and their Relation to CSP Refinement

When referring to testing, we assume a test of an implementation IMP against its specification $SPEC$, which can both be expressed as Untimed CSP processes. In this case, the intuitive understanding of correctness of an implementation may be formally expressed using different types of CSP refinement relations, as already introduced in section 2.5.4. The relations between correctness requirements and refinement is explained in the following, which are an excerpt from the authors diploma thesis.

Safety

The implementation IMP should only perform executions pre-planned in the specification $SPEC$. This can be expressed by demanding that all possible traces of the implementation should also be produced by the specification.

$$traces(IMP) \subseteq traces(SPEC)$$

Requirements Coverage

After performing an initial execution s which is possible for both specification and implementation, the implementation should never refuse a service which is not refused by the specification. This implies that a trace which can never be refused by the specification will also be performed by the implementation. Additionally sufficient requirements coverage allows to refuse a service in the implementation completely if it may be refused according to the specification.

$$\forall s \;:\; traces(SPEC) \cap traces(IMP) \;\bullet$$
$$refusals(IMP \setminus s) \subseteq refusals(SPEC \setminus s)$$

Non-Divergence

Apart from blocking a service, non-availability may be caused by performing an infinite sequence of internal events invisible to the environment, or by showing completely unpredictable system behaviour. This is denoted by divergence and the implementation should diverge – if at all – only after traces where the specification also diverges.

$$divergences(IMP) \subseteq divergences(SPEC)$$

Robustness

Robustness requires that every trace pre-planned in the specification should also be performable in the implementation. Such robustness properties for example are required for specifications, which contain non-determinism for exception handling. In addition to the the non-divergence requirements, robustness requires that non-deterministic exceptional behaviour described by the specification is also covered by the implementation, which is not ensured by the requirements coverage property.

$$traces(SPEC) \subseteq traces(IMP)$$

The following table describes the correspondence between the correctness properties and the refinement notations. *'yes'* means that the safety requirement is implied by the refinement relation.

Property	$\sqsubseteq_T$	$\sqsubseteq_F$	$\sqsubseteq_{FD}$	$\sqsubseteq_{FDR}$
Safety	*yes*	*yes*	*yes*	*yes*
Requirements Coverage	*no*	*yes*	*yes*	*yes*
Non-Divergence	*no*	*no*	*yes*	*yes*
Robustness	*no*	*no*	*no*	*yes*

This result show that it is sufficient to verify a SUT against a specification in the failures-divergences model to cover the safety, requirements coverage and non-divergence requirements at the same time. If the robustness of the system must be ensured as well, a simple trace refinement $IMP \sqsubseteq_T SPEC$ after the refinement proof $SPEC \sqsubseteq_{FD} IMP$ is sufficient. For the testing considerations it is obvious that a test case should be evaluated in the failures-divergences model to validate the most important test requirements.

10.2.2 Hennessy Tests

The testing methodology Matthew Hennessy describes in [ ] applies to reactive systems, which produce outputs at their system interfaces as a result of inputs, that were given to the SUT. To check, whether a test is successful, an *experiment*[1] is conducted, during which an input has to be send to the system. If the resulting output is the expected result, the test was a success. If on the other hand an unexpected or no output can be observed, the test has failed.

For non-deterministic systems these tests get more complicated. If after a certain input event i a system may diverge, or produce arbitrary events, a single test run does not suffice to check, whether the system may eventually produce the expected output o. In fact three different outcomes of the experiments may occur:

a) All experiments fail, i.e. all computations of the system after the input i never lead to the output o.

b) All experiments succeed, i.e. all computations of the system after the input i always leads to the output o.

c) Some experiments fail and some succeed. In this case, there are certain computations of the system after the input i, which result in the expected output o, but some also lead to an unexpected output o'.

Since this simple view with only one input and output is not applicable to real systems, Hennessy extended his notions to experimenters as processes U running in parallel with the system P. The alphabet of events of the implementation has to be a subset of the alphabet of the experimenter: $\alpha(P) \subset \alpha(U) = \alpha(P)$. If an experiment was identified to be successful, the specific event $\omega \in \alpha(U) \setminus \alpha(P)$ is produced by the experimenter.

Those interconnected systems (denoted as $P \parallel U$) communicate on all common events $\alpha(U) \cap \alpha(P)$: only if both processes can produce an event, both processes must evolve. If after a trace of events $s \in traces(P \parallel U)$ the test is successful the events ω is produced: $s^\frown\langle\omega\rangle \in traces(P \parallel U)$.

---

[1]The term *experiment*, which Hennessy has used in [ ], was previously introduced in this thesis as *test case*. Both terms can be used synonymously.

Based on this observations Peleska et al. [ ] defined test cases U on a system P, which specify the expected results:

Definition 10.1 *May and Must Tests:*

1. P may *satisfy the test case* U, *if a result of type b) or c) can be observed:*

$$P \text{ may } U \equiv (\exists s : traces(P).s\char`^\langle\omega\rangle \in traces(P \parallel U))$$

2. P must *satisfy the test case* U, *only if results of type b) can be observed.*

$$P \text{ must } U \equiv (\exists Q.(P \parallel U) \setminus (\alpha(U) \setminus \{\omega\}) = \omega \rightarrow Q)$$

A may test only requires, that at least one trace of the system P running in parallel with the test case U produces the ω event to indicate a successful test. On the contrary a must test requires all possible runs of the system to produce the ω event. This is expressed by P must U in definition 10.1: the parallel system of P and U can only produce the ω event, if $P \parallel U$ does neither block nor produce an infinite number of events other than ω before indicating success. This requirement is ensured by $(P \parallel U) \setminus (\alpha(U) \setminus \{\omega\})$, since all events of U except the event ω are hidden from the parallel system. Since $\alpha(P) \subset \alpha(U)$ holds, the event ω must be produced immediately in all test runs to pass the must test. The process Q after signalling success is an arbitrary one, since the test case may terminate immediately after a successful run.

Unfortunately it is impossible to specify an additional event, that indicates the failure of a test case, since the system P may diverge or block, such that no event can ever be produced anymore. Therefore a test error can only be identified by the test system failing to produce the ω event. In real world applications this is no problem, since this can easily be solved with timeouts.

Based on Hennessy's may and must tests and the correctness requirements introduced in the previous section, it is possible to define test cases in CSP which detect certain types of failures:

Definition 10.2 *Let U be a test case.*

1. U *detects a safety failure* s *iff*

$$\forall P.P \text{ must } U \Rightarrow s \notin traces(P)$$

2. U *detects a requirements coverage failure* (s, A) *iff*

$$\forall P.P \text{ must } U \Rightarrow (s, A) \notin failures(P)$$

3. U *detects a divergence failure* s *iff*

$$\forall P.P \text{ must } U \Rightarrow s \notin divergences(P)$$

4. *U detects a robustness failure s iff*

$$\forall P.P \text{ may } U \Rightarrow s \in traces(P)$$

Such test cases can principally be specified in any (formal) mechanism, since checking those conditions requires only a generated trace of the SUT running in parallel with the test case. In the following only the formal language CSP is considered.

Additionally it is possible to restrict the test cases to a smaller class of *admissible test cases*, as introduced in [ ]. Only those test cases are relevant for tests, for which at least one process successfully performs a must-test. All other test cases do not contribute to finding errors in the SUT. Additionally only those test cases are relevant, which require only a finite number of events, before the situation that should be tested occurs. Finally a termination event is required for the test driver, that indicates, whether a test case is completed. The termination event may occur, as soon as the test case was successfully passed, or directly when it has been established that the test case cannot be completed.

This leads to the definition of four different test classes and a framework for the corresponding test cases specified in CSP:

Definition 10.3 *Hennessy Test Classes*
For the following definitions s always denotes an arbitrary trace consisting only of elements of the alphabet of the system P: $s \in \alpha(P)^*$. Additionally $a \in \alpha(P)$ denotes an element of the alphabet of P, and $A \subseteq \alpha(P)$ is a subset of the alphabet.

1. *Safety Tests $U_S(s, a)$ detect safety failures $s^\frown \langle a \rangle$:*

$$U_S(s, a) = \textbf{if } s = \langle \rangle$$
$$\textbf{then } \omega \to SKIP \ \square \ a \to SKIP$$
$$\textbf{else } \omega \to SKIP \ \square \ head(s) \to U_S(tail(s), a)$$

2. *Requirements Coverage Tests $U_C(s,A)$ detect requirements coverage failures (s,A):*

$$U_C(s, A) = \textbf{if } s = \langle \rangle$$
$$\textbf{then } a : A \to \omega \to SKIP$$
$$\textbf{else } \omega \to SKIP \ \square \ head(s) \to U_C(tail(s), A)$$

3. *Divergence Tests $U_D(s)$ detect divergence failures s:*

$$U_D(s) = \textbf{if } s = \langle \rangle$$
$$\textbf{then } \omega \to SKIP$$
$$\textbf{else } \omega \to SKIP \ \square \ head(s) \to U_D(tail(s))$$

4. Robustness Tests $U_R(s)$ detects robustness failures s:

$$U_R(s) \quad = \quad \textbf{if } s = \langle \rangle$$
$$\textbf{then } \omega \rightarrow SKIP$$
$$\textbf{else } head(s) \rightarrow U_R(tail(s))$$

Safety tests $U_S(s, a)$ are detecting, whether an event a can be produced after the SUT has performed the events of the trace s. To do so – confirming to definition 10.2 – for all possible traces of the system P the test case $U_S(s, a)$ must terminate successfully, except for the trace $s^\frown\langle a\rangle$. Exactly this behaviour is specified in definition 10.3-1: if the system runs in parallel with $U_S(s, a)$, the test case may produce an ω event after each trace of the SUT, but it may also refuse to after the safety violating trace.

Requirements coverage tests $U_C(s, A)$ – also known as *failures tests* in the CSP terminology – check whether the set of events A is refused after the system has produced the trace s. In analogy to the safety tests, the requirements coverage tests may indicate success after each possible trace of the SUT, additionally it accepts any event of the set A after the trace s has been produced. All other events after s are refused to be generated, thus no ω events is being emitted. Therefore these type of tests are detecting requirement coverage failures (s, A).

Divergence tests $U_D(s)$ are detecting divergences failures on traces s. To achieve this, the test specification must create positive test results for all traces other than s. Additionally it must terminate successfully, if the trace s has been produced without diverging. If the SUT diverges during or after the trace s, the test specification cannot produce the required ω event and the must-test fails, since there is at least one run of the system, which does not lead to a successful termination, hence the required property of definition 10.3-3 fails.

Robustness test $U_R(s)$ have to ensure, that the SUT can produce a specified trace s. The corresponding test case must only accept those events in the order as appearing in the trace. If the SUT refuses any event of the trace at any time, the test deadlocks and therefore fails, since the SUT and the test specification can only produce events simultaneously. But since the robustness tests are only may-tests, it is sufficient, to have at least one run of the SUT, which produces the trace P.

As Peleska proves in [ ] a direct relationship between Hennessy's test classes and the CSP refinement operators can be established.

Theorem 10.1 *The classes $U_S(s, a)$, $U_C(s, A)$, $U_D(s)$ and $U_R(s)$ of test cases are related to T-, F-, FD- and FDR-refinement as follows.*

1. *If* $\forall\, a \in \alpha(SPEC), s \in \alpha(SPEC)^*.SPEC$ must $U_S(s,a) \Rightarrow IMP$ must $U_S(s,a)$
   then SPEC $\sqsubseteq_T$ *IMP.*

2. *If* $\forall\, s \in \alpha(SPEC)^*, A \subseteq \alpha(SPEC)$. *SPEC* $\sqsubseteq_T IMP \wedge SPEC$ must $U_C(s,A)$
   $$\Rightarrow IMP \text{ must } U_C(s,A)$$
   then SPEC $\sqsubseteq_F$ *IMP.*

3. *If* $\forall\, s \in \alpha(SPEC)^*.$ *SPEC* $\sqsubseteq_F IMP \wedge SPEC$ must $U_D(s) \Rightarrow IMP$ must $U_D(s)$
   then SPEC $\sqsubseteq_{FD}$ *IMP.*

4. *If* $\forall\, s \in \alpha(SPEC)^*.$ *SPEC* $\sqsubseteq_{FD} IMP \wedge SPEC$ may $U_R(s) \Rightarrow IMP$ may $U_R(s)$
   then SPEC $\sqsubseteq_{FDR}$ *IMP.*

These results can be employed to formulate a thrustworthy test driver for Untimed CSP based specifications of safety critical reactive systems. Such test driver will be presented in section 11.1. The extension of this results to Timed CSP has been accomplished by Oliver Meyer's structural decomposition theorem, which been explained earlier in this section.

10.3 Automated Test Systems

Testing of embedded systems gets more and more important, since an increasing number of computer systems are used to control safety critical processes in everyday-life products. The systems tend to gain complexity, which makes it almost impossible to give a complete formal specification of the systems behaviour, so that the systems could be formally verified. This is where specification based testing fills a gap between classical manual testing and formal verification. *Specifications* in languages with a formally defined semantics allow an precise interpretation of the specified behaviour, which is usually not possible with informal, natural language documents. Testing based on such specifications allows an automated test case generation and online test evaluation.

In this section we are going to explain a general structure of a test automation system. After that the components of an actual implementation of such automated test systems – the RT-Tester – are described in detail, since later chapters of this thesis will introduce mechanisms for automated testing with synchronisation terms and high level transition graphs, implemented as an RT-Tester module.

10.3.1   General Structure of Automated Test Systems

Figure 10.3 illustrates the structure of an conceptual test automation system. In the following we are going to introduce those terms, which can be found in the figure in more detail.

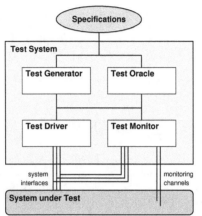

Figure 10.3: Structure of a Test Automation System

The basis for automated testing are *specifications*, in a language with a well defined semantics, that allow automatic interpretation. Possible specification formalisms are for example timed automata, state charts, trace assertions or CSP specifications. Not all formalisms can be applied to each of the following building blocks, but they can easily be used for at least one of them.

The task of creating test cases from formal specifications is performed by the *Test Generator*. Since the only possibility to influence the SUT is via its interfaces, the test generator requires a specification of the environments behaviour. It must be able to generate all possible sequences of events, that can be produced by the environment. If the SUT is non-deterministic, it is not only sufficient to generate inputs of the SUT, but also to receive its outputs, which allows to determine which state the system is in. Depending on the determined state, new test cases have to be created immediately, which is expressed by the term *on-the-fly test generation*. Another advantage of this approach is, that the on-the-fly test generation allows non-terminating environment specifications. Therefore it is not necessary, to develop one environment specification for each test case, but it is sufficient to have one, from which all relevant behaviour can be determined. Typical specification languages for the test generator are CSP specifications and state charts. Other formalisms like trace assertions are not appropriate, since it is not possible to specify non-terminating behaviour with this formalisms.

But not only the continuous production of events by the test generator is required for testing purposes. Sometimes it is also required, that a SUT must produce outputs, if no input data is provided. Therefore the test generator must also be able to *refuse* certain inputs to the system under test, to inspect the outcome of those tests. This type of testing is called *refusal testing*.

The *Test Driver* accesses the interfaces of the SUT and interprets the test cases generated by the test generator. To achieve this, each action of the test case is translated into data on the input interfaces, which simulates an accordingly behaving environment. Outputs of the SUT are either used to change the internal simulation of the environment or translated to information, which can be processed by the other components of the automated test system.

As stated before, the test generator can produce an infinite number of inputs for the SUT, but it cannot determine, whether all relevant test cases have been produced, to achieve the required *test coverage*. This is the task of the *Test Monitor*. It inspects the input and output interfaces of the SUT and collects information, which relevant test cases already have been executed. Additionally it may monitor the internal state of the SUT via monitoring channels, e.g. to check, whether the required test coverage has already been achieved; or it may even force the SUT into states, which cannot be reached by controlling the input interface.

The fourth building block of the generic automated test system is the *Test Oracle*, which is also called *Test Evaluator*. It observes the generated inputs from the test generator and the outputs of the SUT. A formal specification of the SUT's behaviour is applied to check, whether the recorded traces are conforming to the system specification. These checks can be done by any formalism, which allows to partially describe the systems behaviour, e.g. trace assertions, CSP specifications, etc. The test oracle must be able to find all violations of the specified behaviour. Therefore the specification used for this purpose is usually more complex than the one used for test generation, since not only the environments behaviour, but also the systems responses has to be modelled.

Additionally the test oracle should do an *on-the-fly test evaluation*, which determines in real-time, whether a test case was successfully passed or failed. This is necessary, since it is not desirable for automated tests to stop after each single error. On the contrary, the test oracle should be able to find a valid execution step, after which a failed test can be resumed. Especially for long-term tests, which usually runs for days and weeks, this property is important.

10.3.2   RT-Tester

One software product, which can be used for specification based testing is the RT-Tester tool, developed in cooperation of Verified Systems International GmbH and University Bremen. "The RT-Tester tool has been designed to perform automated *hardware-in-the-loop tests* and *software component tests* on process or thread level for embedded real-time systems." [   ] In figure 10.4 the structure of RT-Tester's modules can be observed, which will be described on the following pages.

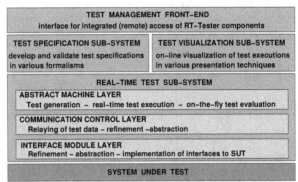

Figure 10.4: Structure of the modules of the RT-Tester

Structure of the RT-Tester Components

The core component of the automated test system RT-Tester is the *Real-Time Test Sub-System*, since the modules belonging to this system are representing the four test components that have been described in the previous section.

Communication between the different components in this subsystem- employs an event passing mechanism, that is implemented in the *Communication Control Layer* (CCL). Each event that is produced as an output by any component of the real-time test sub-system functions as an input for several other components. To achieve this the CCL requires an event map table, which describes all possible communications between the modules for the current test configuration.

The interfaces of the SUT, are accessed from modules in the *Interface Module Layer*. Each *interface module* (IFM) functions as an abstraction module, which translates abstract events that are received via the CCL to concrete data on the systems interfaces. Concrete outputs on the interfaces of the SUT are conversely abstracted to events, that can be passed by the CCL to other modules of the real-time test sub-system. The abstractions implemented in the interface modules must usually be adapted for each SUT separately, since the abstraction function differs for each project, even if the systems interface is a standardised component, since the payload is usually not standardised.

Generating test cases and on-the-fly test evaluation are tasks of the *Abstract Machine Layer*. Therefore each *abstract machine* (AM) implements the behaviour of a timed state machine, which describes the desired behaviour of the SUT under changing environment conditions. During test execution each AM may change the state of the simulated environment as well as check whether the outputs of the SUT are allowed by the system specification. The functionality of an embedded controller is usually so complex, that it is not possible to model everything inside only one AM. Therefore it is possible to have several AMs running in parallel each testing a subset of the desired requirements. A useful design pattern is to have specialised AMs, which stimulate the changes of the environment simulation, while other machines are specialised only on checking the results of the SUT. The test evaluation, which checks for the correctness of timing, input/output sequences or produced data values, can occur in real-time during test execution or later by replaying the log files of each test run.

In the *Test Specification Sub-System* the specifications of the tests for the SUT are developed, validated and translated into a form, that can easily be interpreted in real-time from abstract machines. The commonly used mechanism in the RT-Tester tool are CSP specifications. With a model checker like FDR it is possible to make refinement checks of the developed specifications, to prove that the CSP specification satisfies the requirements of the system specification. Additionally FDR is used in RT-Tester to transform the CSP specification into a transition system, which binary representation can be interpreted in real-time by an abstract machine, as will be explained later.

Another possibility to develop abstract machines are *Customised Abstract Machines*. A well defined framework for customised AMs can be used to implement the behaviour of an AM completely in a C/C++ program, which seamlessly integrates into the abstract machine layer. This mechanism is especially useful, if a checking abstract machine specified in CSP would result in a state explosion of the transition system. This occurs often for larger processes which are heavily data dependant. For such applications customised abstract machines are often easier and faster to implement than to develop several formal specifications that do not state explode.

The *Test Visualisation Sub-System* allows different views on ongoing and already performed tests, by visualising the recorded traces by graphical means, which is especially useful during the debugging of a specification, that is currently been developed. One component of the sub-system is provided in the RT-Tester software distribution. This module visualises events using textual displays, radio buttons, y/t-diagrams or histograms. More complex abstractions like a 3D simulation of the application domain can be developed separately and are easily integrated.

Managing test execution is the task of the *Test Management Front-End*. Under UNIX there exists several command line programs, that can be used in a flexible way, to achieve the desired tasks. Additionally a test management server exists, allowing remote access to the most common functions of the RT-Tester, like editing specifications, executing and stopping test and creating test documentation. This server can be accessed by clients of various platforms due to the open interface definition available for the test management server.

Abstract Machines

As described above the abstract machines of the RT-Tester provide the functions of the test generator and test oracle simultaneously. Even though there are several different types of abstract machines in the RT-Tester system available, the most commonly used is the one, which interprets a transition systems of CSP specifications.

The task of converting CSP into transition systems is performed by the model checker FDR, which creates a normal form transition system from a CSP specification. This type of transition graphshave already been introduced in section 2.5.5. Such normal form graphs do not contain any non-determinism and internal τ actions. This structure allows a simple and efficient way to traverse the graphs within bounded time, because no backtracking is necessary to decide, whether a certain event is possible in any state.

Since each abstract machine interacts with other modules in the AML, it is necessary to define the interfaces for each specification on which the components interact. To achieve this, the channel definitions of the CSP specification are enriched with additional meta information specifying which channels are used as input or output channels to communicate with other abstract machines. Additionally some channels may be marked as internal channels, which are used only for internal communication of processes inside the AM. The timed behaviour of each CSP specification is modelled by timers, that can be set by the specification. As soon as a previously set timer elapses, the abstract machine offers to produce a corresponding elapsed timer event. Finally there are events marking test errors and test warnings. *Test errors* mark situations, from which the abstract machine cannot recover, while *test warnings* only indicate, that something unexpected has occurred, but the system may still act according to the specification afterwards (e.g. a timeout has elapsed, but the system may still produce the expected outputs later).

An abstract machine based on CSP specifications testing a SUT in the failure-divergences model can be implemented as follows: For each state the abstract machine may be in, it is necessary to check first, what events are possible at the moment. This step has to be repeated at certain user defined intervals, since there are special events in the specifications, which deals with setting and elapsed timers. As soon as a timer has elapsed the transition marking this incident may be taken immediately.

The separation of input and output events of an abstract machine requires the use of refusals during evaluating which event can be accepted in the next step. Refusals ensure, that the abstract machine wait for external inputs, rather then producing possible outputs immediately. Therefore all set-timer and output events are removed from a selected acceptance set (which directly corresponds to a refusal), that is used to determine the next event.

As soon as the set of accepted events for the current state are determined, the abstract machine checks if progress can be made. First all special events marking test errors or test warnings are produced if possible, since the specification is in a state, where a test error has been discovered. If marked active in the acceptance set, all events dealing with timers are processed next. If several of those events can be produced in the current state, only one set or elapsed timer event is chosen non-deterministically. Should none of the conditions above lead to the production of an event, the abstract machine checks, whether it may produce any internal or output events.

Finally the AM processes the next input event, that have been sent via the CCL. If the event is in the acceptance set, the abstract machine accepts it to be produced. Otherwise a target system output error occurrs, since another abstract machine or the SUT sent an event, that is not allowed in the current state. In this case the abstract machine produces an error output and stays in the current state to try continuing the test.

After the event selection algorithm has finished, the abstract machine takes the transition labelled with the selected event and continues from the beginning. The selected event is sent to other modules in the abstract machine layer via the CCL, if the event was marked as an output event.

The procedure above and the normal form transition graph guarantees that there is exactly one transition, that can be taken in this step. This whole algorithm can be executed within a bounded amount of time, since it can be determined *a priori*, how many events can occur at maximum in any given state of the transition graph, and additionally the normal form ensures, that no backtracking is required to find out, what events are possible in any state. Therefore this algorithm can be used to test any real-time reactive systems, if only the computer executing the abstract machine is fast enough to execute the algorithm.

Chapter 11

Testing with normalised Transition Graphs

In chapter 10 the basic concepts for testing embedded reactive real-time systems have been explained. This chapter introduces testing algorithms for normalised transition graphs like Roscoe-style normalisation graphs or normal form synchronisation terms, which can directly be derived from parallel high level transition graphs by normalising it according to the algorithms introduced in chapter 8.

The algorithm for testing based on Roscoe-style normalisation graphs, which is explained in section 11.1, is implemented as a CSP abstract machines in the RT-Tester toolkit. As proven in [ ] this implementation is a trustworthy test driver for CSP based transition systems, since it checks an implementation of a system not only by its traces, but also using the failures of the specification.

Based on this, a testing algorithm for parallel systems using synchronisation terms will be introduced in section 11.2. This will allow – under certain restrictions – the checking of specifications against an actual implementation in real-time, without the need to unfold the whole transition system. These restrictions, which allows the evaluation in real-time, will be explained as design patterns for CSP specifications, that will allow the use of normalised synchronisation terms instead of completely unfolded graphs, without effecting the real-time capability of the test algorithm.

11.1   Testing with Roscoe Style Graphs

The RT-Tester tool, as explained earlier in section 10.3, uses formal methods to generate test-cases and perform an on-the-fly evaluation of the test-results. To achieve this, *abstract machines* are interpreting transition systems, which are generated from CSP specifications by the FDR2 model checking tool. Those transition systems have to be normalised, since the execution in real-time requires, that an upper bound for the calculation of the next events, which are allowed by the specification, can be given. This is only possible for normalised transition systems, since otherwise τ-events or non-determinism may require the use of backtracking to determine the following state in the transition system after an event has been produced.

Below a trustworthy test driver for $\sqsubseteq_{FD}$-refinement will be given, which was suggested by Jan Peleska [, p. 132] and is implemented in the RT-Tester abstract machines. This test driver requires a specification of the abstract behaviour $ASYS$ of the target system and an additional environment specification E, which is simulated by the test driver itself. The implementation SYS of the target system is the only required input, since the generated trace, consisting of elements of the set of observable actions I, is used to check the systems behaviour against its specification. The set of observable actions I containing those events on which the environment E communicates with the target systems SYS or $ASYS$.

In the following specification an abbreviation P_I is used, which hides all events but those in I from a process P: $P_I = P \setminus (\alpha(P) \setminus I)$. A trustworthy test driver for $\sqsubseteq_{FD}$-tests is defined by the collection of test cases $\mathcal{U} = \{U(n) \mid n \in \mathbb{N}\}$, where $U(n)$ is defined as follows:

$$U(n) = U(n, \langle \rangle)$$
$$U(n, s) =$$
$$(\#s = n \lor A(s) = \emptyset) \,\&\, (\omega \to SKIP)$$
$$\square$$
$$(\#s < n) \,\&\, (e : ([E_I/s]^0 \setminus [ASYS_I/s]^0) \to \dagger \to SKIP)$$
$$\square$$
$$(\#s < n-1 \land R(s) \neq \emptyset) \,\&\, (\textstyle\bigsqcap R : R(s) \bullet U(n, s, [(E \parallel ASYS)_I/s]^0 \setminus R))$$
$$\square$$
$$(\#s = n-1 \land A(s) \neq \emptyset) \,\&\, (\textstyle\bigsqcap R : refMax(E_I/s), A : A(s) \bullet U(n, s, A \setminus R))$$
$$U(n, s, M) = e : M \to U(n, s^\frown \langle e \rangle))$$

where

$$A(s) = \{\, A : \mathcal{P}(I) \mid A \subseteq [(E \parallel ASYS)_I/s]^0$$
$$\land\, (\forall R : Ref((E \parallel ASYS)_I/s) \bullet A \not\subseteq R)$$
$$\land\, (\forall X : \mathcal{P}(A) - \{A\} \bullet (\exists R : Ref((E \parallel ASYS)_I/s) \bullet X \not\subseteq R))\}$$
$$R(s) = \{R : Ref(E_I/s) \mid [(E \parallel ASYS)_I/s]^0 \setminus R \neq \emptyset\}$$

The test algorithm $U(n)$ specified in CSP produces traces with a maximum length of n, starting with the empty trace. An execution of the specification simulates the environment E, while test cases $U_S(s, a)$ and $U_C(s, A)$ are exercised on the target system. Such simultaneous simulation of the test oracle and generation of test cases is called *on-the-fly test evaluation*.

First we start with a description of the auxiliary functions A and R: $A(s)$ denotes a set of event sets, which cannot be completely refused by $(E \parallel ASYS)_I$

after the trace s. $R(s)$ denotes a set of those refusals of the environment E_I after the trace s, that do not block the operation of $(E \parallel ASYS)_I$ completely.

For each trace s, which has not reached its maximum length n, the algorithm $U(n, s)$ checks in its second branch, if the target system SYS can produce any event e, which can be produced by interacting with E_I/s. If this event cannot be produced by $ASYS_I/s$ as well, a test error has been discovered, that is being marked with the event †. The test execution stops after this event, since the abstract target system specification cannot be used any longer to check the behaviour of the implemented system, since either the specification $ASYS$ is incomplete or the target system SYS does not behave according to its specification.

If $(\#s < n-1)$ and the set of refusals $R(s)$ is not empty, the test driver non-deterministically chooses one of the current refusals and tries to exercise those events on the target system, that are possible by $(E \parallel ASYS)_I/s$, but which are not in the selected refusal. The target system may now only produce those selected events. If other events are being generated a test error has occurred. Alternatively the system may block after the trace s, which is covered by the first branch of the test algorithm, since in this case $A(s)$ is empty. In that case, or if the maximum length of the trace s is reached, the test case signals success by producing the event ω.

With these combination of test cases, the test driver can detect trace failures up to a length of $n-1$. Additionally $U(s, n)$ detects requirement coverage errors occurring after a trace s of the length of $n-1$.

Even though this test driver algorithm works on CSP specifications it can also by applied to normalised transition systems as well. As already shown earlier, each CSP specification can be transferred into a normalised labelled transition system, where for each node l the initial events $[l]^0$ and the refusals $refusals(l)$ can be derived. Additionally we have also stated earlier, that each trace s produced by any CSP process P leads to exactly one state in the corresponding labelled transition system, which is represented by P/s.

If it is possible to specify an abstraction for the other formalisms introduced in this thesis, which allows an interpretation of the formalism as a normalised transition system, the test driver algorithm can be used without any changes for all other formalisms.

11.2 Testing with Synchronisation Terms

Testing based on CSP specifications requires them to be transformed into a labelled transition system. The testing algorithm, that has been explained in section 11.1 requires a normal form transition system, in which all non-determinism has been eliminated and which nodes are marked with the initial events and refusals or acceptances, such that the system under test can be checked against its specification in the failures model of CSP.

The interpretation of synchronisation terms has already been introduced in definition 5.31, giving rules on how the structure of the synchronization term changes, as soon as an event is produced. Additionally a normal form of synchronisation terms has been explained in section 8.3, in which all τ- and π-events and the non-determinism has been removed from the high level transition graphs representing the sequential components of the parallel system. Using these normal forms of synchronisation terms and high level transition graphs, an on-the-fly normalisation for synchronisation terms is introduced in this section, which allows the use of the unchanged test driver algorithm from section 11.1.

11.2.1 Multiple Synchronisation Terms

Using the abstraction of synchronisation terms as labelled transition systems to interpret them, as explained in section 5.2.3, allows a simple view on which all considerations of conventional labelled transition systems can be applied to. E.g. the transition system may be non-deterministic, which means, that there can be more than one synchronisation term that can be generated by producing a single event. In the area of testing non-deterministic transition systems cannot be used to specify a systems behaviour to check against in real-time. This problem occurs, since it is not possible to determine a unique following state in a non-deterministic transition system. It may be required to use backtracking to find a state, which satisfies the observed trace of the system under test. To prevent such problems transition system used for testing purposes are normalised according to the algorithms in chapter 8.

Synchronisation terms cannot be completely normalised, since this would require to unfold the transition system, which should be prevented by this approach. But they can be normalised as far as possible as described in section 8.3. Therefore we are going to introduce another representation for synchronisation terms, which allows to model several different synchronisation terms in a single representation. Each subterm of a *multiple synchronisation terms* may therefore contain not only one, but a set of terms. This allows to simultaneously model several states of the parallel system in one representation, which can be used to describe an on-the-fly normalisation for processes, to determine a deterministic following multiple synchronisation term for any state the system is in.

Definition 11.1 *Multiple Synchronisation Terms*
A multiple synchronisation term can be used to describe a set of synchronisation terms using one single representation. In the following $s \subseteq \Sigma$ is a synchronisation set and $h \subseteq \Sigma$ denotes a hiding set.

$$
\begin{aligned}
\Lambda^* \quad := \quad & (HLTG_i, l_i, \varepsilon_i) & & \textit{where } l_i \in L_i \textit{ is a location of } HLTG_i \\
& & & \textit{and } \varepsilon_i \in Env \textit{ is an environment for } HLTG_i. \\
| \quad & (h, \Lambda_h^*) & & \textit{where } \Lambda_h^* \subseteq \Lambda^* \\
| \quad & (s, \Lambda_{s_1 \times s_2}^*) & & \textit{where } \Lambda_{s_1 \times s_2}^* \subseteq \Lambda^* \times \Lambda^*
\end{aligned}
$$

In contrast to definition 5.30, where each λ in a term references only one synchronisation term, each Λ in definition 11.1 references a set of multiple synchronisation terms. If each Λ in a multiple synchronisation term contains exactly one element, it is semantically equivalent to a synchronisation term as explained in 5.2.3. Based on this observation it is possible to define, whether or not a multiple synchronisation term is representing a deterministic transition system.

Definition 11.2 *Determinism:*
A multiple synchronisation term Λ^* is deterministic, if there exists no interpretation starting at the initial term, in which there exists a set of the resulting terms containing more than one multiple synchronisation term.

The multiple synchronisation terms allows the representation of several different synchronisation terms in a single representation, which reuses identical parts of the terms. Minimal differences in the leafs of the tree structure of two synchronisation term are represented as two elements of the set at the leafs of the multiple synchronisation term representing both terms in one representation. This ability to represent more than one synchronisation term in one term implies, that the use of the abbreviation, which has been employed for synchronisation terms, is not ingenious.

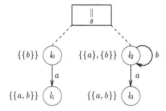

Figure 11.1: A Synchronisation Term for the Process SYS

Since the multiple synchronisation terms differ slightly form the synchronisation terms that have been introduced earlier, an example will be given to illustrate the usage of these terms. For that the following **CSP** specification will be used, which describes two interleaved processes, which share the common set event $\{a\}$, without synchronising on it.

$$SYS = P \;|||\; Q$$
$$P = a \rightarrow STOP$$
$$Q = P \sqcap b \rightarrow Q$$

As a result of the normalisation of the process SYS the synchronisation term $((HLTG_P, l_0, \varepsilon_P), \emptyset, (HLTG_Q, l_2, \varepsilon_Q))$ is returned, which is illustrated in figure

11.1. Since the synchronisation term is in its normal form, the high level transition graphs $HLTG_P$ and $HLTG_Q$ are normalised to a labelled transition system without conditions and assignments. For the execution this initial synchronisation term has to be transformed in its corresponding multiple synchronisation term, which looks as follows: $(\emptyset, \{((HLTG_P, l_0, \varepsilon_P), (HLTG_Q, l_2, \varepsilon_Q))\})$.

A multiple synchronisation term representing more than one state pairs can be used to express non-determinism. Therefore we consider the multiple synchronisation term that results, if the event a is executed in the initial state. The result could be any of the two following synchronisation terms, depending on which transition has been taken:

$$\left(\emptyset, \left\{\left((HLTG_P, l_0, \varepsilon_P), (HLTG_Q, l_3, \varepsilon_Q)\right)\right\}\right)$$
$$\left(\emptyset, \left\{\left((HLTG_P, l_1, \varepsilon_P), (HLTG_Q, l_2, \varepsilon_Q)\right)\right\}\right)$$

The multiple synchronisation term representing both states simultaneously would look as follows:

$$\left(\emptyset, \left\{\left((HLTG_P, l_0, \varepsilon_P), (HLTG_Q, l_3, \varepsilon_Q)\right), \left((HLTG_P, l_1, \varepsilon_P), (HLTG_Q, l_2, \varepsilon_Q)\right)\right\}\right)$$

11.2.2 On-the-fly Normalisation of Multiple Synchronisation Terms

In this section we are going to describe an on-the-fly normalisation for multiple synchronisation terms which allows an interpretation as normalised labelled transition system. Such abstraction is employed to use multiple synchronisation terms for automated testing of real-time systems.

To achieve this, an interpretation of multiple synchronisation terms will be introduced in definition 11.3. This interpretation already creates a deterministic multiple synchronisation term for non-deterministic systems, that results from shared alphabets of parallel processes without synchronising on these events. Even though the normalisation of the sequential processes removes all τ-events, those events are produced again during the interpretation by the hiding operators in the multiple synchronisation term. Those τ-events will be eliminated again later during the on-the-fly normalisation of the multiple synchronisation terms.

Definition 11.3 *Interpretation of Multiple Synchronisation Terms:*
If a multiple synchronisation term λ_1^* produces an event α, its structure changes to λ_2^*, which is denoted by $\lambda_1^* \xrightarrow{\alpha} \lambda_2^*$, where the following rules apply:

1. *λ_1^* denotes a leaf of the multiple synchronisation term.*

$$(HLTG_i, l_i, \varepsilon_i) \xrightarrow{\alpha} (HLTG_i, l_i', \varepsilon_i')$$
$$\Leftrightarrow l_i, \varepsilon_i \xmapsto{\alpha} l_i', \varepsilon_i'$$

2. λ_1^* *represents a hiding operator* (h, Λ_h^*):

$$(h, \Lambda_h^*) \xrightarrow{\alpha} (h, \Lambda_h^{*\prime})$$
$$\Leftrightarrow \Lambda_h^{*\prime} = \{\lambda^{*\prime} \mid \exists \lambda^* \in \Lambda_h^* \ . \ (\ (\lambda^* \xrightarrow{\alpha} \lambda^{*\prime} \wedge \alpha \notin h)$$
$$\vee (\exists \alpha' \in h \ . \ \lambda^* \xrightarrow{\alpha'} \lambda^{*\prime} \wedge \alpha = \tau))\}$$
$$\wedge \Lambda_h^{*\prime} \neq \emptyset$$

3. λ_1^* *represents a parallel operator* $(s, \Lambda_{S1 \times S2}^*)$:

$$(s, \Lambda_{S1 \times S2}^*) \xrightarrow{\alpha} (s, \Lambda_{S1 \times S2}^{*\prime})$$
$$\Leftrightarrow \Lambda_{S1 \times S2}^{*\prime} = \{(\lambda_1^{*\prime}, \lambda_2^{*\prime}) \mid (\lambda_1^*, \lambda_2^*) \in \Lambda_{S1 \times S2}^* \wedge$$
$$((\lambda_1^* \xrightarrow{\alpha} \lambda_1^{*\prime} \wedge \lambda_2^* = \lambda_2^{*\prime} \wedge \alpha \notin s)$$
$$\vee (\lambda_1^* = \lambda_1^{*\prime} \wedge \lambda_2^* \xrightarrow{\alpha} \lambda_2^{*\prime} \wedge \alpha \notin s)$$
$$\vee (\lambda_1^* \xrightarrow{\alpha} \lambda_1^{*\prime} \wedge \lambda_2^* \xrightarrow{\alpha} \lambda_2^{*\prime} \wedge \alpha \in s))\}$$
$$\wedge \Lambda_{S1 \times S2}^{*\prime} \neq \emptyset$$

Such multiple synchronisation term can be applied not only to high level transition graphs but also to normal form transition systems like normalised high level transition graphs. In those cases the environment of the references to the sequential graphs is always empty, since normalised graphs do not contain any conditions, expressions or assignments anymore.

For the further considerations a notation will be required, that is going to be introduced below. The notation $\lambda^* \xrightarrow{\sigma} \lambda^{*\prime}$ with $\sigma = \alpha_1 \cdot \ldots \cdot \alpha_n$ denotes that it is possible to reach the target multiple synchronisation term $\lambda^{*\prime}$ from an initial multiple synchronisation term λ^* via the trace of events $\langle \alpha_1, ..., \alpha_n \rangle$.

Definition 11.4 *Repeated Interpretation Steps:*

$$\lambda^* \xrightarrow{\sigma} \lambda^{*\prime} = \exists \lambda_0^*, ..., \lambda_n^* \ . \ \lambda_0^* \xrightarrow{\alpha_1} \lambda_1^* \wedge ... \wedge \lambda_{n-1}^* \xrightarrow{\alpha_n} \lambda_n^*$$
$$\wedge \lambda^* = \lambda_0^* \wedge \lambda^{*\prime} = \lambda_n^* \wedge \sigma = \alpha_1 \cdot \ldots \cdot \alpha_n$$

Each execution step of a multiple synchronisation term results in a new term representing the target state of the transition system. The test execution in real-time requires, that transition systems are deterministic so that no backtracking is required during the traversal of the transition system. The rules for the interpretation of the multiple synchronisation terms already deal with the non-determinism, that could be introduced by the parallel operator. Additionally the sequential transition systems represented by the leafs of the terms are also completely normalised and hence deterministic. Thus only the hiding operator can introduce non-determinism by the production of τ-events. The following definition describes a normalisation instruction for the hiding operator:

Definition 11.5 *On-the-fly Normalisation:*
Hiding events from a multiple synchronisation term leads to the introduction of
τ-*events to the specification. The function* $normalise(\lambda^*)$ *for the hiding operator,*
denotes a multiple synchronisation term, in which all possible chains of τ-*events*
have been taken. For the other operators the functions is the identity.

1. $normalise(HLTG_i, l_i, \varepsilon_i) = (HLTG_i, l_i, \varepsilon_i)$

2. $normalise(h, \Lambda_h^*) = (h, \{\lambda^{*'} \mid \lambda^* \xrightarrow{\sigma} \lambda^{*'} \wedge \lambda^* \in \Lambda_h^* \wedge \sigma = \alpha_1 \cdot ... \cdot \alpha_n$
   $\wedge \forall i \in \{1, ..., n\} . \alpha_i \in h\} \cup \Lambda_h^*)$

3. $normalise(s, \Lambda_{S1 \times S2}^*) = (s, \Lambda_{S1 \times S2}^*)$

To apply the test algorithm described in section 11.1 to multiple synchronisation term, it is necessary that it is possible to determine the initial actions and
maximal refusals or minimal acceptances for any state the system may be in.

The initial actions of a multiple synchronisation term are those events, that
can be directly produced from the on-the-fly normalised term. The on-the-fly
normalisation of the term is required, since otherwise a hiding subterm could introduce τ-events in the set of initial events, which would violate the requirements
of the test algorithm.

Definition 11.6 *Initial Actions*
The initial actions $[\lambda^*]^0$ *of a multiple synchronisation term* λ^* *are defined as*
follows:

$$[\lambda^*]^0 = \{\alpha \mid \exists \lambda^{*'} . normalise(\lambda^*) \xrightarrow{\alpha} \lambda^{*'}\}$$

For a testing algorithm still the computation of the refusals or acceptance sets
is required. The following rules for the calculation of the refusals of a multiple
synchronisation term are adopted from the corresponding rules in the stable-
failures model of the denotational semantics. The acceptance sets for multiple
synchronisation terms can be determined according to the rules described in
section 3.2.3.

Definition 11.7 *Refusal calculation for Multiple Synchronisation Terms.*

1. $refusals(HLTG_i, l_i, \varepsilon_i)$ *denotes the refusals of the location* l_i*. The refusals*
   have been calculated during the normalisation process and are available as
   attributes to the locations of the high level transition graphs.

2. $refusals(h, \Lambda_h^*)$ *are the refusals resulting from the process of hiding the events*
   from h *in all multiple synchronisation terms in* Λ_h^**. Therefore all those*
   multiple synchronisation term have to be computed, that can be reached from
   Λ_h^* *via any chains of events from* h*, which is described by* $normalise(h, \Lambda_h^*)$*.*

According to the rules of the denotational semantics only those refusals of the multiple synchronisation terms are contained in the normalised node, which contain all events from the hiding set:

$$refusals(h, \Lambda_h^*) = \{R \mid \exists \Lambda_h^{*\prime} \, . \, (h, \Lambda^{*\prime}) = normalise(h, \Lambda_h^*) \wedge$$
$$\exists \lambda^* \in \Lambda^{*\prime}. \, h \cup R \in refusals(\lambda^*)\}$$

3. $refusals(s, \Lambda_{S1 \times S2}^*)$ *denote the refusals of the parallel system consisting of the pairs of multiple synchronisation terms in $\Lambda_{S1 \times S2}^*$, synchronising on the events in s.*

$$refusals(s, \Lambda_{S1 \times S2}^*) = \{R_1 \cup R_2 \mid (\lambda_1^*, \lambda_2^*) \in \Lambda_{S1 \times S2}^*$$
$$\wedge R_1 \in refusals(\lambda_1^*)$$
$$\wedge R_2 \in refusals(\lambda_2^*)$$
$$\wedge R_1 \setminus (s \cup \{\checkmark\}) = R_2 \setminus (s \cup \{\checkmark\})\}$$

An Example for the Parallel Operator

In the following an exemplary interpretation using multiple synchronisation terms is going to be described in detail. For this the example from section 11.2.1 and figure 11.1 is going to be considered again, but here an examplary execution of the specification is presented.

The initial multiple synchronisation term for the execution of the process SYS is $\lambda_0^* = (\emptyset, \{((HLTG_P, l_0, \varepsilon_P), (HLTG_Q, l_2, \varepsilon_Q))\})$ and the execution begins with determining, which events are possible for the parallel system, by examining the sequential subprocesses. $HLTG_P$ in location l_0 can only produce the event a, while in location l_2 of $HLTG_Q$ either a or b can be produced. Therefore the initial events of this location are the events a or b, from which only the event b can be refused to be produced according to rule 3 of definition 11.7.

Producing the event b results in a new multiple synchronisation term, where all sets, that may contain multiple synchronisation terms, consists of exactly one element. The resulting multiple synchronisation term still remains in the locations l_0 and l_2, since the event b is not in any synchronisation set and can only be produced in $HLTG_Q$. Since $(HLTG_Q, l_2, \varepsilon_Q) \xrightarrow{b} (HLTG_Q, l_2, \varepsilon_Q)$ and the application of rule 3 of definition 11.3 the result looks as follows: $(\emptyset, \{((HLTG_P, l_0, \varepsilon_P), (HLTG_Q, l_2, \varepsilon_Q))\})$, which is identical to λ_0^*.

$$\lambda_0^* \xrightarrow{b} \lambda_0^*$$

In contrast to that is the production of the event a in the initial state: since a is not in the synchronisation set of the multiple synchronisation term and it can be performed in both high level transition graphs it cannot be determined from the outside, in which state the SUT is. Therefore the multiple synchronisation term has to be normalised on-the-fly, which means, that the term should represent all possible states of the system simultaneously.

Since either $(HLTG_P, l_0, \varepsilon_P) \xrightarrow{a} (HLTG_P, l_1, \varepsilon'_P)$ or $(HLTG_Q, l_2, \varepsilon_Q) \xrightarrow{a}$ $(HLTG_Q, l_3, \varepsilon'_Q)$ can be performed, the multiple synchronisation term representing the following state must contain both combinations of locations in it: $\lambda_1^* = (\emptyset, \{((HLTG_P, l_1, \varepsilon'_P), (HLTG_Q, l_2, \varepsilon_Q)), ((HLTG_P, l_0, \varepsilon_P), (HLTG_Q, l_3, \varepsilon'_Q))\})$.

$$\lambda_0^* \xrightarrow{a} \lambda_1^*$$

The resulting multiple synchronisation term λ_1^* represents two possible combinations of location pairs. Therefore the refusals of the represented state must be computed using the refusals for the pairs (l_0, l_3) and (l_1, l_2) simultaneously. For the following calculation it is important to note, that the refusals in figure 11.1 represent only the maximal refusals of the corresponding node.

$$
\begin{aligned}
refusals(HLTG_P, l_0, \varepsilon_P) &= \{\{b\}, \{\}\} \\
refusals(HLTG_Q, l_3, \varepsilon_Q) &= \{\{a, b\}, \{a\}, \{b\}, \{\}\} \\
refusals(HLTG_P, l_1, \varepsilon_P) &= \{\{a, b\}, \{a\}, \{b\}, \{\}\} \\
refusals(HLTG_Q, l_2, \varepsilon_Q) &= \{\{a\}, \{b\}, \{\}\} \\
refusals(\emptyset, \lambda_1^*) &= \{R_1 \cup R_2 \mid\ (\lambda_1^*, \lambda_2^*) \in \Lambda_{S1 \times S2}^* \\
&\qquad\qquad \wedge R_1 \in refusals(\lambda_1^*) \\
&\qquad\qquad \wedge R_2 \in refusals(\lambda_2^*) \\
&\qquad\qquad \wedge R_1 \setminus \{\checkmark\} = R_2 \setminus \{\checkmark\}\} \\
&= \{\{a\}, \{b\}\}
\end{aligned}
$$

If the next event that can be observed is the event b it is clear, that the state of the system must have been (l_1, l_2), since b is only available in the location l_2. The interpretation rules must produce the only following state (l_1, l_2), that the system can have after producing the trace $\langle a, b\rangle$. The computation for rule 3 of definition 11.3 takes all pairs of multiple synchronisation terms containd in its set $\Lambda_{S1 \times S2}^*$ and checks, if one of those terms can produce the selected event, which is not in the synchronisation set. If the event cannot be produced by a selected pair of locations, this combination cannot represent the original state of the SUT, which generated the observed trace. Therefore the pair of locations must be disregarded for the following interpretation step. The resulting multiple synchronisation term after the production of the trace $\langle a, b\rangle$ is once again completely deterministic:

$\lambda_1^* \xrightarrow{b} \lambda_2^*$, with
$\lambda_2^* = (\emptyset, \{((HLTG_P, l_1, \varepsilon'_P), (HLTG_Q, l_2, \varepsilon_Q))\})$

On the other hand the production of the event a in the non-deterministic state after the trace $\langle a\rangle$, leads also to a deterministic following state, since both combinations of state pairs in the multiple synchronisation term set of the parallel term lead to the same target state:

$$\lambda_1^* \xrightarrow{a} \lambda_3^* , \text{ with}$$
$$\lambda_3^* = (\emptyset, \{((HLTG_P, l_1, \varepsilon_P'), (HLTG_Q, l_3, \varepsilon_Q'))\})$$

In this resulting multiple synchronisation term no events can be produced at all, since both locations l_1 and l_3 are representing a $STOP$-state, that can refuse all events to be produced, resulting in the maximum refusal set $\{\{a, b\}\} = \{\Sigma\}$.

An Example for the Hiding Operator

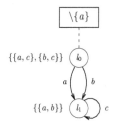

Figure 11.2: Interpreting a Multiple Synchronisation Term with Hiding

In this second example the effect of the multiple synchronisation term representing the hiding operator will be explained. The multiple synchronisation term in figure 11.2 could represent the following simple process with the alphabet $\Sigma = \{a, b, c\}$.

$$SYS = (a \to C \sqcap b \to C) \setminus \{a\}$$
$$C = c \to C$$

The multiple synchronisation term $\lambda_0^* = (\{a\}, \{(HLTG, l_0, \varepsilon)\})$, which represents the process from above, can produce in the initial step the events b and c, since the definition 11.3 states, that λ_0^* can only produce the events τ and b. But the event a, that leads from l_0 to l_1 has to be hidden by the multiple synchronisation term and therefore the event c has to be offered, which is the next visible event reachable from the term.

The on-the-fly normalisation described so far can only cope with multiple synchronisation terms which have completely normalised high level transition graphs containing no τ-events. Since the hiding operator is the only one that can introduce τ-events into such multiple synchronisation terms, only this operator requires a normalisation for the represented nodes. It is therefore necessary to use the function *normalise*, that has been introduced in definition 11.7 to determine which multiple synchronisation term represents the normalised system with all events from the hiding set hidden from the environment.

$$
\begin{aligned}
normalise(\lambda_0^*) &= (\{a\}, \{\lambda^{*\prime} \mid \lambda^* \xrightarrow{a} \lambda^{*\prime} \wedge \lambda^* \in \{(HLTG, l_0, \varepsilon)\}\} \\
&\quad \cup \{(HLTG, l_0, \varepsilon)\}) \\
&= (\{a\}, \{(HLTG, l_0, \varepsilon), (HLTG, l_1, \varepsilon)\}) = \overline{\lambda_0^*}
\end{aligned}
$$

This resulting normalised multiple synchronisation term contains all those terms, which can only produce events, that are not in the hiding set. On this term the rules from definition 11.3 can be applied. The possible events from this multiple synchronisation term are b and c:

$\overline{\lambda_0^*} \xrightarrow{b} \lambda_1^*$ and $\overline{\lambda_0^*} \xrightarrow{c} \lambda_1^*$, with $\lambda_1^* = (\{a\}, \{(HLTG, l_1, \varepsilon)\})$, because $(HLTG, l_0, \varepsilon) \xrightarrow{b} (HLTG, l_1, \varepsilon)$ and $(HLTG, l_1, \varepsilon) \xrightarrow{c} (HLTG, l_1, \varepsilon)$.

Finally the refusal calculation for λ_0^* can be done:

$$
\begin{aligned}
refusals(HLTG, l_0, \varepsilon) &= \{\{a, c\}, \{b, c\}, \{a\}, \{b\}, \{c\}, \{\}\} \\
refusals(HLTG, l_1, \varepsilon) &= \{\{a, b\}, \{a\}, \{b\}, \{\}\} \\
refusals(\lambda_0^*) &= \{R \mid \exists \Lambda_h^{*\prime}. \ (\{a\}, \Lambda^{*\prime}) = normalise(\lambda_0^*) \wedge \\
&\qquad \exists \lambda^* \in \Lambda^{*\prime}. \{a\} \cup R \in refusals(\lambda^*)\} \\
&= \{\{a, b\}, \{a, c\}, \{a\}, \{b\}, \{c\}, \{\}\} \\
refusals_{max}(\lambda_0^*) &= \{\{a, b\}, \{a, c\}\}
\end{aligned}
$$

After performing either b or c on the multiple synchronisation term λ_0^* it is once again required to normalise the multiple synchronisation term λ_1^*, to determine, from which terms only visible events can be performed.

$$
\begin{aligned}
normalise(\lambda_1^*) &= (\{a\}, \{\lambda^{*\prime} \mid (HLTG, l_1, \varepsilon) \xrightarrow{a} \lambda^{*\prime}\} \cup \{(HLTG, l_1, \varepsilon)\}) \\
&= (\{a\}, \{(HLTG, l_1, \varepsilon)\}) = \overline{\lambda_1^*}
\end{aligned}
$$

The refusals then can computed as follows:

$$
\begin{aligned}
refusals(\lambda_1^*) &= \{R \mid \exists \Lambda_h^{*\prime}. \ (\{a\}, \Lambda^{*\prime}) = normalise(\lambda_1^*) \wedge \\
&\qquad \exists \lambda^* \in \Lambda^{*\prime}. \{a\} \cup R \in refusals(\lambda^*)\} \\
&= \{R \mid \{a\} \cup R \in refusals(HLTG, l_1, \varepsilon)\} \\
&= \{\{a, b\}, \{a\}, \{b\}, \{\}\} \\
refusals_{max}(\lambda_1^*) &= \{\{a, b\}\}
\end{aligned}
$$

The interpretation allows the production of the event c leading back to the same state: $\overline{\lambda_1^*} \xrightarrow{c} \overline{\lambda_1^*}$, which completes the generation of the interpretation, since the multiple synchronisation term $\overline{\lambda_1^*}$ in the following can only produce an infinite number of c events.

11.2.3 Design Patterns for Evaluation in Real-Time

The evaluation and interpretation of multiple synchronisation terms for testing purposes is in general not possible in hard real-time, since no upper bound can be given, on how many elements the current term may get during an interpretation run.

One possibility would be to compute in advance all possible combinations of multiple synchronisation terms that may occur and determine on the way the largest term that occurred. This approach is not reasonable, since it would mean the computation of the whole state space, which is exactly what should be prevented by this approach.

Another possibility is the use of design patterns during the development of a test specification, which ensure that the evaluation of the test results can be done in real-time. There are two different ways, on how a multiple synchronisation term contains more that one element in any of the sets of terms: non-determinism of the underlying processes or τ-events introduced by hiding.

Non-determinism is introduced, if two processes, which run in parallel, share events, on which the two do not synchronise. This is the only way, how non-determinism can be introduced by the parallel operator, since the sequential subprocesses are completely normalised and deterministic.

The first design pattern is therefore, to use unique alphabets for each sequential subprocess, except if the shared events are in the synchronisation set of that parallel operator, that connects the two processes.

The hiding operator can introduce non-determinism or even divergences if any event from the subprocesses is hidden. But for testing purposes the hiding operator is not as important as for model checking. Model checking two CSP processes against each other in any refinement model of CSP sometimes requires, that the internal implementation is hidden from the other process, which is done by the hiding operator. In testing with RT-Tester this is not required, since those events, that must not be visible to the SUT or other abstract machines, just need not to be mapped by the CCL. If those channels are marked as *AM_INTERNAL* in the channel definition part of the specification, those events are not processed by the event mapping mechanism and are therefore not visible for the other participants of the test.

The second design pattern for testing with multiple synchronisation terms is therefore not to use hiding, but instead declare those channels, that are to be hidden, as internal.

Additionally there are further ways to use multiple synchronisation terms for testing, even if those design patterns are not used during the design of the test cases in CSP. Even though it is not possible to use multiple synchronisation terms for hard real-time test evaluation, the mechanisms can still be used to evaluate the test results on the fly. While abstract machines, that generate inputs to the SUT are required to do so in hard real-time, the test evaluation can be performed with a slight delay. It is not necessary, that a test-error or a test-warning is indicated in the moment it occurs, it is sufficient, that these evaluation results are shown within a reasonable amount of time, e.g. a few seconds. Such algorithm is introduced in section 12.4.

Since an explosion of the size of the multiple synchronisation terms occur only under rare circumstances, the evaluation is in most cases performed in that moment an input from the SUT or other abstract machines occurs. Only in a few cases the on-the-fly normalisation of the multiple synchronisation terms creates such large terms, that this cannot be accomplished within a bounded amount of time. But as soon as more events are occurring, the term is usually simplified that much, that the evaluation is still possible again in bounded time.

Chapter 12

Testing with High Level Transition Graphs

The benefit of the high level transition graphs against Roscoe-style normalisation graphs is the use of variables and expressions in conditions and events, which often leads to a smaller graph representation of a process. This chapter describes techniques to represent high level transition graphs in a way, that they can be used for testing and the possibilities of using high level transition graphs for test generation and test verification.

12.1 Representation

A high level transition graph as defined in section 5.1 consists of five sets representing different elements of the graph. If they should be used for automated testing, it is necessary to find a machine readable, efficient representation of these sets.

12.1.1 Variables and Types

A high level transition graph can contain variables as parameters of processes or introduced by events. These variables must be represented for the test engine, because their values can only be determined at runtime. To be able to give a representation of these values, the type of each variable must be determined. There are different possibilities to achieve this. In some cases, it is possible to calculate the type of a variable during the context analysis of the CSP specification. This can be very complex for some specifications. Alternatively, the type of a variable can explicitly be declared in the specification or the type can be calculated using the high level transition graph. In this case, the HLTG is traversed until all possible variable assignments are collected. This calculation of the type is similar to creating the Roscoe-style normalisation graph of the specified process, except that the result is a number of types and not a possibly huge transition graph. Which method is the best one, depends on the CSP process and how it is specified. Calculating the type of a variable using the high level transition graph of a process always results in the minimal type for the variable, as only the values that can be reached by a process are collected.

After the type of a variable is determined, the values can be encoded in a binary representation[1]. To do so, for each variable v with the type t, a new binary type t^{bit} is introduced with $t^{bit} = \{0, 1\}^n$ and $n = log_2(|t|)$. The elements e of the type t are mapped to elements $e^{bit} \in t^{bit}$ using an injective function. In other words, the elements of t are coded in bit-vectors of the length $log_2(|t|)$. For each type t^{bit}, an array of pairs (e^{bit}, ASCII *representation of* e) is created containing all elements of t^{bit} and the ASCII representation of their corresponding element $e \in t$.

Every variable in a high level transition graph can be identified by its unique number. Because there can exist multiple values with the same bit representation, every variable has a reference to a type definition of its possible values. These type definitions can be shared by variables of the same type. References are represented by an array of references to binary encoded types. The type of a variable can be found in the array at the position of the number of the variable.

Example: Lets take a high level transition graph contains the variables x of the type $t_1 = \{\langle a, b, c \rangle, true, 100\}$, y of type t_2 which is equal to the type t_1 ($t_2 = t_1$) and z of type $t_3 = \{1, 2, 4, 8\}$. The binary encoding of the types can be seen in tables 12.1 and 12.2.

bit-vector	ASCII representation
00	<a,b,c>
01	true
10	100

Table 12.1: The lookup table for the binary encoded values t_1^{bit} of the types t_1 and t_2.

The variable x gets the index 1, y the index 2 and z the index 3. The array of type references for the variables would be $[t_1^{bit}, t_1^{bit}, t_3^{bit}]$. In this example, the binary values 00, 01 and 10 are ambiguous as long as it is not clear in which type they have to be interpreted. A concrete value can be expressed by a pair (b, t) of its bit-vector b and a reference for its type t.

---

[1]This is similar to finding a binary encoding for the domain of a function. Binary encoded domains of functions and BDDs are described in chapter 4

bit-vector	ASCII representation
00	1
01	2
10	4
11	8

Table 12.2: The lookup table for the binary encoded values t_3^{bit} of the type t_3.

12.1.2 Environments

The environment of a high level transition graph contains a value for every variable v_i of the represented process. It can be represented using an array of binary encoded values (bit-vectors of variable length). The value of variable v_i can be found in the array at the position of the number, the variable can be identified with. The type, the value has to be interpreted in, can be taken from the array of types, defined above. Again, the position in the array is the number of the variable. During the interpretation of a high level transition graph, the values of the variables in the *current environment* are altered if transitions labelled with assignments are taken. The array $[10, 01, 01]$ would be a possible environment for the above example. In this case, the variable x would have the value 100, y would have the value true and z would have the value 2.

12.1.3 Expressions

One of the benefits of high level transition graphs is, that the expressions that occur in events and conditions need not to be evaluated to generate the graph. When interpreting the graph at runtime, the expressions have to be evaluated under the current environment ε. Because CSP$_M$ has a powerful expression language, this can be complex to implement. Evaluating complex expressions also can take an undefined amount of time since it can involve recursive functions with unknown complexity. For these reasons, an explicit representation using BDDs is suggested. Another alternative to BDDs would be a representaion of the expressions as C/C++ functions. Together with libraries for complex types like sets and sequences, this would be the most efficient representation. The disadvantage is that the functions in general cannot be evaluated in real-time, because recursive functions can occur. In the following, the BDD representation will be discussed because it supports evaluation in real-time. The representation as C/C++ functions can be used for transition graphs that need not be evaluated in realtime or if the BDDs of the expressions are growing too big.

Every expressions e with free variables $x_1, ..., x_n \in vars(e)$ of a high level transition graph can be seen as a function $f : D_1 \times ... \times D_n \rightarrow R_f$ with D_i being the type of variable x_i, R_f being the range of f and $f(x_1, ..., x_n) = e$. Let

$f^{bit} : D_1^{bit} \times ... \times D_n^{bit} \rightarrow R_f^{bit}$ be a function equivalent to f that uses binary domains D_i^{bit} and a binary range R_f^{bit}. In section 12.1.1, a binary representation t^{bit} of the type t_i was defined for each variable of the specification. The binary range of the function can be defined as $R_f^{bit} = \{0,1\}^m$ with $m = log_2(\mid R_f \mid)$. Because each variable that occurs in e already have a binary coded type definition, the binary encoded types t_i^{bit} of the free variables x_i can be used: $D_i^{bit} = t_i^{bit}$. A definition of these binary encoded functions is given in chapter 4, section 4.2.

Let f^{BDD} be a boolean function that determines if for the binary encoding $v_{11}, ..., v_{1k}, ..., v_{n1}, ..., v_{nl}$ of a set of variable values $v_1, ..., v_n$ possible for f (which is $\forall i \in 1, ..., n . v_i \in t_i$) and an element $y_1, ..., y_m \in R_f^{bit}$ of the binary encoded range of f, the following equation holds:

$$f^{bit}(v_{11}, ..., v_{nl}) = (y_1, ..., y_k)$$

As introduced in chapter 4 the original expression e can be represented using the ROBDD of f^{BDD} together with a list of its free variables $x_1, ..., x_n$ and a type definition for the range of the expression. If e has to be evaluated during the execution of the high level transition graph, the values of $x_1, ..., x_n$ are taken from the current environment ε. As already defined, the environment holds a binary encoded value for the current value of each variable. Because the binary encoded domains of the variables of e that were used to create the BDD use the same encoding as the type of the variable, the values in the environment can directly be taken to evaluate the BDD.

There exists exactly one path in the BDD of e for a given set of binary encoded variable values $(x_{11}, ..., x_{nl}$ that leads to the result node 1 of the BDD. The result of e can be collected in its binary encoding as values of the result variables $y_1, ..., y_k$ on this path. The result can be interpreted using the type definition of the range of the expression.

In high level transition graphs, expressions can occur in events, conditions and assignments. A condition is a boolean expression so the result type of the BDD always is $\{(0,\texttt{false}), (1,\texttt{true})\}$. Assignments are pairs (v, e) of a variable and an expression being assigned to the variable. The expression e is represented as a BDD with the range type R_e^{bit} being the type of the variable v.

It is not necessary to represent function *definitions*. Instead, every function *reference* $f(a_1, ..., a_n)$ can be represented as an expression e of the *term* of the function *definition* in which all parameters have been replaced by the values of the function *reference*. As function *references* can use parameters or expressions as values for parameters, the expression e still can contain variables. The number of these variables is less or equal to the number of parameters of the function and the types of these variables are a subset or equal to the type of the parameters. Therefore the ROBDD of e can only be smaller than the ROBDD of the function *definition*. The result type of the ROBDD of e can be set according to the context of the function *reference*, so that no type conversion of the result is necessary. The disadvantage is that a ROBDD has to be created for every *reference* of a function instead of one for the function *definition*. If representing the function definition, the ROBDD can be greater than necessary and a type conversion may be necessary for each function reference.

12.1.4 Events

Two sets of events have to be represented for a high level transition graph: $\Sigma^{\pi\tau\checkmark}$, being the alphabet of the specification extended by $\{\pi, \tau, \checkmark\}$ with $\forall e \in \Sigma^{\pi\tau\checkmark}.comms(e) = e$ and a set S of events that occur in the graph. The events in S are either explicit events that are also elements of the alphabet $e \in \Sigma^{\pi\tau\checkmark}$ or contain variables or expressions that have to be evaluated under an environment ε. The elements of $\Sigma^{\pi\tau\checkmark}$ have unique numbers so that every event can be identified by its number. A label in a high level transition graph always contains a set E of pairs (e, a) of an event $e \in S$ and a set of assignments a.

Every definition of a typed channel results in a number of type definitions according to section 12.1.1 that represent the type of the channel. For a channel definition `channel b:{1..3}.{true,false}` for example, two binary types $t^{bit}_{\{1..3\}}$ and $t^{bit}_{\{true,false\}}$ for the binary type $t^{bit}_b = t^{bit}_{\{1..3\}} \times t^{bit}_{\{true,false\}}$ of the channel would be created. The channel b itself would be represented as a special variable with an extra type $t^{bit}_{chan} = [(0, \texttt{<name of the channel>})]$.

The alphabet Σ extended by the events π, τ and $\checkmark$ is represented as an array of the unique number of the event and its ASCII representation.

The events of S always have the form c for events of untyped channels and $c.d$ for events of typed channels with c being a channel and d being a dotted expression. The dotted expressions carry the values that are communicated on the channel. They may contain variables and expressions that have to be evaluated under the current environment.

The CSP events $e \in S$ of the high level transition graph are represented as arrays of either a variable, a BDD or a pair (b, t) of a bit-vector and its type. Variables are used to represent the channel of an event or the explicit occurrence of a variable in the dotted expression. BDDs are used to represent expressions in dotted expressions and pairs of a bit-vector and its type are used to represent concrete values. An event $a.x.3.(y+1)$ for example could be represented as the array $[a_{ref}, x_{ref}, (011, t_3), ROBDD_{y+1}]$ of the variables of the channel a and the parameter x, a pair of the bit-vector 011 and its type t_3 and the reduced ordered BDD of the expression $y + 1$. The result type of $ROBDD_{y+1}$ would be the binary encoding t^{bit}_{a3} which is part of the type $t^{bit}_a = t^{bit}_{a3} \times t^{bit}_{a2} \times t^{bit}_{a3}$ of the channel a.

12.1.5 Transitions and Locations

The locations of a high level transition graph must have unique names. This can be achieved by counting them. A location than is represented by its number.

The transitions of a high level transition graph are tuples (l_S, c, E, l_T) of a source location l_S, a target location l_T, a label consisting of a condition c and a set E of pairs (e, a) of an event e and a set of assignments a. Because the representation of these elements has already been defined, transitions can be represented as an array of the elements of their tuples.

12.2 Exploring the State-Space

Representing conditions and assignments as BDDs has been described in the previous section 12.1. Especially for variables representing traces, sets or other complex data types, the computation of the possible values of the variable is important. Only if all values are known, a BDD representing an expression using that variable can be created in a way, that can be efficiently evaluated. Therefore in this section an algorithm is going to be introduced, that computes all possible values for any variable that occurs in a CSP specification.

Small BDD representations of expressions are only possible, if all possible values of all modelled variables in the BDD have a unique binary representation, which is as small as possible. Depending on the number of possible values n of a variable, the binary encoding requires $log_2(n)$ bits to represent that value. Therefore the computation of a table of reachable values – in the following this is called *look-up-table* – can be directly used, to create a small BDD.

Generating the look-up-table requires to explore the complete state space of the transition system represented by the high level transition graph. But this only needs to be done after the generation of the high level transition graph, but not during the execution for testing purposes. For testing still the efficient representation of the high level transition graphs can be used. Additionally the range-calculation, which will be introduced in the following section, makes the testing-algorithm for high level transition graphs real-time capable, as will be explained in section 12.4.

12.2.1 An Algorithm for Range-Calculation

The algorithm, which creates the look-up-table, employs a breadth-first search algorithm, to calculate the possible bindings of all locations in a high level transition graph. For each location a set of bindings is derived, which describes the *range* of possible values for all visible variables in that location. The initial step of the algorithm, which is presented in listing 12.1, requires a high level transition graph and an initial binding for the initial location of the HLTG as arguments. In general this initial binding contains no elements. Only if variable bindings are introduced in the high level structure of the CSP process, those initial bindings contain entries for those variables. If synchronisation terms are used to represent parallel processes, those bindings for the initial location l_0 are represented as ε_0

in the sub-term $(HLTG, l_0, \varepsilon_0)$ of a synchronisation term. Since the *range calculation* has to be performed before the execution of the high level transition graph for testing purposes, it is sufficient to consider only synchronisation terms instead of multiple synchronisation terms, which are only used during the execution of the represented transition system.

```
calculate_ranges(hltg, bind_init)
BEGIN
  hltg ∈ HLTG; loc ∈ LOCATION; bind, bind_init ∈ BINDING; queue ∈ QUEUE

  (* Initialise the ranges for all locations of the HLTG *)
  FORALL loc ∈ L(hltg) DO
    range(loc, hltg) = ∅
  OD
  append(queue, (l₀(hltg), bind_init))

  (* Iterate until all elements from the queue have been processed *)
  WHILE size(queue) > 0 DO
    (* Get the head element from the queue *)
    (loc, bind) = head(queue), queue = tail(queue)

    (* Check, if the pair of loc and bind has already been processed *)
    IF bind ∉ range(loc, hltg) THEN
      (* Append bind to range of loc and extend the look-up-table *)
      range(loc, hltg) = range(loc, hltg) ∪ { bind }
      extend_look_up_table(bind)

      (* Calculate bindings for the target locations of loc *)
      next_bindings(loc, hltg, queue, bind)
    FI
  OD
END
```
Listing 12.1: The initial step of the range calculation

The function `range(loc,hltg)` denotes a mapping of a location from a HLTG to a set of bindings, which can be reached from any location using a transition leading to loc. At the beginning of the algorithm those sets of bindings are initialised to the empty set for all locations in the high level transition graph.

Breadth-first search algorithms, as explained in [, p. 531], usually employs a queue of nodes, which have to be considered later in the search. The implementation suggested in this section also uses a queue to store elements, which have to be considered later in the range calculation. A difference to breadth-first search is, that this algorithm does not visit each location in the high level transition graph only once, but once for each possible binding. Therefore the queue stores pairs of locations and bindings, instead of locations only. Before the range calculation itself can be started, an initial element must be appended to the queue, which consists of the pair of the initial location and the initial binding, that was specified as an argument to the algorithm.

```
next_bindings(loc, hltg, queue, bind)
BEGIN
    hltg ∈ HLTG; loc, loc' ∈ LOCATION; bind, bind' ∈ BINDING
    tra ∈ HLTRANS; ev ∈ EVENT; assign ∈ ASSIGNMENT; queue ∈ QUEUE

    (* Perform the following loop for all transitions of loc *)
    FORALL tra ∈ {(l_S, c, E, l_T) ∈→_CA (hltg) | l_S = loc} DO
        (* Does the binding hold under the condition of the transition? *)
        IF eval(c(tra), bind) THEN
            (* Determine the target location of the selected transition *)
            loc' = l_T(tra)
            FORALL (ev, assign) ∈ E(tra) DO
                (* Calculate the bindings for the target location *)
                bind' = apply(assign, bind)

                (* Append the pair (loc', bind') to the queue *)
                append(queue, (loc', bind'))
            OD
        FI
    OD
END
```

Listing 12.2: Calculating the bindings of a following location

After that a loop is entered, which only terminates if the queue is empty. Since there is already one element in the queue, this loop is processed at least once. The first element is removed from the queue and the references to the location and binding are stored in the variables loc and bind. If the binding is already in the set of the ranges for the location, this pair can be disregarded for the following computations, because these values have already been used to perform them earlier.

If the binding is not in the set range(loc,hltg), this combination has to be used to compute all possible pairs of the following locations and corresponding bindings, that can be reached from the pair under consideration. Before these calculations are performed, the current binding is added to the set of bindings, that have already been processed for the current location. Additionally the values in the binding are used to extend the look-up-table for the corresponding variables by calling the function extend_look_up_table(bind). Finally the function next_bindings(loc, hltg, queue, bind) is called, which calculates the bindings for the target locations of the transitions leading from loc.

The function next_bindings(), that is presented in listing 12.2, processes sequentially each transition leading from the current locations. First it checks, whether the condition at the label of the transition holds under the binding, that was passed as the functions argument. All labels, which condition do not hold, are disregarded in the following. The other ones are used to determine the target location of the corresponding transition. Then each event-assignments pair at the label is processed and the assignments are applied to the current binding, to derive a new binding, which is valid for the following location. The actual event at the label is not required for these considerations and can be ignored here. The new pair of target location and new binding is added to the queue, which enables the algorithm to continue processing this pair later. As soon as all all event-assignment pairs at the label of all transitions of the source location have been processed, this function terminates and the algorithm continues in `calculate_ranges()` by processing the next element from the queue.

As soon as the queue in the while-loop of `calculate_ranges()` is empty, the whole algorithm terminates. At that point, all possible bindings for the locations in the high level transition graphs have been computed. Additionally the look-up-table is filled with the possible values, that the different variables can carry in a run of the system.

Using the algorithm for parallel systems, which are represented by synchronisation terms, is also possible. The range calculation for synchronisation terms differs only in that way, that the algorithm is not only executed for one high level transition graph, but for all sub-terms $(HLTG, l_0, \varepsilon_0)$, that are contained in the synchronisation term. Since the function `range` requires not only a location, but also a high level transition graph as arguments, the ranges of the synchronisation term are unique for each location of any of the references high level transition graphs.

The algorithm for the range-calculation as explained above, shares many ideas from the normalisation algorithm for high level transition graphs introduced in chapter 8. But there are also some differences, between the two approaches:

One difference, which simplifies the range-calculation in contrast to the normalisation, is that the range-calculation do not process any events being attached to the transitions of a high level transition graph. Especially there is no difference whether an event at a label is visible or not. In contrast to that, for the normalisation it is necessary to repeatedly follow all possible chains of τ or π events, that are possible for a given location. The range-calculation on the contrary processes each pair of location and binding only once. Additionally it is not necessary to perform a calculation of the acceptances or refusals, since this can be done later on runtime, as will be explained in section 12.4.1.

12.2.2 Example

The following CSP specification will be used to explain the algorithm with an exemplary execution. The result of the high level transition graph generation process is shown in figure 12.1.

```
1   channel a : {0..99}
2   SYS  = P(0)
3   P(x) = a.x -> P((x+1) % 2)
```

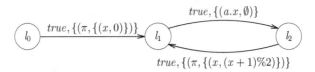

Figure 12.1: High level transition graph of the Process SYS

At the beginning of the algorithm the ranges of the locations l_0, l_1 and l_2 are initialised to empty sets of bindings and the queue is filled with the pair $(l_0, \emptyset)$, since there are no visible variables in the location l_0. The algorithm then takes this pair from the queue and checks, whether the empty set is an element of the ranges of l_0, which is not the case. Therefore the empty set is added to the ranges of l_0, and the function next_bindings() is called with the l_0 and $\emptyset$ as current values for the current location and binding.

Since there exists only one transition leaving from l_0, which condition holds under the given binding, the new target location of the algorithm is identified as l_1. The assignment at the label of the transition creates a new binding for the target location, which is $\{(x, 0)\}$, since x is a visible variable of the location l_1. Thus the pair $(l_1, \{(x, 0)\})$ is appended to the queue for further processing. Since there are no further event-assignment pairs and no other transitions to be processed, the function terminates and returns to calculate_ranges().

The top element is once again removed from the queue and the ranges algorithm begins with the processing of the next pair $(l_1, \{(x, 0)\})$, which has not been processed before. Calling next_bindings() again results is a new queue element $(l_2, \{(x, 0)\})$. The algorithm continues producing further pairs $(l_1, \{(x, 1)\})$ and $(l_2, \{(x, 1)\})$ representing states, which all have not been explored earlier. At this stage the ranges of the locations look as follows:

$$ranges(l_0, hltg) = \{\}$$
$$ranges(l_1, hltg) = \{\{(x, 0)\}, \{(x, 1)\}\}$$
$$ranges(l_2, hltg) = \{\{(x, 0)\}, \{(x, 1)\}\}$$

Applying the function next_bindings() to the pair $(l_2, \{(x, 1)\})$ generates a new queue element $(l_1, \{(x, 0)\})$. As soon as the element is removed from the queue, it is checked, whether the binding $\{(x, 0)\}$ is in the ranges of l_1. Since this is the case, processing the elements of this pair would not result in the production of new bindings for any location. Therefore the algorithm ignores the pair and tries to get the next element from the queue. But the queue does not contain any more elements and therefore the algorithm terminates, because the whole state space have been explored.

During the algorithm the look-up-table for the variable x has been filled. The channel definition for the channel a would allow all values from 0 to 99 to be communicated, and therefore these values would in general be possible for the variable x. But the algorithm identifies, that only the values 0 and 1 are used.

Representing the expressions of the high level transition graph as BDD is more efficient now, since it is only necessary to model the values with one bit in the BDD. With other mechanisms it could have been guessed, that x could be in the range of 0 to 99. Representing 100 different values for a variable in a BDD requires 7 bits, which is a significant difference to representing the really used values with 1 bit.

12.2.3 Applications of the Algorithm

The results of the range-calculation can be used to find efficient representations for modelling variables in BDDs. But this is not the only application ranges can be used for: the range-calculation is the foundation for an algorithm, that can determine whether or not a high level transition graph is divergent. Roscoe-style normalisation graphs like the ones produced by **FDR** can easily be used to find divergent nodes, since it is sufficient to find a loop in the graph, which contains only τ events at the transitions. In high level transition graphs this is not sufficient, since the labels at the transitions can contain conditions and assignments, which changes the environment. Therefore a high level transition graph is divergent, only if there is a chain of τ or π events, leading from a certain location with a corresponding binding, to the same location with the same binding.

An implementation of an algorithm detecting divergences could be sketched as follows: The first step requires a search algorithm, which detects all possible loops of transitions labelled with τ or π events. In this stage the conditions or assignments labelled to the transition can be disregarded, since the result represents all loops, which could possibly lead to divergency. If there are no such loops, the high level transition graph cannot be divergent and the algorithm may terminate. Otherwise it is necessary to start a range calculation.

The results of the range calculation can now be used to perform a depth first search, whether or not any of the previously identified loops leads to divergence. The algorithm starts by selecting a random location with one of its possible bindings and marks it in the range of the location. The search takes only transitions labelled with τ or π events, if the condition holds under the current binding, and then applies the assignments. In the next step it is checked, if the resulted binding is already been marked as processed in the range of the target location. In this case the location-binding-pair would have been visited by the algorithm previously and thus the specification would be divergent in this location. If the binding is not yet marked, the algorithm continues exploring the identified loops.

Basically the same algorithm can also be used to calculate the maximum length of chains of τ and π events. This maximum length can be used for the calculation of the upper bound of the time that is required to evaluate high level transition graph until the next visible event is being produced. These considerations will be described in more detail in 12.4 and 12.5.

To calculate the ranges of the high level transition graphs embedded in a synchronisation term, it is only necessary to do the calculation for those sub-terms referencing a HLTG. Calculating the ranges of the whole synchronisation term itself is in general also possible. But this would require to identify all pairs of combinations of the ranges of the sequential high level transition graphs, which is basically computing the complete product graph of the modelled system. Therefore this approach would have the same disadvantages, like state explosion, as the Roscoe-style normalisation graphs for parallel systems. As will be discussed in section 12.5, the range-calculation for synchronisation terms is not necessary, since it is sufficient to identify the maximum length of the τ/π-chains in each high level transition graph to specify an upper bound of steps required for an on-the-fly normalisation. Combining these results with the considerations about synchronisation terms will result in a real-time capable testing algorithm for synchronisation terms using high level transition graphs.

12.3   Trace Generation

CSP process terms can contain high and low level operators. In chapter 7, a strict hierarchy of these operators is postulated. The transformation of high level operators result in a synchronisation term and processing the low level sub-processes results in high level transition graphs. In this section, the execution of HLTGs representing low level sub-processes is discussed first and after this, the concept is extended for the trace generation using synchronisation terms containing unnormalised high level transition graphs.

12.3.1   Trace Generation with HLTG

High level transition graphs can be used to simulate a specified process and generate traces of events. To generate a possible trace of a low level process, its high level transition graph is traversed, starting at the start location and with the start environment. Transitions labelled with the special event π are used to represent process references and this event does not appear in the trace. The event τ is not represented in traces as well, because it is invisible to the environment. To add a new element $\alpha \in \Sigma$ to the trace of a HLTG with the current location l and the current environment ε, it must hold that

$$\exists\, l' \in L, \varepsilon' \in Env \,.\, l, \varepsilon \xmapsto{\alpha'} l', \varepsilon' \text{ with } eval(\alpha', \varepsilon) = \alpha$$

Because of the definition of $\overset{\alpha}{\mapsto}$, there can exists multiple π-labelled transitions that have to be traversed, before the transition marked with the event α' can be taken. Each execution step that creates a new trace member therefore can require a number of steps

$$l, \varepsilon \overset{c,(\alpha',a)}{\succ\!\!-\!\!-\!\!-\!\!\longrightarrow} l', \varepsilon' \ \text{with} \ \alpha' \in \{\pi\}$$

unnormalised high level transition graphs can contain τ-events, as well, so that there can be several execution steps with invisible events necessary before the next trace element can be calculated.

If all possible environments have been calculated as described in the previous section 12.2, for each location the maximum number of steps with invisible events before the next visible event can be calculated. This is only possible if all possible variable values of a location are known, because otherwise the conditions on the labels of transitions could not be evaluated.

For a step $l, \varepsilon \overset{c,(\alpha,a)}{\succ\!\!-\!\!-\!\!-\!\!\longrightarrow} l', \varepsilon'$ of a current location l with a current environment ε, all transitions of l are examined, to see if their labels condition holds under the current environment ε. One of the possible transitions then is selected non-deterministically. Since labels can contain more than one event, one of the events together with its assignment set has to be selected. The assignments are applied to the current environment. If the event is visible, it is appended to the trace. The graph is traversed until a location is reached from which no transition can be taken anymore. This is described in the following algorithms step(hltg, l, env,t) in listing 12.3, which defines $l, \varepsilon \overset{c,(\alpha,a)}{\succ\!\!-\!\!-\!\!-\!\!\longrightarrow} l', \varepsilon'$ and trace(hltg,env$_0$) in listing 12.4, which generates a trace for a HLTG and a given start environment ε_0 until a stop location is reached.

Because π-events have been especially created for high level transition graphs and do not affect the behaviour of a process, it has to be assured, that reaching a stop location using a π-transition, implies that there are no other possible labels for the source location of the π-transition, that would result in a new trace item. The only locations that can contain multiple transitions including π-labels are the start locations of *if-then-else* or *external choice*.

For *if-then-else*, the choice between the transition representing the *then* case and the transition representing the *else* case is deterministic and depends on the value of the condition of the operator evaluated under the current environment. Thus if the possible transition carries a π-label and leads to a stop location, the process has to stop, because the else-case is not possible.

For *external choices*, the π-transitions are part of the sub-graph $HLTG_{\tau_P \times \tau_{Q'}}$ which is the product graph of the invisible beginnings of the sub-graphs of the sub-terms of the *external choice* operator. Invisible events do not affect the selection of an external choice operator. Therefore a stop location in $HLTG_{\tau_P \times \tau_{Q'}}$ implies that the whole process stops.

```
step(hltg,l,env,t)
BEGIN
    hltg ∈ HLTG;  l,l' ∈ LOCATION;  tra ∈ HLTRANS;  initials ⊂ HLTRANS
    env,env' ∈ ENVIRONMENT;  e ∈ EVENT;  a ∈ ASSIGNMENT;  t ∈ TRACE

    (* calculate set of possible transitions of l *)
    initials = ∅;
    FORALL tra ∈ {(l_S, c, E, l_T) ∈→_CA (hltg) | l_S = l} DO
        (* Does the condition of the label hold under the environment? *)
        IF eval(c(tra), env) THEN
            initials = initials ∪ { tra }
        FI
    OD
    (* return unchanged values if no transition is possible *)
    IF initials = ∅ THEN
        RETURN (l,env,t)
    FI
    (* if there exist possible transitions, select a label *)
    tra ∈ initials;  (e,a) ∈ E(tra)
    env' = apply(a,env);  l' = l_T(l);  t' = t
    IF ((e ≠ τ) ∧ (e ≠ π)) THEN
        t' = t ^ eval(e,env)
    FI
    RETURN (l',env',t)
END
```

Listing 12.3: Find and execute a step $l, \varepsilon \rangle \xrightarrow{c,(e,a)} l', \varepsilon'$

```
trace(hltg,env_0)
BEGIN
    hltg ∈ HLTG;  l,l' ∈ LOCATION;  env_0,env,env' ∈ ENVIRONMENT;  t,t' ∈ TRACE

    (* start algorithm at start location and with start environment *)
    l = l_0(hltg);  env = env_0;  t = ⟨⟩

    (* execute steps until a stop location is reached *)
    DO
        (l',env',t') = step(hltg,l,env,t)
    WHILE ((l' ≠ l) ∨ (env' ≠ env) ∨ (t' ≠ t))
    RETURN t
END
```

Listing 12.4: Generating a trace t for a HLTG hltg with a start environment env_0

12.3.2 Trace Generation with Synchronisation Terms

This section describes a method to generate traces of synchronisation terms containing unnormalised high level transition graphs. For each execution step, the possible events α together with the transitions of each synchronisation sub-term $\lambda_i = (HLTG_i, l_i, \varepsilon_i)$, that have to be taken when emitting α, must be calculated. Then the rules for the interpretation of synchronisation terms must be applied to calculate the set of transitions. One of the possible events together with its label has to be selected and the synchronisation term λ evolves to λ'. The function *initials* calculates the set of all tuples (α, C) of a synchronisation term. The tuples contain an element of the alphabet $\alpha \in \Sigma$ of the synchronisation term and a set C of tuples $(HLTG_i, l_T, \varepsilon_t)$ of a high level transition graph $HLTG_i$, a target location $l_T \in L_i$ and a target environment ε_t. Every tuple represents a new current state of $HLTG_i$ if α is executed. $HLTG_i$ together with its current location l_i and its current environment ε_i must be a sub-term of the synchronisation term. The set of all events α that occur in $initials(\lambda)$ is equal to the initial actions of the synchronisation term λ.

Definition 12.1 *The function initials calculates the possible execution steps in a state of a synchronisation term. It is defined in three cases according to the different types of synchronisation terms:*

1. *λ represents a hiding operator $(\lambda_h, hide)$:*

$$initials((\lambda_h, hide) = \quad \{(\alpha, C) \in initials(\lambda_h) \mid \alpha \notin hide\} \\ \cup \{(\tau, C) \mid \exists (\alpha, C) \in initials(\lambda_h) \wedge \alpha \in hide\}$$

2. *λ represents a parallel operator $(\lambda_1, sync, \lambda_2)$:*

$$initials((\lambda_1, sync, \lambda_2)) = \quad \{(\alpha, C) \in initials(\lambda_1) \mid \alpha \notin sync\} \\ \cup \{(\alpha, C) \in initials(\lambda_2) \mid \alpha \notin sync\} \\ \cup \{(\alpha, C_1 \cup C_2) \mid \ \exists (\alpha, C_1) \in initials(\lambda_1) \wedge \\ \exists (\alpha, C_2) \in initials(\lambda_2) \wedge \\ \alpha \in sync\}$$

3. *λ denotes a leaf of the synchronisation term $(HLTG_i, l_i, \varepsilon_i)$:*

$$initials((HLTG_i, l_i, \varepsilon_i)) = \\ \{(\alpha, \{(HLTG_i, l_T, \varepsilon_t)\}) \mid \ \alpha \in \Sigma, l_T \in L_i, \varepsilon_t \in Env \wedge \\ \exists \ l' \in L_i, \varepsilon' \in Env \ . \\ (l_i, \varepsilon_i \overset{\sigma}{\mapsto} l', \varepsilon' \wedge l', \varepsilon' \overset{c_i, (\alpha', a)}{\succ\!\!\longrightarrow} l_T, \varepsilon_t \wedge \\ \forall \ c_i, (\alpha_i, a_i) \in \sigma \ . \ \alpha_i \in \{\tau, \pi\} \\ \alpha = eval(\alpha', \varepsilon') \ \}$$

Definition 12.2 *The initial actions* $[\lambda]^0$ *of a synchronisation term* λ *can be calculated from initials*(λ) *as follows:*

$$[\lambda]^0 \;=\; \{\alpha \mid \exists(\alpha, C) \in initials(\lambda)\}$$

Progress now is made by selecting one of the elements of *initials*(λ), adding α to the trace and setting the new current location and environment in all affected $HLTG_i$.

12.4 Testing

In this section, methods and algorithms to use high level transition graphs for refusal testing are defined. These methods are extended later to enable testing with synchronisation terms of unnormalised high level transition graphs.

12.4.1 Testing with HLTG

Another intention of high level transition graphs is to use them for testing purposes. In this case the graph has to be traversed and for each location, the acceptances or refusals and initial actions have to be calculated. Non-determinism of a HLTG increases the complexity of a suitable test algorithm, because it can not be guaranteed, that a test trace leads to a unique location. If an error is detected, all other possible current locations have to be checked as well, to ensure that the behaviour in fact is wrong according to the specification. This can require backtracking to find the other possible current locations, which can be avoided using an on-the-fly normalisation of the current location, where all possible current locations are joint into a single normalised location.

On-the-fly Normalisation of HLTG

When testing with on-the-fly normalised high level transition graphs, the current location always is a normalised location representing a set of possible current locations together with their corresponding environment. The algorithm to calculate the normalised location and its refusals or acceptances[2] is similar to the one used to generate the stage-1 normalisation of a HLTG, described in section 8.1. The main difference is, that only the current location is normalised and that the algorithm is defined recursively and does not use a stack of next iteration steps. The algorithm is described in listing 12.5.

---

[2]The term *refusals* is used as a short form for the term *maximal refusals*, as well as *acceptances* is used to describe the *minimal acceptances*. The acceptances can be used to calculate the refusals of a location and vice versa. In the algorithms, normally the acceptances are calculated because they are usually smaller than the refusals.

```
eliminateTaus_{on-the-fly}(nloc, hltgloc, hltg, env, acc, viapi,hide)
BEGIN
    hltg ∈ HLTG; hltgloc, nloc ∈ LOCATION; a ∈ ASSIGNMENT
    env, env' ∈ ENVIRONMENT; acc, acc' ∈ ACCEPTANCE; tra, tra' ∈ HLTRANS
    e,e' ∈ EVENT; viapi ∈ BOOL; hide ⊂ EVENT

    (* If hltgloc is stable a new acceptance set is created *)
    IF stable(hltgloc, hltg, env) ∧ viapi THEN acc' = acc
    ELSE acc' = ∅  FI
    (* Perform the following loop for all transitions of hltgloc *)
    FORALL tra ∈ {(l_S, c, E, l_T) ∈ →_CA (hltg) | l_S = hltgloc} DO
        (* Does the condition hold under the environment? *)
        IF eval(c(tra), env) THEN
            FORALL (e, a) ∈ E(tra) DO
                (* Calculate environments for the target state *)
                env' = apply(a, env)
                CASE e
                τ) eliminateTaus_{on-the-fly}(nloc, l_T(tra), hltg, env', ∅, false)
                π) eliminateTaus_{on-the-fly}(nloc, l_T(tra), hltg, env', acc', true)
                *) (* evaluate event and add it to initials *)
                    e' = eval(e,env)
                    IF e' ∈ hide THEN
                        (* hidden events are treated as τ-events. *)
                        eliminateTaus_{on-the-fly}(nloc, l_T(tra), hltg, env', ∅, false)
                    ELSE
                        [nloc]^0 = [nloc]^0 ∪ {e'}
                        (* calculate acceptances for stable locations *)
                        IF stable(hltgloc, hltg, env) THEN
                            acc' = acc' ∪ {e'}
                        FI
                        (* Extend normalised location *)
                        nloc = nloc ∪ {(l_T(tra), acc')}
                    FI
            ESAC
            OD
        FI
    OD
    (* Add acceptance to nloc if hltgloc was not reached by a π-event *)
    IF stable(hltgloc, hltg, bind) ∧ not(viapi) THEN
        acceptances(nloc) = acceptances(nloc) ∪ {acc'}
    FI
END
```

Listing 12.5: HLTG on-the-fly-normalisation for a single location.

The execution of a high level transition graph hltg using on-the-fly normalisation always start with calculating the normalisation of the start location l_0(hltg) using the start environment env_0. This is done by

$$\texttt{eliminateTaus}_{on-the-fly}(\{(l_0(\text{hltg}), \emptyset)\}, l_0(\text{hltg}), \text{hltg}, \text{env}_0, \emptyset, false)$$

If an element of the acceptances is executed, the next normalised location is calculated using all transition labelled with the selected event that are possible for the locations represented by the current normalised location. This is defined in algorithm $\texttt{evolve}_{on-the-fly}$ in listing 12.6.

```
evolve_{on-the-fly}(hltg,normloc,e)
BEGIN
   hltg ∈ HLTG; normloc, normloc', loc, loc' ∈ LOCATION; tra ∈ HLTRANS
   env,env' ∈ ENVIRONMENT; acc' ∈ ACCEPTANCE; e,e' ∈ EVENT
   a' ∈ ASSIGNMENT

   (* Create an empty normalised location and an empty acceptance set *)
   normloc' = ∅; acc' = ∅; init' = ∅
   (* For all pairs (loc, env) of current normalised location do *)
   FORALL (loc, env) ∈ normloc DO
      FORALL tra ∈ {(l_S, c, E, l_T) ∈→_{CA} (hltg) | l_S = hltgloc ∧ eval(c, env) = true ∧
                                                      ∃(e', a') ∈ E(tra) . eval(e', env) = e}
      DO
         (* get target location and target environment *)
         (loc',env') = evolve_{loc}(tra, e, env)
         (* Extend the next normalised location *)
         eliminateTaus_{on-the-fly}(normloc', loc', hltg, env', acc', false)
      OD
   OD
   RETURN (normloc', acc')
END
```

Listing 12.6: The calculation of the next current normalised location.

An algorithm for $\texttt{evolve}_{loc}$(tra,e,env) is given in listing 12.7. It can be used to determine the target location and target environment of a transition tra when emitting the event e under the current environment env.

12.4.2 Testing with HLTG and Synchronisation Terms

A method to use synchronisation terms of normalised high level transition graphs has been introduced in section 11.2. It uses an on-the-fly normalisation of the synchronisation term into a multiple synchronisation term. To use synchronisation terms of unnormalised high level transition graphs for testing, it is possible to combine the on-the-fly normalisation of the HLTGs in the synchronisation term together with the on-the-fly normalisation of the synchronisation term.

```
evolve_loc(tra,e,env)
BEGIN
   tra ∈ HLTRANS
   env,env' ∈ ENVIRONMENT; e,e' ∈ EVENT; a ∈ ASSIGNMENT

   FORALL (e',a) ∈ E(tra)  DO
      (* if the events matches, apply assignments to environment *)
      IF eval(e',env) = e THEN
         env' = apply(a,env)
         RETURN (l_T(tra),env')
      FI
   OD
   (* if no event matches, return source location and current env *)
   RETURN (l_S(tra),env)
END
```

Listing 12.7: Calculating the target location and environment of a transition and a given event.

The methods defined for synchronisation terms of normalised high level transition graphs require a normalised current location l_i of each high level transition graph $HLTG_i$ in the synchronisation term together with its acceptances or refusals and initial actions $[l_i]^0$. This can be assured by the on-the-fly normalisation of high level transition graphs. It is as well required, that such a current location must be able to evolve to the next normalised location under a given event, which is included in the acceptances of the current location. This can be achieved using the algorithm $evolve_{on-the-fly}$. The only difference between testing with synchronisation terms of normalised or unnormalised high level transition graphs therefore is the complexity of calculating the next execution step.

12.5 Real-Time Capabilities

In this section, the real-time capabilities of the different types of transition graphs and synchronisation term/transition graph combinations are discussed.

Trace Generation of HLTG

Selecting one of the labels of a transition requires to lookup all transitions of a location l. Transitions as defined in section 12.1.5 are tuples (l_S, c, E, l_T) of a source location l_S, a target location l_T a condition c under which the transition can be taken and a set E of pairs (α, a) of an event and a set of appropriate assignments for the event. Transitions are represented as a list of these tuples. Finding all transitions of a location requires to search this list for all tuples with $l_S = l$. For each of the labels of these transitions, the condition c must be evaluated under the current environment ε. Conditions are represented as BDDs so that for each label, a BDD has to be evaluated. After all possible transitions have been collected, one of them has to be chosen non-deterministically. Finding all possible transitions is linear to the number of transitions and with the complexity of evaluating the BDD of the condition of the transitions label. An upper bound for this operation is the maximum number of transitions that occur for a location in the graph times the complexity of evaluating the deepest BDD of all conditions.

For this transition, a pair (e, a) of an event e and a set of assignments a out of E has to be selected. The event e can contain expressions or variables. It has to be evaluated under the current environment. Events are represented as lists which elements are either variables, BDDs or pairs (b, t) of a bit-vector and its type. Each element of the list has to be evaluated. Each result has to be interpreted using the according type definition and the resulting ASCII representations are concatenated as dotted communication fields. The result is the ASCII representation of e under the current environment. The cost of evaluating an event therefore is linear to the number of communication fields of the event. An upper bound is the maximum number of sets that occur in the type definition of the channels of the specification times the complexity of evaluating the deepest BDD of all expressions of the representation. The trace of the specified process is a sequence of events $\alpha \in \Sigma$ of the alphabet of the specification. The alphabet is represented as an array of the unique number of the event together with its ASCII representation. If the evaluated event e is a visible event, its number must be determined using the representation of $\Sigma^{\pi\tau\checkmark}$ and this number has to be added to the trace.

Before proceeding the trace generation with the target location l_T, the assignments $a_1, ..., a_n$ of a have to be applied to the current environment ε to get the new current environment ε' of l_T. Assignments are pairs $(var, expr)$ of a variables var and an expressions $expr$. For each variable $var \in \textit{Variables}$ of the high level transition graph, there can be at most one assignment $(var_i, expr_i)$ in a with $var = var_i$. The values of assignments are represented as either a variable, a BDD or a pair (b, t) of a bit-vector and its type. The values of the assignments have to be evaluated under the current environment ε. The results are stored in the new environment ε'. The values of all variables that are not effected by the assignments in a remain unchanged. The cost of creating the new environment is linear to the number of assignments to be evaluated. Because there can only be one assignment for each variable, an upper bound is the number of variables times the complexity of evaluating the deepest BDD of all expressions of the HLTG. The just described calculations are necessary for every step of the trace generation. An upper bound for the calculations necessary for every single step can be determined for every high level transition graph, so every step can be done in hard real-time.

Generating a new element $\alpha \in \Sigma$ of the trace can require a number of steps of invisible events τ or π. Only if an upper bound for the number of execution steps of invisible events can be determined, the generation of a new visible event

α of a trace can be done in real-time. The upper bound for this is the longest path of τ- or π-transitions in the graph. As shown in section 12.2, the longest path of transitions with invisible events can only be calculated if all possible environments for all locations of the graph have been calculated before. This is equal to exploring the complete state space of the high level transition graph. Because these calculation can be done before the graph is executed, it is then possible to calculate and select one next visible event of the HLTG in hard real-time during the execution. If the state space of the HLTG has not been calculated before, no upper bound can be calculated and therefore no trace generation in real-time is possible.

Trace Generation of Synchronisation Term

Creating traces for synchronisation terms of unnormalised high level transition graphs is more complex than generating the trace for a single high level transition graph, because all possible transitions must be calculated according to the operational semantics of the parallel or hiding operators represented by the synchronisation term. It is not sufficient to choose any transition that is possible for one of the HLTGs, because the events labelled to this transition can occur in synchronisation sets or hiding sets of high level operators. Therefore the complete initial actions of the synchronisation term must be calculated as defined in section 12.3.2.

The calculation of the initial actions of a current location l for a current environment ε of an unnormalised HLTG requires to find all location l' with an environment ε' such that $l, \varepsilon \overset{\alpha}{\mapsto} l', \varepsilon'$ and $\alpha \notin \{\tau, \pi\}$. This requires a recursive algorithm that is similar to eliminateTaus$_{on-the-fly}$, except that no acceptance set is created. Because the algorithm is recursive, the cost of calculating the initial actions of a current location depends on the depth of the τ/π-paths of the location. To determine the maximum depth of these paths for a HLTG, all possible environments for each location have to be calculated because the conditions of the transitions can enable or disable them according to the current environment. It is not possible to assume that all transitions are enabled when calculating the maximum depth of τ/π-paths, because this could lead to circles of τ/π-paths which would not be possible for valid environments.

According to the definition 12.1, the initial actions of a synchronisation term of unnormalised HLTG is a set expression with sub-terms for every high level operator and the initial actions of the high level transition graphs as set values in these sub-term. The complexity of this set expression depends on the complexity of the high-level structure which therefore can be used to determine an upper bound for the calculation of the initial actions of the synchronisation term together with the maximal length of τ/π-paths of each high level transition graph of the synchronisation term.

Calculating an upper bound for the calculation of a possible next trace item requires the calculation of the maximal number of invisible events that can be selected. This can only be done in general if the complete state space of the synchronisation term has been calculated. Thus, traces for synchronisation terms of unnormalised HLTG can in general only be generated in hard real-time if the complete state space of the synchronisation term has been calculated previously which can cause state explosions.

When using normal form synchronisation terms together with applying the design patterns for evaluation of multiple synchronisation terms of normalised high level transition graphs in real-time, discussed in section 11.2.3, trace generation in hard real-time can be achieved without calculating the state space of the whole synchronisation term. Only the state space of each high level transition graph of the synchronisation term has to be calculated which can be significantly smaller. In this case, all possible environments for each location of a HLTG have to be calculated which is equal to calculating its state space. With this information, an upper bound for the maximum length of τ/π-paths of the HLTG can be determined. The normal form synchronisation term together with the design patterns guarantees, that all events, that occur in hiding sets of a synchronisation term are not used for synchronisation of high level transition graphs in the synchronisation term. This allows to include them in the calculation of the maximum length of the τ/π-paths of each HLTG without taking attention to any high level operators represented by the synchronisation term. Therefore it is not necessary to calculate the whole state space of the synchronisation term.

Testing with HLTG

The on-the-fly normalisation of a current location l with a current environment ε calculates the normalised node together with its initial actions and its acceptances or refusals. An upper bound for this calculation can only be determined, if all possible environments of all locations have been created previously. In this case, the conditions of the transitions of a location can be evaluated so that the maximal length of all τ/π-paths of each location can be determined. This maximal length limits the complexity of the on-the-fly normalisation of a location.

Because calculating all environments of all locations is equivalent to calculating the complete state space of the high level transition graph, this can result in a state explosion. If no environments have been calculated, no test execution and verification in real-time is possible. In this case, the graph can still be used for a delayed evaluation that not necessarily is done in real-time. This *delayed evaluation* is described in the following section 12.6.

Testing with Synchronisation term

The real-time capabilities of refusal testing with synchronisation terms of unnormalised HLTG depend on the just described real-time capabilities of the on-the-fly normalisation of unnormalised high level transition graphs. This on-the-fly normalisation can only be done in real-time if all possible environments of all locations have been previously computed. To prevent the synchronisation term from introducing τ-actions and non-determinism by the use of hiding operators, the design patterns of section 11.2.3 have to be regarded and the synchronisation term has to be in normal form. In this case, the calculation of the initial actions and acceptances or refusals of all high level transition graphs of the synchronisation term can be done in real-time. If the restrictions of the design patterns cannot be regarded or the state space of the high level transition graphs is too large, the graph can still be used for *delayed evaluation* that not necessarily is done in real-time.

12.6   Delayed Evaluation

A test system contains a *test generator*, that creates test cases that can be based on the outputs of the SUT and a *test oracle*, that evaluates the test results. As stated in the previous section, it cannot be guaranteed, that refusal testing with unnormalised HLTGs or synchronisation terms of unnormalised HLTGs can be done in real-time. Therefore they are not suitable for the test generator if new test inputs to the SUT have to be calculated in real-time. The test oracle, that monitors the inputs SUT and outputs of the SUT and has to validate these test results, does not have to do this in real-time, because no interaction takes place between the test oracle and the SUT. Even an offline validation of the test results, after the test is finished, is possible, though this obviously has disadvantages for long time tests.

In this section, a test algorithm for a delayed test evaluation is developed, based on the test main loop of the RT-Tester test engine. It starts together with the test but uses a local clock, that can fall back behind the global time of the test system. The algorithm is designed to be able to catch up with the global time, again. A local time is necessary, because it cannot be guaranteed that the calculation of the initials and refusals of the current state can be done in real-time. This local time can be different to the global time of the test system but it must be assured that it is never before the global time. It is only allowed to be behind the global time or synchronised with it. Inputs of the test AM are stored in a queue together with a time-stamp of the global time, at which they occurred. If the local time of the test process is equal to the global time, the inputs of the test AM (the outputs of the SUT or other AMs) must be included in the calculation of the test algorithm immediately. If the local time is behind the global time, only those events with a time-stamp that is behind or equal to the local time are involved in the test algorithm.

The test algorithm of the RT-Tester is implemented in the main loop of the abstract machines that processes the graph representation of the test processes. For every execution step, the set of accepted events is calculated and one of them is selected according to the test strategy of the abstract machine. This event is written to the test log and the next current state is calculated. If no event can be executed, the test AM is suspended for a period of time or increases its local time, before checking for new outputs of the SUT. The test algorithm for *delayed evaluation* is only suspended for one time-unit using the function sleep(1), if its local time is synchronised to the global time. Otherwise the local time is simply increased to check if new events from the input queue or new *elapsed timer* events must be involved in the event calculation. Inputs from the SUT or other AMs and *elapsed timer* events are the only type of events that can become available in a current state of the test AM by increasing the local time.

Outputs from the test AM to the SUT can only be produced if both times are synchronised, because otherwise they are logged with the local time of the AM but actually occur at the SUT at a different global time. This invalidates the test results. Logging them with the current global time could be wrong too, because there could be input or elapsed timer events left to process by the AM before the local time reaches the current global. So if the delayed evaluation algorithm is used for a test generator, that can have both: input and output events, it has to be assured that there does not exist any or only sufficient soft timing requirements for the interaction between AM and SUT.

In listing 12.8 the main loop for a test algorithm implementing delayed evaluation is presented. The function getAcceptedEvents() used in the algorithm calculates the initial actions and refusals of a current state. If the graph structure requires on-the-fly normalisation, it is done in this function, as well. The function nextEvent() selects the next event according to the test strategy. The next event is selected from a set of events that is the union of three sets: the initial events, excluding the input events and the elapsed timer events of the AM, the intersection of the elapsed timer events of the AM and the elapsed timer events that are generated for the current local time and the set of outputs of the SUT for the current local time. The current state of the AM is changed using the selected event, if the selected event does not cause a TARGET-SYSTEM-OUTPUT-ERROR which indicates, that it is not allowed in the current state of the AM. Finally the function putTestDriverEvent() adds the event to the trace of the test process and sends output Events to other AMs or the SUT via the CCL. Because the delayed evaluation algorithm is designed to even work with graph representations that are not capable of calculating the initial actions and refusals in real-time, it will work with real-time capable graph representations as well. Only the functions getAcceptedEvents() and nextEvent() must be adjusted for each graph structure, because they contain the details of how the

initials and refusals are calculated, whether or not the current state has to be
normalised and how progress is made for the specific graph structure.

```
main_loop(simstate)
BEGIN
    simstate ∈ SYNCTERM;  e ∈ EVENT;  init ⊂ EVENTS;  ref ∈ REFUSALS
    localtime, globaltime ∈ TIMETICK;  evolve ∈ BOOL

    evolve = true
    WHILE true DO
        DO
            IF evolve THEN
                (* Calculate initials and refusals *)
                (init,ref,simstate) = getAcceptedEvents(simstate)
                evolve = false
            FI
            IF init ≠ ∅ THEN
                (* Select next event from initials and evolves simstate *)
                (e,simstate,evolve) = nextEvent(init,ref,simstate,localtime)
                putTestDriverEvent(e,localtime)
            FI
        WHILE init ≠ ∅

        IF localtime ⩾ globaltime THEN
            (* if not behind the clock:  sleep one time unit *)
            sleep(1)
            localtime = globaltime
        ELSE
            (* if behind the clock:  increase local time *)
            localtime = localtime + 1
        FI
    OD
END
```

Listing 12.8: The algorithm of a delayed evaluation main loop.

Example

The following example shows the operating sequence of the algorithm for a SUT
emitting the events a and b and the specification P describing the desired behaviour. The timer event $setT$ indicates starting a timer that waits 5 time-ticks
and the event $elaT$ can be produced after the timer is elapsed.

```
1    #pragma AM_INPUT
2    channel a,b
3
4    #pragma AM_WARNING
5    channel warning
6
```

```
7    #pragma AM_SET_TIMER
8    channel setT
9
10   #pragma AM_ELAPSED_TIMER
11   channel elaT
12
13   P = a -> setT -> Q
14   Q = (b -> STOP) [] (elaT -> warning -> STOP)
```

Figure 12.2 illustrates the delayed evaluation of the SUT where the event b is emitted in time while in figure 12.3, the timer expires before the event is received by the checking abstract machine. Both examples start at time 0 for the global time, which is also the local time of the abstract machine (AM) representing the test process P. In this example, the AM works on an unnormalised HLTG of the process, but delayed evaluation can be used with any of the graph structures presented in this thesis.

To calculate the acceptances or refusals and initial actions, the start location is normalised using the on-the-fly normalisation defined in section 12.4.1. In the example, this calculation takes 2 time-ticks. At global time 1, the SUT produces the event a. This event is received by the test engine and stored in the input queue of the AM for P together with its corresponding time tick 1. This is illustrated in the figure as $[(a,1)]$. At this time, the AM is still normalising its current location. At global time 2, the current state of the AM is normalised and the AM is ready to handle the next events. The local time of the AM still is 0, so no events are possible in the queue. Because the only event that is possible for the test process is an output event of the SUT, the AM cannot produce an event. In this example, the calculation of the next event lasts 0.5 time-ticks. Normally an AM is suspended for a time-tick, if no actions are possible and no input from the SUT are in the queue. For delayed evaluation, the AM simply increases its internal clock so that the local time changes from 0 to 1 at global time 2.5. Now the event a is accessible to the AM and is written to the log file. The event is logged at global time 3 but with the local time 1 stored as the timing information in the log.

The AM now changes to a new current state. The on-the-fly normalisation of the next state again takes 2 time-ticks and is finished at global time 5. At the same time, the next input of the SUT is received by the test driver and stored in the input queue of the AM. The next event of the test process is $setT$. Because this is a timer event, it can be produced by the AM immediately at local time 1 (global time 5.5).

Again the next current state together with the acceptances or refusals and initial actions is calculated. This take two time-ticks to global time 7.5. The only events allowed by the test process at this point are b and $elaT$. The event $elaT$ is a timer event that is not possible until the local time is 6 and the event

b is a SUT output that has to be in the input queue of the AM together with a time-stamp that is equal or less than the local time. The event b is already in the input queue but it occurred at global time 5 so it is only accessible to the AM at local time 5. The AM now increases the local time as long as neither b nor $elaT$ is possible. Each check with an increased local timer takes 0.5 time-ticks so at global time 9.5, the AM increases its local time to 5. With this local time, the event b of the input queue becomes available. It is selected as the next event and logged at global time 10 with the time-stamp 5 of the local time.

The next current state is calculated. No events are possible at this state, because the test process stops. Still the AM is checking for input events of the SUT, because they would result in TARGET-SYSTEM-OUTPUT-ERRORs. At global time 12.5, the local time is increased to 6. From now on, the local time is increased every 0.5 time ticks after the input queue for the current local time is checked. At global time 19, the local time and the global time are both 19. As long as the local time is equal or greater than the global time, the AM behaves as a real-time AM and is suspended for 1 time-tick.

The second case, illustrated in figure 12.3, starts exactly with the same actions and timings. Up to global time 9.5 the only difference to the just described case of figure 12.2 is that the event b is not send by the SUT at global time 5 and therefore is not in the input queue of the AM. At global time 10, the AM increases the local clock to 6 and the event $elaT$ is generated. Because it is the only possible event at this time, it is chosen and the next current state is calculated. Still the local time is 6. The next possible event is *warning*. Because its the only event possible at this time (global time 12.5, local time 6), it is selected at global time 13 and the next current state is calculated. Because the event *warning* is declared as AM_WARNING, the event is logged as a TEST-WARNING.

The process P stops after the event *warning*, so no events are possible at global time 15 and therefore no event can be selected. The AM increases its timer and checks for inputs until global time 19, where the local time is increased to 14. Now the event b, that has been received from the SUT at global time 14, becomes available. Because this event is not possible for the test process P, a TARGET-SYSTEM-OUTPUT-ERROR of the event b is written to the log file of the AM. Because no event of the test process was executed, no new current state has to be calculated and the AM can go on increasing its local time. At global time 24, both clocks are synchronised. As in the previous example, the AM is suspended for 1 time-tick.

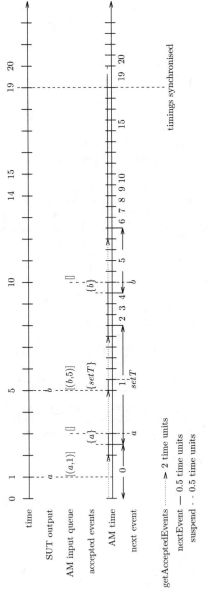

Figure 12.2: Example for delayed verification of P with the event b in time.

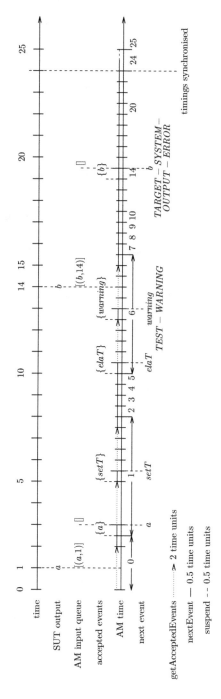

Figure 12.3: Example for delayed verification of P with the event b not in time.

Chapter 13

Implications for Test-Designs

In this chapter the different approaches to represent CSP specifications as transition systems for testing purposes are compared with each other, to evaluate, which type of transition system is well suited for which testing scenario.

The first section deals with the comparison of the approaches itself, where for example the size or the ease of the evaluation of the different approaches are put in contrast to each other. First the comparisons are realised only on the sequential process level with high level transition graphs and Roscoe-style transition graphs later these considerations are extended to synchronisation terms and Roscoe-style normalisation graphs.

Concluding this part of this thesis, the second section of this chapter summarises the considerations for the use of the different representations for testing purposes. Roscoe-style normalisation graphs are usually well suited for the most testing scenarios, but there are some situations, in which testing with any of the new representations for CSP based transition systems provides a powerful alternative to computing the completely unfolded transition system.

13.1 Comparison of Transition Systems

This section discusses the differences between the new transition system representations introduced in this thesis and the Roscoe-style transition graphs. Those benefits and weaknesses of the new approaches will be used in the following section 13.2, which will discuss, which formalisms to use for different testing objectives.

13.1.1 High Level Transition Graphs

As indicated earlier, high level transition graphs are usually smaller than Roscoe-style transition graphs, since the high level transition graphs allow to have more than one event at each transition. This approach is useful for CSP specifications, which store state information in the transition graph. This is done for example in processes modelling variables.

The language CSP itself has no concepts of variables. The assignments to variables, which are modelled in the high level transition graph approach are derived from a pattern matching mechanism, which is part of CSP_M. Even though CSP does not support any variables, it is possible to model the behaviour of variables in a CSP specification. This is done by a process, that runs in parallel to other processes, which always offers to communicate the current contents of a local process parameter to other processes. Additionally the process allows a communication, that can be used to change the contents of a process parameter and therefore changes the value of the modelled variable. Such process could be defined as follows:

```
VAR(x) = input?y -> VAR(y)
         []
         output!x -> VAR(x)
```

The size of the process as a transition graph depends of the definition of the channels *input* and *output*. Figure 13.1 shows the resulting transition graph of this process, if the channels *input* and *output* may communicate the values 1, 2 or 3. For each additional value that may be communicated, the size of the graph grows by one state, since each state represents an actual value of the modelled variable. Additionally new transitions from each existing state to the new one are created – each one labelled with the event *input.⟨value⟩*. One of the outgoing transitions from the new state, which leads back to the same state, is labelled with the event *output.⟨value⟩*. The other transitions are labelled with *input.⟨value⟩* events leading to the states representing the communicated value. These type of graphs can be huge, especially if large sets of values have to be communicated.

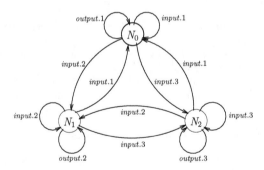

Figure 13.1: A variable process in Roscoe-style normalisation graph form.

Processes of this kind are a strength of the high level transition graph approach. As shown in figure 13.2 the size of the graph does not grow with an increasing number of communicated values, since there is always the same number of locations and transitions representing the behaviour of the process. The only thing that grows is the number of assignments at the transition representing the *input?y* event. An implementation, which generates and evaluates these high level transition graphs can use the knowledge on the type of a channel to create an internal representation of these event-assignment pairs, from which all combinations can be derived without the need to explicitly calculate all pairs. Therefore this representation can be significantly smaller than Roscoe-style transition graphs.

Another difference between the high level transition graphs and the Roscoe-style transition graphs can be observed in figure 13.2: in high level transition graphs process references are modelled as π-events, whereas FDR produces no event for process references. Hence it is possible that Roscoe-style transition graphs are smaller, since there is no need to model assignments to variables at process references.

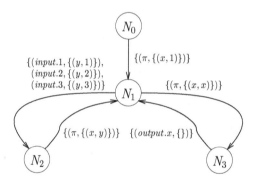

Figure 13.2: A variable process in high level transition graph form.

Those π-events tend to add more locations to a HLTG, which may lead to the effect, that Roscoe-style transition graphs are significantly smaller than the corresponding HLTG, as shown in the following example:

```
1    channel a, b : {1..2}
2
3    START = A(1) [] B(2)
4    A(x)  = a!x -> STOP
5    B(y)  = b!y -> STOP
```

The process **START** can only produce two events: $a.1$ and $b.2$. The resulting Roscoe-style transition graph as shown in figure 13.3 is simple, since it consists only of two states and two transitions leaving from the start state to the end state. Unlike Roscoe-style transition graphs the corresponding high level transition graph is much more complex, since there are internal π-events, which do not effect the decision of the external choice operator. Therefore the HLTG contains all possible combinations of assignments, that can take place at π-events, leading to a larger graph shown in figure 13.4.

Figure 13.3: Roscoe-style transition graph for process $START$

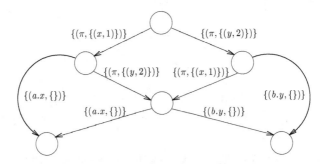

Figure 13.4: External choice and process references

On page 96 the difference between infinite states and finite HLTG was established. This problem indicates another strength of the ClaO system: It is theoretically possible to use infinite (or at least finite, but very large) transition systems for testing purposes, which would not be possible with tools like **FDR2**.

The normalisation of both types of transition systems generates exactly the same results, since in both approaches the non-determinism, which is introduced by τ-events or multiple transition labelled with the same event leaving from one state, is completely eliminated, such that after any trace of the system a unique state in the normalised transition system can be identified in which the system is in.

13.1.2 Synchronisation Terms

Even though the normalisation of the high level transition graphs and Roscoe-style transition graphs for identical processes are resulting in the same normal form graph, the approach suggested in this theses has its special strength with interleaved or parallel systems. In contrast to Roscoe-style normalisation graphs, which requires all parallelism to be completely unfolded, the synchronisation terms, which provide a representation for parallel high level transition graphs, do not have this disadvantage. Synchronisation terms model the synchronisation information for parallelism or additional hiding information within its own structure and allows the computation of the behaviour of the parallel system using the rules of the operational semantics for CSP. Those terms can be applied either to high level transition graphs as described in chapter 5, or to normal form graphs, which are the result of the normalisation of any transition system.

Applying synchronisation terms to unnormalised high level transition graphs allows an interpretation of the term as an unnormalised unfolded transition system. Therefore the interpretation of synchronisation terms can e.g. be used to apply the normalisation algorithm for transition systems directly to the term. This would allow the generation of the normal form graph without the need to completely compute the unfolded transition system first. Since those unfolded transition system may be rather large, it is possible to compute the normal form of larger CSP specifications in contract to ordinary approaches, because this intermediate step is no longer necessary.

An alternative to the complete normalisation of the synchronisation terms with unnormalised high level transition graphs is the on-the-fly normalisation, which was introduced earlier in section 12.4. For testing purposes this mechanism allows to use very large and even infinite CSP specifications. The disadvantage is that it is no longer possible to evaluate those representations in hard real-time.

This disadvantage does no longer exist for synchronisation terms, if they are applied to normal form transition systems. Under certain restrictions, which have been discussed in section 11.2.3, the evaluation of synchronisation terms is possible in hard real-time, since for each term there is exactly one following term representing the new state of the parallel system. The designer of the test cases have only to ensure, that the specifications do not introduce non-determinism by its high level synchronisation and hiding structure, which would violate the real-time capability of the evaluation algorithm for synchronisation terms.

On the other hand using normal form transition systems in the leafs of synchronisation terms usually results in a larger representation in contrast to the use of high level transition graphs at the leafs. This is the case, since the normalisation of high level transition graphs usually produces larger representations for the behaviour of the sequential systems. But those HLTG representations cannot be evaluated in real-time, which relativises this advantage.

Comparing synchronisation terms using normalised high level transition graphs with unfolded Roscoe-style normalisation graphs of parallel systems leads to two important differences: Unfolded Roscoe-style normalisation graphs of interleaved systems tend to be large, since the interleaving operator allows all possible interactions of the systems to happen. If instead the set of events to synchronise on or the set of hiding events is rather large, a lot of those possible interactions cannot occur. Especially for those types of specifications the resulting normal form transition system is in general smaller then the unnormalised graphs. On the contrary for synchronisation terms the resulting structure of the terms and the underlying transition systems, do not depend on the number of elements in the synchronisation set or hiding information of the high level CSP operators.

The second difference is the real-time capability of the evaluation algorithm. If the design patterns mentioned above are used, both types of transition system representations can be evaluated for testing purposes in real-time. Only if those patterns, which pose no large restriction on the testing specifications, cannot be applied and evaluation in real-time is required, it is more efficient to use Roscoe-style normalisation graph for testing purposes. This is the case, since nondeterminism introduced by the high-level CSP operators can only be prevented by the multiple synchronisation terms. But those multiple synchronisation terms cannot be evaluated in real-time.

13.2   Test Case Design

In the previous section the strength and weaknesses of the different approaches of representing CSP specifications as transition systems have been discussed in detail. The following four different type of representations for labelled transition systems have been discussed, and their corresponding test algorithms have been explained in this part:

   I. Roscoe-style normalisation Graphs

  II. Synchronisation Terms with Roscoe-style normalisation Graphs

 III. High Level Transition Graphs

 IV. Synchronisation Terms with High Level Transition Graphs

Testing with Roscoe-style normalisation graphs is already well understood and implemented in tools like the RT-Tester. Recent experience of working with the RT-Tester and the underlying Roscoe-style normalisation graphs helped to identify different applications for the abstract machines in a test case. In the following the different purposes, that abstract machines can be used for, are

described, where at least three different types of applications of the abstract
machines in test scenarios have been identified:

Stimulation

Some abstract machines are used only to stimulate the input channels of
the system under test. Those machines need not interact with any other
abstract machine, but only produces outputs at certain points in time.
Therefore these *stimulators* do not process any inputs, but requires the
production of traces in hard real-time. Often the environment of a SUT or
non-reactive parts of the system specification can be represented by such
stimulators.

Control

Abstract machines which *control* the test execution are used to produce
outputs to the SUT or other abstract machines as a result of a sequence
of input events. Since the generation of traces consisting of input and
output events is vital for this kind of abstract machine, the evaluation
of the structure of the underlying normalised transition system must be
performable in hard real-time. This type of abstract machine is used to
generate different test cases depending on the outputs of the SUT or other
abstract machines, while the following results are verified simultaneously.

Checking

A third type of application for abstract machines are the ones checking, if
the output of the SUT is correct according to a specification. Especially
these checking machines occasionally have to be implemented for the RT-
Tester as *customised abstract machines* in C/C++, if the CSP specification
would produce a transition system that causes a state explosion. These
machines usually take only input events and produce no output events.

These checks need not necessarily be performed in hard real-time, since it
is sufficient to evaluate the test results with a slight delay. But still the
checking should be done during test execution, so it is possible to stop an
already failed test. Therefore an offline test evaluation is often not desirable.

The table 13.1 shows, which type of transition system is well suited for which
of the test applications described above. Checking abstract machines can be
required to process inputs of the SUT or other abstract machines in hard real-
time, or it may suffice to use a delayed checking algorithm as described in section
12.6. Each of the four possible applications has different requirements to timing
constraints or what information to be calculated from the transition system.

The *stimulation* requires only the transition system to be traversed in such
a way, that one of the possible following events can be determined in real-time.
This is possible for Roscoe-style normalisation graphs and synchronisation terms

	I	II	III	IV
Stimulation	×	×[1]	×[2]	×[1,2]
Control	×	×[1]	×[2]	×[1,2]
Checking in Hard Real-Time	×	×[1]	×[2]	×[1,2]
Delayed Checking	×	×	×	×

[1] Only if the design-patterns for the evaluation of synchronisation
terms in real-time as described in section 11.2.3 are used.
[2] Only if the range-calculation algorithm was used to determine the
maximum length of τ/π-chains in the high level transition graph.

Table 13.1: Transition Systems for Testing Applications

with Roscoe-style normalisation graphs, since both allow the computation of
the initial events in hard real-time. The only restriction for synchronisation
terms with Roscoe-style normalisation graphs are that the design patterns from
section 11.2.3 are required to be applied. In principle high level transition graphs
can also be used to produce traces in real-time, but that requires an a priori
investigation of the complete state space of the specification, to determine the
longest chain of τ/π-events, which specifies the upper bound for evaluating the
high level transition graph. Such a priori investigation of the complete state space
has already been introduced as the *range calculation* in section 12.2. Finally, if
such range calculation can be performed for all high level transition graphs of a
synchronisation term and the design patterns are applied to the synchronisation
term itself, it is in general also possible to perform a trace generation for graphs
of type IV. as well.

Control abstract machines and the ones performing *checking in hard real-time*
demand the most from the underlying transition systems, since the computation
of the initials and refusals as well as the evaluation of test results for input and
output events are required to be computed in real-time. This can be achieved
for all types of transition system representation. Since if the constraints from
a above are met, the computation of the initials and refusals in each state are
possible in real-time.

Delayed checking abstract machines can employ any transition system abstraction introduced in this thesis, since it is not required, that the computation
of the initials and refusals and the deduction of following state must be performable in real-time. It is sufficient, if the algorithm is fast enough to keep up
with the execution, even if sometimes the abstract machine cannot process the
incoming events in real-time. An algorithm for the delayed checking abstract
machines has been introduced in section 12.6.

The different types of transition system abstractions described in this part can
therefore all be used for delayed checking, which is one of the achievements of
this thesis. Additionally it has been shown, that all transition system abstraction

using synchronisation terms or high level transition graphs are equally well suited for testing purposes as the completely unfolded Roscoe-style normalisation graphs used in the current implementation of the RT-Tester. The only restriction is that the design patterns for the test specifications have to be used and that the range-calculation is possible for all high level transition graphs.

Using synchronisation terms with Roscoe-style normalisation graphs for testing results in a slightly more complex evaluation of the initial events and the refusals of the current state, but the gain is a significantly lower memory consumption during test execution, since the representations for the modelled transition systems are more compact. All other formalisms require an even large ammount of time to compute the initial events and the refusals of the next state of the modelled transition system, but this can still be done in bounded time.

Another improvement in the field of testing is achieved by using the combination of delayed checking abstract machines with synchronisation terms applied to high level transition graphs. This allows to use significantly larger CSP specifications for checking purposes as possible with Roscoe-style normalisation graphs. Even infinite specifications with a finite representation as high level transition graph can now be used for testing, since the on-the-fly normalisation only processes those parts of the state space that is currently been explored by the test. Therefore many checkers, which have to be implemented as customised abstract machines until now, can in the future be implemented as CSP specifications. It is important to note, that it is not possible to use infinite specifications for testing in real-time, since the range-calculation is not possible for that types of graphs.

Part IV

The CIaO System

This part describes the tool ClaO, which has been implemented by the authors. The first version of ClaO was developed as part of the authors diploma thesis [ ]. The intention was to develop an interpreter for CSP based on the operational semantics, which is the reason why ClaO is called "CSP Interpreter applying the Operational semantics". Further information about early versions of ClaO can be found at http://www.ciao-team.de, where a copy of the diploma thesis and the source of ClaO-1.0 can be obtained. That thesis includes a lot of information about the theory behind ClaO-1.0 and the implementation of the three tools csp_parser, ciao and xciao. Additional information about abstract syntax trees and how to use them for interpreting CSP processes can also be found there.

For this PhD-thesis ClaO has been extended to not only interprete CSP specifications on-the-fly, but also to generate high level transition graphs and synchronisation terms from CSP specifications. These generated transition systems can be normalised according to the algorithms introduced in the previous part. This functionality has been implemented in two additional tools: csp2rtt and csp2alpha. A third tool has been developed to integrate the new transition graph representations in the automated testing software RT-Tester: an abstract machine rttctgam, which can be used to use high level transition graphs and synchronisation terms for real-time testing.

Chapter 14 explains the different tools from the users point of view. For each tool a small description is given, what tasks can be achieved using the tool. An exemplary run of the tool then explains how the functions of the tools can be used and what the results are. Each section closes with a list of command line arguments that can be given to each tool to change the behaviour of the tool.

A different view on the tools is given in chapter 15, which describes the implementation of the ClaO system. This starts with a description of the abstract syntax tree and its corresponding implemented classes, which are used to represent the syntax of CSP specification. In the following section a brief description of the classes required for the interpretation of CSP specifications, generating and representing high level transition graphs and synchronisation terms are described in detail. That chapter is especially useful for persons, who are interested in extending the functionality of the ClaO system.

266

Chapter 14

Applications

The ClaO system consists of several different programs, which represent different frontends to the functionality, implemented in the ClaO core system. Throughout this chapter these tools will be introduced and their usage will be explained in detail. The tools can be divided into three different categories, which are going to be described briefly in the following.

Debugging of CSP specifications

Developing CSP specifications for testing or model checking purposes is a complex task. Therefore the resulting code for any non-trivial application will probably contain mistakes causing the test or model-check to fail. Understanding and correcting such errors is often difficult, since especially for systems containing parallelism and hiding small changes in one component can have strong effects on other parts of the systems. This non-trivial task can be supported by tools in different ways. Usually a model-checker or a test-system shows a trace of the system leading to the faulty state. Especially for large non-deterministic specifications this means, that the parts of the system responsible for generation the observed outputs, can be distributed all over the specification. Detecting such errors manually is difficult.

Computer aided debugging allows the developer to inspect the states of the different components of the system, where at the same time he must still be able to oversee the state of the whole system. It is possible to interactively observe and influence the systems progress, while events are produced. With such debugging tools effects between different components of the system are easier to detect, and therefore it is simpler to debug the specification. Several tools of ClaO have been developed to serve these purposes:

- csp_parser is a parser for CSP specifications, that loads a file and parses its syntax. If there is a syntax error in the specification, the line and a brief description of the error is displayed as a result. This tool is explained in more detail in section 14.2.

- `ciao` and `xciao` are debuggers for CSP specifications using the operational semantics to interprete the specification. Their functionality is presented in sections 14.3 and 14.4.

Transition Graph Generation

A second application area of ClaO is the generation of transition graphs from CSP specifications. The tool `csp2rtt`, which is presented in section 14.5, generates a high level transition graph from a CSP specification and transforms it in such a way, that is can be used for testing or model-checking purposes.

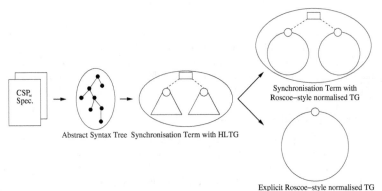

Figure 14.1: Stages of the Transition Graph Generation

Figure 14.1 illustrates the different stages of the transition graph generation. First the abstract syntax tree is created from a CSP specification, which is transformed into a synchronisation term using high level transition graphs. In an optional following normalisation stage either only the high level transition graph is normalised into a Roscoe-style normalisation graph or the whole tranistion system is unfolded.

Testing Components

The third component of the ClaO suit are the tools `csp2alpha` and `rttctgam`, which are both implemented for the RT-Tester system. `csp2alpha`, as explained in section 14.6, parses a CSP specification and extracts all information about the channel-definitions in the file. Those information is enriched with RT-Tester meta information on different types of channels (e.g. input, output or timing channels) and exported in a format, that the different RT-Tester tools can read. The `rttctgam` is an exemplary RT-Tester abstract machine, that illustrates the use of synchronisation terms with Roscoe-style normalisation graphs for testing purposes. Its usage is described in section 14.7.

In the following sections the tools serving the different purposes are explained. For each tool its main application area and some examples are stated, such that is becomes clear to the user on how to use the tool. The concluding part of each section is a short reference to the commands, that can be used with each tool.

14.1 Strict Alternation

This section introduces the specification `strict-alternation.csp`, which will be used as an example throughout this chapter. The specification gives a CSP abstraction of the algorithm for mutual exclusion by strict alternation. Such algorithm has been suggested by Tanenbaum in [ ].

$GOOD\_MUTEX$ is an abstract process that specifies a correct mutual exclusion. It indicates, that it is never possible to have two processes in a critical section at the same time. The events *enter* and *leave* represent the beginning and the end of the critical section. Additionally the communicated values on those channels show, which of the two processes is currently entering or leaving the critical section.

The processes SYS specifies a system consisting of two processes, and their turn variable. By using the FDR model checker, it can be shown, that SYS refines $GOOD\_MUTEX \mid\mid\mid CHAOS(\Sigma \setminus \{\mid enter, leave \mid\})$ in the traces model of CSP.

```
1   ----------------------------------------------------------------
2   -- CSP abstraction of  the  algorithm for mutual exclusion
3   -- by strict alternation (c.f. Tanenbaum, Modern Operating Systems,
4   -- Section 2.2.3)
5   ----------------------------------------------------------------
6
7   -- simple type definitions
8   Pid = { 0, 1 }
9
10  -------------------------------------------------------------
11  -- Event and channel declarations
12  -------------------------------------------------------------
13
14  -- events notifying that process i enters/leaves its
15  -- critical section: enter.i/leave.i
16  pragma AM_INPUT
17  channel enter : Pid
18  channel leave : Pid
19
20  -- events denoting that process i does uncritical things
21  pragma AM_OUTPUT
22  channel doNonCritical : Pid
23
```

```
24   -- channels for CSP definition of the turn variable:
25   channel rdTurn : Pid
26   channel wrTurn : Pid
27
28   ----------------------------------------------------------------
29   -- CSP implementation of the turn variable
30   ----------------------------------------------------------------
31   turn(pid) = rdTurn!pid -> turn(pid)
32                 []
33                 wrTurn?newPid -> turn(newPid)
34
35   ----------------------------------------------------------------
36   -- the CSP version of an active wait enterregion function
37   ----------------------------------------------------------------
38   enterregion(pid) = rdTurn?id ->
39                           ( if (id == pid )
40                             then SKIP
41                             else enterregion(pid) )
42
43   ----------------------------------------------------------------
44   -- the CSP version of an leaveregion function
45   ----------------------------------------------------------------
46   leaveregion(pid) = wrTurn!(1-pid) -> SKIP
47
48   ----------------------------------------------------------------
49   -- Two processes, entering and leaving their
50   -- critical sections:
51   ----------------------------------------------------------------
52   P(pid) = doNonCritical.pid
53               -> enterregion(pid);
54                  enter.pid -> leave.pid
55               -> leaveregion(pid);
56                  P(pid)
57
58   ----------------------------------------------------------------
59   -- the system consisting of the 2 processes and their turn
60   -- variable
61   ----------------------------------------------------------------
62   SYS = ( P(0) ||| P(1) )
63           [| {| wrTurn , rdTurn |} |]
64         turn(0)
65
66   SYSFD = SYS \ DONT_CARE
67
68   ----------------------------------------------------------------
69   -- an abstract process denoting correct mutual
70   -- exclusion
71   ----------------------------------------------------------------
72   GOOD_MUTEX = enter.0 -> leave.0 -> GOOD_MUTEX
73                  |~|
74                  enter.1 -> leave.1 -> GOOD_MUTEX
```

```
75
76   GOOD_MUTEX2 = enter.0 -> leave.0 -> enter.1 -> leave.1 -> GOOD_MUTEX2
77
78   -----------------------------------------------------------
79   -- the abstract system specifying correct operation:
80   -- behaviour of GOOD_MUTEX on the enter/leave channels,
81   -- with respect to the other events don't care
82   -----------------------------------------------------------
83   DONT_CARE = {| wrTurn, rdTurn, doNonCritical |}
84
85   SAFE = GOOD_MUTEX ||| CHAOS(DONT_CARE)
86
87   SAFEFD = SAFE \ DONT_CARE
```

14.2 csp_parser

The application **csp_parser** can be used to check the syntactical correctness of
CSP$_M$ specifications. For an overview of the supported syntax of the ClaO system
see section 15.3.

csp_parser requires the path to a CSP specification as its command line
argument. As soon as the program is started, the contents of the file is read
and the program tries to parse it according to the syntax of CSP$_M$. A grammar,
which can be used to describe the syntax of CSP$_M$ specifications, is presented in
appendix C. If the specification is syntactically incorrect, the parsing process will
fail and the program will display an output like the following:

```
*** parse error near line 74 of strict-alternation.csp
*** last parsed symbol was 'enter.1' at line 74
```

This error message helps to find the mistake in the CSP specification. The
error message from above could for example be produced, if the following lines
were part of a CSP specification the parser had to analyse:

```
68   -----------------------------------------------------------
69   -- an abstract process denoting correct mutual
70   -- exclusion
71   -----------------------------------------------------------
72   GOOD_MUTEX = enter.0 -> leave.0 -> GOOD_MUTEX
73               |~|
74               enter.1 ; leave.1 -> GOOD_MUTEX
```

The error message helps to find the simple mistake in line 74, which can be
corrected by replacing the sequential composition operator ";" with the prefix
operator "->".

If the specification can successfully be parsed, a context analysis is started
which divides the different parts of the specification into categories: processes,

functions, channels, constants and identifiers. The result of this context analysis is written to the console. Below follows an exemplary output of the `csp_parser`, which successfully has parsed a CSP specification. Since the output is rather long, it has been shortened at several points, which is marked by "..." in the output.

```
processes:
    turn = rdTurn!pid -> turn(pid)
           []
           wrTurn?newPid -> turn(newPid)
    enterregion = rdTurn?id -> if (id == pid)
                    then (SKIP)
                    else (enterregion(pid))
    ...

identifier:
    Pid
    enter
    leave
    ...

channels:
    enter
    leave
    doNonCritical
    rdTurn
    wrTurn

constant values:
    { 0, 1 }
    {| doNonCritical, rdTurn, wrTurn |}

functions:

    ..
```

An additional option, that can be passed to `csp_parser` is the option `-v`. With this option, the parser is put into verbose mode, which generates much more output illustrating the internal structure of the CSP specification in the ClaO system.

14.2.1   Command Line Options

`csp_parser` expects the filename of the specification to be parsed as command line argument. The full command line options of `csp_parser` read as follows:

```
usage: csp_parser filename [-v]
```

    -v   Generate verbose output during execution.
    filename   The name of the CSP_M specification.

14.3   ClaO

The application ClaO is a command line CSP interpreter. It is able to parse a
CSP$_M$ specification and execute a selected process, defined in the specification.
During the execution, it creates a trace of the events produced from the speci-
fication by interpreting the syntax of the process in the operational semantics.
Figure 14.2 shows an exemplary run of ClaO.

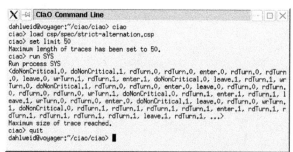

Figure 14.2: ClaO in a terminal window

After `ciao` is started, it optionally parses a CSP specification given as an
command line option and then shows the prompt and accepts user commands. If
no file was specified, ClaO generates a command line prompt and waits for user
inputs. Additionally the user can also provide a command file containing ClaO
instructions. If such a command file is given as an argument, ClaO executes the
instructions in the file sequentially.

There are several ways of loading the CSP specification into the ClaO-system.
One way, as already explained above, is to specify the filename as an argument
to the call of `ciao`. In the following the result of starting `ciao` in verbose mode
with a CSP specification as argument can be seen. Without the verbose-option,
only the prompt `ciao>` would be printed.

```
dahlweid@voyager:~> ciao strict-alternation.csp -v
loading file strict-alternation.csp:
parsing file ... (creating predefined functions) (creating predefined types) done
calculating types ... done
cecking types ... done
parsing complete.
ciao>
```

The other possibility is using the `load`-command in ClaOs command line interface. In both cases the files is loaded into the system, and if parsing the
specification was successful, it can be processed further with other ClaO commands.

```
dahlweid@voyager:~> ciao
ciao> load strict-alternation.csp
ciao>
```

Executing a CSP process by its operational semantics can be achieved by entering the run-command with the name of the process to be started. The list-command can be used to determine the name of all identifiers, that have been defined in the specification. This list of identifiers contains all names of channels, types, functions and processes of the specification.

```
ciao> list
global identifier:
Pid
enter
leave
doNonCritical
rdTurn
wrTurn
turn
enterregion
leaveregion
P
SYS
SYSFD
DONT_CARE
GOOD_MUTEX
GOOD_MUTEX2
SAFE
SAFEFD
ciao>
```

The process SYS is one of the processes without parameters of the CSP specification that can be used for the interpretation. Now it would be possible to use the command run SYS to execute that process by using the rules of the operational semantics. But the process SYS in non-terminating and ClaO would therefore execute the process infinitely. To prevent this, the command set limit n can be used, that instructs ClaO that the execution of the process should be interrupted, if a trace of the specified size n has been produced:

```
ciao> set limit 50
Maximum length of traces has been set to 50.
ciao>
```

If no limit is required, the command set limit 0 can be entered, which prevents the interruption of the process. Now that a limit has been set, the process SYS can be executed:

```
ciao> run SYS
Run process SYS
<doNonCritical.1, doNonCritical.0, rdTurn.0, rdTurn.0, enter.0, rdTurn.0,
rdTurn.0, rdTurn.0, rdTurn.0, rdTurn.0, rdTurn.0, leave.0, rdTurn.0, wrTurn.1,
rdTurn.1, enter.1, doNonCritical.0, rdTurn.1, leave.1, wrTurn.0,
doNonCritical.1, rdTurn.0, rdTurn.0, rdTurn.0, rdTurn.0, rdTurn.0, rdTurn.0,
rdTurn.0, rdTurn.0, enter.0, leave.0, wrTurn.1, doNonCritical.0, rdTurn.1,
enter.1, leave.1, wrTurn.0, doNonCritical.1, rdTurn.0, enter.0, rdTurn.0,
rdTurn.0, leave.0, wrTurn.1, doNonCritical.0, rdTurn.1, rdTurn.1, rdTurn.1,
rdTurn.1, enter.1, ...>
Maximum size of trace reached.
ciao>
```

Looking closely at the resulting trace reveals that no τ-events are displayed to the user, instead only those events are shown, that can also be observed by the environment. For the trace generation ClaO non-deterministically chooses one of the possible τ-events without displaying it. This behaviour can be changes with the **set tau on** command. If this command is given and the same process is started once again, the resulting trace now also contains τ-events, which are written as _tau. Any occurrence of $\checkmark$ would represented by the event _tick in the trace. Since usual event names must not start with an underline-character, this choice for the names of these special events imposes no restrictions to the names of the other events.

```
ciao> set tau on
ciao> run SYS
Run process SYS
<doNonCritical.0, rdTurn.0, _tau, enter.0, leave.0, wrTurn.1, _tau,
doNonCritical.0, doNonCritical.1, rdTurn.1, rdTurn.1, _tau, enter.1, leave.1,
rdTurn.1, rdTurn.1, wrTurn.0, rdTurn.0, _tau, enter.0, leave.0, _tau,
wrTurn.1, _tau, doNonCritical.0, doNonCritical.1, rdTurn.1, rdTurn.1, _tau,
rdTurn.1, rdTurn.1, rdTurn.1, enter.1, leave.1, wrTurn.0, _tau,
doNonCritical.1, rdTurn.0, rdTurn.0, rdTurn.0, rdTurn.0, rdTurn.0, rdTurn.0,
rdTurn.0, rdTurn.0, _tau, rdTurn.0, enter.0, leave.0, rdTurn.0, ...>
Maximum size of trace reached.
ciao>
```

For debugging a CSP specification it might be useful to step through a specification and inspect the initial events of the current state. The can be achieved by the **set user on** command, which switches on the interactive mode during trace generation. For each step that the operational semantics allows, all possible initial events are printed to the command line. The user just has to select one of the events to be executed. For τ-events a special handling has been implemented: each τ-event is printed with an additional information field that states, which event is originally responsible for the production of the τ-event. This is especially useful for specifications using hiding, since the original name of the event is still visible during the interactive mode, though it is visible in the trace as

τ-event. After finishing the interpretation by entering 0, which stops the process execution, the complete generated trace is printed to the console. An exemplary run of the interactive mode can be seen in the following:

```
ciao> set user on
Interactive mode on
ciao> run SYS
Run process SYS

0: stop process execution
1: doNonCritical.0
2: doNonCritical.1
> 1
doNonCritical.0
0: stop process execution
1: doNonCritical.1
2: rdTurn.0
> 2
rdTurn.0
0: stop process execution
1: doNonCritical.1
2: _tau (_tau)
> 2
_tau
0: stop process execution
1: enter.0
2: doNonCritical.1
> 1
enter.0
0: stop process execution
1: leave.0
2: doNonCritical.1
> 1
leave.0
0: stop process execution
1: doNonCritical.1
2: wrTurn.1
> 2
wrTurn.1
0: stop process execution
1: doNonCritical.1
2: _tau (_tau)
> 0
<doNonCritical.0, rdTurn.0, _tau, enter.0, leave.0, wrTurn.1,
Debugging session terminated.
ciao>
```

But in ClaO it is not only possible to run and debug processes. There are further commands like eval, that expects an identifier of an expression or function as its argument. If the identifier represents a function call, the arguments must be specified in following brackets. The expression or function is evaluated and its value is returned. Lets for example take the following simple specification:

```
1   A = { 1, 2, 3 }
2   foo(x) = x*2
```

With ClaO it is possible to do the following evaluations:

```
ciao> eval A
{ 1, 2, 3 }
ciao>eval foo(3)
6
ciao> quit
```

The first command evaluates the expression represented by A yielding in returning the set $\{1, 2, 3\}$. The second example is a function call, which passes the value 3 for the argument x of the function. The expression is evaluated using the specified bindings and returns the resulting value.

14.3.1 ClaO Commands

The commands `ciao` accepts as inputs are explained in the following. Some of the commands have already been explained above.

clear
> This command removes the abstract syntax tree from the runtime environment of ClaO. This is normally necessary before loading a new specification.

compile *id*
> With the command `compile`, it is possible to generate the high level transition graph of the process with name *id*. The selected process must not require any arguments. As a result of this process the number of locations and labels that have been generated are shown.

eval *id*[(*args*)]
> The command `eval` evaluates expressions. It expects an identifier of an expression or function as its argument. If the identifier refers to a function, the arguments must be specified as a comma separated list in the brackets.

help
> The command `help` prints the list of all commands that can be used in ClaO.

list
> The `list` command displays a list of all global identifiers in the abstract syntax representation of the currently loaded process. The list contains the names of all defined processes, channels, datatypes and functions.

load *filename*

> Using the command load, users can instruct ClaO to load and parse a CSP specification.

print [*id*]

> This command prints the ASCII-representation of all elements of the abstract syntax representation. If the optional *id* is specified, the output is only generated for the given identifier.

quit

> quit can be used to end a ClaO session.

run *id*

> With the command run, it is possible to start a process id. id must be an identifier referencing a CSP process. The process must not require any arguments.

set *option value*

> is used to set options that are required for execution.

> set limit *number*
>
> > With this version of the set command, the maximum length of a trace, the ClaO produces during the execution of a CSP process, can be defined. The default value is 0 meaning unlimited traces.

> set tau on|off
>
> > With this command it is possible to decide whether τ-events should be displayed in the generated traces or not. The default value is off, which means that no τ-events are shown in the resulting traces.

> set user on|off
>
> > This option toggles whether for each step of the execution ClaO should wait for the user to select the next event or just choose one itself. The default value is off meaning that ClaO generates traces without user interaction.

14.3.2   Command Line Options

In addition to the commands, which triggers certain functionality of the ClaO system, it is also possible to specify some options at program start, which changes the overall behaviour of ciao. The following options can be set by the user as command line options of the program:

```
usage: ciao --help ( -h, -? )          help: prints this message
       ciao [-v] [-w[0-9]] [-e] [-P] [-T] [-i csp_spec]
            [-I include_dir[:include_dir]] [csp_file] [ciao_cmd_file]
```

-v	Ciao produces verbose output during execution.
-w[0-9]	This option sets the warning level to a value between 0 and 9. Using a warning level of 0 would force the application to show only critical errors while with warning level 9, all warnings would be shown, that are for example generated during the context analysis or during the transition graph generation.
-e	This option forces the parser to calculate a special set called *Events*, which contains the alphabet Σ of the specification. For the execution of processes this is not necessary, but the option allows a print Events command in ClaO to inspect the set of events.
-P	This option can be used to suppress the creation of the hard-coded predefined functions and types. The predefined functions are: *set union*, *set intersection*, *set difference* and *head* and *tail* for sequences. Currently, the only predefined type is *Bool*.
-T	This option stops the parser from calculating and checking the types of the definitions in the CSP specification.
-i csp_spec	This option can be used to specify the name of a CSP specification that contains definitions that should be parsed before the main CSP specification. This is an alternative mechanism to the include statement in CSP specifications.
-I include_dir	Use this option to specify a colon separated list of include directories in which included CSP specifications are searched.
csp_file	The name of the file containing the CSP specification that will be parsed at program start.
ciao_cmd_file	The name of a file containing the ClaO commands that will be executed after the CSP specification is successfully loaded and parsed.

14.4   XClaO

One design-goal during the development of the shell-interface of ciao was to provide a simple command-line interface, which provides the basic means to debug CSP specifications. But this is not the only user interface the the functionality of the ClaO system. The graphical user-interface of the ClaO system is called XClaO, which was designed to function as a comfortable debugger for CSP.

Programming a debugger for CSP is in certain points more complex than to implement one for other sequential programming languages, since in CSP it is necessary to provide means to access any parts of parallel systems, which participate in the generation of the next possible events. As other debuggers, it must also be possible to inspect the variables, that are visible in the current state of the system. Selecting one of the initial events must trigger the production of that event and generate the new current state the system is in. A graphical user interface provides better means to see the hierarchy of processes involved in the production of events, than it would be possible with command line tools.

In addition to the hierarchy of processes a detailed inspection of the individual processes is necessary. This includes to indicate, which parts of a process have already been executed, which could be executed in the next step, and which parts are currently not available for execution. To make the debugging easier, this should all be possible on the syntax representation of the processes. Doing so on transition system would make the task of determining which parts of the system participate in the generation of which events more difficult.

While these features provide means for investigating a process in a specific state, executing CSP processes also requires an interactive selection of one of the initial events available in the current state. This event is used to execute the next step and transfer the system it into its target state.

14.4.1   Basic functions of XClaO

After starting xciao an empty window is shown, displaying a menu, a status bar, a white and a yellow area. The white area on the left hand side of the window is called the *process tree*, containing all channels, expressions and processes defined in the currently loaded specification. The *process view* on the right hand side displays the syntactical structure of a process, that can be selected in the process tree. The first step in XClaO usually is loading a CSP specification from a file. For this the *Load* command from the *File* menu can be used. After selecting that entry from the menu, a dialog opens, allowing the user to select a file.

If the file is loaded successfully, all expressions, channels and unparametrised processes are listed in the process tree. Double-clicking any of the defined processes changes the displayed process in the process view. A graphical representation of the selected process is displayed in a hierarchical way as shown in figure 14.3.

Each operator of the CSP specification is represented in the graphical representation of the abstract syntax tree using a button, which can be selected by pression a mouse button. These buttons are connected by lines representing the hierarchy of the operators in the process definition. If one of these buttons is selected, another window opens showing the events that are offered to the environment by the operational semantics of the represented operator.

Not only the processes can be selected in the process tree, but also the expressions and channels. Double-clicking those objects triggers an output of detailed information about that expression or channel, e.g. the possible communication values of the channel or the syntactic structure of the expressions. One extension

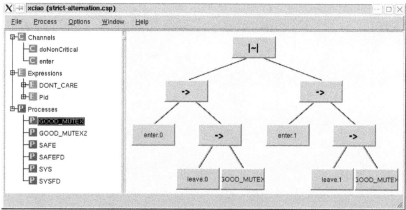

Figure 14.3: Displaying a selected process

of this mechanism, that could be implemented in future versions of XClaO would
be to evaluate the expressions under arguments, that could be provided by the
user. Such functionality is already implemented in the ClaO tool and could easily
be adopted for XClaO.

14.4.2 Executing Processes

In oder to execute a selected CSP process, the item *Run* from the *Process*-menu
has to be activated. In the following example the CSP specification
strict-alternation.csp from section 14.1 was loaded and the process SYS was
executed.

When XClaO is executing a specification, the usage of the process tree and the
process view changes. The process tree does not contain expressions or channel
definitions anymore, but only the currently running processes and the history
of already generated events is displayed. The history representing the recently
generated trace is initially empty and the process tree shows all processes, that
are initially participating in the generation of events. Different colouring of the
boxes in the process view indicate different states of the operators: green buttons
indicate, that the represented CSP operator may contribute in the execution of
the next step generated by the system. A light grey button indicates that these
parts of the specification cannot be executed at this stage, since the execution
has not yet evolved that far. Finally there are buttons in dark grey representing
part of a specification, that have already been used to execute the process.

The process view displays only one process at a time. The high level structure of the processes is indicated in the process tree, showing which processes

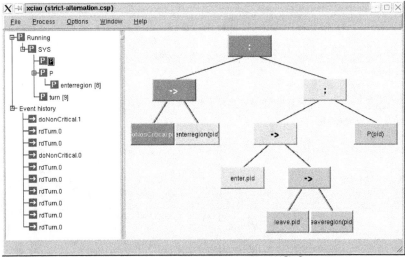

Figure 14.4: Executing a process in XClaO

have been called from which other process. Double-clicking any of the displayed processes in the tree, switches the process view to display the selected process.

In order to proceed with the execution of a CSP specification the user has to choose an event for the next step. All currently available events are presented in the *event-list*-window, which is shown in figure 14.5. There are three different classes of events, that are shown in that window, where only the first two types may be selected by the user to proceed with the execution of the process.

1. Visible events, that can be selected by the environment. Those events are marked in the event-list-window by a blue icon.

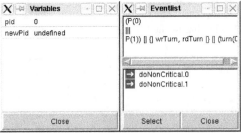

Figure 14.5: Displaying the variables and currently accepted events

2. Invisible or τ-events. These events are marked by a red icon, indicating that those events are internal events and can be produced at any with without interaction of the environment.

3. Visible events, that cannot be produced by the modelled system due to restrictions that may be imposed by the high level structure of the processes. Those events are displayed in a grey colour marking them unavailable at the moment.

An additional window is available during the execution of processes: the *variables* window as shown in figure 14.5. In that window all local variables or parameters of the currently running process can be displayed. During the execution of a process the user can always switch between any of the currently active processes and inspect the contents of the variable.

Selecting an event from the event-list window results in the production of the event, which is inserted in the event history. Additionally the operational semantics of all operators involved in producing the selected event is applied and the state of the system is changed accordingly. During this step the marking of the different operators in the processes change to reflect the new state of the system.

14.4.3   Command Line Options

The command line options of `xciao` are basically identical to the ones of `ciao`. The only differences is, that no command file can be specified, since XClaO is an interactive tool.

```
usage: xciao --help ( -h, -? )        help: prints this message
       xciao [-v] [-w[0-9]] [-u] [-e] [-P] [-T] [-i csp_spec]
             [-I include_dir[:include_dir]] [csp_file]
```

14.5   csp2rtt

The second category of tools, that are part of the ClaO tool suit are the ones required for transition graph generation. `csp2rtt` is currently the only tool in this category. In contract to the debugging tools, this one does no longer execute the abstract syntax of processes, but creates transition graphs from the syntax tree. These transition graphs can be exported in a textual representation and in a graphical description format. Through these exports, it is possible to use the transition graphs as an input format for other programs as for example the test system RT-Tester.

`csp2rtt` is a command line tool, since its only purpose is generating transition systems from CSP specifications which does not require any user interaction. All parameters, that are required for the compilation process, is the path to the CSP specification and the name one of its processes.

The command `csp2rtt strict-alternation.csp SYS` for example, loads the specified file `strict-alternation.csp` from the current directory and generates a synchronisation term with high level transition graphs representing the process *SYS*. During the following normalisation step the state space of the specification is partially unfolded and normalised according to the algorithm described in chapter 8. The result of executing this program are several output files, that have been created during the compilation process: an alphabet file, two files representing the generated synchronisation term with the normalised transition system and finally a file containing the acceptances, that are valid for the states of the sequential transition system. The format of those files are explained in detail in section 14.5.1.

The output files generated by `csp2rtt` follow a naming convention: the name of the file with CSP specification without its extension is appended with the process name, which was specified as second argument to `csp2rtt`. To the resulting string different extensions are appended, marking the different output types, which are explained in table 14.1. The only exception to this rule is the name of the alphabet file, which carries only the name of the CSP specification with a different extension, since the alphabet does not depend on any process.

Suffix	File Type
`.csp`	CSP specifications
`.t`	Alphabet files listing all possible events of the CSP specification
`.tg`	ASCII-Representation modelling a normal form transition graph
`.sync`	ASCII-Representation modelling a synchronisation term
`.acc`	Acceptances of the states in the transition graph
`.dot`	Graphical output of the generated transition graph

Table 14.1: File types and their corresponding extensions

Adding the option `-g` to the command line call of `csp2rtt` enables an additional output filter: the Graphviz-output. The UNIX tool `dot`, which is a part of the Graphviz tool suite, has been developed by the AT&T Bell Laboratories. Its purpose is to draw directed graphs as hierarchies. "It reads attributes graph text files and writes drawings, either as graph files or in a graphics language such as PostScript." [ ]

Especially for small specification those created graph outputs can be useful to understand the behaviour of a transition system, since every trace generated by the CSP specification leads to a unique state in the transition graph. An exemplary output for the process *SYS* of `strict-alternation.csp` can be seen in figure 14.6.

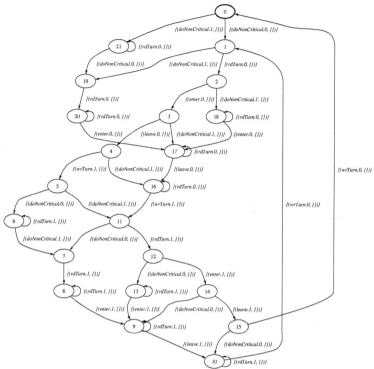

Figure 14.6: Normalised transition graph of SYS

The tool **csp2rtt** not only produces normal form graphs, but also can generate outputs representing synchronisation terms using Roscoe-style normalisation graphs or high level transition graphs. Selecting which type of graph is generated is done by specifying the type of normalisation for the generation process.

There are two different ways to specify, which types of transition system should be exported by **csp2rtt**: the command line switch **-n** or **pragma**-definitions within the CSP specification. Such **pragma**-definition must occur in the CSP specification before the process is specified. The defined type of normalisation applies to all process definitions below that definition, until the end of the file or until another pragma-definition occurs changing the normalisation type. If no normalisation type has been specified in a CSP specification a Roscoe style normalisation is assumed. Command line options can be used to overwrite the behaviour specified in the CSP specification. Setting the different types of normalisation by command line options or pragma-definitions is shown in table 14.2.

Resulting Transition System	Command line	CSP specification
Synchronisation Term with High level transition graphs	-n 0	NORM_NONE
Synchronisation Term with Roscoe-style Normalisation Graphs	-n 1	NORM_LOWLEVEL
Roscoe-style Normalisation Graphs	-n 2	NORM_UNFOLD

Table 14.2: Setting the Type of Normalisation in csp2rtt

Calling csp2rtt for the same specification and process as above, but with the the command line options -g -n 1, generates a transition system that can be seen in figure 14.7. The normalisation for the synchronisation term with high level transition graphs representing the specified process is only performed on the sequential components of the system and the synchronisation term is put into its normal form. The same result could also have been produced by stating the processing instruction **pragma NORM_LOWLEVEL** above the definition of the process SYS in the CSP specification.

The resulting output of this stage slightly differs from the one generated by the Roscoe style normalisation: an additional file is produced containing the structure of the synchronisation term representing the high level structure of the system, which format is described in section 14.5.1. Also the format of the exported graphical representation changed, because synchronisation terms are modelled as a tree structure connecting the sequential subprocesses, as can be observed in figure 14.7. The information about the synchronisation and hiding events can be seen in the .sync-file, but are not illustrated in the graphical representation of the high level structure.

Finally, if csp2rtt is configured to perform no normalisation at all by using the -n 0 option or the pragma NORM_NONE, the program exports the synchronisation term with high level transition graph representation of the transition system. An exemplary graphical output of this process can be seen in figure 14.8.

A closer look at this figure reveals that each variable and parameter name is extended by a number. This mechanism is used to uniquely identify all variables and parameters, since it is possible to use the same names at different places in a CSP specification. These extended names allow an easy way of identifying, which variables are identical and which only have the same name in the CSP specification.

At the current stage of development of csp2rtt, no other information about the generated high level transition graph other than the graphical export can be produced. The considerations from chapter 12 still need to be implemented: a range calculation has to be done on the sequential high level transition graphs and the expressions have to be transformed into corresponding BDDs. Finally an export function for the synchronisation term with high level transition graphs

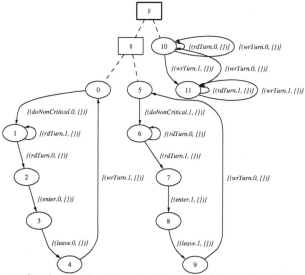

Figure 14.7: Synchronisation Term with Roscoe-style Normalisation Graphs of the process SYS

has to be developed. Except from the range calculation, which has already been implemented, these parts still have to be developed in the future.

14.5.1 Output Formats

In the following the different formats of the output files generated by csp2rtt are going to be described. Some of these file formats are adopted from RT-Tester tools like csp2alpha or TGgen to keep the compatibility with RT-Tester.

Alphabet Files

Alphabet files provide a mapping between events and corresponding numbers, which identify that event uniquely. The representation of an event in any of the following file formats always use the corresponding number in this file. This allows to store the events more efficiently, since the complete string containing the ASCII-representation of the event, needs to be stored only once.

An additional information field in the alphabet file is the classification of the events as input, output or timer events. The annotated CSP specifications, which

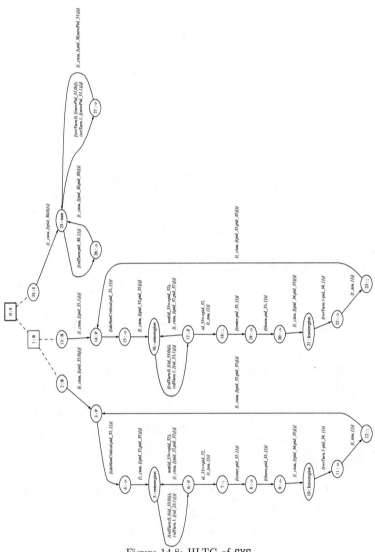

Figure 14.8: HLTG of SYS

contains pragma definitions of the form **pragma AM_**[1] are used to determine for each event the corresponding type. The generated output for the specification **strict-alternation.csp** looks as follows:

```
0 enter.0 & AM_INPUT
1 enter.1 & AM_INPUT
2 leave.0 & AM_INPUT
3 leave.1 & AM_INPUT
4 doNonCritical.0 & AM_OUTPUT
5 doNonCritical.1 & AM_OUTPUT
6 rdTurn.0 & AM_OUTPUT
7 rdTurn.1 & AM_OUTPUT
8 wrTurn.0 & AM_OUTPUT
9 wrTurn.1 & AM_OUTPUT
```

The first column of each line is the number under which the event, that is stored in column two, is referenced. The character & is a field separator, that allows an easier parsing process for the input/output type of the event, which is stored in the fourth column.

This generated file format is identical to the format of **csp2alpha** of the RT-Tester tool suit. A difference is, that **csp2rtt** automatically sorts the entries in the required order, which is for example that all **AM_INPUT** events must be listed before the **AM_OUTPUT** events. Such internal requirements of the RT-Tester had to be ensured by the user, when the script **csp2alpha** has been used.

Roscoe-style Normalisation Graphs

Roscoe-style normalisation graphs or the sequential transition graph components of synchronisation terms with Roscoe-style normalisation graphs are stored in files with the extension .tg – the transition graph files. The format of this file is simple. Each line contains a triple of numbers representing one transition in the graph. The first and third number represents the source respective target state of the transition. If the graphical export of the transition system has been used during the generation of the transition graph, each of these numbers is denoting exactly that state in the graphical export, that carries the same number. The second number of the triple is a reference to one of the events in the alphabet file.

An exemplary output for the process *SYS* of **strict-alternation.csp** can be found below, which is describing the graph from figure 14.7. The generated type of transition system is a synchronisation term with Roscoe-style normalisation graphs, but this output represents only the sequential part of those graphs.

---

[1]A complete list of all **pragma AM_** definitions can be found in the syntax reference in section 15.3.6.

```
0 4 1
1 6 2
1 7 1
2 0 3
3 2 4
4 9 0
5 5 6
6 6 6
6 7 7
7 1 8
8 3 9
9 8 5
10 6 10
10 8 10
10 9 11
11 7 11
11 8 10
11 9 11
```

Synchronisation Terms

The sequential transition system represented above show three different sub-graphs. Those subgraphs are not connected, since the generated type of transition system was a synchronisation term with Roscoe-style normalisation graphs.

As already explained in 8.3, each synchronisation term can be transformed into its normal form, where each sub-term of the term is either a reference to a location in the embedded transition system or another synchronisation term of the form $(\lambda_1, s, h, \lambda_2)$. This finding has been used for the design of the output file format for synchronisation terms.

Each line in the generated output file with the extension .sync either represents another synchronisation term or a state of the sequential transition graph which has been exported to the .tg file. A line in a synchronisation term file, which only contains one number is such a reference to a state in the transition graph. The other possibility is that a line is starting with the character {. In this case the line will represent a node in the normal form synchronisation term, which contains synchronisation and hiding information. The first set in the line contains those numbers of events, that the two sub-terms of the current term must synchronise on, and the second one represents the set of hiding events.

In the next line below the synchronisation and hiding sets, there may occur another set, which would introduce a sub-term of the synchronisation term, or just a reference to a location. Below all other sub-terms, which may have been defined within the first reference, a second term must occur, which represents the second part of the synchronisation term. This second term may once again be just a reference to a location or a complete synchronisation term.

An exemplary output for the synchronisation term belonging to the transition system from above can be seen in the following:

```
{ 6 7 8 9 } { }
{ } { }
0
5
10
```

This output represents the following synchronisation term, where *HLTG* is the sequential transition graph already exported in the Roscoe-style normalisation graph file, and l_0, l_5 and l_{10} correspond to the states 0, 5 and 10 of that file. All environments of the contained high level transition graphs have to be empty, since normalised transition graphs do not carry any variables information at their transitions.

$$(((HLTG, l_0, \emptyset),$$
$$\{\}, \{\},$$
$$(HLTG, l_5, \emptyset)),$$
$$\{ rdTurn.0, rdTurn.1, wrTurn.0, wrTurn.1, \}, \{\},$$
$$(HLTG, l_{10}, \emptyset))$$

In the case of a completely normalised graph, this file contains only one single number containing the start state of the generated Roscoe-style normalisation graph. If the normalisation option -n 2 is set, the resulting .sync file is identical to a .startstate file required by RT-Tester.

Acceptances

Creating and exporting the acceptances of the states in the Roscoe-style normalisation graphs is the final task, that has to be performed by csp2rtt. The created output file has the extension .acc. The first line contains the acceptances for state 0 of the generated Roscoe-style normalisation graph, the second line contains them for state 1, and so on. Each set representing the acceptances of one state may contain none, one or multiple sets of numbers, where each number again represents one of the events in the alphabet file. The following output is the generated acceptances for the example from above.

```
{ { 4 } }
{ { 6 7 } }
{ { 0 } }
{ { 2 } }
{ { 9 } }
{ { 5 } }
{ { 6 7 } }
{ { 1 } }
{ { 3 } }
{ { 8 } }
{ { 6 8 9 } }
{ { 7 8 9 } }
```

This output means for example, that the node with the number 0 in figure 14.7, which represents a location, accepts only the event *doNonCritical*.0, and location 10 in the transition graph representing the variable process accepts all events from the set {*rdTurn*.0, *wrTurn*.0, *wrTurn*.1}.

The format of the acceptances file is slightly different from the one RT-Testers TGREFgen produces:

- The output of TGREFgen puts all sets for all states in one single line, which makes it more difficult to find the acceptances for one state manually.

- The output of csp2rtt contains spaces before and after each curly bracket.

Those differences have been implemented intentionally to increase readability of the generated output. Adapting this output file format for RT-Tester just requires small changes in the parsing function of rttmkref, which is the tool that creates a machine readable binary representation of the acceptances sets.

14.5.2   Command Line Options

The application csp2rtt has command line options, similar to those of the other applications but with a few extensions that are explained in the following table:

```
csp2rtt - converting CSP specifications into transition graphs

usage:    csp2rtt [options] [specification] [process]
          csp2rtt --help ( -h, -? )
options:  -v        be verbose
          -w [0-9]  set warning level (0 - quiet, 9 - verbose)
          -n [0-2]  set normalisation level (default: 2)
                    0 - syncterm with unnormalised HLTG
                    1 - syncterm with normalised HLTG
                    2 - Roscoe style transition graph
          -g        export graphical representation of transition graph
          -p        show visible parameters at each node and transition
          -I IncludeDir[:IncludeDir:...]
                    search include specs in IncludeDir(s)
          -i predefined_definition_spec
                    name of the file holding the predefined definitions
```

-n [0-2]   Specifies the type of normalisation, that is going to be used during the generation of the transition graph. The options argument represent one of the following normalisation types:

   0 – Synchronisation Term with High Level Transition Graphs

   1 – Synchronisation Term with Roscoe-style normalisation Graphs

   2 – Roscoe-style normalisation Graphs

-g   If this option is set, a graphical representation of the tran-
              sition graph will be exported.
-p   This option can be used to show the visibility of the param-
              eters in the high level transition graph as used in section
              5.1.2, definition 5.18.
specification The file containing the CSP specification.
process   The name of the process, that the generation algorithm of
              the transition graph starts with. Note that a CSP speci-
              fication file may contain several process definitions which
              can be selected as the start process.

14.6 csp2alpha

The tool csp2alpha provides a part of the functionality that is included in
csp2rtt as well: the generation of the alphabet of a CSP specification and exporting the result to a file. In contrast to csp2rtt this tool requires only a CSP
specification as argument. The specified file is loaded and parsed. csp2alpha
processes all information, that is required for the calculation of the whole alphabet of the CSP specification, which is done by evaluating the channel-definitions.

The produced output is written to a file with the same name as the CSP
specification where only the extension of the filename is changed to .t.

14.6.1 Command Line Options

The application csp2alpha has command line options, similar to those of the
other applications that have already been explained in detail and will therefore
not be explained here anymore.

```
csp2alpha - generate alphabet files from CSP specifications

usage:    csp2alpha [options] specification [output file]
          csp2alpha --help ( -h, -? )
options: -v       be verbose
         -w [0-9] set warning level (0 - quiet, 9 - verbose)
         -I IncludeDir[:IncludeDir:...]
                  search include specs in IncludeDir(s)
         -i predefined_definition_spec
                  name of the file holding the predefined definitions
```

14.7 rttctgam

Generating Roscoe-style normalisation graphs is one of the currently implemented
normalisation functions in csp2rtt. Testing based on the resulting output files
is possible, since most files can directly be processed by RT-Tester tools. The

other generated files, that cannot be processed directly, can easily be converted to match the requirements of the RT-Tester.

But testing with the second currently implemented output format – synchronisation terms with Roscoe-style normalisation graphs – is not possible with the standard abstract machines of the RT-Tester. Therefore an abstract machine rttctgam has been implemented, which is already part of the RT-Tester software distribution. This abstract machine reads the binary form of the output produced by csp2rtt and creates an internal representation of the sequential transition system and the synchronisation term, which allows an interpretation of the modelled transition graph in real-time.

The transformation of the format produced by csp2rtt into the binary representation, which rttctgam reads, is performed by the script HLTGgen and the command line tool rttmkctg. Those tools have been developed based on the already existing tools TGgen and rttmktg of the RT-Tester.

Compiling a CSP specification into a synchronisation term with Roscoe-style normalisation graph just requires a call of HLTGgen with two arguments: the filename of the CSP specification without its extension .csp and the start process. For strict-alternation.csp and the process *SYS* this call looks as follows: HLTGgen strict-alternation SYS. The resulting output files are the same as with csp2rtt and additionally the binary representation of the transition system are produced.

The test algorithm used in this abstract machine and its restrictions have already been discussed in detail in section 11.2. Therefore only the usage of this special abstract machine and its required shell-scripts will be explained in this section.

14.7.1   Command Line Options

Using an abstract machine in a test configuration is explained in detail in the RT-Tester User Manual [ ] and will not be discussed here any further. Starting the specialised abstract machine rttctgam manually during a test run can be achieved by giving the following activation command:

```
rttctgam AMID [config-file] [-s] [-o output-file] [-u IP-address:port]
```

AMID	This number specifies the section in the configuration file, in which the required information for this abstract machine is stored.
config-file	Specifies the path to the configuration file.
-s	If this option is set, the output of the abstract machine is printed to standard output. If none of the options -s, -o or -u is set, the results are also printed to standard output.

-o output-file   Specifies the name of the file to which the output of the
                      abstract machine should be stored.
-u IP-address:port   The third possibility of redirecting the generated outputs
                      is sending the results to a server with the specified IP-
                      address, which listens on the given UDP-port.

Chapter 15

ClaO Implementation

In the previous chapter an introduction to the several tool, that are implemented in the ClaO system, has been given. This chapter is going to explain the internal structure of the implementation. Based on the authors diploma thesis, several classes have been designed and implemented, which provide the functionality for executing CSP specifications and transforming them to transition systems.

This chapter on the other hand provides an overview about the different components in the ClaO system and how they interact. Figure 15.1 gives a small impression of the structure and dependencies of the different components. Each of the implemented tools required a CSP specification and produces an abstract syntax graph of that specification. The parser `csp_parser` stops as soon as the syntax graph is built, because in that case the specification was syntactical correct.

The tools `ciao` and `xciao` are using a class `csp_interpreter` to execute the rules of the operational semantics on the graph representation. Both programs are using the same components of the ClaO library, because the only difference is, that `xciao` does not produce random traces like `ciao`, but allows to interactively simulate CSP processes.

`csp2rtt` uses other algorithms on the syntax graphs defined in the classes `rtt_export` and `tg_generator` to create and normalise different types of transition graphs, which can be exported to be used by other tools.

The ClaO components use complex data structures as interfaces to interact with each other. In order to understand how the ClaO components work together, these interfaces will be explained here. A more detailed description of the different components will be given in later sections of this chapter.

Abstract Syntax Tree

The abstract syntax tree is a special form of a parse tree and is generated by the class `csp_parser`. The abstract syntax tree will be called *abstract syntax representation* or *abstract syntax* in this document.

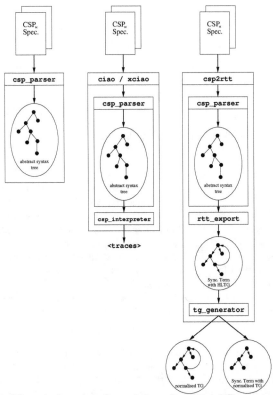

Figure 15.1: The relations, interfaces and results of the different parts of ClaO.

If an object of the class `csp_parser` is used to parse a CSP_M specification, it creates the abstract syntax tree of this specification by traversing its parse tree. During this process, the `csp_parser` creates the abstract syntax tree using C++ objects representing the different CSP operators, which are derived from the class `absy_symbol`. The abstract syntax contains all information of the CSP_M specification except layout information, since this is disregarded during the parsing process. The syntactical structure of the specification is checked when creating the parse tree.

A further description of the structure and the design of the abstract syntax representation and its implementation in the class `csp_parser` will be given in section 15.1. Following those implementation details, a description of the base classes of the abstract syntax will be given in section 15.2, which are used to implement the abstract syntax tree. Since certain process operators are not available in some tools of the ClaO system, an overview about the supported syntax of CSP specification in the different tools will be given in section 15.3, which concludes this part about the abstract syntax in this chapter.

Interpretation

Based on this abstract syntax tree an interpretation of the represented CSP specification is possible, if the rules of the operational semantics are directly applied to represented syntax. Therefore a short description of applying the operational semantics to the elements of the syntax tree will be given in section 15.4, which closes with the description of the class `csp_interpreter` and its derived classes. These classes are are used to compute the operational semantics of the objects of the abstract syntax tree and execute processes by this means.

High Level Transition Graphs

The third topic in this chapter is the generation of transition systems from the abstract syntax tree and their normalisation. First a general description on how a transition system can be generated from a abstract syntax tree and the implementation of the algorithms in the classes `rtt_export` and `tg_generator` will be given in section 15.5.

Finally this chapter closes with the description of the classes actually implementing the high level transition graph structure with conditions, events, assignments, locations and transitions in section 15.6.

15.1   Abstract Syntax

This section provides an overview of the abstract syntax trees which has to be constructed by a CSP parser for each definition of a specification. Such representation of CSP_M is necessary for all ClaO applications, since `ciao` and `xciao` work directly on the abstract syntax for the symbolic execution of a process. The tool `csp2rtt` creates the high level transition graphs based on the abstract syntax of the processes.

First a general overview on the intended structure of the abstract syntax tree will be provided, before the actually implemented class `csp_parser` of the ClaO system will be explained.

15.1.1   Structure of the Abstract Syntax

For each CSP_M specification there exists a parse tree using the syntactical elements, like process operators, as nodes. The abstract syntax representation of ClaO is similar to such parse tree.

Figure 15.2 shows the parse tree of the process x -> y -> SKIP. This parse tree uses the rules of the grammar defined in appendix C.2 and the lexer definition in appendix C.1. The leaves of this tree contain the terminal symbols 'x', '->', 'y', '->' and 'SKIP'. A lexical token is assigned to each terminal symbol. These are written in capital letters. All other nodes represent non-terminal symbols.

In the figure, parts of the tree have been combined to units. These units are indicated by rectangular boxes. When creating the ClaO representation, these units are replaced by instances of special ClaO classes as can be seen in figure 15.3. Those classes will be explained in detail in section 15.2 of this chapter. The representation ClaO uses is called abstract syntax tree, because it abstracts from the complete set of non-terminals and creates only the relevant structure.

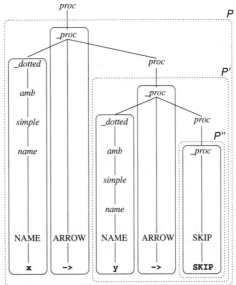

Figure 15.2: The parse tree of the process x -> y -> SKIP

In both figures, the dotted rectangular boxes indicate the process P and its included subprocesses P' and P'', which are :

$$P \ = \ x \rightarrow y \rightarrow SKIP$$
$$P' \ = \ y \rightarrow SKIP$$
$$P'' \ = \ SKIP$$

The abstract syntax representation in the ClaO system uses an object of the class `simple_prefix` to represent the *prefix* operators. The events x and y are represented by objects of the class `dot_seq` and an object of the class `skip` is used to represent the *SKIP* process.

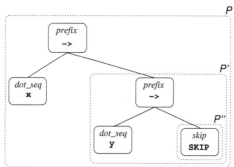

Figure 15.3: The abstract syntax tree of the process x -> y -> SKIP

The abstract syntax tree contains all relevant information of the syntax of a CSP_M specification, such as definitions of processes, channels and expressions. Processes and expressions are always implemented as trees of ClaO objects. Beginning in section 15.2 those classes are introduced that are used to build the abstract syntax tree, but before that the class `csp_parser` will be explained, which is responsible for creating the abstract syntax tree from a CSP specification.

15.1.2   The Class `csp_parser`

Every time one of the ClaO applications creates an abstract syntax tree of a CSP specification, this is done by an instance of the class `csp_parser`. Having successfully parsed a specification, the parser creates a *runtime environment* of the specification which consist of five lists containing all identifiers, channel definitions, process definitions, functions and named expressions of the specification. The runtime environment is stored in the `csp_parser` object which provides public member functions to access it. Finally, a context analysis is started on the runtime environment, which ensures unique identifiers for all parameters and calculates and checks the types, where this is possible.

Class Member Variables:

`char *fileName`
> This attribute contains the filename of the CSP specification to be parsed.

```
                    ┌──────────────────────────────────────────┐
                    │                csp_parser                 │
                    ├──────────────────────────────────────────┤
                    │ -fileName: char*                           │
                    │ -_ids: id_map                              │
                    │ -_channels: absy_stack                     │
                    │ -_procs: proc_stack                        │
                    │ -_funcs: func_stack                        │
                    │ -_consts: expr_stack                       │
                    ├──────────────────────────────────────────┤
                    │ +csp_parser()                              │
                    │ +~csp_parser()                             │
                    │ +set_parserin(char*): void                 │
                    │ +parse(): void                             │
                    │ +build_runtime_env(absy_stack*): void      │
                    │ +store_id(id*): void                       │
                    │ +store_channel(s:absy_symbol*): void       │
                    │ +store_proc(s:csp_proc*): void             │
                    │ +store_func(s:csp_func*): void             │
                    │ +store_constant(s:expr*): void             │
                    │ +clear(): void                             │
                    │ +ids(): id_map*                            │
                    │ +procs(): proc_stack*                      │
                    │ +funcs(): func_stack*                      │
                    │ +repl_tree(): void                         │
                    │ +deref_ids(): void                         │
                    │ +calculate_types(): void                   │
                    │ +check_types(): void                       │
                    │ +set_channel_type(channel_type): void      │
                    │ +get_channel_type(): channel_type          │
                    │ +set_norm_type(rtt_norm_type): void        │
                    │ +get_norm_type(): rtt_norm_type            │
                    │ +calculate_Events(): event_set*            │
                    │ +export_Events(std::ofstream*): void       │
                    │ +print(): void                             │
                    │ +sprint(): void                            │
                    └──────────────────────────────────────────┘
```

Figure 15.4: Class csp_parser

id_map _ids

absy_stack _channels

proc_stack _procs

func_stack _funcs

expr_stack _consts

These attributes are container classes for the definitions of the specification. They found the runtime environment.

Class Member Functions:

csp_parser()

csp_parser()

The constructor and destructor of the class. If predefined functions are not disabled in the command line options, they are created by the constructor.

void set_parserin(char *)

This function sets the filename of the specification that ought to be parsed.

void parse()

This function parses the file specified by fileName and creates a stack of symbols of the abstract syntax. Each symbol on the stack is the root symbol of the abstract syntax tree of a definition of the specification. This stack then is used to create the runtime environment using the function build_runtime_environment.

```
void build_runtime_env(absy_stack *)
```
> This member function sorts the symbols from the stack created during the function **parse** into the different stack of the runtime environment.

```
void store_id(id *)
void store_channel(absy_symbol *s)
void store_proc(csp_proc *s)
void store_func(csp_func *s)
void store_constant(expr *s)
```
> These functions are used to store the different kinds of symbols in the respective stack.

```
void clear()
```
> This function clears the whole runtime environment and all symbols created from a specification. It can be used to prepare an application to load new specification.

```
id_map *ids()
proc_stack *procs()
func_stack *funcs()
```
> The access to the runtime environment can be gained through these member functions.

```
void repl_tree()
void deref_ids()
```
> These functions are part of the context analysis. They ensure unique numbers for all identifiers and dereference identifiers in symbols of the abstract syntax representation.

```
void calculate_types()
void check_types()
```
> The type of parameters is calculated and checked by these functions, where this is possible. Because CSP is not strictly typed, in some cases, the amount of a complete and exact type calculation is as complex as calculating the state space of a process.

```
void set_channel_type(channel_type)
channel_type get_channel_type()
```
> This member function sets and retrieves the value of the role attribute for all channel definitions that are parsed before this function is called again with another value. This function is called during parsing of the specification and is activated by a channel pragma definition beginning with AM.

```
void set_norm_type(rtt_norm_type)
rtt_norm_type get_norm_type()
```
> Pragmas beginning with TG cause a **set_norm_type** which specifies the normalisation type of all following process definitions before the next pragma.

The type is retrieved using **get_norm_type**, every time a process definition is created.

```
event_set *calculate_Events()
void export_Events(std::ofstream *)
```
These member functions calculate and export the set **Events** which is equal to the alphabet Σ of the specification.

```
void print()
void sprint()
```
These member functions can be used to call the equally named functions for all symbols of the runtime environment. This causes an output of all definitions as they are stored in the parser.

15.2   Classes of the Abstract Syntax

The previous section introduced the concepts of the abstract syntax of the ClaO system. For each operator supported by the syntax of ClaO there exists one specialised C++ class, which implements its functionality. All elements of the abstract syntax graphs are derived from one base class called **absy_symbol**. This class defines functions, which are required for all elements in the graph.

Most syntactic elements of CSP_M can be categorised into two different basic kinds: expressions and process terms. This leads to the design of two generic classes representing these kinds:

The class **expr** is the generic class for all *expressions*. The most important function, that all derived classes share, is the function **eval2expr**, that evaluates a syntax tree of expression items to one expression object containing the result of the expression. To achieve this, the expression classes are calling the **eval2expr** function for each syntax tree item representing a sub-expression, before their own implementation of the function is applied.

A similar functionality is implemented for classes derived from the class **proctree**, which forms the basis for all *process operators*. Each class must implement three generic functions, that are required for the proper functionality of the ClaO components: **acc()**, **evolve()** and **compileTG()**.

ciao and **xciao** require the functions **acc()** and **evolve()** which are implementing the rules of the operational semantics. **acc()** returns the events, that this class can produce by the rules given in section 2.4 and **evolve()** is necessary for the symbolic execution of a selected event.

The transition graph generation component **csp2rtt** has different requirements. During the construction of the high level transition graph the function **compileTG()** is called recursively for each object in the syntax tree. This function creates new transitions and locations in the transition system based on the rules of the operational semantics. For each process operator there are different rules, how the graph must be created. These rules are described in section 5.1.

The class **event** implements another basic concept of CSP: the *events*. Every time a CSP process communicates internally or with the environment an event is produced. Each instance of the class **event** can represent one or more events of a single *channel*. The statement **communicate?in!out** for example is represented by only one object, although an arbitrary number of different events can be generated by it. The member function **comms()** can be used to calculate the set of events that are represented by an instance of the class **event**.

The abstract syntax representation of a CSP specification is created and stored when parsing a specification. This is done by an instance of the class **csp_parser**. This object can be used to access all definitions of the specification. For this purpose the **csp_parser** provides the ClaO *runtime environment*. It consists of five lists containing all process definitions, channel definitions, function definitions and named expressions like $A = \{1, 2, 3\}$. The fifth list contains all global identifiers. Because every definition has a global identifier, this list can be used to access all definitions stored in the other lists. The lists of processes, functions and identifiers can be accessed by the member function **procs**, **funcs** and **ids** of the class **csp_parser**.

The list of processes contains instances of the class **csp_proc**, which is a derived class of **proctree**. This class stores a list of the local variables and parameters for each process.[1] Every time a process is referenced during execution, the parameters are set accordingly to the actual values and the variables are initialised. This is necessary to implement different scopes of identifiers.

15.2.1 The Class absy_symbol

The class **absy_symbol** is the generic abstract class for all symbols of the abstract syntax. Most of the functions are virtual and some are abstract so that this class can never be instantiated. It defines the minimum attributes and interfaces of all derived classes.

Figure 15.5 shows the directly derived classes. They are the class **csp_channel** which is used to represent channel definitions, the class **id** which represents identifiers and the two abstract classes **proctree** and **expr**. The classes derived from **proctree** are used to represent the process definitions and process terms and derived classes from **expr** are used to represent expressions that occur in a specification. Figure 15.6 shows the most relevant attributes and member functions of the class **absy_symbol** .

---

[1]Process parameters are defined by left side of a process definition. local variables are introduced by input fields of events in the process term. See section 2.2.4 and 2.2.5.

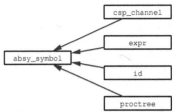

Figure 15.5: Class-Hierarchy `absy_symbol`

```
                            absy_symbol
#_base: absy_type
#_type: absy_type
#_valid: bool
#_line: int
+absy_symbol()
+~absy_symbol(): virtual
+operator ==(absy_symbol&): bool
+operator <(const absy_symbol&): bool
+base(): absy_type
+type(): absy_type
+set_line(i:int): void
+get_line(): int
#set_valid(b:bool): void
+valid(): virtual bool
+print(): virtual void
+sprint(): virtual void
+deref_id(): virtual void
+repl_tree(): virtual void
+repl_id(absy_symbol*,absy_symbol*): virtual bool
+repl_param(parameter*,absy_symbol*): virtual void
+acc(bool=true): virtual acc_set*
+evolve(event*): virtual proctree*
+runtime_error(i:int,in_file:char *,in_line:int,errormsg:char *): int
```

Figure 15.6: Class `absy_symbol`

Class Member Variables:

`absy_type _base`

`absy_type _type`

> Every symbol of the abstract syntax has a base and a type assigned to it.
> The base is the general type of the symbol while the type is the exact type
> of the class. These attributes can be used to distinguish between different
> kinds of symbols

`bool _valid`

> This attribute indicates whether the symbol is complete and can be used
> or if it is incomplete or corrupt

`int _line`

> This attribute stores the linenumber of the original syntax that the symbol
> of the abstract syntax represents.

Class Member Functions:

`absy_symbol()`

> The constructor of the class. Default values are set for all attributes. They
> ought to be redefined by the constructors of the derived classes

```
virtual  absy_symbol()
```
> The destructor of the class.

```
bool operator ==(absy_symbol&)
```
> The equality operator can be used to compare two symbols of the abstract syntax. It is implemented in the class `absy_symbol`.

```
bool operator <(const absy_symbol&)
```
> This operator defined an order on the symbols of the abstract syntax. This order for example is necessary for efficient storage of `absy_symbol` classes in set.

```
absy_type base()
absy_type type()
```
> These member functions can be used to access the attributes `_base` and `_type`.

```
void set_line(int)
int get_line()
```
> These member functions set and get the line number information of the symbol.

```
void set_valid(bool)
virtual bool valid()
```
> The value of the attribute `_valid` can be set or retrieved using these functions.

```
virtual void print()
```
> This function prints the relevant attribute values of a symbol of the abstract syntax.

```
virtual void sprint()
```
> This function returns a short ASCII representation of the symbol that is similar to the original syntax.

```
virtual void deref_id()
```
> This function is part of the context analysis. If a derived class of `absy_symbol` has attributes that can contain values that are represented by an identifier, this class redefined `deref_id` so that the identifier is replaced with its value.

```
virtual void repl_tree()
virtual bool repl_id(absy_symbol *, absy_symbol *)
virtual void repl_param(parameter *, absy_symbol *)
```
> These functions are part of the context analysis and ensure, that unique identifiers and corresponding parameters are created for each parameter that is introduced by input fields of dotted expressions.

`virtual acc_set *acc(bool)`

> This function calculates the initial events of a symbol. It is only relevant for derived classes of **proctree** described in section 15.2.5.

`virtual proctree *evolve(event *)`

> This function is used during the symbolic execution of the abstract syntax tree and implements a state change of the process. It is further described in section 15.2.5.

`int runtime_error(int, char *, int, char *)`

> This function provides an error message output for symbols that encounter a runtime error. A given error message is printed and attributes of the symbol are displayed. The function rises a `runtime_exception`.

15.2.2   The Class `id`

Identifiers can occur in several places in a CSP specification and can represent different kinds of values. If the parser creates a new **id** object, it is checked if this identifier has already been parsed before or not. If not, a new unique number is assigned to the identifier and it is stored in the list of all identifiers for further lookups. Otherwise no new object is created and a reference to the old one is used.

During the context analysis, The values of all defined identifiers that occur as an attribute of a symbol of the abstract syntax, are assigned to the appropriate attributes of the symbol. It is also checked if there exist undefined identifiers – identifiers that have no assigned value.

Figure 15.7: Class `id`

Class Member Variables:

`char *_name`

> This member variable holds the name of the identifier as a string.

`int _num`

> The unique number of the identifier is stored in this attribute. The numbers are assigned during parsing and the context analysis.

`absy_symbol *_value`

> Identifiers normally are used as references to named values. The value of the identifier can be any symbol of the abstract syntax like a function or process, a parameter, a channel or a named expression or type.

Class Member Functions:

`id()`

> The constructor of the class. The number is set to the illegal value -1, to indicate that it has not been assigned by the parser, yet.

`id()`

> The destructor of the class.

`bool operator==(id *)`

> This operator can be used to check for the equality of two `id` objects. Two identifiers are equal if they have the same name and number.

`void set_name(const char *)`
`void set_name_ref(char *)`
`char *id_name()`

> These member functions are used to set and get the name of the identifier. `set_name` creates a copy of the given string while `set_name_str` does not. `id_name` returns a copy of the name string of the `id` object.

`void set_num(int)`
`int id_num()`

> The number of an identifier are set and retrieved using these member functions.

`void set_value(absy_symbol *)`
`absy_symbol *value()`

> The value, the identifiers refers to, is set and retrieved by these member functions.

15.2.3 The Class `expr`

The class `expr` is an abstract class, that defines the common interface of all symbols of the abstract syntax that represent expressions. Figure 15.8 displays the class hierarchy of its derived classes.

Expressions are evaluated to a single value which is a element of the type of the expression. The type of expressions that are supported by ClaO are numbers, booleans, sets, sequences, tuples, intervals, data types, communication expressions and Cartesian products. During the context analysis, only the type of the parameters of an expression is determined, not the type of the expression itself. Therefore every expression can be evaluated to an expression that represents a

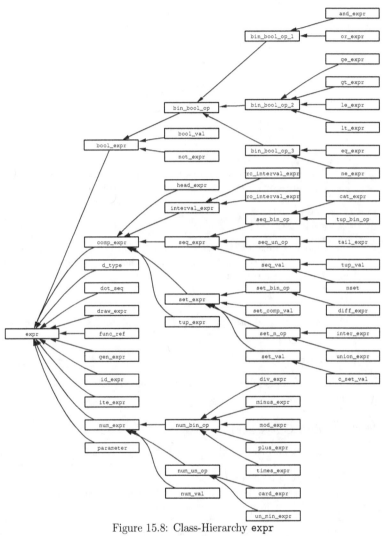

Figure 15.8: Class-Hierarchy **expr**

value in the type of the expression. Using the member function **base** and **type**, the type of this expression can be determined. Every expression implements a member function **eval** that returns a native representation of the value of the expression, but because the return type of this function can be different for each class inherited from **expr**, this function can not be declared in this class. If an expression is evaluated, all parameters of this expression must have assigned values. Otherwise a runtime error message is displayed and a **runtime exception** occurs.

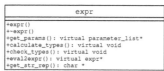

```
                            expr
+expr()
+~expr()
+get_params(): virtual parameter_list*
+calculate_types(): virtual void
+check_types(): virtual void
+eval2expr(): virtual expr*
+get_str_rep(): char *
```
Figure 15.9: Class **expr**

Class Member Functions:

expr()
expr()
> The constructor and destructor of the class.

virtual parameter_list *get_params()
> This member function returns a list of all parameters of an expression. It recursively traverses the complete syntax tree of the expression.

virtual void calculate_types()
> This function is used during the context analysis to calculates the type of the parameters of an expression. The type of an parameter is stored as an attribute of the parameter.

virtual void check_types()
> During the context analysis, this function is used, to check if the type of a parameter is valid for the expression, it is used with.

virtual expr *eval2expr()
> This function return an expression that represents the value of the expression. All parameters of the expression must have assigned values. Otherwise a **runtime exception** occurs.

15.2.4   The Class **parameter**

The class **parameter**, as its name says, is used to represent parameters in the abstract syntax tree. They are derived from the class **expr** and therefore can be

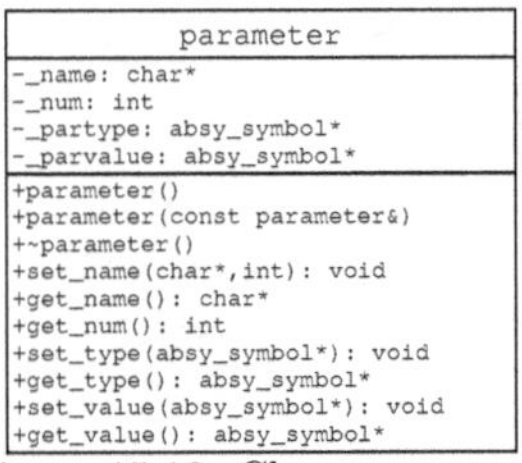

```
                  parameter
-_name: char*
-_num: int
-_partype: absy_symbol*
-_parvalue: absy_symbol*
+parameter()
+parameter(const parameter&)
+~parameter()
+set_name(char*,int): void
+get_name(): char*
+get_num(): int
+set_type(absy_symbol*): void
+get_type(): absy_symbol*
+set_value(absy_symbol*): void
+get_value(): absy_symbol*
```

Figure 15.10: Class `parameter`

evaluated, returning the value of the expression, the parameter refers to. If a
parameter currently has no values assigned to it, a runtime error occurs.

Every parameter has a name and a number which are the name and the
number of the identifier referring to the parameter. Parameters have an attribute
containing the type of values, that can be assigned to the parameter and an
attribute containing the actual value of the parameter. Parameters can be used
to refer to any kind of expression.

Class Member Variables:

`char *_name`

> The name of the parameter. This is identical to the name of the identifier
> referring to the parameter.

`int _num`

> The number of the parameter. It is identical to the number of the identifier
> referring to the parameter.

`absy_symbol *_partype`

> The type of possible values of the parameter.

`absy_symbol *_parvalue`

> This attributes specifies the current value of the parameter. It can be any
> kind of expression.description.

Class Member Functions:

`parameter()`

> The contructor of the parameter. The _base and _type attribute of the pa-
> rameter are set to `parameter_def`.

`parameter(const parameter &)`

> The copy constructor of the class.

`parameter()`

> The destructor of the class.

`void set_name(char *, int)`
> This function sets the name and the number of the parameter. The arguments must be a valid name and number of an identifier. A copy of the name string is stored.

`char *get_name()`
> This member function returns a copy of the name attribute of the object.

`int get_num()`
> This member function can be used to retrieve the number of a parameter.

`void set_type(absy_symbol *)`
> During the context analysis, the type of the parameter is set using this member function.

`absy_symbol *get_type()`
> This function can be called to retrieve the type of a parameter.

`void set_value(absy_symbol *)`
> The value of a parameter can be assigned using this member function.

`absy_symbol *get_value()`
> This function returns the current value of a parameter. For parameters with no value assigned, this would be `NULL`.

15.2.5 The Class `proctree`

Interpreting CSP processes or generating transition systems from them requires an internal representation of the syntax of the processes. The class `proctree`, which is directly derived from the class `absy_symbol`, is the base class for all classes in the ClaO system, that represent process operators. This class and all classes that are derived from it implement the functionality, which is required for the representation and interpretation of CSP processes and the generation of transition systems from them.

The derived classes from `proctree`, which are illustrated in figure 15.11, can be divided into three different categories of process operators:

1. Classes representing other processes, like SKIP, STOP and CHAOS. But also classes representing process definitions or process references fall into this category. All these classes are directly derived from `proctree`.

2. Classes representing process operators, which only have one process as argument, are derived from the class `unary_proctree`, which encapsulates all functionality concerning the referenced process. Operators in this category are prefixing, guards and hiding. Additionally all replicated operators are

Figure 15.11: Class-Hierarchy **proctree**

derived from `unary_proctree`, since the semantics of those operators instantiates any number of processes from one specified process in the syntax tree.

3. Classes representing process operators, which only have two processes as arguments. The semantics of the CSP operators representing choices, sequential composition, parallelism and conditions requires to determine the semantics of the two specified underlying processes. Therefore the classes representing those kind of operators are derived from `binary_proctree`, which encapsulates all functionality concerning the two referenced processes.

But the basic functionality for all classes is identical. There are functions, that allow the creation of the abstract syntax tree, which represents the structure of the original CSP process. This syntax tree allows to perform a type analysis which will detect errors in the CSP specification used to build the abstract syntax tree. During this phase the visibility of all variables, that are contained in the processes can be computed and is stored for each item in the abstract syntax tree.

As soon as the analysis of the processes is completed, the resulting abstract syntax trees can be used to execute the processes based on the rules of the operational semantics. From these rules it can be determined, which elements initially participate in the generation of events. Only some of the objects in the abstract syntax tree may participate in the generation. Those objects are considered to be active, the others are unused.

The execution requires basically two functions: one to retrieve the initial events of the currently represented state of the system and one that changes the state of the abstract syntax tree to reflect the new state after the production of the event. That new state is reflected by changing the objects in the syntax tree. Objects which participated in the generation of the event change their state to **processed**, while other formerly unused states may become **active**.

A third main functionality provided by the **proctree** classes are the functions that are used to generate a high level transition graph from the abstract syntax tree. Those functions have to call the transition graph generation methods from the referenced process operators, and connect the transitions, that are generated by the rules of the corresponding operator to the high level transition graph returned by the previously called methods. The complete high level transition graph is then returned as result.

Class Member Variables:

`acc_set *_evset`

Almost all classes derived from the class **proctree** are required to store an acceptance set of events once the functions `acc()` has been called. This variable is used to store this information.

`parameter_list _visible_params`

This variable stores a list of visible parameters for each object of the ab-

proctree
#_evset: acc_set*
#_visible_params: parameter_list
#_state: proc_state
+proctree()
+~proctree(): virtual
+operator ==(proctree&): virtual bool
+set_visible_params(parameter_list*): void
+get_visible_params(): parameter_list*
+add_visible_param(absy_symbol*,absy_symbol*): void
+set_proc_state(proc_state): virtual void
+is_active(): bool
+is_processed(): bool
+is_unused(): bool
+set_child_state(proc_state): virtual void
+calculate_types(): virtual void
+check_types(): virtual void
+acc(bool): virtual acc_set *
+evolve(event *): virtual proctree *
+compileTG(event_set *,event_pair_list *,rtt_proc_stack *,rtt_location *): virtual rtt_label*

Figure 15.12: Interface-definition of the class `proctree`

stract syntax tree, that is an instance of this class. The visible parameters are for example required for the range calculation and the transition graph generation algorithms.

proc_state _state

During the interpretation of the abstract syntax tree, this variable stores the current state of the represented object. The possible values of the variable are `active`, `processed` and `unused`.

absy_type _base

This variable is an inherited attribute from the class `absy_symbol`. For the class `proctree` and all classes that are derived from that class, the value of `_base` is always `proctree_def`.

Class Member Functions:

proctree()

The constructor of the class `proctree` initialises the three global variables. Initially the set `_evset` and the list `_visible_params` contain no elements and the `_state` is set to `unused`.

virtual bool operator==(proctree&);

The equality-operator checks, whether or not two specified objects, that are derived from `proctree`, are semantically identical. This function has to be redefined in all derived classes.

void set_visible_params(parameter_list *)
parameter_list *get_visible_params()

These two functions can be used to retrieve and set the set of visible parameters for an object of the class `proctree`.

void add_visible_param(absy_symbol *, absy_symbol *)

This function allows to change the list of visible parameters for any object of this class. Both arguments are pointers to elements of the base class absy_symbol, but for proper functionality both values should be references to identifiers.

If the constraints are met, the function searches the list of visible parameters until it finds the identifier referenced by the first argument and replaces it by the identifier in the functions second argument. The function ensures, that each identified is only contained once in the list of visible events.

```
void set_proc_state(proc_state)
bool is_active()
bool is_processed()
bool is_unused()
```
Changing and retrieving the state during the interpretation of the abstract syntax tree, can be achieved by using these functions.

```
void set_child_state(proc_state)
```
This function works basically like the set_proc_state() function from above, but does not only change the status of the current object, but also for all other referenced *proctree* objects. This function is redefined in the derived classes to ensure its functionality.

```
virtual void calculate_types()
```
The function calculate_types() implements the context analysis on process level. For each variable and parameter it is tried to derive the corresponding type. This function needs to be redefined in most derived classes.

```
virtual void check_types()
```
As soon as the context analysis is completed this function, which has to be redefined in most derived classes, checks for type violations in the syntax tree. This can be achieved by calling this functions on all referenced expression objects derived from the class expr. Especially for process references this function has to ensure, that the arguments of a process reference match to the types of the process definition. Otherwise a type error must be produced.

```
virtual acc_set *acc(bool)
```
The function acc() uses the current status of the abstract syntax tree to calculate all initial events of the represented state. The returned value is a set, which contains all events that are possible by the current operator object. To compute the own set of acceptances, it might be necessary to call this method on other objects in the syntax tree, which result is required for the computation of the own return value, as for example with the choice operators.

The functions argument is a boolean value, which is implemented only for efficiency reasons. If this value is *true* a previously computed result is being reused instead of computing the acceptance set again. The default value for this parameter is *false*.

`virtual proctree *evolve(event*)`

evolve() changes the state of the objects in the abstract syntax tree to reflect the new state, which will be valid, if the specified event is being produced. This function has to be redefined for each derived subclass.

`virtual rtt_label *compileTG(event_set *hide, event_pair_list *rename,`
                          `rtt_proc_stack *stack, rtt_location *current)`

To generate a high level transition graph from an abstract syntax tree, it is necessary to call this method on the root element. compiteTG() takes a set of hiding events and a renaming relation as arguments which allows to change events at transitions in the generated high level transition graph already at compile time. Additional arguments are a stack of processes, which represents the hierarchy of previous process calls, and a current location, to which the sub-graph of the generated high level transition graph must be connected. For each derived class, the behaviour of this method has to be redefined, to reflect the semantical behaviour of the represented CSP operator. In most cases this method will call itself on other objects, until the complete high level transition graph is computed. The implemented algorithm has been described in detail in chapter 7.

15.2.6   The Classes `csp_proc_func`, `csp_proc` and `csp_func`

Some of the classes, that are derived from the class **proctree** are of special interest for the interpretation and high level transition graph generation algorithms: for example the classes **csp_proc_func**, **csp_proc** and **csp_func**, which represents the definition of processes or functions. Both functions and processes share some common attributes: each one has a name, under which it can be referenced, an arbitrary number of parameters and a body, which either consists of an expression or an abstract syntax tree. Those common functionality is implemented in the class **csp_proc_func**. The derived classes **csp_proc** and **csp_func** then implement the functionality that is specific for processes or functions.

Those three classes are used to build the runtime-environment directly after the parsing process. The runtime-environment contains container classes for processes and functions, which are used later by algorithms that need to identify the target of a process or function reference. Those containers are filled with all objects referencing processes and functions, that are created during the parsing process.

Additionally there is a third container in the runtime environment, which temporarily holds all those **csp_proc_func** objects, for which could not be determined during the parsing process, whether it represents a function or a process. Such definition could for example be the process or function P = Q(1). From the definition of P cannot be derived if it is a process or a function. As soon as the runtime-environment is built, it is possible in a second stage to determine, whether $Q(1)$ is a function or a process. From this result the type of P can also be determined. This results in moving the object from the temporary container to the one storing the corresponding type. Such categorisation process has to be performed, until it has been determined for all csp_proc_func objects in the temporary container, what type they are representing and moving them to the correct container object. As soon as the runtime-environment is completely built, there exist no more csp_proc_func objects, but only objects either of the class csp_proc or csp_func.

The class csp_proc_func stores in addition to the parameters all variables that are local to the references process or function. The difference between variables and parameters in the ClaO system is characterised as follows: the list of parameters contains only references to those variables, that represent the arguments of the process or function. The list of variables on the other hand contains references to all identifiers, that are bound at any point inside the process or function definition, which includes the arguments of the process or function.

Using the process or function definition as a container for all parameters and variables is especially useful during the interpretation of processes. Since the local parameter list as well as the variable list contains only references to the objects containing their current value, changing the value of one parameter also effects the value of the local variable in the whole process.

Individual attributes of the processes are a reference to the actual proctree object, which is the root element of the abstract syntax tree that forms the body of the process. Additionally there are information, which are required during the interpretation of the process: a set of currently accepted events and a reference to a proctree object, which participates in the generation of the next event. Functions require only one additional attribute to the ones of the class csp_proc_func: a reference to the body of the function which is of the base type expr.

The Class `csp_proc_func`

csp_proc_func
#_name: id*
#_local_ids: id_map
#_local_params: param_list
#_local_vars: param_list
#_proc_or_func: absy_symbol*
#_norm_type: rtt_norm_type
+csp_proc_func()
+~csp_proc_func()
+operator ==(proctree&): virtual bool
+set_name(id*): void
+get_name(): id*
+get_name_str(): char*
+set_proc_or_func(absy_symbol*): void
+get_proc_or_func(): absy_symbol*
+add_par(): parameter*
+num_par(): int
+set_param(int,absy_symbol*): void
+get_param_list(): param_list*
+get_params(csp_proc_func*): void
+get_params(proc_ref*): void
+add_var(): parameter*
+get_var_list(): id_map*
+get_vars(csp_proc_func*): void
+set_norm_type(rtt_norm_type): void
+get_norm_type(): rtt_norm_type
+store_id(id*): void

csp_proc
-_value: proctree
-_current: proctree*
+csp_proc()
+csp_proc(csp_proc&)
+~csp_proc()
+set_proc(absy_symbol*): void
+get_rhs_proctree(): proctree*

csp_func
-_value: expr*
+csp_func():
+csp_func(csp_func&):
+~csp_func()
+set_func(absy_symbol*): void
+get_func(): expr*
+eval(): expr*

Figure 15.13: Interface-definitions of the classes `csp_proc_func`, `csp_proc` and `csp_func`

Class Member Variables:

`id *_name`
> An identifier containing the name of the function or process as defined in the CSP specification.

`id_map _local_ids`
`param_list _local_params`
`param_list _local_vars`
> These three lists store all identifiers, parameters and variables, that are local to the represented process. The contents is required for the interpretation of the abstract syntax tree of the process, since this allows to directly access all required information for a process at one central point. This information could also have been stored directly in the objects of the syntax tree, but that would have made the interpretation more difficult, since each occurrence of a variable would have resulted in a search of the object carrying its definition.

`rtt_norm_type _norm_type`
> During the parsing process this attribute is set for each `csp_proc` and `csp_proc_func` object. It stores the type of normalisation, that should be used if this process is used to generate a high level transition graph from it. The currently available values for this variable are `rtt_norm_complete` for Roscoe-style normalisation graphs, `rtt_norm_lowlevel` for synchronisation terms with Roscoe-style normalisation graphs and `rtt_norm_none`

for no normalisation at all. An additional value `rtt_norm_undefined` indicates, that in the CSP specification no pragma definition has been found, which indicates the normalisation type for this process.

`absy_symbol *_proc_or_func`

This attribute stores a reference to an object, which is the body of the process or function definition that is represented by a `csp_proc_func` object. The referenced object is usually a reference to a process or function, which type cannot be determined during the parsing process.

Class Member Functions:

`csp_proc_func`

The constructor of this class initialises all local attributes and sets the inherited attribute `_base` to the value `proc_def`, which remains unchanged for all derived classes.

`virtual bool operator==(proctree&)`

A virtual function which allows to call the equality operator == for any objects that are derived from `csp_proc_func`.

`void set_name(id *)`
`id* get_name()`
`char *get_name_str()`

These functions allow to set and retrieve the value of the member variable `_name`.

`void set_proc_or_func(absy_symbol *)`
`absy_symbol *get_proc_or_func()`

These functions allow to set and retrieve the value of the member variable `_proc_or_func`.

`parameter *add_par()`

Appends a new parameter object to the lists of parameters and variables. The reason for this has been explained at the beginning of this sub-section. A reference to the newly created parameter is returned, which allows to set its attributes.

`int num_par()`

Returns the number of parameters of the `_proc_or_func` object.

`void set_param(int, absy_symbol*)`

This function is used to set the values of the parameters of a CSP process during the interpretation. The first argument is the number of the parameter to be changed: 0 denotes the first parameter, 1 the second and so on. The second argument of this function is the value of the parameter. Since the values of all parameters and variables for a process are all stored in the class `csp_proc_func`, this function changes the value for all occurrences of the corresponding variable in the complete process or function.

`param_list *get_param_list()`

> This functions returns a copy of the local parameter list of the `_proc_or_func` object.

`void get_params(proc_ref *)`
`void get_params(csp_proc_func *)`

> These two functions are specialised functions to retrieve and set parameters in one single step. The argument is either a process reference or another process, which values for the parameters are already set. This functions retrieves these values and set the parameter values of the current `_proc_or_func` object accordingly.

`parameter *add_var()`

> This function is similar to **add_par()**, except that the newly created parameter is only added to the list of local variables and not to the list of local parameters.

`id_map *get_var_list()`

> This functions returns a copy of the local variable list of the `_proc_or_func` object.

`void get_vars(csp_proc_func *)`

> This function is similar to **get_params(proc_ref *)**, except that the local variable list is copied from the referenced `csp_proc_func` object.

`void set_norm_type(rtt_norm_type)`
`rtt_norm_type get_norm_type()`

> Sets and retrieves the normalisation type, that is defined for the process referenced by the current object.

`void store_id(id *)`

> Adds the specified identifier to the list of local identifiers.

The Class `csp_proc`

Class Member Variables:

`proctree *_value`

> A reference to the proctree object, which is the root element of the abstract syntax tree that forms the body of the process.

`proctree *_current`

> During an execution of the process, this reference always points to the first element of the abstract syntax tree, that is responsible for the generation of the next events. In the redefinition of the function `evolve()` in this class, this variable is changed to reflect this behaviour. At the beginning of the execution this reference points to the same object as `_value`.

Class Member Functions:

`csp_proc()`

> The constructor of the class `csp_proc` initialises all local attributes, that are not initialised by inherited constructors.

`csp_proc(csp_proc &)`

> A copy-constructor which initialises a new object with the same local attributes then the specified object. But not only the attributes are copied, but also a copy of the complete abstract syntax tree is created as well.

`void set_proc(absy_symbol *)`

> This function takes any object, that is of the class `proctree` and stores it as the root of the abstract syntax tree in the variable `_value`. For other objects, which are not derived from `proctree` an error message is issued.

`proctree* get_rhs_proctree()`

> Returns that object that represents the root element of the right hand side of the process definitions abstract syntax tree. This is basically the object referenced by `_value`.

The Class `csp_func`

Class Member Variables:

`expr *_value`

> A reference to the object, which contains the expression that forms the body of the function.

Class Member Functions:

`csp_func()`

> The constructor of the class `csp_func` initialises all local attributes, that are not initialised by inherited constructors.

`csp_func(csp_func &)`

> A copy-constructor which initialises a new object with the same local attributes then the specified object and copies the expression representing the body of the function.

void set_func(absy_symbol *)

> This function takes any object, that is of the class expr and stores it in the variable _value. For other objects, which are not derived from expr an error message is issued.

expr *get_func()

> Returns the expression stored in the variable _value.

expr *eval()

> Returns the evaluated value of the expression in the variable _value. Please refer to the documentation of the class expr for details.

15.2.7   The Classes dot_seq, event, csp_channel

Events in CSP$_M$ consist of a single channel name or a channel name or a channel name followed by a field expression. The field expression itself can contain multiple communication fields. A detailed description of the structure of events and communication fields is given in 5.1.1. This concept of events has been directly carried into the classes representing events in the abstract syntax tree. The class csp_channel represents the channel of an event, objects of the class dot_seq can be used to represent communication expressions which communication fields are represented by objects of the class dot_seq_elem. To be able to represent an event by a single object and not through a csp_channel and a dot_seq, events with communication fields can be represented as dot_seq object, where the first dot_seq_elem contains the csp_channel object of the event.

The classes csp_channel, dot_seq and dot_seq_elem are used to represent events in the syntax tree. During the execution, events are represented by objects of the class event. Every object of class event can represent one or more events of the same channel.

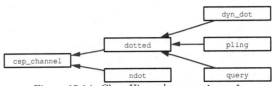

Figure 15.14: Class-Hierarchy csp_channel

The class csp_channel

Objects of the class csp_channel are used to represent channel definitions of a CSP specification and can be used to represent the channel of an event in the syntax tree. They are also used as an attribute of the class event to represent the channel of an event.

Figure 15.15: Class `csp_channel`

Class Member Variables:

`id *_name`
> This attribute stores the name of the channel.

`channel_type _inout_type`
> This attribute specifies the role of the channel. The roles of events are specific for the RT-Tester and are assigned by `pragma` definitions in the specification. This attribute is part of the RT-Tester integration of ClaO.

`expr *_csp_type`
> The type of a channel is stored in this attribute of `csp_channel`.

`id *_type_id`
> If the type is named, this attribute stores a reference to its identifier.

Class Member Functions:

`csp_channel()`
> During the construction of a `csp_channel`, the `_name`, `_csp_type` and `_type_id` attributes are set to NULL.

`virtual csp_channel()`
> The destructor of the class.

`void set_name(id *i)`
`id *get_name()`
> This member function gen be used to set and retrieve the value of the `_name` attribute.

`char *get_name_str()`
> This member function returns a string representation of the name of a `csp_channel` object.

```
void set_type(absy_symbol *)
absy_symbol *get_type()
```
> The _csp_type attribute can be set and retrieves with this member function.

```
id *get_type_id()
```
> This member function returns the identifier of the type if it is set or NULL otherwise.

```
void set_inout_type(channel_type)
channel_type get_inout_type()
```
> The role of the channel is defined and retrieved by this member function.

```
virtual event *comms()
```
> This function calculates the set of all events that are possible for this channel according to its channel definition. Note that the return type is a single object of the class event.

The Classes dot_seq and dot_seq_elem

The class **dot_seq** is used to represent communication expressions of events in the abstract syntax tree. It uses objects of the class **dot_seq_elem** to represent the communication fields. For a more flexible use of **dot_seq** objects as expressions, a **dot_seq_elem** object in the current implementation can contain **dot_seq** objects to represent multiple communication fields. This leads to a tree form of communication expressions. Every tree form **dot_seq** can be transformed into a sequential form **dot_seq** using the member function **serialize**.

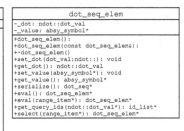

Figure 15.16: Class dot_seq

The Class `dot_seq_elem`

Class Member Variables:

`ndot::dot_val _dot`
> This attribute specifies the input/output role of the communication field. It can contain values for `!`, `?` and `.` or can be unspecified.

`absy_symbol *_value`
> The value of a communication field is stored in this attribute. It can be any expression including another communication expression.

Class Member Functions:

`dot_seq_elem()`
`dot_seq_elem(const dot_seq_elem &)`
`dot_seq_elem()`
> The constructor, copy constructor and destructor of the class.

`void set_dot(ndot::dot_val)`
`ndot::dot_val get_dot()`
> With this member functions, the attribute `_dot` can be defined or retrieved.

`void set_value(absy_symbol *)`
`absy_symbol *get_value()`
> This member functions can be used to set or retrieve the value of a communication field.

`dot_seq *serialize()`
> This member function can be used to create a sequential form of a `dot_seq_elem` object. This is only necessary for objects that contain `dot_seq` objects as their `_value`.

`dot_seq_elem *eval()`
> This member function evaluates the `_value` of a `dot_seq_elem` object. If the attribute contains an expression with undefined parameters, a `runtime exception` occurs.

`dot_seq_elem *eval(range_item *)`
> This member function as well evaluates the `_value` attribute, but it used the parameter bindings of the argument to do so. This is necessary to evaluate events when creating the high level transition graph of a specification, because in this case, the parameters have no values.

`id_list *get_query_ids(ndot::dot_val *)`
> This member function returns a list of all identifiers that refer to parameters of input fields of a `dot_seq_elem`. If the objects contains a `dot_seq`

as its value, the function is used on this object, too and the results are concatenated.

`dot_seq_elem *select(range_item *)`
> Events containing input fields can represent multiple elements of the alphabet Σ. For input fields, this function returns an output field `dot_seq_elem` where the parameter of the input field is set according to the bindings given as the argument of the function. For non input fields, a copy of the field expression is returned.

The Class `dot_seq`

Class Member Variables:

`seq_elem_list _seq_elems`
> This member function contains a list of all `dot_seq_elem` objects of a communication expression. If the `dot_seq` is in sequential form, these are all communication fields of the expression

Class Member Functions:

`dot_seq()`
`dot_seq()`
> The default constructor and destructor of the class.

`dot_seq(event_data *)`
> A constructor that creates a `dot_seq` object out of a given **event** object.

`bool operator==(dot_seq &)`
> This operator can be used to check the equality of `dot_seq` objects.

`void push_front(dot_seq_elem *)`
`void push_back(dot_seq_elem *)`
> Member functions to add `dot_seq_elem` objects to the `dot_seq`.

`unsigned long size()`
> This member function returns the size of the communication expression. It is defined as the number of the communication fields of the expression.

`dot_seq_elem *first_elem()`
`dot_seq_elem *next_elem(dot_seq_elem*)`
`dot_seq_elem *previous_elem(dot_seq_elem*)`
`dot_seq_elem *last_elem()`
> These member functions are used to access the `dot_seq_elems` of the object.

`dot_seq *serialize()`
> This function returns a sequential form of the `dot_seq` where none of its `dot_seq_elems` contains `dot_seq` objects as values.

`dot_seq *eval()`
> This member function returns an evaluated form of the object, where all expressions have been evaluated, It is required, that all parameters have assigned values.

`dot_seq *eval(range_item *)`
> Like `eval()`, this member function evaluates a `dot_seq`, but this time, the parameter bindings of the argument are used.

`id_list *get_query_ids(ndot::dot_val *`
> This member function uses the equally named member function of its `dot_seq_elems` to returns a list of all identifiers that refer to parameters of input fields of a `dot_seq_elem`.

`dot_seq *select(range_item *)`
> This member function selects that single event out of all events, the `dot_seq` can represent, that uses the parameter bindings of the argument for all parameters of input fields. It calls the equally named member function on all its `dot_seq_elems`.

`event *comms(bool eval_expr)`
> This member function returns an `event` object containing all events that are represented by the `dot_seq` object.

`event *rtt_comms(range_item *)`
> This member function is equal to `comms`, but uses the bindings of its argument for non-input-fiels parameters.

The Class event

Objects of the class **event** are used to represent events during the execution of a CSP specification. They are designed to be able to represent multiple elements of the alphabet Σ of the same channel.
Class Member Variables:

`bool _tic`
> This attribute specifies whether the **event** is the special event $\checkmark$ or not.

`bool _tau`
> This attribute specifies whether the **event** is the special event τ or not.

```
                          event
┌─────────────────────────────────────────────┐
│                  event                        │
├─────────────────────────────────────────────┤
│ -_ctau: bool                                  │
│ -_tau: bool                                   │
│ -_tic: bool                                   │
│ -_vis: bool                                   │
│ -_channel: csp_channel*                       │
│ -_values: expr*                               │
├─────────────────────────────────────────────┤
│ +event()                                      │
│ +event(e:const event&):                       │
│ +event(tt)                                    │
│ +~event()                                     │
│ +operator ==(event&): bool                    │
│ +set_tau(t:bool): void                        │
│ +is_tau(): bool (query)                       │
│ +set_tic(t:bool): void                        │
│ +is_tic(): bool (query)                       │
│ +set_ctau(t:bool): void                       │
│ +is_ctau(): bool (query)                      │
│ +set_visible(b:bool): void                    │
│ +is_visible(): bool (query)                   │
│ +set_channel(csp_channel*): void              │
│ +get_channel(): csp_channel* (query)          │
│ +set_values(expr*): void                      │
│ +get_values(): expr* (query)                  │
│ +add(event*): void                            │
│ +sub(event*): void                            │
│ +div(event*): void                            │
│ +get_str_rep(eval:bool): char*                │
│ +print(): void                                │
│ +sprint(): void                               │
└─────────────────────────────────────────────┘
```

Figure 15.17: Class **event**

`bool _ctau`
   This attribute specifies whether the **event** is the special event π or not.

`bool _vis`
   This attribute specifies whether the **event** is visible or not – including the case of hidden events and invisible events like τ and π.

`csp_channel *_channel`
   The channel of an **event** object is stored in this attribute.

`expr *_values`
   This attribute contains the communication expression(s) of the **event**.

Class Member Functions:

`event()`
`event(const event &)`
`event()`
   The constructor, copy constructor and destructor of the class.

`event(tt)`
   A constructor creating a ✓, τ or π **event**.

`bool operator==(event &)`
   This operator can be used to check the equality of two **event** objects.

`void set_tau(bool)`
`bool is_tau()`
   This member function sets or retrieves the value of the attribute `_tau`.

```
void set_tic(bool)
bool is_tic()
```
This member function can be used to set or retrieve the _tic attribute.

```
void set_ctau(bool)
bool is_ctau()
```
This member function sets or retrieves the value of the attribute _ctau.

```
void set_visible(bool)
bool is_visible()
```
The visibility status of an event can be set or retrieved with this member function.

```
void set_channel(csp_channel*)
csp_channel *get_channel()
```
This function sets or retrieves the channel of an **event** object.

```
void set_values(expr*)
expr *get_values()
```
This member function sets or retrieves the **expr** object containing the communication expression(s) of an **event**.

```
void add(event *)
void sub(event *)
void div(event *)
```
An **event** object can represents more than one element of the alphabet Σ. These member functions provide set operations for the set of elements of Σ that are represented bat the event. Note that all represented events must be of the same channel.

```
char *get_str_rep(bool)
```
Returns a string representation of the event.

```
void print()
```
This member function prints information about the attributes of the event.

```
void sprint()
```
This member function returns an ASCII representation of the events represented by an object.

15.3 Supported Syntax

Since the ClaO system is still in a prototype state, not all elements of CSP_M are currently supported by all tools of the ClaO suit. This section describes which part of the syntax is supported or unsuported by which tools. Additionally some new syntactical constructs have been developed, which are used for the RT-Tester integration. Those elements will also be described in this section.

15.3.1 Expressions

ClaO supports the same set of expressions for all its applications. It therefore is not necessary to tell which expressions are supported by which tool. In section 2.2.1 a description of the CSP$_M$ expressions is given. ClaO does support nearly all expressions listed there with some restrictions.

Numbers Numbers are represented using the C++ type `long integer`. This limits the numbers to values between -2147483648 and 2147483647.

Sets Because ClaO only supports numbers from -2147483648 to 2147483647, open intervals are represented as closed intervals $m..2147483647$. Like all closed ranges, they are expanded when inserted into a set. So use them with care, because this usually requires a lot of memory.

Some functions like `empty(a)`, `member(x,a)` and `card(x)` are not implemented in the ClaO system, but are defined in CSP specifications that are automatically included before any CSP specification is loaded.

Sequences Unlike in FDR, it is not necessary that all elements in a sequence have the same type. This is not checked and therefore there is no difference between homogeneous and heterogenous sequences.

Like for sets, the definition of functions like `null(s)` are automatically loaded on program start for a CSP specification. Therefore these functions can be used even though they are not directly implemented as classes derived from the class `expr`.

Functions ClaO supports functions definitions without pattern matching. In CSP it is not necessary to define the range and domain of a function. A function consists of a name, an optional tuple of parameters and a function body. The function body is an supported expression as described here. Functions can not have functions as parameters. *Let* expressions are currently not supported.

15.3.2 Types

CSP$_M$ as supported by FDR knows three different kinds of types: *simple types*, *named types* and *datatypes*. ClaO supports simple types and named types as defined in section 2.2.2. Datatypes in ClaO are less powerful than in FDR . The current version of ClaO only supports the definition of sets of enumerations like:

```
datatype T = A | B | C
```

15.3.3 Channels

ClaO supports the full range of channel definitions as described in section 2.2.3. The types are limited to the supported types described before.

15.3.4 Events

CSP_M events are supported in ClaO as described in section 2.2.4. Events can be explicit members of Σ, e.g. $a.3$ or can introduce new variables using input fields like $a?x$. Expressions and parameters can be used as in $a.f(3)$ or $a!x + 4$. The parameters in an expression can also represent dotted expressions like $a.x$ with the parameter binding $x = 3.4?y$, which evaluates to the event $a.3.4?y$.

15.3.5 Process Operators

The following table shows, which CSP operator is supported in which of the ClaO tools. For each operator there is an additional field in the table, which states, wheather there are any restrictions for the use of the operator in CSP specifications.

Operator	Kind of support	csp-parser	ciao/xciao	csp2rtt
STOP	The basic process STOP is fully implemented.	×	×	×
SKIP	The basic process SKIP is fully implemented.	×	×	×
Prefixing	The prefix operator itself is completely implemented.	×	×	×
Sequential Composition	All processes of the kind $P; Q$ can be used if P and Q are valid processes.	×	×	×
Internal Choice	Processes of the kind $P \sqcap Q$ can be parsed, if P and Q are processes or identifiers representing process definitions.	×	×	×
External Choice	Processes of the kind $P \square Q$ can be parsed, if P and Q are processes or identifiers representing process definitions.	×	×	×
Hiding	The hiding operator $P \setminus B$ is implemented in the current version of ClaO.	×	×	×
Renaming	The renaming operator is currently not supported. The parser can parse specifications containing renaming operators but does not create an abstract syntax tree. This is not implemented yet, since this operator is rarely used in testing specifications.	×		

continued on next page

Operator	Kind of support	csp_parser	ciao/xciao	csp2rtt
Interrupt	The interrupt operator is currently not supported. The parser can parse specifications containing renaming operators but does not create an abstract syntax tree. This is not implemented yet, since this operator is rarely used in testing specifications.	×		
Interleaving	The interleaving operator $P \;\|\|\|\; Q$ works for all kind of supported processes P and Q.	×	×	×
Parallel	Both variations of the parallel operator are supported. It is possible to use the simple kind of the operator with definitions like $P \parallel Q$ or the alphabetised parallel operator with process definitions of the form $P \underset{a\ b}{\parallel} Q$, where P and Q are processes and a and b are sets of events.	×	×	×
Conditions	Process definitions of the kind *if b then P else Q* are supported, if b is a supported boolean expression and P and Q are supported processes.	×	×	×
Guarded Commands	Guarded Commands of the form $b\&P$ are supported, if b is a boolean expression.	×	×	×
Replicated Functions	Replicated Functions are supported by the parser but no by the current version of the interpreters.	×		×
Chaos	The process $CHAOS(a)$ is implemented for the interpretation, but its application is limited by the restriction of the supported set-definitions. For transition system generation the syntactical abbreviation from 2.4 can be used instead.	×	×	

Table 15.1: The supported CSP operators in the different ClaO tools.

15.3.6   Syntax Enhancements

ClaO does support the include of other CSP specifications and pragma definitions.

Include statements

Include statements can be used to include other specifications into a specification. The included specification is inserted at the point where the include statement occurs. The syntax for include statements is:

```
include "<filename>"
```

For compatibility reasons with the RT-Tester also #include can be used instead of just include. ClaO automatically avoids cyclic includes by only including each file once, which is completely sufficient, since CSP does not require any forward declaration of processes as other programming languages do.

Pragmas

Pragma definitions are used to provide meta information to definitions of a CSP specification. The syntax for pragmas is:

```
pragma <identifier>
```

ClaO accepts two types of **pragma** definitions. All pragmas identifiers beginning with AM_ specify classes of channels and pragmas beginning with NORM_ specify a normalisation form for the high level transition graph of a process. They may occur between two definitions in a CSP specification. All other pragms definitions are ignored by the tools of the ClaO system.

Channel Pragmas

When using CSP specifications together with a test engine like RT-Tester, it can be necessary to apply special roles to events. Because all events except τ and $\checkmark$ are defined by channel definitions, ClaO provides a mechanism to attach a role to a channel. In this case, all events of that channel are bound to that role.

Because ClaO was designed to support RT-Tester, all roles known by RT-Tester can be applied using channel pragmas. A channel pragma stays active, until another channel pragma is parsed. The role defined by the pragma is applied to every channel definition that is parsed while the pragma is active. If no process pragma is parsed, the default pragma AM_INTERNAL is active. The different channel pragmas are:

AM_INPUT
This pragma applies the *input* role to the following channels.

AM_OUTPUT
This pragma applies the *output* role to the following channels.

AM_ERROR
This pragma applies the *error* role to the following channels.

AM_WARNING
This pragma applies the *warning* role to the following channels.

AM_SET_TIMER
This pragma applies the *set timer* role to the following channels.

AM_ELAPSED_TIMER
This pragma applies the *elapsed timer* role to the following channels.

AM_RESET_TIMER
This pragma applies the *reset timer* role to the following channels.

AM_INTERNAL
This pragma applies the *internal usage* role to the following channels.

Process Pragmas

Process pragmas can be used to add information to process definitions. The following pragmas specify which normalisation algorithm should be used when creating the normalised form of the transition graph of the related process. Note that the transition graph of a process is always normalised in one way. It is not possible that subgraphs, that represent subprocesses of the top level process, are normalised in another way than the rest of the transition graph even if they are marked with a different pragma. Like for channel pragmas, a process pragma stays active until another process pragma is parsed. If no process pragma is parsed, the default pragma NORM_COMPLETE is active.

NORM_COMPLETE When this pragma appears, all following processes are marked to be normalised using an algorithm that produces a Roscoe-style normalisation graph.

NORM_LOWLEVEL When this pragma appears, all following processes are marked to be normalised using an algorithm that produces a synchronisation term using a Roscoe-style normalisation graph.

NORM_NONE When this pragma appears, all following processes are marked not to be normalised at all.

15.4   Interpretation of CSP Specifications

This section covers the topic of interpreting CSP specifications using the operational semantics. First a short description will be given, on how the operational semantics can be applied to an abstract syntax tree. After that the class csp_interpreter will be explained, which implements the on-the-fly execution of CSP processes in the CIaO system. A more detailed description of the applied techniques and mechanisms can be found in [ ].

15.4.1   Operational Semantics in the Syntax Tree

Since the abstract syntax representation of a CSP specification contains all semantic information that is given in the specification, the operational semantics that is defined in section 2.4, can directly be applied to the proctree classes in the abstract syntax tree.

Figure 15.3 shows the abstract syntax tree of the process P which is defined as x -> y -> SKIP as specified in section 15.1.1. Consequently the subprocesses P' and P'' of P are defined as P' = y -> SKIP and P'' = SKIP.

To determine the operational semantics of P, it is possible to directly apply definition 2.2 of section 2.4. The adopted rule reads:

$$\frac{}{e \to P \ \xrightarrow{a} \ subs(a, e, P)} \quad (a \in comms(e))$$

As described in section 15.2, the class of objects that can be used to represent the event x provides a member function event *comms() that can be used to calculate all events $a \in comms(x)$. These are represented using objects of the class event. For the event x of the example from above $comms(x) = \{x\}$.

The classes that are used to represent process operators provide a member function proctree *evolve(event *a) that implements exactly the operational semantics of that operator. In this example, the class prefix that is used to represent the *prefix* operator defines a specialised evolve() function that implements the behaviour of emitting the given event a and returning a pointer to the next process operator P. By producing the event a, one of the events from $comms(e)$ is selected and the corresponding assignments are executed, which results in creating bindings for those variables, that are introduced by e. The reference to P being returned by evolve() is therefore identical to $subs(a, e, P)$ of the operational semantics, since the function *subs* performs a textual replacement of the bound variables in the new process, which yields to the same result.

The example above shows how the operational semantics of the operators can be applied directly to the process operators in the abstract syntax tree. This mechanism is valid for all process operators. The rules of the operational semantics are implemented as member functions if the classes derived from proctree itself, but the interpretation, which can be achieved by applying these rules, is implemented in the class csp_interpreter and its derived classes, which are going to be described in the following.

15.4.2 The Class csp_interpreter

The csp_interpreter class and its derived classes contain the implementations for the CSP debuggers as described previously in chapter 14. The derived classes usually implement only the different interfaces: shell_interpreter implements the command line interpreter of ClaO and qinterpreter is used for the graphical user interface XClaO.

This base class implements all the common functionality of those derived classes, like loading a CSP specification starting and stopping executions, producing events, inspecting the structure of processes and variables and finally compiling CSP specifications to transition systems. While the derived classes must

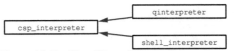

Figure 15.18: Class-Hierarchy `csp_interpreter`

implement the user interface abstraction of the interpreter, this class only implements the functionality which is required to achieve the intended task without
considering the user interface abstraction.

Figure 15.19: Class `csp_interpreter`

Class Member Variables:

`bool show_tau`

> This status variable is required for the execution of processes and stores,
> whether or not τ-events are displayed in a generated trace.

`csp_proc *running`

> As soon as a process is selected for execution, this variable contains a ref-
> erence to the top element of the abstract syntax tree representing that
> process. This top element of a process is always of the type `csp_proc`,
> since important status information for the execution of processes is stored
> in that class, as explained earlier in section 15.2.6.

`acc_set *_evset`

> During execution of processes, this variable stores a set of events that are
> accepted by at least one of the process operators in the current state of
> execution. This variable is set as soon as the function `acc()` has been
> called.

Class Member Functions:

`csp_interpreter()`

> The constructor of this class initialises all local attributes. Initially the two

reference types are not referring to any objects, and τ-events are not displayed in traces.

`void load(char *file)`

This function is a frontend to several parser functions, which are called sequentially. First the specified file is loaded and parsed. Then the context analysis is started, which computes the visibility of all identifiers, checks the types of the variables and derives the alphabet from the channel definitions.

`virtual void help()`

This virtual function has to be redefined in each derived class. In the `shell_interpreter` class this function just displays the implemented command line functions. Since the type of help differs for each interface, it is not useful to implement this function in this base class.

`int run_proc (absy_symbol *)`

This function can be used to start the execution of a process. The referenced `absy_symbol` has to be of the type `proc_def`, since otherwise an interpretation is not possible. For the execution, a copy of the abstract syntax tree of the referenced process is created. The member variable `running` is changed to reference this newly created syntax tree. A return value of 0 means success, all other values indicate an error.

`int stop_proc()`

This function stops the execution of the currently running process, by removing the running copy of the current process tree and reinitialising all the corresponding local variables. A return value of 0 indicates that the process was terminated.

`csp_proc *get_running()`

Returns a reference to the `csp_proc` object, that is the root object of the currently running syntax tree. If no process is currently running a *NULL*-reference is returned.

`acc_set *acc(absy_symbol *)`

This function is a wrapper function, that calls a function with the same name and arguments on the `proctree` object this is the root of the current abstract syntax tree. The returned value is the set of initial events of the process in its current state during execution.

`bool can_evolve()`

This function checks whether or not during execution of a process a deadlock has been encountered. A return value of *true* means that the process can still produce events, hence no deadlock has been encountered.

`bool can_execute(class event*)`

> This function checks whether the specified event can be produced in the current state of execution.

`proctree *execute_event(class event *)`

> If `can_execute()` returned, that the specified event can be produced, this function is usually called, which changes the state of the currently used abstract syntax tree, that is being used for execution. A new system state is generated by calling the function `evolve()` on the root `proctree` object of the abstract syntax tree. Then the function `acc()` is called to calculate the initial events of the process in its new state. This set of initials is stored in the classes attribute `_evset`.

`int execute_tau()`

> This function is a wrapper for `execute_event()`, which just executes τ-events.

`virtual void print(absy_symbol*)`

> This abstract function has to be redefined in each class, to display information about the specified `absy_symbol` object. In the derived class `shell_interpreter` this function e.g. calls the print function on the referenced object and displays the result on the console.

`void clear()`

> Calling this function stops any process in execution and removes it from the programs memory.

15.5 Compiling HLTGs

The operational semantics can not only be used to interpret CSP processes but also to generate transition graphs from them which is described in [ ]. Interpreting a specified process results in one possible trace for the process. Generating the transition graph results in a new representation of the same process, that is semantically equivalent to the syntax representation.

In section 15.5.1 the generation algorithm implemented in the ClaO system, that is based on the description in chapter 7, will be explained with two examplary processes. After that the two relevant classes `rtt_export` and `tg_generator` are introduced in detail, which implement the transition graph generation and normalisation algorithms.

15.5.1 Implementation of the Generation Algorithm

ClaO generates a high level transition graph from a CSP process by applying the operational semantics to the abstract syntax tree of a process. For each CSP operator, a special subgraph is created and all subgraphs later are connected to build the whole high level transition graph.

The algorithm traverses the abstract syntax tree from the root to the leafs and back. On the way down to the leafs, information about processes and process references are collected. A stack of processes and a corresponding start locations is created. On the way back, the subgraphs of the process operators are generated and connected starting with the right most operator. Each process operator starts the algorithm with its child processes, getting back the start location of the subgraph. The following examples illustrate the compilation of high level transition graphs from the abstract syntax trees of two simple processes.

Example 1: P = a -> SKIP

The abstract syntax tree of the process P = a -> SKIP is shown in figure 15.20. This form of the syntax tree is discussed in section 15.1. It contains the CSP process P as the root and the CSP operator for prefixing -> and the SKIP process.

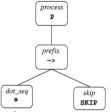

Figure 15.20: The abstract syntax tree of the process P.

When compiling the high level transition graph, the algorithm traverses the syntax tree down to the SKIP operator. Now the first subgraph is created. It consists of a transition with the event ✓ leading from an unnamed location to the special location Ω. The location Ω is special because it indicates the successful termination of a process. It always is an end-location of the transition graph with no transition leaving it. The subgraph of the SKIP operator is shown in figure 15.21. The SKIP operator returns the unnamed location to the prefix operator. The location P in the figure, that is not connected to the rest of the graph was created by the process P as the algorithm did traverse the syntax tree to the leafs. This location is necessary for recursive processes as will be illustrated in the next example.

For the prefix operator, a new location named -> and a transition with the event a leading to it is created. Then it connects the ✓-transition of the SKIP operator to the new location. The a-transition is connected to a new unnamed location. This location is returned to the process P. The subgraph of the prefix operator can be seen in figure 15.22.

Figure 15.21: The subgraph of the *SKIP* operator.

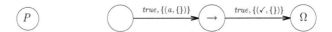

Figure 15.22: The subgraph of the prefix operator.

As mentioned above, the object representing the process *P* has already created a location *P*. The location, that was returned by the prefix operator is replaced with this location *P*, which becomes the start location of the high level transition graph. The complete high level transition graph is illustrated in figure 15.23.

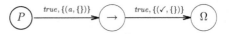

Figure 15.23: The high level transition graph of the process *P*.

Example 2: Q = a -> Q

This example is only a little more complex, as the process *Q* includes a recursion. The syntax tree is similar to the one of the process *P* from the previous example and is shown in figure 15.24. The main difference is that the process operator SKIP is replaced by the process reference to *Q*.

When compiling the high level transition graph, the algorithm traverses the syntax tree down to the *process reference* *Q*. On the way down, the object that represents the *process Q* in the abstract syntax tree (the root object), creates a *location Q* and puts it on a stack. When the algorithm reaches the *process reference Q*, it starts generating its subgraph. It searches the stack for a *location Q* representing an already existing start location of the *process Q*. If no appropriate location can be found on the stack, the *process reference* operator copies the abstract syntax tree of the *process* it references and builds the high level transition graph of it. Because the *location Q* generated by the *process Q* is found on the stack, the resulting subgraph of the *process reference* is a transition to this location. The label of the tranistion contains the special event π. It is connected to a new unnamed location. The unnamed location is returned to the prefix operator. The subgraph so far is shown in figure 15.25.

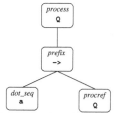

Figure 15.24: The abstract syntax tree of the process Q.

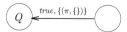

Figure 15.25: The subgraph of the process reference to Q.

The subgraph returned by the prefix operator is similar to the one in the previous example. A new location marked with "->" is created and connected to the beginning of the π-transition and a transition with the event a is created pointing to the new location. This transition is connected to a new location that is unnamed. The resulting subgraph is displayed in figure 15.26.

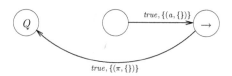

Figure 15.26: The subgraph of the prefix operator.

When the algorithm reaches the object representing the *process* Q, the high level transition graph is nearly complete, except that the unnamed location returned by the prefix operator must be replaced by the location Q which must be marked as the start location. The complete high level transition graph generated for the process defition of Q = a -> Q can be seen in figure 15.27.

The two classes rtt_export and tg_generator, which will be explained in the following, are used by the ClaO tool csp2rtt to generate high level transition graphs from an abstract syntax tree and normalise it according to different normalisation algorithms, which have been introduced earlier in this thesis.

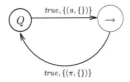

Figure 15.27: The high level transition graph of the process Q.

15.5.2   The Class rtt_export

The class **rtt_export** encapsulates all functionality from the parser, interpreter and transition graph generation into one class, and provides a simple interface, that allows to load CSP specifications use any of the defined processes to generate the corresponding high level transition graph or even perform the whole export of the transition system for RT-Tester with one single function call.

rtt_export
-_cspfile: char * -_cspprocess: char * -_parser: csp_parser* -_interpreter: csp_interpreter -_start: rtt_label* -_events: event_log
+rtt_export() +~rtt_export() +load(cspfile:char *): bool +do_export(cspprocess:char*): bool +compileTG(cspprocess:char*): bool +get_start(): rtt_label* +export_events(): void +calculate_ranges(): void +eval2expr(expr*,range_item*): expr*

Figure 15.28: Class rtt_export

Class Member Variables:

char *_cspfile
> This string contains the path in the filesystem to the CSP specification that is used to generate an abstract syntax tree from.

char *_cspprocess
> The name of the start process for the transition graph generation algorithms. The name of the process must be defined in the CSP specification referenced by the variable above.

csp_parser *_parser
> A reference to a **csp_parser** object, which is responsible for parsing a CSP specification and build its runtime-environment.

csp_interpreter _interpreter
> The **csp_interpreter** object in this context is not used to interprete CSP

specifications on-the-fly, but several auxiliary functions are implemented in that class, that process the abstract syntax tree. These functions are required for the transition system generation algorithm.

`rtt_label *_start`

As soon as a high level transition graph from a CSP specification has been generated, this label contains a reference to the start location of the newly created graph.

`event_log _events`

This object provides the means to generate the alphabet of a CSP specification and to access the mapping from concrete events to event numbers, which are exported to the alphabet files.

Class Member Functions:

`rtt_export()`

The constructor of this class initialises all local attributes.

`~rtt_export()`

The destructor of this class, removes the generated transition system from the computers memory.

`bool load(char *cspfile)`

This function is responsible for loading the specified CSP specification file. It initialises the parser and interpreter objects and employs their functionality to check for errors in the CSP specification. If the specification was successfully parsed and the abstract syntax tree has been generated, the functions returns the value *true*, otherwise *false* is returned.

`bool do_export(char *cspprocess)`

The `do_export()` function implements the functionality, that is required for the command line tool `csp2rtt`, which has already been explained in section 14.5. It creates a high level transition graph from the specified process of the already loaded CSP specification and finally normalises it according to the command line options or pragma definitions. Then it creates all export files and call those methods, that are responsible to produce their contents.

`bool compileTG(char *cspprocess)`

`compileTG()` is the function responsible to generate a high level transition graph from a CSP specification and a process name. To achieve this it gets a copy of the abstract syntax tree from the interpreter object and calls the method `compileTG()` on the root element of that tree, which returns the start location of the generated high level transition graph.

`rtt_label *get_start()`
> After `compileTG()` has been called, this function returns a reference to the initial label `_start`.

`void export_events()`
> This function calculates the set of all events possible in the loaded CSP specification. If the global options are set accordingly the output is directly written to a file instead of collecting the whole set in the programs memory.

`void calculate_ranges()`
> This function implements the range calculation algorithm from listings 12.1 and 12.2 in section 12.2. As soon as this algorithm terminates, each location in the transition system carries a set of all possible simultanious variable values, that are possible in that location.

`expr *eval2expr(expr *, range_item *)`
> This static member function takes an expression, which has free variables and a range item object, which contains pairs of variables and their corresponding values, and evaluates the expression under the bindings from the `range_item`. The result of this process is a completely evaluated expression object.

15.5.3 The Class `tg_generator`

The `tg_generator` class implements the normalisation algorithms based on high level transition graphs. To start the normalisation algorithm, it is completely sufficient to call the method `tg_normalise()` which only parameter is a reference to the start location of the high level transition graph to be normalised. Depending on the command line options or the pragma definitions in the CSP specification which was used to generate the high level transition graph the normalisation type is automatically determined.

The normalisation algorithm for Roscoe-style normalisation graphs is implemented in the auxiliary function `tg_normalise_fdr()`, and the function `tg_normalise_ctg()` contains the normalisation algorithm which creates synchronisation terms with Roscoe-style normalisation graphs. All normalisation functions return a reference to the location, that forms the start location of the generated transition system.

Finally there exists a public export function in the class, that writes the generated normalised transition system to a file. The output file formats have been described in detail in section 14.5. All other functions, that are going to be described below are helper functions, that are called during the normalisation processes. Adding a new type of normalisation simply requires to add a new function, that implements a new normalisation algorithm.

The precise functionality of the normalisation algorithms has already been explained in chapter 8 and will therefore not be explained here. Instead it will just be sketched, how the functions operate together.

tg_generator
#_start: norm_location*
-tg_loc: location_map*
-tg_stack: tg_norm_stack*
+tg_generator()
+~tg_generator()
+tg_normalise(start:rtt_location*): void
+tg_normalise_ctg(start:rtt_location*): norm_location*
+tg_normalise_fdr(start:rtt_location*): norm_location*
+get_start_location()(): norm_location*
+export_fdr_graph(basename:char*): void
#tg_normalise_graph(start:rtt_location*): norm_location*
#tg_fdr_norm_highlevel(norm_location*,rtt_location*,range_item*,acceptances*,event_set*): void
#tg_fdr_norm_node(start:rtt_location*): void
#tg_collect_tau_locations(norm_location*,rtt_location*,range_item*,acceptances*,event_set*): void

Figure 15.29: Class `tg_generator`

Class Member Variables:

`norm_location *_start`
> The variable contains the start location of the normalised transition system, that have been generated by the function `tg_normalise()`.

`location_map *tg_loc`
`tg_norm_stack *tg_stack`
> These two private variables are only required during the normalisation process. `tg_log` provide means to determine, whether or not a location/binding pair has already been processed during the normalisation. The `tg_stack` is a stack of locations that still have to be processed for the normalisation.

Class Member Functions:

`tg_generator()`
> The constructor of this class initialises the local attributes.

`void tg_normalise(rtt_location *start)`
> The functions determines from the command line options or from the pragma commands in the CSP specification which normalisation algorithm should be used. The selected algorithm is executed and optionally a graphical representation of the generated transition systems is generated. This function returns the start location of the generated normal form graph.

`norm_location *tg_normalise_ctg(rtt_location *start)`
> This function implements the type of normalisation, that results in a synchronisation term using Roscoe-style normalisation graphs. This is achieved by first generating the normal form of the synchronisation term by calling the function `tg_fdr_norm_highlevel()` and then applying the normalisation algorithm to the leafs of the generated term with the function

`tg_fdr_norm_node()`. This function returns the start location of the generated normal form graph.

`norm_location *tg_normalise_fdr(rtt_location *start)`
  This function implements the type of normalisation, that results in a completely unfolded Roscoe-style normalisation graph. It uses the result from the normalisation resulting in a synchronisation term using Roscoe-style normalisation graphs to compute the product graph, that is created by evaluation the synchronisation term structure. This function returns the start location of the generated normal form graph.

`void export_fdr_graph(char *basename)`
  This function exports the generated normal form transition system – either as Roscoe-style normalisation graph or as synchronisation term using Roscoe-style normalisation graphs – to be used with the RT-Tester tools.

`norm_location *tg_normalise_graph(rtt_location *start)`
  This function implements the functionality that has been described earlier in the algorithm 8.1. It repeatedly calls the τ-elimination process, until the sequential graph is completely normalised.

`void tg_fdr_norm_node(rtt_location *start)`
`void tg_fdr_norm_highlevel(norm_location *, rtt_location *, range_item *,`
`                             acceptances*, event_set *)`
  These two functions implement the functionality that has been described earlier in the algorithms 8.3 and 8.4: they normalise a high level transition graph and result in a synchronisation term using Roscoe-style normalisation graphs.

`void tg_collect_tau_locations(norm_location *, rtt_location *, range_item *,`
`                               acceptances *, event_set *)`
  This function implements the τ-elimination process, the has been described in detail the algorithm 8.2.

15.6   High Level Transition Graph Classes

This sections describe those classes in the ClaO system, that are used to model high level transition graphs. First the classes are introduced, that are required for the labels of the high level transition graphs: the conditions, events and assignments. As soon as those classes are introduced and explained, those two classes are going to be described, that are used to implement the structure of the high level transition graphs: the location and transition classes.

15.6.1 The Class rtt_condition

The conditions at the labels of a high level transition graph are represented by objects of the class rtt_condition. The class rtt_condition is a container for objects of the abstract syntax that represent the boolean expression of condition. These objects of the abstract syntax can either be **parameter** objects or derived from the class **bool_expr**.

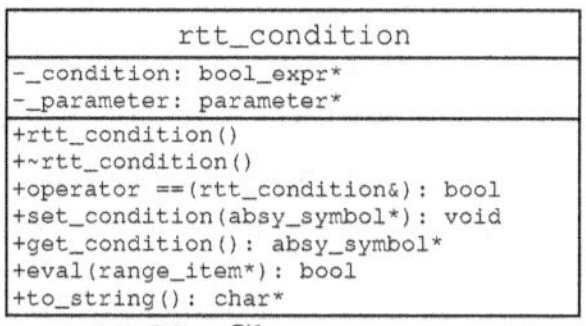

```
┌─────────────────────────────────────────┐
│              rtt_condition               │
├─────────────────────────────────────────┤
│ -_condition: bool_expr*                  │
│ -_parameter: parameter*                  │
├─────────────────────────────────────────┤
│ +rtt_condition()                         │
│ +~rtt_condition()                        │
│ +operator ==(rtt_condition&): bool       │
│ +set_condition(absy_symbol*): void       │
│ +get_condition(): absy_symbol*           │
│ +eval(range_item*): bool                 │
│ +to_string(): char*                      │
└─────────────────────────────────────────┘
```

Figure 15.30: Class rtt_condition

Class Member Variables:

bool_expr *_condition

> This attribute refers to the object of the abstract syntax that represents the condition. The default value is NULL.

parameter *_parameter

> This attributes refers to a **parameter** object. The default value is NULL.

Class Member Functions:

rtt_condition()

rtt_condition()

> The constructor and destructor of the class.

bool operator==(rtt_condition &)

> This operator can be used to check the equality of to rtt_condition objects. It returns true, if the conditions and parameters of both objects are undefined (NULL), if the conditions are set and equal according to the equality of symbols of the abstract syntax or if the conditions are NULL but the parameters are set and have the same number.

void set_condition(absy_symbol *)

absy_symbol *get_condition()

bool eval(range_item *)

> This function evaluates the symbol of the abstract syntax that represents the condition and returns its value. If the abstract syntax object is a **parameter**, the value of the parameter is set according to the bindings of the argument.

`char *to_string()`
    This member function returns a string representation of the condition

15.6.2   The Class `rtt_assign`

The assignments at the labels of transition in high level transition graphs are
represented by objects of the class `rtt_assign`. There exist two types of assignments: assignments of parameter values of process references and assignments
of parameters introduced by input fields of events. To achieve an implicit representation of the set of event-assignments-set pairs of the transitions of a high
level transition graph, the assignments for input field parameters assign the set
of all possible values to the parameter and are marked as being ambiguous. For
example the event $e?x$ of the channel e with the channel definition `channel`
`e : {1,2,3}` is represented at a transition as a single `rtt_event` $e?x$ and a
list of `rtt_assign` objects $\langle(x, \{1, 2, 3\})\rangle$. These two objects represent the set
$\{(e.1, \{(x, 1)\}), (e.2, \{(x, 2)\}), (e.3, \{(x, 3)\})\}$ of event-assignments-et pairs that
is part of the label according to the definition of high level transition graphs.

Figure 15.31: Class `rtt_assign`

Class Member Variables:

`id *_var_id`
    This attribute contains the identifier of the parameter of the assignment.

`parameter *_var`
    This attribute contains the parameter of the assignment.

`id *_range_id`
    This attribute can specify an identifier that references the value that should
    be assigned to the parameter of the assignment.

`parameter *_range_par`
> If the value of the assignment itself is a parameter, this attribute is used to store this parameter.

`expr *_range_expr`
> This parameter can contain an expression representing the value of the assignment.

`set_val *_range;`
> This parameter is used to store all possible values of an ambiguous assignment.

`bool _ambiguous`
> This attribute specifies whether an assignment is ambiguous or not.

Class Member Functions:

`rtt_assign()`
`rtt_assign()`
> The constructor and destructor of the class.

`bool operator==(rtt_assign &)`
> This operator checks the equality of two **rtt_assign** objects. Two assignments are equal if they assign the same value to the same parameter.

`void set_id(id*)`
`id *get_id()`
> These functions set and retrieve the identifier of the parameter of an assignment.

`void set_var(parameter *)`
`parameter *get_var()`
> The parameter of an assignment can be set and retrieved by these member functions.

`void set_range_par(id *)`
`parameter *get_range_par()`
`id *get_range_id()`
> A parameter which value is assigned to the parameter of the assignment, can be set and retrieved by these functions.

`void set_range_expr(expr *)`
`expr *get_range_expr()`
> These functions set and retrieve the expression describing the value of a assignment.

```
void set_range(set_val *)
set_val *get_range()
```
These member functions set and retrieve the set of all possible values for an ambiguous assignment.

```
void set_ambigious(bool)
bool ambigious()
```
Whether or not an `rtt_assignment` is ambiguous can be specified and retrieved using these functions.

```
parameter_range *apply()
```
This member function returns the set of bindings created by the assignment.

```
char *to_string()
```
This member function returns an ASCII representation of an `rtt_assign` object.

15.6.3   The Class `rtt_event`

The class `rtt_event` was designed to represent events at the transitions of a high level transition graph or normalised HLTG. It used objects of the the class `dot_seq` to store the events of the specification. A high level transition graph contains sets of pairs (e, a) of an event e and a set of assignments a. Because multiple events for a transition are only created through input fields in the original event, an implicit representation of the events and assignments was chosen for the implementation. All events that occur in the set of events are represented by a single `rtt_event` that contains input fields.

```
                    rtt_event
-_event: dot_seq*
-_type: event_type
+rtt_event()
+rtt_event(rtt_event&)
+rtt_event(p:event_data*)
+~rtt_event()
+operator ==(rtt_event&): bool
+set_tau(): void
+is_tau(): bool
+set_ctau(): void
+is_ctau(): bool
+set_tick(): void
+is_tick(): bool
+get_event_type(): event_type
+set_event(dot_seq*): void
+get_event(): dot_seq*
+select_event(range_item*): dot_seq*
+get_num(): long int
+to_num(): char*
+to_string(): char*
```

Figure 15.32: Class `rtt_event`

Class Member Variables:

`dot_seq *_event`

    This attribute contains the event that is represented by an `rtt_event` object. The first `dot_seq_elem` of the `dot_seq` object of this attribute contains the `csp_channel` of the event.

`event_type _type`

    This attribute specifies the `event_type` of an `rtt_event`. The enumeration `event_type` is defined as {`rtt_else, rtt_tick, rtt_tau, rtt_ctau`}. It specifies whether the event is one of the special events $\checkmark$, τ and π or consists of a channel and a possibly empty communication field.

Class Member Functions:

`rtt_event()`
`rtt_event(rtt_event&)`
`rtt_event()`

    The constructor, copy constructor and destructor of the class.

`rtt_event(event_data *)`

    a special constructor, that creates an `rtt_event` object out of an `event_data` object. `event_data` objects are used to represent sets of `event` objects.

`bool operator==(rtt_event &)`

    This operator can be used to check the equality of two `rtt_event` objects. Two `rtt_events` are equal if they both have the type `rtt_tick, rtt_tau` or `rtt_ctau` or if the assigned `dot_seq` objects are equal.

`void set_tick()`
`void set_tau()`
`void set_ctau() bool is_tau()`

    These functions set the `_type` attribute to `rtt_tick, rtt_tau` or `rtt_ctau`.

`bool is_tick()`
`bool is_tau()`
`bool is_ctau()`

    These function check if the `_type` attribute is set to `rtt_tick, rtt_tau` or `rtt_ctau`.

`event_type get_event_type()`

    This member function can be used to retrieve the current `_type` of an `rtt_event` object.

`void set_event(dot_seq*)`
`dot_seq *get_event()`

    These member functions are used to set and retrieve the events of an `rtt_event` object.

`dot_seq *select_event(range_item *)`
> The `dot_seq` objects of an `rtt_event` can contain input fields, so that they can represent more than one event. This member function can be used to select that events out of all events represented by the `dot_seq`, where all parameters of input fields are bound according the argument of the function.

`long int get_num()`

`char *to_num()`
> This function returns the number of the events as exported in the alphabet file described in section 14.5.

`char *to_string()`
> This member function returns a string representation of an `rtt_event`.

15.6.4   The Class `rtt_location`

The class `rtt_location` works in collaboration with the class `rtt_label` to model high level transition graphs in the ClaO system. Objects of `rtt_location` carry information about its unique node number and references those objects of `rtt_label` that represents transitions leaving from the current location to another. Additionally is carries a list of parameters, that are visible in the current location.

This class is not only used to model the locations in the sequential high level transition graphs but also to model synchronisation terms. For modelling synchronisation terms there are three attributes in addition to those required for modelling high level transition graphs: `_level` stores, whether the current locations has to be considered as an element of a tree representing synchronisation terms. For each location which attribute `_level` has the value `loc_highlevel`, the attributes `_sync` and `_hide` must be set, which are representing the sets of synchronisation and hiding events for the corresponding term in the synchronisation term.

Finally this class is also used to model normalised Roscoe-style normalisation graphs, which are created during the normalisation of the high level transition graphs. Even though there are more efficient ways to model those graphs with adjacency-lists or adjacency-matrices (see [, Chapter 22] for more information about that topic), this approach was chosen, since the design goal was just to create and export those graph structures. It is therefore not inalienable to use a representation which allows a fast and efficient access to the represented graph structures. In later versions of ClaO is might nevertheless be useful to change the representation of normalised transition system.

```
                         rtt_location
─────────────────────────────────────────────────────────
#_num: long int
#_name: char*
#_labels: rtt_export::label_list
#_visible_params: parameter_list
#_range: parameter_range*
#_accset: acceptance_set*
#_level: loc_level
#_sync: expr*
#_hide: expr*
#_norm_type: rtt_norm_type
─────────────────────────────────────────────────────────
+rtt_location()
+~rtt_location(): virtual
+set_num(long int): void
+get_num(): long int {query}
+continual_numbers(): void
+set_name(char*): void
+get_name(): char*
+add_label(rtt_label*): void
+first_label(): rtt_label*
+prev_label(rtt_label*): rtt_label*
+next_label(rtt_label*): rtt_label*
+last_label(): rtt_label*
+find_event(rtt_event*): rtt_label*
+num_labels(): int
+has_label(ev:rtt_event*,target:rtt_location*): bool
+has_tau_labels(): bool
+has_tau_labels_only(): bool
+set_visible_params(parameter_list*): void
+add_visible_params(parameter_list*): void
+get_visible_params(): parameter_list*
+has_visible_params(): bool
+set_range(parameter_range*): void
+add_range_item(range_item*): void
+get_initial_actions(): acceptances*
+range(): parameter_range*
+prune_ranges(): void
+is_in(range_item*): bool
+is_stable(ri:range_item*,hide:event_set*=NULL): bool
+set_acceptance_set(acceptance_set*): void
+add_acceptances(acceptances*): void
+get_acceptance_set(): acceptance_set*
+set_level(typ:loc_level): void
+get_level(): loc_level
+is_lowlevel(): bool
+set_sync(expr*): void
+get_sync(): expr*
+sync_events(ri:range_item*): event_set*
+set_hide(expr*): void
+get_hide(): expr*
+hide_events(ri:range_item*): event_set*
+set_norm_type(rtt_norm_type): void
+get_norm_type(): rtt_norm_type
+graph_size(loc:int*, lab:int*): void
+do_graphviz_export(nodeinfo:bool): virtual void
─────────────────────────────────────────────────────────
```

Figure 15.33: Class rtt_location

Class Member Variables:

`long int _num`
> This attribute stores the internal number of the location in the high level transition graph. Each location must have a unique number.

`char *_name`
> An optional name, which might help to identify the process, which was responsible for the creation of the current location. E.g. a process operator creates a location, which name is set to the name of the current process.

`rtt_export::label_list _labels`
> A list of transitions that leave the current location in the represented high level transition graph. This list contain references to other objects of the class `rtt_label`.

`parameter_list _visible_params`
> A list of the parameters, that is visible in the process state, which is represented by the location. These visible parameters are for example required during the normalisation or range calculation.

`parameter_range *_range`
> This attribute represents a set of possible variable values, that can be reached during execution. The range calculation algorithm fills this set with all possible combinations of values, that can be reached from the start location on the represented high level transition graph.

`acceptance_set *accset`
> The set of event sets, that models the acceptances of the current location. These acceptance set is computed during the normalisation process.

`loc_level _level`
> If the value of this attribute is `loc_lowlevel`, the corresponding object represents a location in a high level transition graph. Otherwise the object is an element of a tree structure representing a synchronisation term. In that case the attributes `_sync` and `_hide` must be set.

`expr *_sync`
`expr *_hide`
> Two sets of events modelling synchronisation and hiding information, if the object represents a part of a synchronisation term.

`rtt_norm_type _norm_type`
> This attribute is set only for high level transition graphs, which are directly created from the abstract syntax tree. The value of this attribute contains the preferred normalisation type of the represented process as states in the original CSP specification using `pragma` statements.

Class Member Functions:

`rtt_location()`
> This constructor initialises the object. Initially each object is considered to represent a location in a high level transition graph and no element of a synchronisation term. Additionally each newly created object of this class automatically gets a unique number, so that normally the numbers need not to be changed manually.

`~rtt_location()`
> The destructor of this class participates in the clean up process, which removes a high level transition graph from the memory, by marking the referenced `rtt_label` objects as to be deleted.

`void set_num(long int)`
`long int get_num()`
> Changes or returns the unique number, that identifies a location.

`void continual_numbers()`
> During creation of high level transition graphs it cannot always be guaranteed, that the object locations are continuously marked with numbers, since several process operators removes locations that have previously been created from a high level transition graph. This function uses a graph traversion algorithm to provide all locations with new numbers. After this process all locations in a high level transition graph are continuously numbered.

`void set_name(char *)`
`char *get_name()`
> This function is used to provide a location with a name, which is shown in the graphical output of the high level transition graph. Those names need not be unique, since the attribute `_num` already provides this requirement.

`void add_label(rtt_label *)`
> This functions adds the specified transition to the list of transitions of this location.

`void remove_label(rtt_label *)`
> This functions removes an existing transition from the list of transitions of this location.

`rtt_label *first_label()`
`rtt_label *prev_label(rtt_label *)`
`rtt_label *next_label(rtt_label *)`
`rtt_label *last_label()`
> These functions are used to access the transitions, that are referenced by a

location. All functions return a reference to one of the transitions of the locations. `first_label()` and `last_label()` do not require any arguments,
since they return the first or last transition from the objects transition list.
The functions `prev_label()` and `next_label()` require a reference to one
`rtt_label` object of the location and then returns the one before or after
that one in the list. If any end of the list has been reached using these
functions the *NULL* reference is returned.

`rtt_label *find_event(rtt_event *)`

This function is used during the normalisation of a high level transition
graph. It retrieves that tranisition of the normalised location, that already
is marked with the specified event. Since this function returns only the first
occurrence of a transition in the list marked with that event, it can only be
used on normal form transition systems.

`int num_labels()`

Returns the number of transitions that are stored in the transition list.

`bool has_label(rtt_event *ev, rtt_location *target)`

This function checks, whether there exist one transition in the objects transition list, that is marked with the specified event and leads to the specified
target.

`bool has_tau_labels()`
`bool has_tau_labels_only()`

Both functions checks, whether the objects transition list contains τ-events.
`has_tau_labels()` returns *true*, if there exists at least one transition,
whereas `has_tau_labels_only()` only returns *true* if all transitions are
labelled with τ-events.

`void set_visible_params(parameter_list*)`

This function copies the contents of the specified `parameter_list` to the
one of the object. Any previously existing visible parameters are overwrit-
ten.

`void add_visible_params(parameter_list*)`

This functions appends the contents of the specified `parameter_list` to the
already existing one of the object.

`parameter_list *get_visible_params()`

Returns the list of visible parameters of the current object.

`bool has_visible_params()`

Checks if the list of visible parameters of the current object contains any
elements. This function returns *true*, if the object has at least one visible
parameter.

`void set_range(parameter_range *)`

    This function copies the `range_items` from the specified `parameter_range` to the objects attribute `_range`. All previously existing `range_items` are removed from the list.

`void add_range_item(range_item *)`

    This function adds the specified `range_item` to the objects parameter range `_range`.

`parameter_range *range()`

    Returns the objects parameter range.

`void prune_ranges()`

    This function is usually called after new range items have been added to the objects parameter range. It checks, whether all variables or parameters in the elements of the `range_items` are visible in the current location. If this is not the case, those parts of the `range_items` are removed, since their values are not relevant for the represented state.

`bool is_in(range_item *)`

    Checks whether the specified `range_item` is already in the objects parameter range.

`bool is_stable(range_item *ri, event_set *hide)`

    This function is an auxiliary function on an `rtt_location` object, which is required during the normalisation process. The object checks, whether or not any of the referenced transitions would produce a τ-event. Those checks takes the current variables values from the specified range item and also considers the set of hiding events, because both factors are relevant for the checking process.

`void set_acceptance_set(acceptance_set*)`

    This function copies the specified `acceptance_set` to the objects attribute `accset`. All previously existing acceptances in the set are deleted.

`void add_acceptances(acceptances*)`

    Add the specified `acceptances` to the objects acceptances set `accset`.

`acceptance_set *get_acceptance_set()`

    Returns a copy of the acceptances set of the current object.

`void set_level(loc_level typ)`
`loc_level get_level()`

    These functions are used to change and read the type of location, which the objects represents. These functions affect the objects attribute `_level`.

```
bool is_lowlevel()
```
Returns, whether or not the object is representing a location in a high level transition graph. If the objects represents a part of a synchronisation term, the return value is *false*.

```
void set_sync(expr*)
expr *get_sync()
void set_hide(expr*)
expr *get_hide()
```
These functions are used to set and retrieve the expressions, that are representing the synchronisation and hiding sets of the object. This is only useful for objects, which are used as high level operators in synchronisation terms.

```
event_set *sync_events(range_item *ri)
event_set *hide_events(range_item *ri)
```
These two functions evaluate the expressions of their corresponding attribute under the specified `range_item`. This allows the use of variables and parameters in the expressions. The return value is a set containing explicitly all the events in the expression.

```
void set_norm_type(rtt_norm_type)
rtt_norm_type get_norm_type()
```
Set and retrieve the desired normalisation type for the process represented by the object.

```
void graph_size(int *loc, int *lab)
```
This function is an auxiliary function, that is used to determine the number of locations and transitions in a high level transition graph.

```
void do_graphviz_export(bool nodeinfo)
```
This function is called to create the output format for the **dot** tool. It implements a simple graph traversion algorithm to process each location and transition of a high level transition graph only once.

15.6.5 The Class rtt_label

Transitionss represent the state changes in a high level transition graph. They lead from a source location to a target location. Every transition contains a condition, specifying whether it can be taken or not. A transition can only be taken, if its condition is true under the current environment.

As defined in section 5.1.1, labels at transitions of a high level transition graph also contain a set E of pairs (e, a) of an event e and a set of assignments a. Labels with multiple event-assignment-set pairs are created only for events with input communication fields (e.g. a?x). In this case, a pair (α, a) is created for each event $\alpha \in comms(e)$. In the implementation, the set E of event-assignment-set pairs is not represented explicitly. Instead, the original event together with a set of special (ambiguous) assignments is stored at the label. The explicit set E can be calculated out of this information, if it is needed.

```
                          rtt_label
-_source: rtt_location*
-_target: rtt_location*
-_conds: rtt_export::cond_list
-_event: rtt_event*
-_assigns: rtt_export::assign_list
+rtt_label()
+~rtt_label()
+operator ==(rtt_label&): bool
+set_source(rtt_location*): void
+get_source(): rtt_location*
+set_target(rtt_location*,del:bool=true): int
+get_target(): rtt_location*
+set_event(rtt_event*): void
+get_event(): rtt_event*
+set_tau(): void
+set_ctau(): void
+set_tick(): void
+add_cond(rtt_condition*): void
+remove_cond(rtt_condition*): void
+set_conds(rtt_export::cond_list*): void
+get_conds(): rtt_export::cond_list*
+first_cond(): rtt_condition*
+next_cond(rtt_condition*): rtt_condition*
+prev_cond(rtt_condition*): rtt_condition*
+last_cond(): rtt_condition*
+hold_cond(range_item*): bool
+add_assign(rtt_assign*): void
+remove_assign(rtt_assign*): void
+set_assigns(rtt_export::assign_list*): void
+get_assigns(): rtt_export::assign_list*
+first_assign(): rtt_assign*
+next_assign(rtt_assign*): rtt_assign*
+prev_assign(rtt_assign*): rtt_assign*
+last_assign(): rtt_assign*
+apply_assigns(parameter_range*): parameter_range*
+get_assignment_params(): parameter_list*
+do_graphviz_export(bool): void
+print(): void
```

Figure 15.34: Class `rtt_label`

Class Member Variables:

`rtt_location *_source`
`rtt_location *_target`

These attributes specify the source and the target location of a transition.

`rtt_export::cond_list _conds`

The condition of a transition is stores in this attribute.

`rtt_event *_event`

The implicit event representation of the events of a label is stored in this attribute.

`rtt_export::assign_list _assigns`

This attribute specifies the set of assignments of a label for the represented transition.

Class Member Functions:

```
rtt_label()
rtt_label()
```
    The constructor and destructor of the class

```
bool operator==(rtt_label &)
```
    This operator can be used to check the equality of two `rtt_label` objects.

```
void set_source(rtt_location*)
rtt_location *get_source()
```
    These member functions set and retrieve the source location of a `rtt_label` object.

```
int set_target(rtt_location*, bool)
rtt_location *get_target()
```
    These member functions set and retrieve the target location of a `rtt_label` object.

```
void set_event(rtt_event *)
rtt_event *get_event()
```
    The event of a label at the represented transition can be set and retrieved using these member functions.

```
void set_tau()
void set_ctau()
void set_tick()
```
    If a τ, π or *tick* event should be assigned to a `rtt_label`, these member functions can be used to do so.

```
void add_cond(rtt_condition *)
void remove_cond(rtt_condition *)
```
    With these member functions, conditions can be added to or removed from an `rtt_label` object. If an `rtt_label` contains more then one `rtt_condition`, the condition of the label is true, if all conditions of the label evaluate to true.

```
void set_conds(rtt_export::cond_list *)
rtt_export::cond_list *get_conds()
```
    These member functions can be used to set or retrieve the complete list of conditions of an `rtt_label`.

```
rtt_condition *first_cond()
rtt_condition *next_cond(rtt_condition *)
rtt_condition *prev_cond(rtt_condition *)
rtt_condition *last_cond()
```
    These member functions can be used to access the different conditions attached to an `rtt_label`.

`bool hold_cond(range_item *)`
> This member function checks if the conditions of the label for a transition evaluate to *true* if the bindings of parameter the argument are used.

`void add_assign(rtt_assign *)`
`void remove_assign(rtt_assign *)`
> Assignments can be added or removed using these member functions.

`void set_assigns(rtt_export::assign_list *)`
`rtt_export::assign_list *get_assigns()`
> These member functions can be used to set or retrieve the complete list of assignments of an `rtt_label`.

`rtt_assign *first_assign()`
`rtt_assign *next_assign(rtt_assign *)`
`rtt_assign *prev_assign(rtt_assign *)`
`rtt_assign *last_assign()`
> These member functions can be used to access the different assignments attached to an `rtt_label`.

`parameter_range *apply_assigns(parameter_range *)`
> This member function applies all assignments of the transition to a given environment, represented by the **parameter_range** argument.

`parameter_list *get_assignment_params()`
> This member function returns all **parameter** objects that are affected by the assignments of the transition.

`void do_graphviz_export(bool nodeinfo)`
> This function generates the graphical export of the transitions as described in section 14.5.

Chapter 16

Conclusion

The final chapter of this thesis presents a short summary of the work and highlights its scientific contributions. It closes with a section giving an overview of possible extensions of the high level transition graphs and their test theory.

16.1 Summary

Specification based testing of real world systems often leads to the problem of state explosion, when generating a transition system from the formal system specification. To avoid state explosions, the system specification can be divided into sub-specifications that model only parts of the whole system behaviour. Using these components, it is possible to test the specified subset of the system behaviour. One solution is to create several different specifications for a single test case that run in parallel and are capable of communicating with each other and the SUT.

One benefit of high level transition graphs in combination with synchronisation terms is the possibility of modelling larger parts of the system behaviour in a single specification, because it is no longer necessary to unfold the complete state space for specifications used for testing. Through this, the number of specifications used in a test case can be reduced or the test case can check a larger part of the system behaviour.

Because the parameters, conditions and expressions of a CSP specification are preserved in the structure of the corresponding high level transition graph, it is even possible to give a finite representation for specifications that would produce an infinite conventional transition graph. Instead of manually decomposing the whole system into parallel sub-specifications, the whole system can be kept in a single specification where synchronisation terms are used to model the parallel decomposition of the system into sequential components. This requires a strict compliance of the hierarchy of high-level and low-level operators in a test specification.

For real-time testing with conventional transition systems it is necessary to use their normalised forms, because this is the only way to guarantee that the transition system is deterministic. This is required for the calculation of the initial events and refusals of a state of the graph in hard real-time. In this thesis, a normalisation of synchronisation terms and high level transition graphs has been defined, that creates a normal form, which is identical to the corresponding normalised conventional transition graph. In this case, the test theory of conventional transition systems can be applied directly, but the problem of state explosion still remains.

To keep the benefits of the synchronisation terms, they can be converted into their normal form and the subordinate sequential components are completely normalised to a conventional labelled transition system. This approach avoids computing the complete product graph of the parallel system. Together with an on-the-fly normalisation of the synchronisation term, these forms of graphs can be used for real-time testing if certain design patterns are met.

Synchronisation terms with unnormalised high level transition graphs can be used for real-time testing as well. An on-the-fly normalisation of high level transition graphs has been developed to eliminate nondeterminism during a test run. This avoids backtracking in the graph and enables the calculation of the initial actions and refusals in real-time. If all possible parameter values have been calculated for each high level transition graph, an upper bound for each step of the on-the-fly normalisation can be determined. This can be achieved through a complete state space exploration of the respective high level transition graph.

In contrast to the test driver, which must be able to stimulate the SUT in hard real-time, it is sufficient for the test oracle to validate the behaviour of the SUT against the system specification with a slight delay. A delayed evaluation algorithm has been developed in this thesis, that can be used with any type of transition system, in particular with synchronisation terms of unnormalised high level transition graphs. There exist well known methods to efficiently represent general transition systems like adjacency-lists or adjacency-matrices. Still it is necessary to find an efficient representation of the expressions at the transitions of the high level transition graphs. In this thesis, the authors have suggested a way to adjust BDDs such that they can be used for this purpose.

Many of the concepts described above have been implemented as an extension of the ClaO system. The basic ClaO implementation has been developed by the authors as part of their diploma thesis. The implemented extensions include the generation of synchronisation terms with high level transition graphs, several stages of normalisation and the export of the resulting graphs. The on-the-fly normalisation of synchronisation terms has been implemented in a specialised abstract machine of the RT-Tester system.

16.2 Contributions

One of the main scientific contributions of this thesis is the definition of high level transition graphs for the different low-level CSP operators. The structure of high level transition graphs is a representation close to the rules of the operational semantics of CSP. These graphs are usually smaller than the corresponding conventional transition systems. It is shown in appendix A that the high level transition graph of a CSP specification together with the defined semantics on high level transition graphs is semantically equivalent to applying the operational semantics directly to the CSP specification.

The developed concept of synchronisation terms allow to model the CSP high-level operators interleaving, parallel and hiding in an efficient way. Instead of computing an explicit graph representation of the product graph of parallel systems, the synchronisation terms only describe its communication structure. This method prevents one of the main reasons for the occurrences of state explosions.

Normalisation algorithms have been defined for both: high level transition graphs and synchronisation terms. The algorithms result in completely unfolded transition systems, which are semantically identical to the normal form of the corresponding conventional transition system. The developed algorithms are an adaption of Roscoe's normalisation algorithm.

Especially for testing purposes, a normal form of synchronisation terms has been defined, which allows to compute an on-the-fly normalisation for each state of the represented system in real-time. An algorithm for this on-the-fly normalisation has been defined in this thesis, allowing real-time testing without the necessity to compute the whole product graph of parallel systems. This method is restricted by certain design patterns, that have to be applied to the CSP specification used for testing. An additional on-the-fly normalisation has been specified on high level transition graphs, that allows to use unnormalised high level transition graphs for real-time testing, if its state space has been computed previously. This computation is necessary to determine an upper bound for each normalisation step.

Finally a new test algorithm has been developed for the test oracle component of a test system, which does not require the computation of the initial events and refusals of the current state of the employed transition system in hard real-time. This is only possible because the test oracle does not interact with the SUT, but only validates the inputs and outputs of the SUT against a specification. Any transition system type can be used with this delayed test algorithm, especially synchronisation terms with unnormalised high level transition graphs, which is the most compact representation method of the system behaviour described in this thesis.

16.3   Future Work

One of the remaining issues is to extend the developed concepts for high level transition graphs and synchronisation terms to the currently unsupported Untimed CSP operators: timeout and renaming. The timeout operator is a low-level CSP operator, that is only relevant for testing in its timed variant. It is not necessary to define rules for the generation of high level transition graphs for this operator, since according to the structural decomposition theorem for Timed CSP, the timeout operator can be expressed using only supported untimed CSP operators.

Supporting the renaming operator would require an extension of the concepts of synchronisation terms, which also have to represent the renaming relation. Renaming would be useful to instantiate different processes from one single template. Since the renaming operator can introduce non-determinism to a specification this would require to reconsider all definitions and algorithms for the synchronisation terms, especially with regard to real-time aspects.

Another interesting topic not covered in this thesis is the question of test case selection and test coverage. A standard method in testing with conventional transition systems is to mark already processed transitions and, if possible, to select only those which have not been marked. For high level transition graphs it has to be examined, if an additional information about the parameters and conditions at the transitions can support the derivation of classes of relevant test cases for the specified SUT. This could be used to introduce a new term of test coverage for CSP specifications, which does not depend on the covered transitions and states in the represented system, but instead relies on the covered test classes. Finally the currently existing implementation of the ClaO system has to be extended to include all algorithms and concepts developed in this thesis.

Part V

Appendix

Appendix A

Correctness of High Level Transition Graphs

The standard method of creating a transition graph (LTS) for a CSP process uses the rules of the operational semantics. All applied occurrences of process parameters or parameters introduced by input fields of events are substituted by their value, every time a process reference is resolved or an event $\alpha \in comme(e)$ is selected for a prefix term $e \to P$. The operational semantics therefore always uses the concrete values for applied occurrences of parameters that are involved in the current computation.

When creating a high level transition graph (HLTG) from a CSP process, the applied occurrences are *not* substituted by their values. Instead they are represented in the conditions and events of the transitions. Defining occurrences are represented as assignments that manipulate an environment of parameter values when interpreting the graph. The following sections show that a high level transition graph of a CSP process is equivalent to a transition graph of the same process that has been generated using a standard method like the one implemented in FDR2[ ].

Each sub-term of a CSP process can be associated with a state in the standard transition graph of the process. In section A.1, a relation $term_{LTS}$ is defined that labels each state in the LTS with its associated process terms. Applying the operational semantics of process references to a process term does not produce any actions, but defines a new current process term. Therefore multiple process terms can be associated with the same state.

To be able to compare the LTS and HLTG of a process, the locations in the HLTG of a CSP process can as well be associated with sub-terms of the process. This is discussed in section A.2 where a function $term_{HLTG}$ is defined. Because process references are represented by special π-actions, each location can be associated with exactly one sub-term of the process.

In section A.4, a correctness theorem is defined that is used to prove, that the HLTG of a CSP process is semantically equivalent to the standard LTS of the same process. The HLTG of a CSP process is only defined for a subset of low-level CSP operators. Only this subset of CSP and only non-divergent processes are considered here.

A.1   Transition Graphs for CSP Processes

This section describes a standard way of generating transition graphs for CSP processes including the definition of the relation $term_{LTS}$. Transition graphs for process terms can be derived directly from the operational semantics of CSP. The transition graph $LTS_P = (S_{LTS_P}, s_0, \Sigma_{LTS_P}^{\tau\checkmark}, \rightarrow_{LTS_P})$ of a CSP process definition $P = T$ is equal to the transition graph of its process term T. During the generation, the states can be labelled with the associated process terms extending the relation $term_{LTS_P} \subset S_{LTS_P} \times CSPTerm$ where $CSPTerm$ is the set of all CSP process terms. The initial state s_0 can be associated with the process term T so that $(s_0, T) \in term_{LTS_P}$. The LTS is generated by applying each possible rule

$$\frac{c}{T \xrightarrow{\alpha} T'}$$

of the operational semantics of T to the current state s with $(s, T) \in term_{LTS_P}$. For each applied rule, a transition (s, α, s') is created in LTS_P leading from the current state s to a state $s' \in S_{LTS_P}$ that can be associated with the resulting process term T' of the rule so that $(s', T') \in term_{LTS_P}$. The event α of this transition is defined by the rules of the operational semantics. If there already exists a state $s'' \in S_{LTS_P}$ with $(s'', T') \in term_{LTS_P}$, s' and s'' are joined so that there can only exist exactly one state s' for each sub-term T' of T with $(s', T') \in term_{LTS_P}$. The generation continues with all new sub-terms T' and their corresponding states s'.

The process reference operator does not create transitions. As defined in section 2.4, equation 2.3, process references $R(v_1, ..., v_n)$ lead to a textual replacement of $R(v_1, ..., v_n)$ with the process term T'_R which is the process term T_R of the referenced process R with $R(p_1, ..., p_n) = T_R$ where all process parameters $p_1, ..., p_n$ in T_R have been replaced with the corresponding values $v_1, ..., v_n$ of the process reference: $T'_R = subs(\mathcal{C}(R(v_1, ..., v_n)))$. Therefore process references do not create transitions but increase the set of process terms associated with their corresponding state so that

$$(s_R, R(v_1, ..., v_n)) \in term_{LTS_P} \Rightarrow (s_R, subs(\mathcal{C}(R(v_1, ..., v_n)))) \in term_{LTS_P}$$

A.2   HLTG for CSP Processes

High level transition graphs have been defined in section 5.1, together with rules how to execute them. The subgraphs for the different CSP process operators have been defined in chapter 7. In this section, a possible generation method is presented to show that like the states in an LTS of a CSP process, the locations in the HLTG can be associated with corresponding process terms.

Let $HLTG_P = (L_{HLTG_P}, l_0, \Sigma_{HLTG_P}^{\pi\tau\checkmark}, \mathcal{E}_{HLTG_P}^{\pi\tau\checkmark}, \rightarrow_{HLTG_P})$ be the high level transition graph of a CSP process $P = T$. Unlike the process terms of the LTS, the process terms associated with HLTG locations can be parameterised. The function $term_{HLTG} : L_{HLTG_P} \rightarrow CSPTerm$ will be defined during the generation process and maps each location of the HLTG to an associated CSP term.

A.2.1 A Generation Method

A CSP specification can be considered as a set *Spec* of process definitions $P_i = T_i$ of processes P_i and their corresponding process terms T_i. The process terms of P_i can contain process references to P_i itself or to other processes P_j with $P_j = T_j \in Spec$. Initially, a start location l_{P_i0} is created for each process term T_i with $P_i = T_i \in Spec$. An HLTG is always created for a start process $P \in Spec$. The corresponding start location l_{P0} of P is defined to be the start location l_0 of the HLTG. Like an LTS, the HLTG of each process P_i is created top down from the start location of its process term T_i according to the subgraph definitions of chapter 7. Each operator with process term arguments, like the prefix operator $e \rightarrow Q$ of an event e and a process term Q, creates the start location l_{Q0} for process term Q. The generation is continued with the argument process term Q and its start location l_{Q0}. Each start location of a process term is associated with its process term. The only exception to this top down creation is the generation of the HLTG for *sequential composition* and *external choice*, as described below. In the following, the generation procedure for each CSP operator is described together with a definition of the associated process terms. Each location is associated with exactly one process term. Through this, the function $term_{HLTG}$ is defined.

STOP

The process term $STOP$ describes a process that has no possible actions. Therefore no transition or location is created. The start location l_{STOP0} is associated with $STOP$.

$$term_{HLTG}(l_{STOP0}) = STOP$$

SKIP

The only action that is possible for a $SKIP$ process is the successful termination $\checkmark$. Therefore, only a transition $(l_{SKIP0}, true, \{(\checkmark, \emptyset)\}, \Omega)$ from the start location l_{SKIP0} of the $SKIP$ process term to a new location Ω is created. The start location is associated with $SKIP$ and the location Ω is associated with Ω.

$$term_{HLTG}(l_{SKIP0}) = SKIP$$
$$term_{HLTG}(\Omega) = \Omega$$

Process Reference

Process references are not resolved during the HLTG generation, as it would be done for the operational semantics. Instead, the subgraph for the CSP operators of the referenced, possibly parameterised process term is created. As defined in chapter 7, a process reference $R(v_1, ..., v_n)$ of a process R with $R(p_1, ..., p_n) = T$ creates a π-transition $(l_{ref0}, true, \{(\pi, assigns(R(v_1, ..., v_n), R(p_1, ..., p_n)))\}, l_{T0})$ from its start location l_{ref0} to the start location l_{T0} of the subgraph of the referenced process term. Because the start location of each process $P_i \in Spec$ is generated initially and subgraphs are created for each P_i, the transition can be generated, independent of the fact that the referenced subgraph is already created or not. The start location l_{ref0} is associated with the process reference $R(v_1, ..., v_n)$ and the start location of the referenced process is associated with its process term T.

$$term_{HLTG}(l_{ref0}) = R(v_1, ..., v_n)$$
$$term_{HLTG}(l_{T0}) = T$$

Prefix

As defined in chapter 7, definition 7.9, a transition $(L_{\to 0}, true, events(e), l_{Q0})$ is created for a prefix process term $e \to Q$, where $L_{\to 0}$ is the start location of the process term and l_{Q0} is a newly created start location for the process term Q. The generation continues with the process term Q and its start location l_{Q0}. The start location $L_{\to 0}$ is associated with the prefix process term $e \to Q$.

$$term_{HLTG}(L_{\to 0}) = e \to Q$$

if-then-else

The generation of an *if* b *then* Q *else* R process term and its start location l_{ite0} continues with the generation of the HLTG of the sub-terms Q and R. The start location for both sub-terms is the same as for the if-then-else process term. The condition b is added to all initial transitions of the HLTG of Q and $\neg b$ is added to all initial transitions of R. Adding a condition b to a transition (l, c, E, l') is done by creating a new boolean expression c' which is the conjunction $b \wedge c$. The resulting transition is $(l, b \wedge c, E, l')$. The start location l_{ite0} is associated with the if-then-else process term. The locations in the subgraphs of Q and R are associated according to the HLTG generation of Q and R and l_{ite0} is associated with the if-then-else process term.

$$term_{HLTG}(l_{ite0}) = if \; b \; then \; Q \; else \; R$$

Sequential Composition

The sequential composition $Q; R$ of two process terms Q and R requires a complete subgraph for the process term Q, because all $\checkmark$-transitions of Q have to be replaced by τ-transitions leading to the start location of the subgraph of R. A start locations l_{R0} is created for the HLTG of R. An independent new HLTG for Q is generated, using the same set *Spec* of process definitions. New start locations are created for each process definition in *Spec*. This is necessary, because the process references must not lead to start locations in the current set of processes. Otherwise the subgraph of a process $S = SKIP$, referenced by Q and R would be altered by the sequential composition, so that in both cases the $\checkmark$-transition leads to the start location of R. This would be correct for the subgraph referenced by Q, but obviously wrong for the subgraph referenced by R. The generation of the subgraph of Q starts with the start location $l_{Q;R0}$ of the sequential composition process term as start location for Q. After the subgraph $HLTG_Q = (L_{HLTG_Q}, l_{Q;R0}, \Sigma_{HLTG_Q}^{\pi\tau\checkmark}, \mathcal{E}_{HLTG_Q}^{\pi\tau\checkmark}, \rightarrow_{HLTG_Q})$ of Q is completely created, all $\checkmark$-transitions $(l, c, \{(\checkmark, \emptyset)\}, \Omega) \in \rightarrow_{HLTG_Q}$ with $l \in L_{HLTG_Q}$ and $c \in Conditions$ are replaced with τ-transitions $(l, c, \{(\tau, \emptyset)\}, l_{R0})$ leading to the start location l_{R0} of R. The generation then continuous with the generation of the subgraph of R.

During the generation of $HLTG_Q$, associations between locations $l \in L_Q$ and process terms T where created, defining $term_{HLTG_Q}$. These associations have to be altered for $term_{HLTG}$, because the process term Q is part of the sequential composition process term $Q; R$. Each location $l \in L_Q$ that is associated with a process term T, so that $term_{HLTG_Q}(l) = T$, must be associated with the process term $T; R$. The start location l_{R0} of R is associated with the process term R.

$$\forall \, l \in L_{HLTG_Q} \, . \, term_{HLTG}(l) = term_{HLTG_Q}(i); R$$
$$term_{HLTG}(l_{R0}) = R$$

Note that processes of the form $S = a \rightarrow S; STOP$ result in an infinite generation process, because for each process term $a \rightarrow S$, a new set *Spec'* of process definitions would be generated. This is no restriction of this generation method, because the standard LTS generation of such a process also does not terminate. The textual replacement of the process reference S with the process term $a \rightarrow S; STOP$ always contains the process reference itself. In the first instance, it would be $(a \rightarrow S; STOP); STOP$, then $((a \rightarrow S; STOP); STOP); STOP$ and so on.

Internal Choice

During the generation of the HLTG of an internal choice process term $Q \sqcap R$, two transitions $(l_{Q\sqcap R0}, true, \{(\tau, \emptyset)\}, l_{Q0})$ and $(l_{Q\sqcap R0}, true, \{(\tau, \emptyset)\}, l_{R0})$ are created, leading from its start location $l_{Q\sqcap R0}$ to two new created locations l_{Q0} and

l_{R0}. The generation continues with the process term Q together with its start location l_{Q0} and the process term R together with l_{R0}. The start location $l_{Q \sqcap R0}$ is associated with $Q \sqcap R$ and the start locations L_{Q0} and L_{R0} of the sub-terms Q and R are associated with the respective process term Q or R.

$$term_{HLTG}(l_{Q \sqcap R0}) = Q \sqcap R$$

External Choice

The HLTG of an external choice process term $Q \square R$ can be divided into three subgraphs $Q_{remainder}$, $R_{remainder}$ and $\tau_Q \times \tau_{R'}$ and a set V of transitions connecting them. This is described in detail in section 7.2.3. The subgraphs $Q_{remainder}$ and $R_{remainder}$ are subgraphs of the HLTG of Q and R excluding all transitions with invisible actions (τ and π) that can be taken from the start location l_{Q0} respective l_{R0} and the transitions with the initial visible actions of the HLTG. The subgraph $\tau_Q \times \tau_{R'}$ is a new HLTG created for the external choice operator, V is a set of transitions connecting $\tau_Q \times \tau_{R'}$ with $Q_{remainder}$ and $R_{remainder}$.

The subgraph $\tau_Q \times \tau_{R'}$ is the product graph of the invisible beginnings of the subgraphs of Q and R. Therefore the subgraphs of Q and R have to be generated at least up to their first visible actions. If the sub-terms Q and R do not contain process references before any of the first visible actions, the subgraphs of Q with the start location l_{Q0} and R with the start location l_{R0} is generated and $\tau_Q \times \tau_{R'}$ is generated from the invisible beginnings of both subgraphs as defined in 7.19. The start location of $\tau_Q \times \tau_{R'}$ is $l_{Q \square R0}$. If process references are involved in the invisible beginnings of one of the sub-terms Q or R, as for example in $EXT = S(1) \square S(2)$, the HLTG of another process $P_i \in Spec$ is involved. It must be assured, that this process definition is generated at least up to the first visible actions. If it does not exist yet, it has to be generated before the generation of the external choice HLTG can continue. For non-divergent processes, this is always possible, even if the referenced process refers to the process of the external choice process term like in the following example:

```
1    channel a, b
2    P = a -> (P [] Q)
3    Q = b -> STOP
```

If the definition of P in the above example would be P = P [] Q instead, the process P would be divergent and no HLTG could be generated for it.

The process term associated with the start location $l_{Q \square R0}$ is $Q \square R$. The process term associations for the locations in $Q_{remainder}$ and $R_{remainder}$ are created during their generation and the definition of $term_{HLTG_Q}$ and $term_{HLTG_R}$. The locations l_{π_i} in $\tau_Q \times \tau_{R'}$ are identified by pairs (l_{Q_i}, l_{R_i}) of locations from $HLTG_Q = (L_{HLTG_Q}, l_{Q0}, \Sigma_{HLTG_Q}^{\pi \tau \checkmark}, \mathcal{E}_{HLTG_Q}^{\pi \tau \checkmark}, \rightarrow_{HLTG_Q})$ and $HLTG_R = (L_{HLTG_R}, l_{R0}, \Sigma_{HLTG_R}^{\pi \tau \checkmark}, \mathcal{E}_{HLTG_R}^{\pi \tau \checkmark}, \rightarrow_{HLTG_R})$, the two subgraphs of Q and R. The process terms associated with these locations $l_{\pi_i} = (l_{Q_i}, l_{R_i})$ depend on the process terms associated with the locations of their pair, as created during the generation of $HLTG_Q$ and $HLTG_R$. Note that this is true also for the start location $l_{Q \square R0}$ which is identical to the pair (l_{Q0}, l_{R0}).

$$term_{HLTG}(l_{Q \square R0}) = Q \square R$$
$$term_{HLTG}(l_{\pi_i}) = term_{HLTG_Q}(l_{Q_i}) \square term_{HLTG_R}(l_{R_i})$$

A.3   Creating Transition Graphs from High Level Transition Graphs

High level transition graphs, like LTS, can be used to simulate the behaviour of a specified process, as described in section 5.1.3. The execution rules that are defined there, can also be used to create a transition graph describing the same behaviour as the high level transition graph.

Let LTS_P be a transition graph of a CSP process P, generated as described in A.1 and let $HLTG_P = (L_{HLTG_P}, l_0, \Sigma_{HLTG_P}^{\pi\tau\checkmark}, \mathcal{E}_{HLTG_P}^{\pi\tau\checkmark}, \rightarrow_{HLTG_P})$ be the high level transition graph of P. The transition graph $LTS_P' = (S_{LTS_P}', s_0', \Sigma_{LTS_P}^{\tau\checkmark'}, \rightarrow_{LTS_P}')$ can be created from $HLTG_P$ by calculating the complete state space of $HLTG_P$, starting with the start location l_0 and a legal start environment ε_0. The states of LTS_P' are pairs (l, ε) of a location $l \in L_{HLTG_P}$ and an environment $\varepsilon \in Env$. The pair (l_0, ε_0) becomes the start location of LTS_P': $s_0' = (l_0, \varepsilon_0)$. The process term associated with this location is $subst(term_{HLTG_P}(l_0), \varepsilon_0)$.

For each atomic execution step $l_0, \varepsilon_0 \xrightarrow{c,(\alpha,a)} l', \varepsilon'$ with $\alpha \in \mathcal{E}_{HLTG_P}^{\tau\checkmark}$, a new state (l', ε') is added to S_{LTS_P}' and a new transition $(l_0, \varepsilon_0) \xrightarrow{\alpha} (l', \varepsilon')$ is added to $\rightarrow_{LTS_P}'$. The CSP process term associated with the new state can be defined as $subst(term_{HLTG_P}(l'), \varepsilon')$. For each atomic execution step $l_0, \varepsilon_0 \xrightarrow{c,(\pi,a)} l', \varepsilon'$, only a new CSP process term $subst(term_{HLTG_P}(l'), \varepsilon')$ is associated with the existing state (l_0, ε_0).

The process continues with all labels leaving a location l' using the parameter bindings of an environment ε' if the pair (l', ε') is either a new state in LTS_P' or participated in the creation of a new association of a process term to an existing state. Because this process calculates the complete state space and because the state space of P must be finite if LTS_P is finite, the creation terminates for each $HLTG_P$ of a process term P for that a finite transition graph LTS_P can be created.

In definition A.1, a transformation function is given, that creates an LTS for a HLTG of a CSP process using the execution rules for high level transition graphs, as defined in section 5.1.3. During the generation of the LTS, the relation $term_{LTS}$ describing the associated process terms of a state in the LTS is defined, as well.

Definition A.1 *The transformation function*

$$\Psi \quad : \quad HLTG \times LTS \times \mathcal{P}(Env, Transitions) \times \mathcal{P}(Env, Transitions)$$
$$\times \mathcal{P}(Locations \times CSPTerm) \times \mathcal{P}(States \times CSPTerm)$$
$$\rightarrow \quad HLTG \times LTS \times \mathcal{P}(Env, Transitions) \times \mathcal{P}(Env, Transitions)$$
$$\times \mathcal{P}(Locations \times CSPTerm) \times \mathcal{P}(States \times CSPTerm)$$

$$\Psi(HLTG_P, LTS_P, T_{pend}, T_{proc}, term_{HLTG}, term_{LTS})$$
$$= \begin{cases} (HLTG_P, LTS_P, T_{pend}, T_{proc}, term_{HLTG}, term_{LTS}) & if\ T_{pend} = \emptyset \\ \Psi(HLTG_P, LTS'_P, T'_{pend}, T'_{proc}, term_{HLTG}, term'_{LTS}) & otherwise \end{cases}$$

with

$$(\varepsilon, (l, c, E, l')) \in T_{pend}$$
$$\wedge\ HLTG_P = (L_{HLTG_P}, l_0, \Sigma^{\pi\tau\checkmark}_{HLTG_P}, \mathcal{E}^{\pi\tau\checkmark}_{HLTG_P}, \rightarrow_{HLTG_P})$$
$$\wedge\ LTS_P = (S_{LTS_P}, s_0, \Sigma^{\tau\checkmark}_{LTS_P}, \rightarrow_{LTS_P})$$
$$\wedge\ LTS'_P = (S'_{LTS_P}, s_0, \Sigma^{\tau\checkmark'}, \rightarrow'_{LTS_P})$$
$$\wedge\ S'_{LTS_P} = S_{LTS_P} \cup (\bigcup_{(\alpha,a)\in E} \{(l', \varepsilon') \mid l, \varepsilon \xrightarrow{c,(\alpha,a)} l', \varepsilon' \wedge \alpha \neq \pi\})$$
$$\wedge\ \Sigma^{\tau\checkmark'}_{LTS_P} = \Sigma^{\tau\checkmark}_{LTS_P} \cup (\bigcup_{(\alpha,a)\in E} \{eval(\alpha, \varepsilon) \mid l, \varepsilon \xrightarrow{c,(\alpha,a)} l', \varepsilon' \wedge \alpha \neq \pi\})$$
$$\wedge\ \rightarrow'_{LTS_P} = \rightarrow_{LTS_P} \cup (\bigcup_{(\alpha,a)\in E} \{((l,\varepsilon), eval(\alpha, \varepsilon), (l', \varepsilon')) \mid l, \varepsilon \xrightarrow{c,(\alpha,a)} l', \varepsilon' \\ \wedge \alpha \neq \pi\})$$
$$\wedge\ T'_{pend} = T_{pend} \setminus \{(\varepsilon, (l, c, E, l'))\}$$
$$\cup (\bigcup_{(\alpha,a)\in E} \{(\varepsilon', (l', c', E', l'')) \mid l, \varepsilon \xrightarrow{c,(\alpha,a)} l', \varepsilon' \\ \wedge (l', c', E', l'') \in \rightarrow_{HLTG_P}) \\ \wedge (\varepsilon', (l', c', E', l'')) \notin T_{proc}\})$$
$$\wedge\ T'_{proc} = T_{proc} \cup \{(\varepsilon, (l, c, E, l'))\}$$
$$\wedge\ term'_{LTS} = term_{LTS}$$
$$\cup (\bigcup_{(\alpha,a)\in E} \{((l', \varepsilon'), subst(term_{HLTG_P}(l'), \varepsilon')) \mid \alpha \neq \pi\}$$
$$\cup (\bigcup_{(\alpha,a)\in E} \{((l, \varepsilon), subst(term_{HLTG_P}(l'), \varepsilon')) \mid \alpha = \pi\}$$

The transition graph LTS_P of a CSP process P can can be generated from $HLTG_P$ as follows:

$$LTS_P =$$
$$\Psi(HLTG_P, (\emptyset, (l_0, \varepsilon_0), \emptyset, \emptyset), \{(\varepsilon_0, trans(l_0, \varepsilon_0))\}, \emptyset, term_{HLTG}, \{((l_0, \varepsilon_0), T)\})\downarrow_2$$

The relation $term_{LTS_P}$, generated during the generation of LTS_P is defined as:

$$term_{LTS_P} =$$
$$\Psi(HLTG_P, (\emptyset, (l_0, \varepsilon_0), \emptyset, \emptyset), \{(\varepsilon_0, trans(l_0, \varepsilon_0))\}, \emptyset, term_{HLTG}, \{((l_0, \varepsilon_0), T)\})\downarrow_6$$

A.4 Correctness of High Level Transition Graphs

Based on Milners work [,], A.W. Roscoe in [, p. 155] defines a bisimulation of two LTS that can be used to proof the semantical equivalence of different LTS of the same process. If there exists such a bisimulation for LTS_P and LTS'_P, this would show that $HLTG_P$ is a correct representation of P.

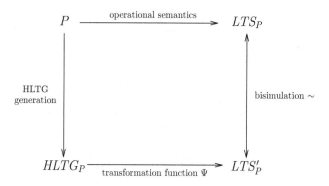

Figure A.1: Transformation diagram

Theorem A.1 Correctness of High Level Transition Graphs
Let $LTS_P = (S_{LTS_P}, s_0, \Sigma_{LTS_P}^{\tau\checkmark}, \rightarrow_{LTS_P})$ be a transition graph of a CSP process P, generated as described in *A.1*. Let $HLTG_P = (L_{HLTG_P}, l_0, \Sigma_{HLTG_P}^{\pi\tau\checkmark}, \mathcal{E}_{HLTG_P}^{\pi\tau\checkmark}, \rightarrow_{HLTG_P})$ be the high level transition graph of the same process, generated as described in *A.2* with a start environment ε_0, and let $LTS'_P = (S'_{LTS_P}, s'_0, \Sigma_{LTS_P}^{\tau\checkmark'}, \rightarrow'_{LTS_P})$ be the transition graph of P that can be generated using the transformation function Ψ, defined in section *A.3*. $HLTG_P$ is a correct representation of P if there exists a bisimulation for LTS_P and LTS'_P and the start locations are labelled with the same process terms.

Lemma *A.1* defines a set of requirements that can be used to show the correctness of a high level transition graph of a CSP process. The following functions *subst* and *ProcRef* are needed for this definition. *subst* substitutes all applied occurrences of a parameter in a CSP_M process term by its assigned value and *ProcRef* is a predicate, that is true if a CSP_M process term contains a process reference that can be resolved according to the operational semantics of the process term.

Definition A.2
The function subst : $\mathcal{L}_{CSP_M} \times Env \rightarrow \mathcal{L}_{CSP_M}$ *denotes the substitution of all applied occurrences of parameters in a* CSP$_M$ *syntax term by their values.*

$subst(T, \varepsilon) = T'$
with $T' = T$ *where for each pair* $(p, v) \in \varepsilon$, *every applied occurrence of* p *has been replaced by* v.

Definition A.3
The function ProcRef : $\mathcal{L}_{CSP_M} \rightarrow \{true, false\}$ *is a predicate that states whether a* CSP$_M$ *process term contains at least one process reference that can be resolved according to its operational semantics.*

$$ProcRef(T) = \begin{cases} true & \textit{if } T \textit{ contains a process reference } R, \\ & \textit{that can be replaced by } subs(\mathcal{C}(R)) \\ & \textit{according to the operational semantics of } T \\ false & \textit{otherwise} \end{cases}$$

The following Lemma defines properties, that can be used to show that the HLTG of a process is semantically equivalent to an LTS of the same process.

Lemma A.1
Let $P = T_P$ *be a CSP process definition and* $LTS_P = (S_{LTS_P}, s_0, \Sigma_{LTS_P}^{\tau\checkmark}, \rightarrow_{LTS_P})$ *be a transition graph of* P, *generated as described in* A.1 *and let* $HLTG_P = (L_{HLTG_P}, l_0, \Sigma_{HLTG_P}^{\pi\tau\checkmark}, \mathcal{E}_{HLTG_P}^{\pi\tau\checkmark}, \rightarrow_{HLTG_P})$ *be the high level transition graph of the same process, generated as described in* A.2 *with a start environment* ε_0. *During the generation of* $HLTG_P$ *and* LTS_P, *the function* $term_{HLTG_P} : L_{HLTG_P} \rightarrow CSPTerm$ *and the relation* $term_{LTS_P} \subset S_{LTS_P} \times CSPTerm$ *have been defined.*

Let $LTS'_P = (S'_{LTS_P}, s'_0, \Sigma_{LTS_P}^{\tau\checkmark}, \rightarrow'_{LTS_P})$ *be the transition graph of* P *that can be generated from* $HLTG_P$ *using* Ψ. *Let* $term'_{LTS_P} \subset S'_{LTS_P} \times CSPTerm$ *be the relation defined during the generation of* LTS'_P.

Let $\sim \subset S_{LTS_P} \times S'_{LTS_P}$ *be a relation with*

$$s \sim s' \Leftrightarrow \exists\, T \in CSPTerm\,.\,(s, T) \in term_{LTS_P} \wedge (s', T) \in term'_{LTS_P}$$

The relation $\sim$ *is a bisimulation on* S_{LTS_P} *and* S'_{LTS_P} *and the start locations are labelled with the same process term, if the following properties hold:*

1. *The start location of* $HLTG_P$ *and* LTS_P *must be associated with the same* CSP *process terms:*
   $(s_0, subst(term_{HLTG_P}(l_0), \varepsilon_0)) \in term_{LTS_P}$

2. *Every action, except π, that is possible in $HLTG_P$ must as well be possible in LTS_P:*

   $\forall\, l, l' \in L_{HLTG_P}, \varepsilon, \varepsilon' \in Env, s \in S_{LTS_P}, \alpha_l \in Events^{\tau\checkmark}, \alpha_s \in \Sigma_{LTS_P}^{\tau\checkmark}$.

   $(s, subst(term_{HLTG_P}(l), \varepsilon)) \in term_{LTS_P} \wedge l_0, \varepsilon_0 \overset{\sigma}{\mapsto} l, \varepsilon \wedge l, \varepsilon \overset{b,(\alpha_l,a)}{\rightarrowtail} l', \varepsilon'$

   $\Rightarrow \exists\, s' \in S_{LTS_P} \, . \, \big(s \overset{\alpha_s}{\rightarrow} s' \wedge \alpha_s = eval(\alpha_l, \varepsilon) \wedge$
   $\qquad\qquad\qquad\quad (s', subst(term_{HLTG_P}(l'), \varepsilon')) \in term_{LTS_P} \big)$

3. *Every action, that is possible in LTS_P must as well be possible in $HLTG_P$:*

   $\forall\, l \in L_{HLTG_P}, \varepsilon \in Env, s, s' \in S_{LTS_P}, \alpha_l \in Events^{\tau\checkmark}, \alpha_s \in \Sigma_{LTS_P}^{\tau\checkmark}$.

   $(s, subst(term_{HLTG_P}(l), \varepsilon)) \in term_{LTS_P} \wedge l_0, \varepsilon_0 \overset{\sigma}{\mapsto} l, \varepsilon \wedge s \overset{\alpha_s}{\rightarrow} s' \wedge$
   $ProcRef(term_{HLTG_P}(l)) = false$

   $\Rightarrow \exists\, l' \in L_{HLTG_P}, \varepsilon' \in Env \, . \, \big(l, \varepsilon \overset{b,(\alpha_l,a)}{\rightarrowtail} l', \varepsilon' \wedge \alpha_s = eval(\alpha_l, \varepsilon) \wedge$
   $\qquad\qquad\qquad\qquad\qquad\quad (s', subst(term_{HLTG_P}(l'), \varepsilon')) \in term_{LTS_P} \big)$

4. *Every π-action in $HLTG_P$ is the result of a process reference and the assignments are correct, so that there exists a corresponding state in LTS_P associated with the process reference and the resulting process term:*

   $\forall\, l, l' \in L_{HLTG_P}, \varepsilon, \varepsilon' \in Env, s \in S_{LTS_P}$.

   $(s, subst(term_{HLTG_P}(l), \varepsilon)) \in term_{LTS_P} \wedge l_0, \varepsilon_0 \overset{\sigma}{\mapsto} l, \varepsilon \wedge l, \varepsilon \overset{b,(\pi,a)}{\rightarrowtail} l', \varepsilon'$

   $\Rightarrow (s, subst(term_{HLTG_P}(l'), \varepsilon')) \in term_{LTS_P}$

5. *For every process reference in a process term, that leads to a situation where a state in LTS_P is associated with the process term containing the process reference and the process term containing the referenced process, there exist an appropriate π-action in $HLTG_P$:*

   $\forall\, l \in L_{HLTG_P}, \varepsilon \in Env, s \in S_{LTS_P}, T_s, T_s' \in CSPTerm$.

   $l_0, \varepsilon_0 \overset{\sigma}{\mapsto} l, \varepsilon \wedge (\, T_s = subst(term_{HLTG_P}(l), \varepsilon) \wedge ProcRef(T_s) = true \wedge$
   $(s, T_s), (s, T_s') \in term_{LTS_P} \wedge T_s' = subs(\mathcal{C}(T_s))$

   $\Rightarrow \exists\, l' \in L_{HLTG_P}, \varepsilon' \in Env$.

   $\qquad (l, \varepsilon \overset{b,(\pi,a)}{\rightarrowtail} l', \varepsilon' \wedge T_s' = subst(term_{HLTG_P}(l'), \varepsilon'))$

A.4.1   Proof: Lemma A.1

Proposition: If the properties 1 to 5 hold for $HLTG_P$ and LTS_P, this implies that $\sim$ is a bisimulation on S_{LTS_P} and S'_{LTS_P} and that the start locations are labelled with the same process term.

According to the definition of HLTG, as described in A.2, it holds that $term_{HLTG_P}(l_0) = T_P$. The definition of Ψ implies that $(s'_0, subst(T_P, \varepsilon_0)) \in term'_{LTS_P}$. Therefore $(s_0, subst(term_{HLTG_P}(l_0), \varepsilon_0)) \in term_{LTS_P}$ implies that $s_0 \sim s'_0$.

Roscoe defines a bisimulation on $S_{LTS_P} \cup S'_{LTS_P}$ as follows:

$$(1)\quad \forall s_1, s_2 \in S_{LTS_P}, s'_1 \in S'_{LTS_P} \ . \ s_1 \sim s'_1 \wedge s_1 \xrightarrow{\alpha_s} s_2$$
$$\Rightarrow \exists s'_2 \in S'_{LTS_P} \ . \ s_2 \sim s'_2 \wedge s'_1 \xrightarrow{\alpha_s} s'_2$$
$$(2)\quad \forall s_1 \in S_{LTS_P}, s'_1, s'_2 \in S'_{LTS_P} \ . \ s_1 \sim s'_1 \wedge s'_1 \xrightarrow{\alpha_s} s'_2$$
$$\Rightarrow \exists s_2 \in S_{LTS_P} \ . \ s_2 \sim s'_2 \wedge s_1 \xrightarrow{\alpha_s} s_2$$

Case (1):

Let $s_1, s_2 \in S_{LTS_P}$, $s'_1 \in S'_{LTS_P}$ with $s_1 \sim s'_1 \wedge s_1 \xrightarrow{\alpha_s} s_2$. Additionally let $T \in CSPTerm$ with $(s_1, T) \in term_{LTS_P} \wedge (s'_1, T) \in term'_{LTS_P}$.

Sub-case $ProcRef(T) = false$:

The definition of Ψ states:

$$(s'_1, T) \in term'_{LTS_P}$$
$$\Rightarrow \exists l \in L_{HLTG_P}, \varepsilon \in Env \ . \ T = subst(term_{HLTG_P}(l), \varepsilon) \wedge$$
$$l_0, \varepsilon_0 \xmapsto{\sigma} l, \varepsilon$$

property 3. then implies

$$\Rightarrow \exists l' \in L_{HLTG_P}, \varepsilon' \in Env \ . \ l, \varepsilon \xrightarrow{b,(\alpha_l, a)} l', \varepsilon' \wedge \alpha_s = eval(\alpha_l, \varepsilon) \wedge$$
$$(s_2, subst(term_{HLTG_P}(l'), \varepsilon')) \in term_{LTS_P}$$

according to the definition of Ψ

$$\Rightarrow \exists s'_2 \in S'_{LTS_P} \ . \ s'_1 \xrightarrow{\alpha_s} s'_2 \wedge$$
$$(s'_2, subst(term_{HLTG_P}(l'), \varepsilon')) \in term'_{LTS_P}$$
$$\Rightarrow s_2 \sim s'_2$$

Sub-case $ProcRef(T) = true$:

The operational semantics of CSP states, that a process reference is always replaced with its corresponding process term, whenever it is possible.

The definition of LTS_P states:

$$(s_1, T) \in term_{LTS_P}$$
$$\Rightarrow (s_1, subs(\mathcal{C}(T))) \in term_{LTS_P}$$

according to the definition of Ψ

$$(s_1', T) \in term'_{LTS_P}$$
$$\Rightarrow \exists l \in L_{HLTG_P}, \varepsilon \in Env . \ T = subst(term_{HLTG_P}(l), \varepsilon) \wedge l_0, \varepsilon_0 \overset{\sigma}{\mapsto} l, \varepsilon$$

property 5. then implies

$$\Rightarrow \exists l' \in L_{HLTG_P}, \varepsilon' \in Env . \ l, \varepsilon \overset{b,(\pi,a)}{\rightarrowtail} l', \varepsilon' \wedge$$
$$subst(term_{HLTG_P}(l'), \varepsilon') = subs(\mathcal{C}(T))$$
$$\Rightarrow (s_1', subs(\mathcal{C}(T))) \in term'_{LTS_P}$$

This implies that if $s_1 \sim s_1'$ according to a process term T that is associated with both states and $ProcRef(T) = true$, this implies that $s_1 \sim s_1'$ according to $subs(\mathcal{C}(T))$. As long as $ProcRef(subs(\mathcal{C}(T))) = true$, the argumentation of this case can be used iteratively, until $ProcRef(subs(\mathcal{C}(T))) = false$. For non-divergent CSP processes, this iteration must be finite. If $ProcRef(subs(\mathcal{C}(T))) = false$, the argumentation of the above sub-case can be used to show that (1) is true if the properties 1 to 5 hold.

Case (2):

Let $s_1 \in S_{LTS_P}$, $s_1', s_2' \in S'_{LTS_P}$ with $s_1 \sim s_1' \wedge s_1' \overset{\alpha_s}{\rightarrow} s_2'$. Additionally let $T \in CSPTerm$ with $(s_1, T) \in term_{LTS_P} \wedge (s_1', T) \in term'_{LTS_P}$.

Sub-case $ProcRef(T) = false$:

The definition of Ψ states:

$$s_1' \overset{\alpha_s}{\rightarrow} s_2'$$
$$\Rightarrow \exists l, l' \in L_{HLTG_P}, \varepsilon, \varepsilon' \in Env . \ l, \varepsilon \overset{b,(\alpha_l, a)}{\rightarrowtail} l', \varepsilon' \wedge \alpha_s = eval(\alpha_l, \varepsilon) \wedge$$
$$l_0, \varepsilon_0 \overset{\sigma}{\mapsto} l, \varepsilon \wedge$$
$$(s_1', subst(term_{HLTG_P}(l), \varepsilon)) \in term'_{LTS_P} \wedge$$
$$(s_2', subst(term_{HLTG_P}(l'), \varepsilon')) \in term'_{LTS_P}$$

property 2. of the Lemma A.1 implies

$$\Rightarrow \exists s_2 \in S_{LTS_P} . \ s_1 \overset{\alpha_s}{\rightarrow} s_2$$
$$\Rightarrow s_2 \sim s_2'$$

Sub-case $ProcRef(T) = true$:

The definition of Ψ states:

$$ProcRef(T) = true$$
$$\Rightarrow \exists\, l, l' \in L_{HLTG_P}, \varepsilon, \varepsilon' \in Env \;.\; l, \varepsilon \xrightarrow{b,(\pi,a)} l', \varepsilon' \wedge l_0, \varepsilon_0 \overset{\sigma}{\mapsto} l, \varepsilon \wedge$$
$$T = subst(term_{HLTG_P}(l), \varepsilon)) \wedge$$
$$(s_1', subst(term_{HLTG_P}(l'), \varepsilon')) \in term'_{LTS_P}$$

property 4. of the Lemma A.1 implies

$$\Rightarrow (s_1, (subst(term_{HLTG_P}(l'), \varepsilon')) \in term_{LTS_P}$$

This implies that if $s_1 \sim s_1'$ according to a process term T that is associated with both states and $ProcRef(T) = true$, this implies that $s_1 \sim s_1'$ according to $subst(term_{HLTG_P}(l'), \varepsilon')$. As long as $ProcRef(subst(term_{HLTG_P}(l'), \varepsilon')) = true$, the argumentation of this case can be used iteratively, until $ProcRef(subst(term_{HLTG_P}(l'), \varepsilon')) = false$. For non-divergent CSP processes, this iteration must be finite. If $ProcRef(subst(term_{HLTG_P}(l'), \varepsilon')) = false$, the argumentation of the above sub-case can be used to show that (2) is true if the properties 1 to 5 hold.

A.4.2   Proof: Correctness of HLTG

In this section, it will be shown that if a finite high level transition graph can be created for a CSP process, as described in section A.2, and a finite transition graph can be created for the same process, using the operational semantics, as described in section A.1, this high level transition graph is always correct according to theorem A.1, because the properties 1 to 5, defined in lemma A.1 are true for the high level transition graph and the transition graph.

Because high level transition graphs are only defined for a subset of CSP operators, only these operators are considered here. As discussed in section 5.1, page 89, it can be assumed, that the identifiers for all variables and parameters are unique and that all overloaded instances have been renamed.

Let $HLTG_P = (L_{HLTG_P}, l_0, \Sigma_{HLTG_P}^{\pi\tau\surd}, \mathcal{E}_{HLTG_P}^{\pi\tau\surd}, \rightarrow_{HLTG_P})$ be the high level transition graph of a CSP process $P = T_P$ generated as described in A.2 with a start environment ε_0. Let $LTS_P = (S_{LTS_P}, s_0, \Sigma_{LTS_P}^{\tau\surd}, \rightarrow_{LTS_P})$ be a transition graph of the same process, that has been generated as described in A.1. During the generation of $HLTG_P$ and LTS_P, the function $term_{HLTG_P} : L_{HLTG_P} \rightarrow CSPTerm$ and the relation $term_{LTS_P} \subset S_{LTS_P} \times CSPTerm$ have been defined.

In chapter 7, the high level transition graphs of the different low-level operators are defined. Each location $l \in L_{HLTG_P}$ in $HLTG_P$ is associated with a process term $T_l = term_{HLTG_P}(l)$ while each state $s \in S_{LTS_P}$ can be associated with a process term T_s such that $(s, T_s) \in term_{LTS_P}$.

According to Lemma A.1, it is sufficient to show, that the properties 1. to 5. hold for $HLTG_P$ and LTS_P. It will be shown, that the property 1. is correct and that for each CSP operator, that can occur as the top-level operator of a process term T_l, the properties 2. to 5. are correct. For the cases of the *if-then-else*, *sequential composition* and *external choice* operators, it will be assumed, that correct subgraphs can be generated for the CSP-term arguments of the operators. This can be done, because it is sufficient to show, that these operators create a correct $HLTG$ if the subgraphs of their arguments are correct.

The Start Location

First, it has to be shown, that the start locations are associated with the correct process terms. As discussed in section A.1 and A.2, the start location l_0 of $HLTG_P$ and the start state s_0 of LTS_P are both associated with the process term T_P of P ($term_{HLTG_P}(l_0) = T_P$ and $(s_0, T_P) \in term_{LTP_P}$). Because an LTS can only be generated for unparameterised start processes, no parameter bindings can occur in the start environment ε_0. Therefore $subst(T_P, \varepsilon_0) = T_P$ which implies that $(s_0, subst(term_{HLTG_P}(l_0), \varepsilon_0)) \in term_{LTP_P}$.

The Bisimulation

Let $l \in L_{HLTG_P}$ be a location in $HLTG_P$ that is associated with a process term T_l so that $T_l = term_{HLTG_P}(l)$ and $\varepsilon \in Env$ be an environment with $l_0, \varepsilon_0 \xrightarrow{\sigma} l, \varepsilon$. Let $s \in S_{LTS_P}$ be a state in LTS_P with an associated process term $T_s = subst(T_l, \varepsilon) = subst(term_{HLTG_P}(l), \varepsilon)$ and $(s, T_s) \in termn_{LTS_P}$.

Because of the definition of $term_{HLTG_P}$, for each location l, the possible transitions are defined by the $HLTG$ definition for the top-level operator of the associated process term T_l, as defined in chapter 7. The transitions of s are defined by the operational semantics of the associated process term T_s. The following case differentiation shows that the properties 2. to 5. hold for each of the CSP operators that are allowed in T_l.

Case $T_l = STOP$

Because of the $HLTG$ definition of $STOP$, as defined in section 7.2.1, it holds that

$$\not\exists l' \in L_{HLTG_P}, \varepsilon' \in Env . l, \varepsilon \xrightarrow{c_i(\alpha_l, a)} l', \varepsilon'$$

Because this is true for any $\alpha_l \in \mathcal{E}_{HLTG_P}^{\pi\tau\checkmark}$, this implies that the properties 2. and 4. are true for each location that is associated with the process term $STOP$.

Because the process term $STOP$ can not contain parameters, it holds that

$$T_s = subst(STOP, \varepsilon) = STOP$$

Because of the operational semantics of $STOP$ it holds that

$$\nexists s' \in S_{LTS_P}, \alpha_s \in \Sigma_{LTS_P}^{\tau\checkmark} \,.\, s \xrightarrow{\alpha_s} s'$$

This implies that the property 3. is true for each location that is associated with the process term $STOP$.

Because the function $subst$ does not affect the type of the CSP operator and $ProcRef(STOP) = false$, the precondition of property 5. cannot be true. Therefore property 5. is true for each location that is associated with the process term $STOP$.

Case $T_l = SKIP$

Because of the $HLTG$ definition of $SKIP$, as defined in section 7.2.1, it holds that

$$\exists l' \in L_{HLTG_P}, \varepsilon' \in Env \,.\, l, \varepsilon \xrightarrow{c,(\alpha_l,a)} l', \varepsilon'$$

and

$$\forall l' \in L_{HLTG_P}, \varepsilon' \in Env \,.\, \left(l, \varepsilon \xrightarrow{c,(\alpha_l,a)} l', \varepsilon' \Rightarrow \alpha_l = \checkmark \wedge \varepsilon' = \varepsilon \right)$$

Because of the definition of $term_{HLTG_P}$, it holds that

$$term_{HLTG_P}(l') = \Omega$$

Because the process term $SKIP$ can not contain applied occurrences of parameters, it holds that

$$T_s = subst(SKIP, \varepsilon) = SKIP$$

Because of the operational semantics of $SKIP$ it holds that

$$\exists s' \in S_{LTS_P}, \alpha_s \in \Sigma_{LTS_P}^{\tau\checkmark} \,.\, s \xrightarrow{\alpha_s} s'$$

and

$$\forall s' \in S_{LTS_P}, \alpha_s \in \Sigma_{LTS_P}^{\tau\checkmark} \,.\, \left(s \xrightarrow{\alpha_s} s' \Rightarrow \alpha_s = \checkmark \right)$$

Because of the definition of $term_{LTS_P}$, it holds that

$$(s', \Omega) \in term_{LTS_P}$$

Because the event $\checkmark$ can not contain applied occurrences of parameters, it holds that

$$eval(\alpha_l, \varepsilon) = eval(\checkmark, \varepsilon) = \checkmark = \alpha_s$$

Because the process term Ω can not contain applied occurrences of parameters, it holds that

$$subst(\Omega, \varepsilon') = \Omega$$

This implies that the properties 2. and 3. are true for each location that is associated with the process term *SKIP*.

Because a location that is associated with the process term *SKIP* can not have π-transitions leaving it, the property 4. is always true for this location.

Because the function *subst* does not affect the type of the CSP operator and $ProcRef(SKIP) = false$, the precondition of property 5. cannot be true. Therefore property 5. is true for each location that is associated with the process term *SKIP*.

Case T_l is process reference $R(v_1, ..., v_n)$

Let $R(p_1, ..., p_n) = T_R \in Spec$ be the CSP process definition that is referenced by $R(v_1, ..., v_n)$. Because of the *HLTG* definition of process references, as defined in section 7.2.1, it holds that

$$\exists\, l' \in L_{HLTG_P}, \varepsilon' \in Env \,.\, l, \varepsilon \xrightarrow{c,(\pi,a)} l', \varepsilon'$$

and

$$\forall\, l' \in L_{HLTG_P}, \varepsilon' \in Env \,.$$
$$\left(l, \varepsilon \xrightarrow{c,(\alpha_l, a)} l', \varepsilon' \Rightarrow \alpha_l = \pi \wedge a = assigns(R(v_1, ..., v_n), R(p_1, ..., p_n)) \right)$$

Because of the definition of $term_{HLTG_P}$, it holds that

$$term_{HLTG_P}(l') = T_R$$

Because no transition can leave the location l with $\alpha_l \neq \pi$, property 2. holds for all locations that are associated with a process reference.

Because the function *subst* does not affect the type of the CSP operator and *ProcRef* is always true for process references, the precondition of property 3. cannot be true. Therefore property 3. is true for each location that is associated with a process reference process term.

According to the definition of $term_{LTS_P}$, each state s that is labelled with a process reference $subst(R(v_1, ..., v_n), \varepsilon)$ is labelled with the process term

$T'_R = subs(\mathcal{C}(subst(R(v_1, ..., v_n), \varepsilon)))$ as well, where T'_R is the textual substitution of the process reference with the actual definition of the process. It holds that

$$(s, subst(R(v_1, ..., v_n), \varepsilon)) \in term_{LTS_P}$$
$$\Rightarrow (s, subs(\mathcal{C}(subst(R(v_1, ..., v_n), \varepsilon)))) \in term_{LTS_P}$$

For property 4., it has to be shown that

$$T'_R = subst(T_R, \varepsilon')$$

According to the definition of $\mathcal{C}$, section 2.4, it holds that

$$subs(\mathcal{C}(subst(R(v_1, ..., v_n), \varepsilon))) =$$
$$subs(subst(R(v_1, ..., v_n), \varepsilon), R(p_1, ..., p_n), T_R)$$

Because $subst$ only substitutes parameters and does not affect the CSP operators, it holds that

$$subst(R(v_1, ..., v_n)) = R(subst(v_1, \varepsilon), ..., subst(v_n, \varepsilon))$$

This means that each argument of the process reference is evaluated under the parameter bindings of the environment ε and the parameters $p_1, ..., p_n$ in T_R are replaced with the evaluated arguments.

According to the definition of $assigns$, $assigns(R(v_1, ..., v_n), R(p_1, ..., p_n))$ is the set of assignments (p_i, v_i) for each parameter p_i of $R(p_1, ..., p_n)$ and the appropriate argument v_i of $R(v_1, ..., v_n)$. As introduced above, $a \in Assignments$ is the set of assignments created by the process reference, so that $a = assigns(R(v_1, ..., v_n), R(p_1, ..., p_n))$. When applying these assignments a to ε as described by $\varepsilon \overset{a}{\leadsto} \varepsilon'$, each argument v_i is evaluated under ε. Therfore it holds that

$$subs(\mathcal{C}(subst(R(v_1, ..., v_n), \varepsilon))) = subst(T_R, \varepsilon')$$

This implies that the property 4. is true for each location that is associated with a process reference.

Because process reference is the only operator that can cause multiple associated process terms for a single state of an LTS, only this operator has to be considered for property 5. of lemma A.1. If two process terms T and T' are associated with a state s of LTS_P and $T' = subs(\mathcal{C}(T))$, this implies that T is a process reference $R(v_1, ..., v_n)$ and T' is the process term T_R of the referenced process $R(p_1, ..., p_n) = T_R$ after the applied occurrences of $p_1, ..., p_n$ have been substituted by the appropriate values $v_1, ..., v_n$ of the process reference $R(v_1, ..., v_n)$.

Because of the *HLTG* definition given in section 7.2.1, for a process reference $R(v_1, ..., v_n)$ referencing $R(p_1, ..., p_n) = T_R$ it holds that

$$\exists \, l' \in L_{HLTG_P}, \varepsilon' \in Env \; . \; l, \varepsilon \xrightarrowtail{c,(\pi, assigns(R(v_1,...,v_n), R(p_1,...,p_n)))} l', \varepsilon'$$

Because of the definition of $term_{HLTG}$, it holds that

$$term_{HLTG_P}(l') = T_R$$

For property 5., it has to be shown that

$$subs(\mathcal{C}(T)) = subst(T_R, \varepsilon')$$

With $T = subst(term_{HLTG_P(l)}, \varepsilon)$, it remains to be shown that

$$subs(\mathcal{C}(subst(R(v_1, ..., v_n), \varepsilon))) = subst(T_R, \varepsilon')$$

This has already been shown before. Therefore the property 5. is true for each state in LTS_P that full-fills its preconditions.

Case T_l is prefixing sub-term $e_l \longrightarrow Q$

Because of the *HLTG* definition of prefixing, as defined in section 7.2.2, it holds that

$$\exists \, l' \in L_{HLTG_P}, \varepsilon' \in Env \; . \; l, \varepsilon \xrightarrowtail{c,(\alpha_l, a)} l', \varepsilon'$$

and

$$\forall \, l' \in L_{HLTG_P}, \varepsilon' \in Env \; .$$
$$\left(l, \varepsilon \xrightarrowtail{c,(\alpha_l, a)} l', \varepsilon' \Rightarrow \alpha_l \in comms(e_l) \wedge a = assigns_{event}(e_l, \alpha_l) \right)$$

Because of the definition of $term_{HLTG_P}$, it holds that

$$term_{HLTG_P}(l') = Q$$

Because the function *subst* only affects applied occurrences of parameters, it holds that

$$subst(e_l \rightarrow Q, \varepsilon) = subst(e_l, \varepsilon) \rightarrow subst(Q, \varepsilon)$$

Let $e_s = subst(e_l, \varepsilon)$ be the CSP event used in the process term T_s. Because of the operational semantics of *SKIP* it holds that

$$\exists \, s' \in S_{LTS_P}, \alpha_s \in \Sigma_{LTS_P}^{\tau\checkmark} \; . \; s \xrightarrow{\alpha_s} s'$$

and

$$\forall\, s' \in S_{LTS_P}, \alpha_s \in \Sigma_{LTS_P}^{\tau\checkmark} \, . \, \left(s \xrightarrow{\alpha_s} s' \Rightarrow \alpha_s \in comms(e_s)\right)$$

Because of the definition of $term_{LTS_P}$, it holds that

$$(s', subs(\alpha_s, e_s, subst(Q, \varepsilon))) \in term_{LTS_P}$$

Because $e_s = subst(e_l, \varepsilon)$, e_l and e_s must have the same defining occurrences for parameters. Because of this and because of the definition of $comms$, it holds that

$$\forall\, \alpha_l \in comms(e_l) \, . \, (\exists\, \alpha_s \in comms(e_s) \, . \, eval(\alpha_l, \varepsilon) = \alpha_s)$$

If $eval(\alpha_l, \varepsilon) = \alpha_s$, the values chosen for the defining occurrences of parameters from the input fields (like x in $a?x$) must be the same in α_l and α_s. Because of the definition of $assigns_{event}$ and $subs$, it holds that during the evaluation of $subs(\alpha_s, subst(e_l, \varepsilon), subst(Q, \varepsilon))$, the values that are used to substitute the applied occurrences of parameters in $subst(Q, \varepsilon)$ are the same values that are bound to these parameters in ε' when applying $assings_{event}(e_l, \alpha_l)$ to ε. This implies that

$$subs(\alpha_s, subst(e_l, \varepsilon), subst(Q, \varepsilon)) = subst(Q, \varepsilon')$$

This implies that the properties 2. and 3. are true for each location that is associated with a process term $e_l \to Q$.

Because a location that is associated with a process term $e_l \to Q$ can not have π-transitions leaving it, the property 4. is always true for this location.

Because the function $subst$ does not affect the type of the CSP operator and $procrefpred$ is always *false* for prefix operator process terms, the precondition of property 5. cannot be true. Therefore property 5. is true for each location that is associated with a prefix process term $e \to Q$.

Case T_l is of the form *if b then Q else R*

According to the *HLTG* definition of *if b then Q else R*, as defined in section 7.2.3, the condition b is added to all transitions leaving the start location of the subgraph of Q and the condition $\neg b$ is added to all transitions leaving the start location of the subgraph of R. Both start locations then are joined into the start location of the *HLTG* of *if b then Q else R*. Therefore if $eval(b, \varepsilon) = true$, only transition, that represent actions of Q can be taken and if $eval(b, \varepsilon) = false$, only transitions representing actions of R can be taken.

Let $HLTG_Q = (L_{HLTG_Q}, l_0, \Sigma_{HLTG_Q}^{\pi\tau\checkmark}, \mathcal{E}_{HLTG_Q}^{\pi\tau\checkmark}, \rightarrow_{HLTG_Q})$ be a high level transition graph of the CSP term Q and $LTS_Q = (S_{LTS_Q}, s_0, \Sigma_{LTS_Q}^{\tau\checkmark}, \rightarrow_{LTS_Q})$ be a transition graph of $subst(Q, \varepsilon)$.

Let $HLTG_R = (L_{HLTG_R}, l_0, \Sigma_{HLTG_R}^{\pi\tau\checkmark}, \mathcal{E}_{HLTG_R}^{\pi\tau\checkmark}, \rightarrow_{HLTG_R})$ be a high level transition graph of the CSP term R and $LTS_R = (S_{LTS_R}, s_0, \Sigma_{LTS_R}^{\tau\checkmark}, \rightarrow_{LTS_R})$ be a transition graph of $subst(R, \varepsilon)$.

The sub-terms Q and R can be divided into two cases: a) the sub-term has the form *if b then S else T* or b) any other operator is used. In case a), this argumentation can be used iteratively, until any other operator is the top level operator of the respective process term. For non-divergent processes, this iteration has to be finite.

For Case b), it can be assumed, that the properties 2. to 5. hold for l_{Q0} and s_{Q0} and for l_{R0} and s_{R0}. In this case, it has to be shown that the correct sub-term is chosen. Because the function *subst* does not affect the structure of a process term, it holds that $subst(if\ b\ then\ Q\ else\ R, \varepsilon) = if\ subst(b, \varepsilon)\ then\ subst(Q, \varepsilon)\ else\ subst(R, \varepsilon)$. Therefore, showing that the correct sub-term is chosen is equal to showing that $subst(b, \varepsilon) = eval(b, \varepsilon)$. This is true because b can only contain applied occurrences of parameters and replacing the parameters in b with the respective values bound to them by ε and then evaluating the expression is obviously the same as evaluating b using the values of ε for the parameters in b.

Case T_l is a sequential composition sub-term $Q; R$

Let $HLTG_Q = (L_{HLTG_Q}, l_0, \Sigma_{HLTG_Q}^{\pi\tau\checkmark}, \mathcal{E}_{HLTG_Q}^{\pi\tau\checkmark}, \rightarrow_{HLTG_Q})$ be a high level transition graph of the CSP term Q and $LTS_Q = (S_{LTS_Q}, s_0, \Sigma_{LTS_Q}^{\tau\checkmark}, \rightarrow_{LTS_Q})$ be a transition graph of $subst(Q, \varepsilon)$.

Let $HLTG_R = (L_{HLTG_R}, l_0, \Sigma_{HLTG_R}^{\pi\tau\checkmark}, \mathcal{E}_{HLTG_R}^{\pi\tau\checkmark}, \rightarrow_{HLTG_R})$ be a high level transition graph of the CSP term R and $LTS_R = (S_{LTS_R}, s_0, \Sigma_{LTS_R}^{\tau\checkmark}, \rightarrow_{LTS_R})$ be a transition graph of $subst(R, \varepsilon)$.

As stated in section A.2, $HLTG_Q$ has to be created completely during the generation of $HLTG_P$. If Q is a sequential composition process term, the argumentation of this case can be applied iteratively, until any other operator is the top level operator of the respective sub-term. For non-divergent processes, this iteration has to be finite. If Q is no sequential composition process term, it can be assumed, that the properties 2. to 5. hold for l_Q0 and s_Q0.

The high level transition graph $HLTG_Q$ is part of $HLTG_P$, except that all $\checkmark$ transitions have been replaced by τ transitions leading to the start location l_{R0}

of R. l is the start location of the modified high level transition graph $HLTG_Q$. The transition graph LTS_Q is part of LTS_P with all $\checkmark$-transitions replaced by τ-transitions to s_{R0}.

If Q occurs in a sequential composition $Q; R$, all process terms T_Q associated with locations of $HLTG_Q$ are extended to $T_Q; R$ in $term_{HLTG_P}$ and all process terms T'_Q associated with states of LTS_Q are extended to $T'_Q; subst(R, \varepsilon)$ in $term_{LTS_P}$. Together with the $HLTG$ definition for sequential composition, as defined in section 7.2.2, this implies that

$$\exists l' \in L_{HLTG_P}, \varepsilon' \in Env \ . \ l, \varepsilon \xrightarrow{b,(\alpha_l, a)} l', \varepsilon' \text{ in } HLTG_P \wedge \alpha_l \notin \{\tau, \pi\}$$
$$\Rightarrow \exists l'_Q \in L_{HLTG_Q} \ . \ l_{Q0}, \varepsilon \xrightarrow{b,(\alpha_l, a)} l'_Q, \varepsilon' \text{ in } HLTG_Q$$

Let $Q'; R$ be the process term associated with l' in $term_{HLTG_P}$. This implies that Q' is associated with l'_Q in $term_{HLTG_Q}$. Because property 2. is assumed to be correct for l_{Q0} and s_{Q0}, this implies that

$$\exists s'_Q \in S_{LTS_Q} \ . \ s_{Q0} \xrightarrow{\alpha_s} s'_Q \text{ in } LTS_Q \wedge \alpha_s = eval(\alpha_l, \varepsilon) \wedge$$
$$(s'_Q, subst(Q', \varepsilon')) \in term_{LTS_Q}$$

Because of the definition of the operational semantics for sequential composition, this implies that

$$\exists s' \in S_{LTS_P} \ . \ s \xrightarrow{\alpha_s} s' \text{ in } LTS_P \wedge \alpha_s = eval(\alpha_l, \varepsilon)$$

Because R can not be affected by defining occurrences of parameters of Q and because of the definition of $term_{HLTG}$, it holds that

$$(s', subst(Q'; R, \varepsilon')) \in term_{LTS_P})$$

This implies that property 2. is true if $\alpha_l \notin \{\tau, \pi\}$.

As stated above, every $\checkmark$-transition in $HLTG_Q$ is replaced by a τ-transition in $HLTG_P$. These new transitions no longer lead to the special location Ω. The target of all these transitions is l_{R0}. The $HLTG$ definition for sequential composition implies that

$$\exists \varepsilon_{R0} \in Env \ . \ l, \varepsilon \xrightarrow{b,(\tau, a)} l_{R0}, \varepsilon_{R0} \text{ in } HLTG_P$$
$$\Rightarrow l_{Q0}, \varepsilon \xrightarrow{b,(\checkmark, a)} \Omega, \varepsilon_{R0} \text{ in } HLTG_Q$$

and

$$\exists l' \in L_{HLTG_P}, \varepsilon' \in Env \ . \ l, \varepsilon \xrightarrow{b,(\tau, a)} l', \varepsilon' \text{ in } HLTG_P \wedge l' \neq l_{R0}$$
$$\Rightarrow \exists l'_Q \in L_{HLTG_Q} \ . \ l_{Q0}, \varepsilon \xrightarrow{b,(\tau, a)} l'_Q, \varepsilon' \text{ in } HLTG_Q$$

Because property 2. is assumed to hold for l_{Q0} and s_{Q0}, it holds that

$$l_{Q0}, \varepsilon \xrightarrow{\ b,(\checkmark,a)\ } \Omega, \varepsilon_{R0} \text{ in } HLTG_Q$$
$$\Rightarrow \exists\, s'_Q \in S_{LTS_Q} . s_{Q0} \xrightarrow{\checkmark} s'_Q \text{ in } LTS_Q \wedge$$
$$(s'_Q, subst(term_{HLTG_Q}(\Omega), \varepsilon_{R0})) \in term_{LTS_Q}$$

Because of the definition of the operational semantics for sequential composition and the relation $term_{LTS_P}$, it holds that

$$\exists\, s' \in S_{LTS_P} . s \xrightarrow{\tau} s' \text{ in } LTS_P$$

Because *SKIP* is the only operator that can create $\checkmark$-transitions and because of the *HLTG* definition of *SKIP*, it holds that

$$\forall\, l, l' \in Locations, \varepsilon, \varepsilon' \in Env \ . \ l, \varepsilon \xrightarrow{\ b,(\checkmark,a)\ } l', \varepsilon' \Rightarrow a = \emptyset \wedge \varepsilon = \varepsilon'$$

Because of the definition of $term_{LTS}$ and because R cannot be affected by defining occurrences of parameters in Q, it holds that

$$(s', subst(R, \varepsilon')) \in term_{LTS_P})$$

Let $Q'; R$ be the process term associated with l'. Because property 2. is assumed to hold for l_{Q0} and s_{Q0}, it holds that

$$\exists\, l'_Q \in L_{HLTG_Q} . l_{Q0}, \varepsilon \xrightarrow{\ b,(\tau,a)\ } l'_Q, \varepsilon' \text{ in } HLTG_Q$$
$$\Rightarrow \exists\, s'_Q \in S_{LTS_Q} . s_{Q0} \xrightarrow{\tau} s'_Q \text{ in } LTS_Q \wedge (s'_Q, subst(Q', \varepsilon')) \in term_{LTS_Q}$$

Because of the definition of the operational semantics for sequential composition, this implies

$$\exists\, s' \in S_{LTS_P} . s \xrightarrow{\tau} s' \text{ in } LTS_P$$

Because of the definition of $term_{LTS}$ and because R cannot be affected by defining occurrences of parameters in Q, it holds that

$$(s', subst(Q'; R, \varepsilon')) \in term_{LTS_P})$$

This implies that property 2. is true for $\alpha_l = \tau$.

The definition of the operational semantics of the sequential composition operator implies that

$$\exists\, s' \in S_{LTS_P}, Q'_s \in CSPTerm . s \xrightarrow{\alpha_s} s' \text{ in } LTS_P \wedge \alpha_s \neq \tau$$
$$(s', Q'_s; subst(R, \varepsilon)) \in term_{LTS_P}$$
$$\Rightarrow \exists\, s'_Q \in S_{LTS_Q} . s_{Q0} \xrightarrow{\alpha_s} s'_Q \text{ in } LTS_Q \wedge (s_{Q0}, subst(Q, \varepsilon)) \in term_{LTS_Q} \wedge$$
$$(s_{Q0}, subst(Q, \varepsilon)), (s'_Q, Q'_s) \in term_{LTS_Q}$$

Because property 3. is assumed to hold for l_{Q0} and LTS_{Q0}, this implies that

$$\exists\, l'_Q \in L_{HLTG_Q}, \varepsilon'_Q \in Env \ . l_{Q0}, \varepsilon \xrightarrow{\ b,(\alpha_l,a)\ } l'_Q, \varepsilon'_Q \text{ in } HLTG_Q \wedge eval(\alpha_l, \varepsilon) = \alpha_s$$
$$\alpha_l \notin \{\tau, \pi\}$$
$$subst(term_{HLTG_Q}(l_{Q0}), \varepsilon) = subst(Q, \varepsilon) \wedge$$
$$subst(term_{HLTG_Q}(l'_Q), \varepsilon') = Q'_s$$

Because of the $HLTG$ definition for sequential composition and the definition of $term_{HLTG_P}$ and because R can not be affected by defining occurrences of parameters in Q, this implies that

$$\exists\, l' \in L_{HLTG_P}, \varepsilon' \in Env \ . l, \varepsilon \xrightarrow{\ b,(\alpha_l,a)\ } l', \varepsilon' \wedge eval(\alpha_l, \varepsilon) = \alpha_s \wedge$$
$$(s', subst(term_{HLTG_P}(l'), \varepsilon')) \in term_{LTS_P}$$

This shows that property 3. is true for $\alpha_s \neq \tau$.

For τ-transitions, the definition of the operational semantics implies that

$$\exists\, s' \in S_{LTS_P}, Q'_Q \in CSPTerm \ . s \xrightarrow{\tau} s' \text{ in } LTS_P \wedge (s', Q'_s; subst(R, \varepsilon)) \in term_{LTS_P}$$
$$\Rightarrow \exists\, s'_Q \in S_{LTS_Q} \ . s_{Q0} \xrightarrow{\tau} s'_Q \text{ in } LTS_Q \wedge$$
$$(s_{Q0}, subst(Q, \varepsilon)), (s'_Q, Q'_s) \in term_{LTS_Q}$$

and

$$\exists\, s' \in S_{LTS_P} \ . s \xrightarrow{\tau} s' \text{ in } LTS_P \wedge (s', subst(R, \varepsilon)) \in term_{LTS_P}$$
$$\Rightarrow \exists\, s'_Q \in S_{LTS_Q} \ . s_{Q0} \xrightarrow{\checkmark} s'_Q \text{ in } LTS_Q \wedge$$
$$(s_Q, subst(Q, \varepsilon)), (s'_Q, \Omega) \in term_{LTS_Q}$$

Because property 3. is assumed to hold for l_{Q0} and s_{Q0}, this implies, for the case with $(s', Q'_s; subst(R, \varepsilon)) \in term_{LTS_P}$, that

$$\exists\, l'_Q \in L_{HLTG_Q}, \varepsilon' \in Env \ . l_{Q0}, \varepsilon \xrightarrow{\ b,(\tau,a)\ } l'_Q, \varepsilon' \text{ in } HLTG_Q \wedge$$
$$term_{HLTG_Q}(l) = Q \wedge subst(term_{HLTG_Q}(l'), \varepsilon') = Q'_s$$

The case with $(s', subst(R, \varepsilon)) \in term_{LTS_P}$ implies that

$$\exists\, l'_Q \in L_{HLTG_Q}, \varepsilon' \in Env \ . l_{Q0}, \varepsilon \xrightarrow{\ b,(\checkmark,a)\ } l'_Q, \varepsilon' \text{ in } HLTG_Q \wedge$$
$$term_{HLTG_Q}(l_{Q0}) = Q \wedge subst(term_{HLTG_Q}(l'_Q), \varepsilon') = \Omega$$

Because of the $HLTG$ definition for sequential composition and the definition of $term_{HLTG_P}$, this implies for $(s', Q'_s; subst(R, \varepsilon)) \in term_{LTS_P}$, that

$$\exists\, l' \in L_{HLTG_P}, \varepsilon' \in Env \ . (s', subst(term_{HLTG_P}(l'), \varepsilon')) \in term_{LTS_P} \wedge$$
$$l, \varepsilon \xrightarrow{\ b,(\tau,a)\ } l', \varepsilon'$$

For $(s', subst(R, \varepsilon)) \in term_{LTS_P}$, it implies that

$$\exists \varepsilon' \in Env \;.\; (s', subst(term_{HLTG_P}(l_{R0}), \varepsilon')) \in term_{LTS_P} \wedge$$
$$l, \varepsilon \xmapsto{b,(\tau,a)} l_{R0}, \varepsilon'$$

This shows that property 3. is true for $\alpha_s = \tau$.

Because of the *HLTG* definition of *sequentialcompostion*, it holds that

$$\exists l' \in L_{HLTG_P}, \varepsilon' \in Env \;.\; l, \varepsilon \xrightarrowtail{b,(\pi,a)} l', \varepsilon' \text{ in } HLTG_P$$
$$\Rightarrow \exists l'_Q \in L_{HLTG_Q} \;.\; l_{Q0}, \varepsilon \xrightarrowtail{b,(\pi,a)} l'_Q, \varepsilon' \text{ in } HLTG_Q$$

Because property 4. is assumed to hold for l_{Q0} and s_{Q0}, this implies that

$$(s_{Q0}, subst(term_{HLTG_Q}(l'_Q), \varepsilon')) \in term_{LTS_Q}$$

Because R can not be affected by defining occurrences of parameters in Q and because of the definition of $term_{LTS_P}$, this implies that

$$(s', subst(term_{HLTG_Q}(l'_Q); R, \varepsilon')) \in term_{LTS_P}$$

Because of the definition of $term_{HLTG_P}$, this implies that

$$(s', subst(term_{HLTG_Q}(l), \varepsilon')) \in term_{LTS_P}$$

This implies that property 4. hold for all location associated with a sequential composition process term.

The operational semantics of **CSP** implies that

$$ProcRef(Q; \; R) = true$$
$$\Rightarrow ProcRef(Q) = true$$

Let $Q_s, Q'_s \in CSPTerm$ with

$$Q_s = subst(term_{HLTG_Q}(l_{Q0}), \varepsilon) \wedge$$
$$ProcRef(Q_s) = true \wedge$$
$$(s_{Q0}, Q_s), (s_{Q0}, Q'_s) \in term_{LTS_Q} \wedge$$
$$Q'_s = subs(\mathcal{C}(Q_s, Q'_s))$$

Because property 5. is assumed to hold for l_{Q0} and s_{Q0}, it holds that

$$implies \; \exists l'_Q \in L_{HLTG_Q}, \varepsilon' \in Env \;.$$
$$(l_{Q0}, \varepsilon \xrightarrowtail{b,(\pi,a)} l'_Q, \varepsilon' \wedge Q'_s = subst(term_{HLTG_Q}(l'_Q), \varepsilon'))$$

Because of the *HLTG* definition of *sequentialcomposition* process terms, this implies that

$$implies \; \exists \, l' \in L_{HLTG_P} \;.(l, \varepsilon \xrightarrow{\; b,(\pi,a) \;} l', \varepsilon'$$

The definition of $term_{HLTG_P}$ implies that

$$Q'_s; \; R = subst(term_{HLTG_P}(l'), \varepsilon')$$

This implies that property 5. hold for all location associated with a sequential composition process term.

Case T_l is an internal choice sub-term $Q \sqcap R$

Because of the *HLTG* definition of $Q \sqcap R$, as defined in section 7.2.3, it holds that

$$\exists \, l' \in L_{HLTG_P}, \varepsilon' \in Env \;.\; l, \varepsilon \xrightarrow{\; b,(\alpha_l,a) \;} l', \varepsilon'$$

and

$$\forall \, l' \in L_{HLTG_P}, \varepsilon' \in Env \;.$$
$$l, \varepsilon \xrightarrow{\; b,(\alpha_l,a) \;} l', \varepsilon' \Rightarrow \alpha_l = \tau \wedge \varepsilon' = \varepsilon$$

Because of the definition of $term_{HLTG_P}$, it holds that

$$term_{HLTG_P}(l') = Q \; \vee \; term_{HLTG_P}(l') = R$$

Because of the definition of *subst*, it holds that

$$subst(Q \sqcap R, \varepsilon) = subst(Q, \varepsilon) \sqcap subst(R, \varepsilon)$$

Because of the operational semantics of $Q \sqcap R$ it holds that

$$\exists \, s' \in S_{LTS_P}, \alpha_s \in \Sigma_{LTS_P}^{\tau\checkmark} \;.\; s \xrightarrow{\alpha_s} s'$$

and

$$\forall \, s' \in S_{LTS_P}, \alpha_s \in \Sigma_{LTS_P}^{\tau\checkmark} \;.\; s \xrightarrow{\alpha_s} s' \Rightarrow \alpha_s = \tau$$

Because of the definition of $term_{LTS_P}$, it holds that

$$(s', subst(Q, \varepsilon')) \in term_{LTS_P} \; \wedge \; (s', subst(R, \varepsilon')) \in term_{LTS_P}$$

Because the event τ can not contain parameters, it holds that

$$eval(\alpha_l, \varepsilon) = eval(\tau, \varepsilon) = \tau = \alpha_s$$

This implies that the properties 2. and 3. are true for each location that is associated with the process term $Q \sqcap R$.

Because a location that is associated with the process term $Q \sqcap R$ can not have π-transitions leaving it, the property 4. is always true for this location.

Because the function *subst* does not affect the type of the CSP operator and $ProcRef(Q \sqcap R)$ is always *false*, the precondition of property 5. cannot be true. Therefore property 5. is true for each location that is associated with an internal choice process term process term $Q \sqcap R$.

Case T_l is an external choice sub-term $Q \square R$

The *HLTG* definition of the external choice operator, as defined in section 7.2.3, defines a renaming of parameters in the invisible beginnings of the subgraphs of the two arguments. This renaming is only necessary to create unique identifiers for each parameter and has already been discussed. In this paragraph, it is assumed, that the identifiers are already unique, so that no renaming is necessary. The correctness of the renaming and the according reassignments remains to be shown.

Let $HLTG_Q = (L_{HLTG_Q}, l_0, \Sigma_{HLTG_Q}^{\pi\tau\checkmark}, \mathcal{E}_{HLTG_Q}^{\pi\tau\checkmark}, \rightarrow_{HLTG_Q})$ be a high level transition graph of the process term Q and $LTS_Q = (S_{LTS_Q}, s_0, \Sigma_{LTS_Q}^{\tau\checkmark}, \rightarrow_{LTS_Q})$ be a transition graph of $subst(Q, \varepsilon)$.

Let $HLTG_R = (L_{HLTG_R}, l_0, \Sigma_{HLTG_R}^{\pi\tau\checkmark}, \mathcal{E}_{HLTG_R}^{\pi\tau\checkmark}, \rightarrow_{HLTG_R})$ be a high level transition graph of the process term R and $LTS_R = (S_{LTS_R}, s_0, \Sigma_{LTS_R}^{\tau\checkmark}, \rightarrow_{LTS_R})$ be a transition graph of $subst(R, \varepsilon)$.

If Q or R is no external choice process term, the argumentation of the appropriate case according to its top-level operator can be used. If Q or R is an external choice process term, the argumentation of this case can be used iteratively, until a process term of another operator occurs. For non-divergent CSP processes, this iteration has to be finite. Therefore it can be assumed, that properties 2 to 5 hold for l_{Q0} and s_{Q0} and for l_{R0} and s_{R0}.

According to the *HLTG* definition of the external choice operator, the beginnings of $HLTG_Q$ and $HLTG_R$ are used to create the *HLTG* of the external choice operator. Therefore for a transition $l, \varepsilon \xrightarrow{c_i(\alpha_l, a)} l', \varepsilon'$ with $l' \in L_{HLTG_P}$ and $\varepsilon' \in Env$, (α_l, a) can be any element of $\mathcal{E}_{HLTG_Q}^{\pi\tau\checkmark} \cup \mathcal{E}_{HLTG_R}^{\pi\tau\checkmark}$.

For $\alpha_l \notin \{\tau, \pi\}$, it holds that

$$\exists\, l' \in L_{HLTG_P}, \varepsilon' \in Env \,.\, l, \varepsilon \xrightarrow{c,(\alpha_l,a)} l', \varepsilon' \text{ in } HLTG_P$$
$$\Rightarrow \exists\, l'_Q \in L_{HLTG_Q} \,.\, l_{Q0}, \varepsilon \xrightarrow{c,(\alpha_l,a)} l'_Q, \varepsilon' \text{ in } HLTG_Q$$
$$\vee$$
$$\exists\, l'_R \in L_{HLTG_R} \,.\, l_{R0}, \varepsilon \xrightarrow{c,(\alpha_l,a)} l'_R, \varepsilon' \text{ in } HLTG_R$$

Because property 2. is assumed to hold for L_{Q0} and s_{Q0} and for l_{R0} and s_{R0}, it holds that

$$\exists\, l'_Q \in L_{HLTG_Q} \,.\, l_{Q0}, \varepsilon \xrightarrow{c,(\alpha_l,a)} l'_Q, \varepsilon' \text{ in } HLTG_Q$$
$$\Rightarrow \exists\, s'_Q \in S_{LTS_Q} \,.\, s_{Q0} \xrightarrow{\alpha_s} s'_Q \text{ in } LTS_Q \wedge$$
$$\quad (s'_Q, subst(term_{HLTG_Q}(l'), \varepsilon')) \in term_{LTS_Q}) \wedge$$
$$\quad \alpha_s = eval(\alpha_l, \varepsilon)$$

and

$$\exists\, l'_R \in L_{HLTG_R} \,.\, l_{R0}, \varepsilon \xrightarrow{c,(\alpha_l,a)} l'_R, \varepsilon' \text{ in } HLTG_R$$
$$\Rightarrow \exists\, s'_R \in S_{LTS_R} \,.\, s_{R0} \xrightarrow{\alpha_s} s'_R \text{ in } LTS_R \wedge$$
$$\quad (s'_R, subst(term_{HLTG_R}(l'), \varepsilon')) \in term_{LTS_R}) \wedge$$
$$\quad \alpha_s = eval(\alpha_l, \varepsilon)$$

Because of the operational semantics of $Q \,\square\, R$, it holds that

$$Q \xrightarrow{\alpha_s} Q' \Rightarrow Q \,\square\, R \xrightarrow{\alpha_s} Q'$$
$$\wedge$$
$$R \xrightarrow{\alpha_s} R' \Rightarrow Q \,\square\, R \xrightarrow{\alpha_s} R'$$

It therefore holds that

$$\exists\, s' \in S_{LTS_P} \,.\, s \xrightarrow{\alpha_s} s' \text{ in } LTS_P$$

Because of the definition of $term_{HLTG_P}$, it holds that

$$subst(term_{HLTG_P}(l'), \varepsilon') = subst(term_{HLTG_P}(l'_Q), \varepsilon')$$

Because of the definition of $term_{LTS_P}$, this implies that

$$(s', subst(term_{HLTG_P}(l'), \varepsilon')) \in term_{LTS_P}$$

This implies that the property 2. hold if $\alpha_l \notin \{\tau, \pi\}$.

Because of the operational semantics of the external choice operator, it holds that for all events $\alpha_s \neq \tau$, $Q \square R$ must evolve to Q' if $Q \xrightarrow{\alpha_s} Q'$, or R' if $R \xrightarrow{\alpha_s} R'$ is possible. It therefore holds that

$$\exists s' \in S_{LTS_P} . s \xrightarrow{\alpha_s} s' \text{ in } LTS_P$$
$$\Rightarrow \exists s'_Q \in S_{LTS_Q} . s_{Q0} \xrightarrow{\alpha_s} s'_Q \text{ in } LTS_Q \vee$$
$$\exists s'_R \in S_{LTS_R} . s_{R0} \xrightarrow{\alpha_s} s'_R \text{ in } LTS_R$$

Because property 3. is assumed to hold for L_{Q0} and s_{Q0} and for l_{R0} and s_{R0}, this implies that

$$\exists l'_Q \in L_{HLTG_Q} . l_{Q0}, \varepsilon \xrightarrow{c,(\alpha_l, a)} l'_Q, \varepsilon' \text{ in } HLTG_Q \wedge$$
$$(s'_Q, subst(term_{HLTG_Q}(l'), \varepsilon')) \in term_{LTS_Q} \wedge$$
$$\alpha_s = eval(\alpha_l, \varepsilon)$$

$\vee$

$$\exists l'_R \in L_{HLTG_R} . l_{R0}, \varepsilon \xrightarrow{c,(\alpha_l, a)} l'_R, \varepsilon' \text{ in } HLTG_R \wedge$$
$$(s'_R, subst(term_{HLTG_R}(l'), \varepsilon')) \in term_{LTS_R} \wedge$$
$$\alpha_s = eval(\alpha_l, \varepsilon)$$

Because of the *HLTG* definition for the external choice operator and the definition of $term_{HLTG_P}$ this implies that

$$\exists l' \in L_{HLTG_P}, \varepsilon' \in Env . l, \varepsilon \xrightarrow{c,(\alpha_l, a)} l', \varepsilon' \text{ in } HLTG_P \wedge$$
$$(s', subst(term_{HLTG_P}(l'), \varepsilon')) \in term_{LTS_P}$$

This implies that the property 3. is true for all transitions with $\alpha_l \neq \tau$.

For τ-transitions, the *HLTG* definition of $Q \square R$ implies that

$$\exists l' \in L_{HLTG_P}, \varepsilon' \in Env . l, \varepsilon \xrightarrow{c,(\tau, a)} l', \varepsilon' \text{ in } HLTG_P$$
$$\Rightarrow \exists l'_Q \in L_{HLTG_Q} . l_{Q0}, \varepsilon \xrightarrow{c,(\tau, a)} l', \varepsilon' \text{ in } HLTG_Q$$
$$\vee$$
$$\exists l'_R \in L_{HLTG_R} . l_{R0}, \varepsilon \xrightarrow{c,(\tau, a)} l', \varepsilon' \text{ in } HLTG_R$$

Because property 2. is assumed to hold for L_{Q0} and s_{Q0} and for l_{R0} and s_{R0}, it holds that

$$\exists l'_Q \in L_{HLTG_Q} . l_{Q0}, \varepsilon \xrightarrow{c,(\tau, a)} l'_Q, \varepsilon' \text{ in } HLTG_Q$$
$$\Rightarrow \exists s'_Q \in S_{LTS_Q} . s_{Q0} \xrightarrow{\tau} s'_Q \text{ in } LTS_Q \wedge$$
$$(s'_Q, subst(term_{HLTG_Q}(l'), \varepsilon')) \in term_{LTS_Q})$$

and

$$\exists l'_R \in L_{HLTG_R} . l_{R0}, \varepsilon \xrightarrow{c,(\tau, a)} l'_R, \varepsilon' \text{ in } HLTG_R$$
$$\Rightarrow \exists s'_R \in S_{LTS_R} . s_{R0} \xrightarrow{\tau} s'_R \text{ in } LTS_R \wedge$$
$$(s'_R, subst(term_{HLTG_R}(l'), \varepsilon')) \in term_{LTS_R})$$

Because of the operational semantics of $Q \square R$, it holds that

$$Q \xrightarrow{\tau} Q' \Rightarrow Q \square R \xrightarrow{\tau} Q' \square R$$
$$\wedge$$
$$R \xrightarrow{\tau} R' \Rightarrow Q \square R \xrightarrow{\tau} Q \square R'$$

It therefore holds that

$$\exists s' \in S_{LTS_P} . s \xrightarrow{\tau} s' \text{ in } LTS_P$$

Because of the definition of $subst$ and $term_{HLTG_P}$ and because τ-transitions never change the environment, it holds that

$$
\begin{aligned}
subst(term_{HLTG_P}(l'), \varepsilon') &= subst(term_{HLTG_P}(l'_Q) \square R, \varepsilon') \\
&= subst(term_{HLTG_P}(l'_Q), \varepsilon') \square subst(R, \varepsilon') \\
&= subst(term_{HLTG_P}(l'_Q), \varepsilon') \square subst(R, \varepsilon)
\end{aligned}
$$

Because of the definition of $term_{LTS_P}$, this implies that

$$(s', subst(term_{HLTG_P}(l'), \varepsilon')) \in term_{LTS_P}$$

This implies that the property 2. is true for all τ-transitions.

Because of the operational semantics of the external choice operator, it holds that for τ-events, $Q \square R$ must evolve to $Q' \square R$ if $Q \xrightarrow{\tau} Q'$, or $Q \square R'$ if $R \xrightarrow{\tau} R'$ is possible. It therefore holds that

$$
\begin{aligned}
&\exists s' \in S_{LTS_P} . s \xrightarrow{\tau} s' \text{ in } LTS_P \\
\Rightarrow \quad &\exists s'_Q \in S_{LTS_Q} . s_{Q0} \xrightarrow{\tau} s'_Q \text{ in } LTS_Q \vee \\
&\exists s'_R \in S_{LTS_R} . s_{R0} \xrightarrow{\tau} s'_R \text{ in } LTS_R
\end{aligned}
$$

Because property 3. is assumed to hold for L_{Q0} and s_{Q0} and for l_{R0} and s_{R0}, this implies that

$$
\begin{aligned}
&\exists l'_Q \in L_{HLTG_Q} . l_{Q0}, \varepsilon \xrightarrow{c,(\tau,a)} l'_Q, \varepsilon' \text{ in } HLTG_Q \wedge \\
&\quad (s'_Q, subst(term_{HLTG_Q}(l'), \varepsilon')) \in term_{LTS_Q} \\
&\vee \\
&\exists l'_R \in L_{HLTG_R} . l_{R0}, \varepsilon \xrightarrow{c,(\tau,a)} l'_R, \varepsilon' \text{ in } HLTG_R \wedge \\
&\quad (s'_R, subst(term_{HLTG_R}(l'), \varepsilon')) \in term_{LTS_R}
\end{aligned}
$$

Because of the $HLTG$ definition for the external choice operator and the definition of $term_{HLTG_P}$ this implies that

$$
\begin{aligned}
&\exists l' \in L_{HLTG_P}, \varepsilon' \in Env . l, \varepsilon \xrightarrow{c,(\alpha_l,a)} l', \varepsilon' \text{ in } HLTG_P \wedge \\
&\quad (s', subst(term_{HLTG_P}(l'), \varepsilon')) \in term_{LTS_P}
\end{aligned}
$$

This implies that the property 3. is true for all τ-transitions.

For π-transitions, the $HLTG$ definition of $Q \,\square\, R$ implies that

$$\exists\, l' \in L_{HLTG_P}, \varepsilon' \in Env \,.\, l, \varepsilon \xrightarrow{c,(\pi,a)} l', \varepsilon' \text{ in } HLTG_P$$
$$\Rightarrow\; \exists\, l'_Q \in L_{HLTG_Q} \,.\, l_{Q0}, \varepsilon \xrightarrow{c,(\pi,a)} l'_Q, \varepsilon' \text{ in } HLTG_Q \vee$$
$$\exists\, l'_R \in L_{HLTG_R} \,.\, l_{R0}, \varepsilon \xrightarrow{c,(\pi,a)} l'_R, \varepsilon' \text{ in } HLTG_R$$

Because property 2. is assumed to hold for L_{Q0} and s_{Q0} and for l_{R0} and s_{R0}, this implies that

$$(s_{Q0}, subst(term_{HLTG_Q}(l'), \varepsilon')) \in term_{LTS_Q}$$
$$\vee$$
$$(s_{R0}, subst(term_{HLTG_R}(l'), \varepsilon')) \in term_{LTS_R}$$

Because of the definition of the operational semantics for external choices it holds that

$$\exists\, Q'' \in CSPTerm \,.\, Q \rightarrow subs(\mathcal{C}(Q, Q''))$$
$$\Rightarrow Q \,\square\, R \rightarrow subs(\mathcal{C}(Q, Q'')) \,\square\, R$$

and

$$\exists\, R'' \in CSPTerm \,.\, R \rightarrow subs(\mathcal{C}(R, R''))$$
$$\Rightarrow Q \,\square\, R \rightarrow Q \,\square\, subs(\mathcal{C}(R, R''))$$

This implies that

$$(s, subst(term_{HLTG_Q}(l'), \varepsilon')) \in term_{LTS_P}$$

This implies that the property 4. holds for external choice operators.

The operational semantics of **CSP** implies that

$$ProcRef(Q \,\square\, R) = true$$
$$\Rightarrow ProcRef(Q) = true \vee ProcRef(R) = true$$

Let $Q_s, Q'_s \in CSPTerm$ with

$$Q_s = subst(term_{HLTG_Q}(l_{Q0}), \varepsilon) \wedge$$
$$ProcRef(Q_s) = true \wedge$$
$$(s_{Q0}, Q_s), (s_{Q0}, Q'_s) \in term_{LTS_Q} \wedge$$
$$Q'_s = subs(\mathcal{C}(Q_s, Q'_s))$$

Because property 5. is assumed to hold for l_{Q0} and s_{Q0}, it holds that

$$\Rightarrow \exists\, l'_Q \in L_{HLTG_Q}, \varepsilon' \in Env\;.$$
$$(l_{Q0}, \varepsilon \xrightarrow{b,(\pi,a)} l'_Q, \varepsilon'\ \text{in}\ HLTG_Q \wedge Q'_s = subst(term_{HLTG_Q}(l'_Q), \varepsilon'))$$

Because of the *HLTG* definition of *externalchoice* process terms, this implies that

$$\Rightarrow \exists\, l' \in L_{HLTG_P}\,.(l, \varepsilon \xrightarrow{b,(\pi,a)} l', \varepsilon'\ \text{in}\ HLTG_P$$

The definition of $term_{HLTG_P}$ and because R cannot be affected by applied occurrences of parameters in Q, this implies that

$$Q'_s \square\, subst(R, \varepsilon) = subst(term_{HLTG_P}(l'), \varepsilon')$$

The same argumentation can be used for $ProcRef(R) = true$. This implies that property 5. hold for all location associated with a sequential composition process term.

Appendix B

Mathematical Notations

This appendix provides a reference for the mathematical notations of this thesis. It is structured into a glossary of symbols and a section describing the meta-language used for the description of the algorithms presented in this thesis.

B.1 Glossary of Symbols

This glossary of symbols provides a brief overview of the most important types, functions and operators, which are introduced and used in this thesis. For each notation a brief description and a reference to a page, where the notation is introduced is given. Functions are denoted by trailing empty brackets. CSP operators are not mentioned in this overview, since they have been explained in detail in chapter 2.

B.1.1 Semantics of CSP

Symbol	Meaning	Page
τ	Internal event τ.	15
$\checkmark$	Event signalling successful termination.	16
Ω	A state reached after successful termination.	16
Σ	Alphabet of a $\mathsf{CSP_M}$ specification.	14
$\Sigma^{\checkmark}$	Alphabet of visible events extended by the termination event $\checkmark$.	20
Σ^{τ}	Alphabet of visible events extended by the internal event τ.	20
$\Sigma^{\tau\checkmark}$	Alphabet of visible events extended by $\checkmark$ and τ.	20
Σ^*	Set of all finite sequences of the events in the alphabet Σ.	15
Σ^{ω}	Set of all infinite sequences over Σ.	47

Symbol	Meaning	Page
$\mathcal{C}_P$	Process context of the process P.	23
$\mathcal{C}()$	Resolve process references in a process context.	27
$\alpha()$	Possible actions of a specification in state.	14
$comms()$	This function calculates the set of events that are represented by an event.	21
$subs()$	Replaces identifiers in a process definition by a value	26
$type()$	Determines all possible values, that can be communicated over a channel.	20
$traces()$	Traces of a process in the traces model of the denotational semantics.	37
$refusals()$	Refusals of a process in the stable failures model of the denotational semantics.	41
$failures()$	Failures of a process in the stable failures model of the denotational semantics.	41
$failures_\perp()$	Failures of a process in the failures-divergences model of the denotational semantics.	45
$divergences()$	Divergences of a process in the failures-divergences model of the denotational semantics.	45
$[P]^0$	Initial events of a process.	51
$s \upharpoonright X$	Restrict a trace s to elements of X.	38
$\sqsubseteq_T$	Trace Refinement	50
$\sqsubseteq_F$	Failures Refinement	50
$\sqsubseteq_{FD}$	Failures-Divergence Refinement	50
$\sqsubseteq_{FDR}$	Failures-Divergences-Robustness Refinement	50
$ProcRef$	predicate that states if a CSP process term contains process references, that can be resolved according to its operational semantics.	380

B.1.2   Labelled Transition Systems

Symbol	Meaning	Page
$\mathcal{L}_{LTS}$	Language of Labelled Transition Systems	53
S	Set of states of an LTS.	53
s_0	Initial state of an LTS.	53
$\Sigma^{\tau\checkmark}$	Set of observable actions including $\checkmark$ and τ.	53
$\rightarrow$	Relation between states.	53
$s \xrightarrow{\alpha} s'$	A transition from state s to s' labelled with the event α.	54
$s \xrightarrow{\tau^*} s'$	There exists a number of τ-transitions leading from state s to s'.	54

Symbol	Meaning	Page
$\tau^*()$	Set of all states, that can be reached from one state via τ-transitions.	61
$[s]^0$	Initial actions of a state of an LTS.	54
$\perp$	Indicates during normalisation, that a CSP term or a state is divergent.	61
$\mathcal{A}$	Convex subset of Σ.	61
$term_{LTS}$	A relation that labels each state in the LTS with its associated process terms.	372

B.1.3 High Level Transition Graphs

Symbol	Meaning	Page
τ	An event representing internal decisions, which cannot be observed by the environment.	85
$\checkmark$	An event indicating successful termination.	86
π	An internal event representing process references.	85
Expressions	The set of all CSP_M expressions.	85
Identifier	The set of all identifiers.	85
Conditions	The set of all boolean CSP_M expressions.	85
Variables	The set of all variables.	85
Assignments	The set of all assignments.	86
Events	The set of all CSP_M events except $\checkmark$ and τ.	86
Events$^{\tau\checkmark}$	The set of all CSP_M events including $\checkmark$ and τ.	86
Events$^{\pi\tau\checkmark}$	The set of all CSP_M events including $\checkmark$ τ and π.	86
Locations	The set of all locations that can occur in HLTGs.	86
Transitions	The set of all possible high-level transitions of HLTGs.	86
Σ	Alphabet of a CSP_M specification.	87
$\Sigma^{\tau\checkmark}$	Alphabet of a CSP_M specification including $\checkmark$ and τ.	
$\Sigma^{\pi\tau\checkmark}$	Alphabet of a CSP_M specification including $\checkmark$, τ and π.	89
$\mathcal{L}_{HLTG}$	Language of High level transition graphs.	89
L	A set of all locations of a HLTG.	89
l_0	Initial location of a HLTG.	89
$\mathcal{E}^{\pi\tau\checkmark}$	A set of tuples of events and assignment sets.	89
(l_S, c, E, l_T)	A transition in a HLTG.	84
$\rightarrow_{CA}$	A relation between locations of a HLTG.	89
$conds_{HLTG}$	Set of all conditions in a HLTG.	90
$assigns_{HLTG}$	Set of all assignments in a HLTG.	90
$vars_{HLTG}$	Set of all variables in a HLTG.	90

Symbol	Meaning	Page
$sigma()$	Demotes the set of all possible events of a channel.	87
$channel()$	This function extracts the name of the channel out of an event.	88
$comms()$	This function calculates the set of events that are represented by an event.	88
$vars()$	This function denotes the set of all variables of an expression.	89
$subst()$	Substitutes applied occurrences of parameters by their value.	379
ε	Environment of a high level transition graph.	90
ε_0	Initial Environment of a high level transition graph.	93
Env	The set of all possible environments.	91
Env_{reach}	Reachable environments of a HLTG.	95
Env_l	Reachable environments of a location.	95
$\varepsilon \overset{a}{\rightsquigarrow} \varepsilon'$	Applying an assignment to an environment.	91
$[l]_\varepsilon^0$	Initial actions of a location under an environment.	94
$l \xrightarrow{c,E} l'$	A label from l to l' exists which is labelled with the condition c and a set E of pairs of events and assignment-sets.	92
$l \xrightarrow{c,(\alpha,a)} l'$	It exist a label such that $l \xrightarrow{c,E} l'$ and (α,a) is an element of E.	92
$l,\varepsilon \xrightarrowtail{c,(\alpha,a)} l',\varepsilon'$	It is possible under the current environment, to take the transition from l to l', producing the event α. ε' is the new environment, the assignments of a have been applied to.	92
$l,\varepsilon \xmapsto{\alpha} l',\varepsilon'$	The same as $l,\varepsilon \xrightarrowtail{c,(\alpha,a)} l',\varepsilon'$, but with the extension that the start location of the label must not be l itself. It can also be a location l'' that can be reached from l using only π-labels.	92
$l,\varepsilon \xmapsto{\sigma} l',\varepsilon'$	It exists a path from l to l' through the high level transition graph, where the event-assignment sets (α_i, a_i), that are selected at the labels, are collected in the sequence σ.	92
$l,\varepsilon \xmapsto{\tau^*} l',\varepsilon'$	A path of transitions, containing only τ events in σ.	92
$eval()$	Evaluation of expressions under an environment.	91
$visible()$	Visible parameters of a location	91
$trans()$	Calculates the set of all transitions leaving a location.	93

Symbol	Meaning	Page
$arguments()$	This function denotes the tuple of arguments of a process or function reference or definition.	118
$assigns()$	This function denotes the set of assignments required for evaluating a function or executing a process with the arguments of a function -or process reference.	118
$assigns_{event}()$	This function denotes the set of assignments that are necessary for the variables with defining occurrences of an event e to evaluate to an event $\alpha \in comms(e)$.	120
$events()$	This function denotes the set of tuples (α_i, a_i) of events and assignment sets with α_i being an element of $comms$ of the event and a_i being the set of corresponding assignments for all defining occurrences of variables in that event.	120
$initialInvisibles()$	This function denotes the set of transitions of a HLTG containing only invisible events and having a source location that can be reached from the starting location using only transitions labelled with invisible events.	127
$initialVisibles()$	This function denotes the set of transitions of a HLTG containing visible events and that can be taken directly from the start location or from a location that can be reached using only transitions labelled with invisible events.	128
$newVars()$	This function denotes a set of tuples (v, v') of new variables v' with a unique variable v in $vars_{HLTG}(HLTG_P)$ of a given HLTG $HLTG_P$.	130
$subst_{HLTG}()$	This function replaces variables in a high level transition graph.	131
$subst_{expr}()$	This function replaces variables in an expression.	132
$reassignEvents()$	This function is used to calculate re-assignment event for an external choice subgraph.	132
$reassignTrans()$	This function denotes the set of transitions of a high level transition graph that contain appropriate reassignments.	132
$assign_{rep}()$	This function denotes the set of assignments, that for each element of a set contain an assignment, assigning the element to the variable argument.	134
$term_{HLTG}$	A function that maps each location of the HLTG to its associated CSP term.	372
$\Psi()$	Transformation function that generates a LTS from a HLTG.	378

B.1.4   Synchronisation Terms

Symbol	Meaning	Page
Λ, λ	Synchronisation terms	100
$(HLTG_i, l_i, \varepsilon_i)$	The leaf of a synchronisation term.	100
(Λ, h)	Synchronisation term representing a hiding operator.	100
(Λ, s, Λ)	Synchronisation term representing a parallel or interleaving operator.	100
(Λ, s, h, Λ)	Abbreviation for $((\Lambda, s, \Lambda), h)$.	100
$\lambda \xrightarrow{\alpha} \lambda'$	Interpretation of a synchronisation term.	102
$\lambda[a]$	Adding assignments a to the environment and extending set of variables for all HLTG in λ.	137
$[\lambda]^0$	Initial actions of a synchronisation term.	103
$initials()$	Calculates the possible execution steps in a state of a synchronisation term.	237

B.1.5   Normalisation

Symbol	Meaning	Page
$stable()$	No τ-transitions can be used to leave the current state under the current environment.	151
$refusal()$	Refusal of a stable location under a current environment.	151
$accept()$	Acceptances of a stable location under a current environment.	151
$refusals()$	Refusal sets of locations in normal form high level transition graphs.	151
$refusals_{max}()$	Maximum refusal sets of locations in normal form high level transition graphs.	151
$acceptances()$	Acceptance sets of locations in normal form high level transition graphs.	152
$acceptances_{max}()$	Minimal acceptance sets of locations in normal form high level transition graphs.	152
$normalise()$	On-the-fly normalisation of synchronisation terms.	216

B.2   Meta Language

The algorithms, which are introduced throughout this thesis, are presented based on a meta language, which is introduced in this section. The formalism is based on functional languages, but allows the use of *sideeffects* of functions. Parameters of functions are used as *call by reference* variables, which means that changes to them in a function also affects their values in the calling functions.

In the following the structure of programs is introduced, which provides a basic understanding of the syntax of the meta language. After that several types and functions working on those types are introduced. This functions provide a efficient way to abstract the relevant parts of an algorithm.

B.2.1 Structure of Programs

The algorithms described in this thesis are composed in a meta language defined as follows:

- The general structure of programs is:

  ⟨ program name ⟩ ((⟨ parameter list ⟩))
  BEGIN
     ⟨ declaration part ⟩
     ⟨ instructions ⟩
  END

- The *program name* can be an arbitrary name, which is used to identify a program.

- The *parameter list* is a comma separated list of names of variables, which are used as parameters of the program. The types of the variables are declared in the *declaration part*.

- Each variable occurring in the programs text must be declared in the *declaration part*. Each type is represented by a set of different values, which can be stored in the variable declared with the type. If more than one variables are of the same type, their names are comma separated. More than one variable declaration in a single line are separated by semicolons.

- Instructions are assignments, function calls, if-then-else statements, case switches, while-loops, for-all-loops and return statements. If more than one instruction is written in one line, they are separated by a comma.

  - Comments are included in programs to explain their functionality and are defined as follows:

    (* This is a comment *)

  - Assignments to variables are written by using the '=' as assignment operator.

  - Function calls are all those above defined auxiliary functions and some functions, which are defined in the respective context.

  - An if-then-else statement is defined as usual:

    IF ⟨ boolean expression ⟩ **THEN**
      ⟨ instructions ⟩
    ELSE
      ⟨ instructions ⟩
    FI

– Case switches are semantically identical to nested if-then-else statement. Only the one case is executed, where the value of the specified expression matches the corresponding guard. If no guard matches the value of the expression the default case is executed.

    CASE expression
    ⟨guard$_1$⟩) *(* Execute this branch if expression = guard$_1$ *)*
          ⟨ instructions ⟩
    ⟨guard$_2$⟩) *(* Execute this branch if expression = guard$_2$ *)*
          ⟨ instructions ⟩
    *)   *(* Otherwise execute this branch *)*
          ⟨ instructions ⟩
    ESAC

– While-loops are defined as usual:

    WHILE ⟨ boolean expression ⟩ **DO**
      ⟨ instructions ⟩
    OD

or

    DO
      ⟨ instructions ⟩
    WHILE ⟨ boolean expression ⟩

– A for-all-loop picks one element out of a given set, assigns that element to a variable and iterates the loop. This continues, until all elements have been selected.

    FORALL ⟨ element ⟩ ∈ ⟨ set ⟩ **DO**
      ⟨ instructions ⟩
    OD

– A value of a variable can be returned by using the *return-statement*:

    RETURN ⟨ variable ⟩

B.2.2   Types and Functions

In this section all those types, which are used in algorithms of this thesis are introduced and explained. Additionally all functions, which can be used on those types are also introduced here.

Basic Types

The following types are representing several well known mathematical concepts. These types are required for almost any mathematical expression in the algorithms of this thesis.

BOOL This type denotes a boolean type, consisting only of the elements *true* and *false*. All of the well known mathematical expressions, like equality, negation, conjunct or quantifiers may be used in boolean expressions.

INT This integer type denotes the set of all natural numbers. All of the usual mathematical functions are available for this type.

SET A set is a finite or infinite collection of objects in which order has no significance, and multiplicity is also ignored. All usual mathematical functions on sets are available in this meta language.

TUPLE n-Tuples are groups of objects, which are linked in some way. The tuple of a, b and c is usually denoted (a, b, c) and is in general considered to be ordered. This type is used to represent tuple of any length n.

EVENT Variables of this type represent any CSP event.

TRACE sequence of events $e \in$ EVENTS. All elements of the trace must be elements of the alphabet Σ.

ACCEPTANCE Acceptances are sets of event sets. Therefore all the functions defined for sets can be used for acceptances as well.

ACCSET Acceptance sets are sets of acceptances. Therefore all the functions defined for sets can be used for acceptances as well.

Complex Types

STACK A stack is a data structure which is a special kind of list in which elements may be added to or removed from the top only. The following functions based on stacks are available in this meta language:

- push(stack, element) puts a new element in the specified stack.
- pop(stack) removes the top element from a stack.
- elem = top(stack) returns the top element from the stack, but does not remove it.
- int = size(stack) returns the number of elements on the stack. The return value is of type INT.

QUEUE A queue is a data structure which allows only to add elements to the back of the queue and remove elements only from the front. This datatype implements a first-in-first-out queue. The following functions based on queues are available in this meta language:

- append(queue, element) adds the specified element to the back of the queue.

- element = head(queue) returns the first element of the specified queue. Calling this function on an empty queue in not permitted.
- queue = tail(queue) returns the complete queue without the first element. Calling this function on an empty queue in not permitted.
- int = size(queue) returns the number of elements in the queue.
- bool = empty(queue) returns *true* if the queue contains no elements.

Types for Transition Systems

The following type definitions are used to represent conventional transition systems and their relevant components. These types are based on the definitions of chapter 3.

STATE Elements of this type represents one state in a conventional transition graph.

- $[s]^0$ represents the initial actions of the specified state in a transition graph, which is a subset of the type EVENT.
- bool = stable(s, tg) checks whether the specified state in the transition system is stable. This is the case, if no τ-transitions are leaving the specified state.
- refusals$_{max}$(s) represents a set of refusal sets of a state in a transition graph.

TRANSITION Elements of this type represent transitions in a transition system. Each element is defined to be a triple (s_S, α, s_T), representing the source state of the transition s_S, an event α and the target state of the transition s_T. The following function are defined to change or retrieve the components of the triple:

- s_S(trans) denotes the source state of the specified transition.
- α(trans) denotes the event at the specified transition.
- s_T(trans) denotes the target state of the specified transition.

TG Variables of the type TG are representing a transition system. As specified in definition 3.1, transition systems are an 4-tuple $(S, s_0, \Sigma^{\tau\checkmark}, \rightarrow)$. The functions defined for transition systems can therefore be used to retrieve and change each of the elements of the tuple:

- S(tg) denotes the set of locations of tg.
- s_0(tg) returns the initial state of the transition system tg.
- $\Sigma^{\tau\checkmark}$(tg) is the set of observable actions of tg and the events τ and $\checkmark$.
- $\rightarrow$(tg) is a set of transitions of the type TRANSITION, representing the transitions of tg.

Types for High Level Transition Graphs and Synchronisation Terms

The following type definitions are used to represent high level transition graphs and their relevant components. These types are based on the definitions of chapter 5.

ENVIRONMENT Environments are sets of pairs of variables names and a corresponding value. They contain variable values for every variable of a given high level transition graph. An environment env $\in$ ENVIRONMENT is valid for a location $l \in$ LOCATIONS if it contains valid values for every variable that is visible in l.

Environments are required to evaluate arbitrary expressions, where any previously introduced variables may be used. Therefore the following function can be used:

- eval(expression, env) evaluates the expression, where the value of any free variable is taken from the specified environment.

BINDING Bindings are sets of pairs of variables names and a corresponding value. Those bindings are a subset of the environments, where only those variables are contained, which are visible in the corresponding location. They can be used to evaluate arbitrary expressions, where any previously introduced variables may be used. Therefore the eval(expression, bind) can be used with bindings, too.

LOCATION Elements of this type represents one location in a high level transition graph.

- Locations for normalised graphs are represented as a set of pairs (loc, bind) of a location loc in the unnormalised graph and a corresponding binding bind. Two normalised locations represented by the same set are considered to be identical.
- $[\text{hltgloc}]^0$ represents the initial actions of a location in a high level transition graph, which is a subset of the type EVENT.
- acceptances(hltgloc) represents the acceptance sets of a location in a high level transition graph, which is of the type ACCSET.
- bool = stable(hltgloc, hltg, bind) returns a boolean value, specifying whether a location of a high level transition graph is stable under a given binding. This functions considers all locations reachable by π-events starting at hltgloc for the check.

ASSIGNMENT Assignments are tuple of variables and their assigned expressions. The type ASSIGNMENT denotes a set of assignments, which can be used in high level transition graphs to change values of variables. This type guarantees that each variable is assigned only one expression.

- env' = apply(assign, env) takes a set of assignments and a variable
  of the type ENVIRONMENT to create a new environment which is a copy
  of the original environment but changed in such way, that all assignments are evaluated using only the bindings from env. Therefore the
  execution order of the assignments is not relevant for the resulting
  environment. The function *apply* can be used with bindings, as well.

CONDITION Conditions are boolean expressions, which may contain free variables.
  These expressions can be evaluated under a specified binding using the
  eval() function introduced earlier.

HLTRANS High level transitions are tuples of the relation $\rightarrow_{CA}$ of high level transition graphs. Each tuple represents a transition leading from a source to
  a target location, labelled with a condition and a set of event-assignments-
  pairs. Therefore the following functions are available on transitions to retrieve the single components of the tuple:

  - l_S(tra) denotes the source location of the specified transition.

  - l_T(tra) denotes the target location of the specified transition.

  - c(tra) is an expression representing the condition guarding the label
    of the transition. This expression evaluates to a boolean value.

  - E(tra) represents the set of pairs of events and assignment sets, which
    is labelled to the transition.

HLTG Variables of the type HLTG are representing a high level transition graph. As
  already defined in definition 5.11, high level transition graphs are a tuple
  $(L, l_0, \Sigma^{\pi\tau\surd}, \mathcal{E}^{\pi\tau\surd}, \rightarrow_{CA})$. The functions defined for high level transition
  graphs can therefore be used to retrieve and change each of the elements of
  the tuple:

  - L(hltg) denotes the set of locations of hltg.

  - l_0(hltg) returns the initial location of the high level transition graph
    hltg.

  - $\Sigma^{\pi\tau\surd}$(hltg) is the set of observable actions of hltg and the events π, τ
    and $\surd$.

  - $\mathcal{E}^{\pi\tau\surd}$(hltg) is the set of tuples of events and assignment sets of the
    given high level transition graph.

  - $\rightarrow_{CA}$(hltg) is a set of transitions of the type HLTRANS, representing the
    transitions of hltg.

SYNCTERM Variables of the type SYNCTERM are representing a synchronisation term as defined in definition 5.30. The values of such variable is either a leaf (hltg,l,bind) containing a reference to a location l in a high level transition graph hltg with the current binding bind, or it represents a parallel or hiding operator, in which case the synchronisation term may look as follows: $(\lambda_1, \text{sync}, \lambda_2)$, (λ_1, hide) or $(\lambda_1, \text{sync}, \text{hide}, \lambda_2)$, where λ_1 and λ_2 are of the type SYNCTERM and sync and hide of the type SET containing only elements of the type EVENTS.

Appendix C

A Grammar for CSP

The grammar that is part of the implementation of ClaO is based on version 2.0 of *CSP lexer* and *Yacc grammar for CSP*, released February 1999 by Bryan Scattergood. The following sections display the modified versions of the lexer definition and the grammar file.

C.1 A flex Input File for CSP

```
%{
/*
  CSP lexer

  Version 2.0

  JBS 22 February 1999
*/

#ifdef input
#undef input
#endif
#ifdef unput
#undef unput
#endif
#ifdef yywrap
#undef yywrap
#endif

#define SWITCHFILE switchfile(yytext);
#define BADCHAR    winge("Ignoring character %d", (int) yytext[0]);

// Fetch input one character at a time, maintaining the line counts
// See flexdoc for flex 2.4 for the basic version of this macro

#define YY_INPUT(buf, result, max_size) \
  { \
```

417

```
    int c = getc(yyin); \
    switch(c) \
    { \
      case EOF:  result = YY_NULL; break; \
      case '\n': setline(location.line() + 1); \
                 /* Fall through */ \
      default:   buf[0] = c; result = 1; \
    } \
  }

%}

alpha          [a-zA-Z]
alnum          [0-9a-zA-Z_]
notalnum       [^0-9a-zA-Z_]
comment        "--".*
discard        [_]
w              ({s}|({comment}[\n]))*
nl             {t}*{comment}?[\n]{w}
s              [\ \r\t\n]
t              [\ \r\t]
int            [0-9]+
exp            [efEF]("-"?[0-9]+)?
primes         [']*
uppers         [A-Z]*
proper         ([A-Za-z0-9 _-]|(\[[A-Z]+\]))+
embed          ("embed"{t}(([^e]|("e"[^em])|("em"[^emb])|("emb"[^embd])| \
               ("embe"[^embd]))*)"embed")
%x             block
%x             soak
%x             sblock

%%

{t}                    { }
"assert"               { return ASSERTION; }
"channel"              { return CHANNEL; }
"datatype"             { return DATATYPE; }
"nametype"             { return NAMETYPE; }
"pragma"{t}.*          { return PRAGMA; }
"transparent"          { return TRANSPARENT; }
"external"             { return EXTERNAL; }
"print"                { return PRINT; }
"module"               { return MODULE; }
"include"{t}.*\n       { SWITCHFILE }
{w}"and"/{notalnum}    { BEGIN soak; return AND; }
{w}"or"/{notalnum}     { BEGIN soak; return OR; }
{w}"not"/{notalnum}    { BEGIN soak; return NOT; }
{w}"if"/{notalnum}     { BEGIN soak; return IF; }
{w}"then"/{notalnum}   { BEGIN soak; return THEN; }
{w}"else"/{notalnum}   { BEGIN soak; return ELSE; }
```

```
{w}"let"/{notalnum}       { BEGIN soak; open_sequence(_let);  return LET; }
{w}"within"/{notalnum}    { BEGIN soak; close_sequence(_within); \
                            return IN; }
{w}"lambda"/{notalnum}    { BEGIN soak; return LAMBDA; }
{w}"ldot"/{notalnum}      { BEGIN soak; return LAMBDADOT; }
"CHAOS"                   { return CHAOS; }
"STOP"                    { return STOP; }
"SKIP"                    { return SKIP; }
"true"                    { return KTRUE; }
"false"                   { return KFALSE; }
{alpha}{alnum}*{primes}   { return NAME; }
{discard}                 { return DISCARD; }
{int}                     { return NUMBER; }
{int}"."{int}{exp}        { return NUMBER; }
"("                       { BEGIN soak; open_sequence(_tuple); return OPEN;}
{w}")"                    { close_sequence(_tuple); return CLOSE; }
"<"                       { BEGIN soak; return LT; }
{w}">"                    { return active_sequence(_sequence)? ENDSEQ : GT;}
"{"                       { BEGIN soak; open_sequence(_set); return LBRACE;}
{w}"}"                    { close_sequence(_set); return RBRACE; }
{w}"[["                   { BEGIN soak; open_sequence(_subst); \
                            return LSUBST; }
{w}"]]"                   { close_sequence(_subst); return RSUBST; }
"{|"                      { BEGIN soak; open_sequence(_pbrace); \
                            return LPBRACE; }
{w}"|}"                   { close_sequence(_pbrace); return RPBRACE; }
{w}"["                    { BEGIN soak; return LSQUARE; }
{w}"]"                    { BEGIN soak; return RSQUARE; }
{w}"<="                   { BEGIN soak; return LE; }
{w}">="                   { BEGIN soak; return GE; }
{w}"["{uppers}"="         { BEGIN soak; return REFINED; }
{w}":["{proper}"]"        { return END_PROPERTY; }
{w}":["{proper}"]:"       { BEGIN soak; return PROPERTY; }
{w}"[|"                   { BEGIN soak; return LCOMM; }
{w}"|]"                   { BEGIN soak; return RCOMM; }
{w}"||"                   { BEGIN soak; return PAR; }
{w}"[>"                   { BEGIN soak; return TIMEOUT; }
{w}"[]"                   { BEGIN soak; return BOX; }
{w}"|~|"                  { BEGIN soak; return NDET; }
{w}"\\"                   { BEGIN soak; return BACKSLASH; }
{w}"|"                    { BEGIN soak; return PIPE; }
{w}"|||"                  { BEGIN soak; return INTL; }
{w}"->"                   { BEGIN soak; return ARROW; }
{w}"<-"                   { BEGIN soak; return BECOMES; }
{w}"<->"                  { BEGIN soak; return TIE; }
{w}":"                    { BEGIN soak; return COLON; }
{w}"/\\"                  { BEGIN soak; return INTR; }
{w}"&"                    { BEGIN soak; return GUARD; }
{w}";"                    { BEGIN soak; return SEMI; }
{w}"."                    { BEGIN soak; return DOT; }
{w}"?"                    { BEGIN soak; return QUERY; }
```

```
{w}"!"                  { BEGIN soak; return PLING; }
{w}"@"                  { BEGIN soak; return AT; }
{w}"@@"                 { BEGIN soak; return AS; }
{w}","                  { BEGIN soak; return COMMA; }
{w}"="                  { BEGIN soak; return EQUAL; }
{w}"+"                  { BEGIN soak; return PLUS; }
"-"                     { BEGIN soak; return MINUS; }
{w}"*"                  { BEGIN soak; return TIMES; }
{w}"/"                  { BEGIN soak; return SLASH; }
{w}"%"                  { BEGIN soak; return MOD; }
{w}"#"                  { BEGIN soak; return HASH; }
{w}"=="                 { BEGIN soak; return EQ; }
{w}"!="                 { BEGIN soak; return NE; }
{w}"^"                  { BEGIN soak; return CAT; }
{w}"~"                  { BEGIN soak; return TIES; }
{w}".."                 { BEGIN soak; return DOTDOT; }
{nl}                    { BEGIN soak; return NEWLINE; }
.                       { BADCHAR }

"{-"                    { ++block_comment_count; BEGIN block; }
<block>"{-"             { ++block_comment_count; }
<block>.                { /* Store the character */ }
<block>[\n]             { /* Store the character */ }
<block>{comment}        { /* Ignore end comments in EOL comments */ }
<block>"-}"             { if(--block_comment_count == 0) BEGIN 0; }

<soak>{w}               { }
<soak>"{-"              { ++block_comment_count; BEGIN sblock; }
<soak>""/.              { BEGIN 0; }

<sblock>"{-"            { ++block_comment_count; }
<sblock>.               { /* Store the character */ }
<sblock>[\n]            { /* Store the character */ }
<sblock>{comment}       { /* Ignore end comments in EOL comments */ }
<sblock>"-}"            { if(--block_comment_count == 0) BEGIN soak; }
```

C.2   A bison Grammer for CSP

```
/*
  Yacc grammar for CSP

  2.0 release, February 1999
*/

%{

/* $Id: csp_raw.y,v 1.1.1.1 2002/03/08 13:43:56 uschulze Exp $ */

%}
```

```
%union {
  absy_symbol*  absy;
  absy_stack*   stack;
  expr*         exp;
  proctree*     process;
  id*           ident;
  Field*         field;
  Text          text;
};

%type<stack>          script
%type<stack>          simple_defns
%type<stack>          defns

%type<absy>           simple_defn
%type<absy>           defn

%type<exp>            _bool
%type<absy>           _dotted
%type<exp>            _numb
%type<process>        _proc
%type<exp>            _seq
%type<exp>            _set
%type<exp>            _tuple
%type<absy>           amb
%type<absy>           simple


%type<absy>           check
%type<absy>           fdr_check
%type<stack>          properties
%type<absy>           rbool
%type<absy>           rdotted
%type<absy>           rset
%type<absy>           rnumb
%type<absy>           rproc

%type<absy>           defn_left


%type<absy>           defn_call_left

%type<absy>           seqtype


%type<absy>           vartype

%type<absy>           branch
%type<absy>           type
```

```
%type<stack>          args
%type<absy>           field
%type<absy>           gen
%type<absy>           pair
%type<stack>          targ, targ0
%type<absy>           tie

%type<ident>          name
%type<exp>            literal
%type<text>           pragma, refined
%type<text>           property,end_property

%type<stack>          anys, ranys
%type<stack>          exprs, rexprs, exprs0
%type<stack>          types
%type<stack>          fields
%type<stack>          gens, optgens
%type<stack>          names
%type<stack>          pairs, pairs0
%type<stack>          ties

/* Reserved for future use */

%token MODULE

/* Real tokens */

%token CHAOS STOP SKIP LBRACE RBRACE LPBRACE RPBRACE EQUAL BECOMES TIE DISCARD
%token COMMA DOTDOT PIPE NAME NUMBER NEWLINE KTRUE KFALSE PRAGMA ASSERTION
%token CHANNEL DATATYPE REFINED PROPERTY END_PROPERTY TRANSPARENT
%token EXTERNAL PRINT NAMETYPE

%nonassoc LET IN LAMBDA LAMBDADOT IF THEN ELSE
%nonassoc COLON AT AS
%left BACKSLASH
%left INTL
%nonassoc LCOMM RCOMM LSQUARE PAR RSQUARE
%left NDET
%left BOX
%left INTR
%left TIMEOUT
%left SEMI
%nonassoc GUARD
%right ARROW QUERY PLING WHERESQ
%right DOT
%left OR
%left AND
%left NOT
%nonassoc EQ NE LT LE GT GE ENDSEQ
%left PLUS MINUS
%left TIMES SLASH MOD
```

```
%left HASH
%left CAT
%left TIES
%token OPEN CLOSE LSUBST RSUBST

%start begin
%%

begin           : script
                                { remember(reverse($1)); }
                ;
script          : newlines0 defns newlines0
                                { $$ = $2; }
                | newlines0
                                { $$ = DefnList(); }
                ;


simple_defns    : simple_defn
                                { $$ = cons($1, DefnList()); }
                | error
                                { $$ = DefnList(); }
                | simple_defns newlines simple_defn
                                { $$ = cons($3, $1); }
                | simple_defns newlines error
                                { $$ = $1; }
                ;


defns           : defn
                                { $$ = cons($1, DefnList()); }
                | error
                                { $$ = DefnList(); }
                | defns newlines defn
                                { $$ = cons($3, $1); }
                | defns newlines error
                                { $$ = $1; }
                ;




simple_defn     : defn_left EQUAL any
                                { $$ = dTerm($1, $3); }
                | NAMETYPE name EQUAL seqtype
                                { $$ = dType($2, $4); }
                | TRANSPARENT names
                                { $$ = dTran($2); }
```

```
                      | EXTERNAL names
                                      { $$ = dExtern($2); }
                      ;




defn              : ASSERTION check
                                      { $$ = dAssert($2); }
                      | CHANNEL names COLON seqtype
                                      { $$ = dChan($2, $4); }
                      | CHANNEL names
                                      { $$ = dChan($2); }
                      | DATATYPE name EQUAL vartype
                                      { $$ = dData($2, $4); }
                      | PRINT any
                                      { $$ = dPrint($2); }
                      | pragma
                                      { $$ = dPragma($1); }
                      | simple_defn
                                      { $$ = $1; }
                      ;

/*
any : _proc | _dotted | _bool | _numb | _set | _seq | _tuple | amb ;
expr        : _dotted | _bool | _numb | _set | _seq | _tuple | amb ;
bool        : _bool | amb ;
dotted      : _dotted | amb ;
numb        : _numb | amb ;
proc        : _proc | amb ;
seq         : _seq  | amb ;
set         : _set  | amb ;
*/




defn_call_left  : name
                                      { $$ = $1; }
              | defn_call_left OPEN CLOSE
                                      { $$ = sApply($1, SyntaxList()); }
              | defn_call_left OPEN anys CLOSE
                                      { $$ = sApply($1, $3); }
              ;


defn_left       : defn_call_left
                                      { $$ = $1; }
                  | _tuple
                                      { $$ = $1; }
```

```
                | _seq
                                { $$ = $1; }
                | _set
                                { $$ = $1; }
                | _dotted
                                { $$ = $1; }
                | _bool
                                { $$ = $1; }
                ;


type            : _set
                                { $$ = $1; }
                | OPEN type COMMA types CLOSE
                                { $$ = sTupleType(cons($2, $4)); }
                | name
                                { $$ = $1; }
                | name OPEN types CLOSE
                                { $$ = sApply($1, $3); }
                ;


rbool           : bool
                                { $$ = $1; }
                ;


rdotted         : dotted
                                { $$ = $1; }
                ;


rnumb           : numb
                                { $$ = $1; }
        ;


rproc           : proc
                                { $$ = $1; }
                ;


rset            : set
                                { $$ = $1; }
                ;


check           : bool
                                { $$ = $1; }
                | fdr_check
```

```
                              { $$ = $1; }
                  ;



fdr_check         : rproc refined rproc
                          { $$ = sRefine($1, $2, $3); }
                  | rproc end_property
                          { $$ = sProperty(singleton_list(PropPair($1, $2))); }
                  | rproc property properties
                          { $$ = sProperty(cons(PropPair($1, $2), $3)); }
                  | NOT fdr_check
                          { $$ = sNot($2); }
                  ;



properties        : rproc
                          { $$ = cons(PropPair($1, Text()), PropList()); }
                  | rproc end_property
                          { $$ = cons(PropPair($1, $2), PropList()); }
                  | rproc property properties
                          { $$ = cons(PropPair($1, $2), $3); }
                  ;



_bool             : NOT bool
                                  { $$ = sNot($2); }
                  | bool AND bool
                                  { $$ = sAnd($1, $3); }
                  | bool OR bool
                                  { $$ = sOr($1, $3); }
                  | expr EQ linkexpr
                                  { $$ = sEq($1, $3); }
                  | expr NE linkexpr
                                  { $$ = sNe($1, $3); }
                  | expr LE linkexpr
                                  { $$ = sLe($1, $3); }
                  | expr LT linkexpr
                                  { $$ = sLt($1, $3); }
                  | expr GE linkexpr
                                  { $$ = sGe($1, $3); }
                  | expr GT linkexpr
                                  { $$ = sGt($1, $3); }
                  | KTRUE
                                  { $$ = sTrue(); }
                  | KFALSE
                                  { $$ = sFalse(); }
```

```
                      | _bool AS bool
                                    { $$ = sAs1($1, $3); }
                      ;


_dotted               : expr DOT expr
                                    { $$ = sDot($1, $3); }
                      | _dotted AS dotted
                                    { $$ = sAs2($1, $3); }
                      ;


_tuple                : OPEN any COMMA anys CLOSE
                                    { $$ = sTuple(cons($2, $4)); }
                      | _tuple AS any
                                    { $$ = sAs1($1, $3); }
                      ;


_numb                 : literal
                                    { $$ = $1; }
                      | numb PLUS numb
                                    { $$ = sPlus($1, $3); }
                      | numb MINUS numb
                                    { $$ = sMinus($1, $3); }
                      | MINUS numb
                                    { $$ = sUminus($2); }
                      | numb TIMES numb
                                    { $$ = sMul($1, $3); }
                      | numb MOD numb
                                    { $$ = sMod($1, $3); }
                      | numb SLASH numb
                                    { $$ = sDiv($1, $3); }
                      | HASH seq
                                    { $$ = sLength($2); }
                      | _numb AS numb
                                    { $$ = sAs1($1, $3); }
                      ;


_proc                 : PAR gens AT LSQUARE rset RSQUARE proc %prec AT
                                    { $$ = sRpar($2, $5, $7); }
                      | NDET gens AT proc                    %prec AT
                                    { $$ = sRndet($2, $4); }
                      | BOX gens AT proc                     %prec AT
                                    { $$ = sRbox($2, $4); }
                      | INTL gens AT proc                    %prec AT
```

```
                              { $$ = sRintl($2, $4); }
      | SEMI gens AT proc                      %prec AT
                              { $$ = sRseq($2, $4); }
      | LCOMM rset RCOMM gens AT proc          %prec AT
                              { $$ = sRshare($2, $4, $6); }
      | TIE gens AT LSQUARE exprs RSQUARE proc
                              { $$ = sRlinkset($2, $5, $7); }
      | LSQUARE ties optgens RSQUARE gens AT proc
                              { $$ = sRlinkseq($2, $3, $5, $7); }
      | proc BACKSLASH set
                              { $$ = sHide($1, $3); }
      | proc INTL proc
                              { $$ = sIntl($1, $3); }
      | proc LCOMM rset RCOMM proc
                              { $$ = sCPar($1, $3, $5); }
      | proc LSQUARE rset PAR rset RSQUARE proc
                              { $$ = sPar($1, $3, $5, $7); }
      | proc LSQUARE ties optgens RSQUARE proc
                              { $$ = sLink($1, $3, $4, $6); }
      | proc NDET proc
                              { $$ = sNdet($1, $3); }
      | proc BOX proc
                              { $$ = sBox($1, $3); }
      | proc TIMEOUT proc
                              { $$ = sTimeout($1, $3); }
      | proc INTR proc
                              { $$ = sInterrupt($1, $3); }
      | proc SEMI proc
                              { $$ = sSeq($1, $3); }
      | bool GUARD proc
                              { $$ = sGuard($1, $3); }
      | dotted fields ARROW proc
                              { $$ = sPick($1, $2, $4); }
      | dotted ARROW proc
                              { $$ = sPick($1, FieldList(), $3); }
      | STOP
                              { $$ = sStop(); }
      | SKIP
                              { $$ = sSkip(); }
      | CHAOS OPEN rset CLOSE
                              { $$ = sChaos($3); }
      | _proc AS proc
                              { $$ = sAs3($1, $3); }
      ;


_seq          : begseq targ0 optgens endseq
                              { $$ = sSeqComp($2, $3); }
      | seq CAT seq
                              { $$ = sCat($1, $3); }
```

```
                    | _seq AS seq
                                { $$ = sAs1($1, $3); }
                    ;



_set                : LBRACE targ0 optgens RBRACE
                                { $$ = sSetComp($2, $3); }
                    | LPBRACE exprs0 optgens RPBRACE
                                { $$ = sESetComp($2, $3); }
                    | _set AS set
                                { $$ = sAs1($1, $3); }
                    ;



amb                 : IF rbool THEN any ELSE linkany
                                { $$ = sCond($2, $4, $6); }
                    | LET simple_defns newlines0 IN any
                                { $$ = sLet(reverse($2), $5); }
                    | LAMBDA args LAMBDADOT any
                                { $$ = sLambda($2, $4); }
                    | BACKSLASH args AT any
                                { $$ = sLambda($2, $4); }
                    | amb AS any
                                { $$ = sAs2($1, $3); }
                    | simple
                                { $$ = $1; }
                    | DISCARD
                                { $$ = sDiscard(); }
                    ;



simple              : name
                                { $$ = $1; }
                    | simple OPEN args CLOSE
                                { $$ = sApply($1, $3); }
                    | simple LSUBST pairs0 optgens RSUBST
                                { $$ = sSubst($1, $3, $4); }
                    | OPEN any CLOSE
                                { $$ = sParen($2); }
                    ;


/********************/
/* Type expressions */



seqtype             : type
```

```
                                        { $$ = $1; }
                        | type DOT seqtype
                                        { $$ = sCross($1, $3); }
                        ;




vartype         : branch
                                        { $$ = $1; }
                        | vartype PIPE branch
                                        { $$ = sChoice($3, $1); }
                        ;




branch          : name
                                        { $$ = sBranch($1); }
                        | name DOT seqtype
                                        { $$ = sBranch($1, $3); }
                        ;


/*******************/
/* Small components */



args            :
                                        { $$ = SyntaxList(); }
                        | anys
                                        { $$ = $1; }
                        ;




field           : QUERY expr
                                        { $$ = fInput($2); }
                        | QUERY expr COLON rset
                                        { $$ = fInputFrom($2, $4); }
                        | PLING expr
                                        { $$ = fOutput($2); }
                        ;




gen             : expr BECOMES expr
                                        { $$ = gDraw($1, $3, "<-"); }
```

```
                | expr COLON expr
                                { $$ = gDraw($1, $3, ":"); }
                | bool
                                { $$ = gFilter($1); }
                ;




tie             : rdotted TIE rdotted
                                { $$ = sTie($1, $3); }
                ;




pair            : rdotted BECOMES rdotted
                                { $$ = sMaplet($1, $3); }
                ;




targ            : anys
                                { $$ = tEnum($1); }
                | rnumb DOTDOT
                                { $$ = tUpFrom($1); }
                | rnumb DOTDOT rnumb
                                { $$ = tBetween($1, $3); }
                ;




targ0           :
                                { $$ = tEnum(SyntaxList()); }
                | targ
                                { $$ = $1; }
                ;

/***********************************/
/* Simple tokens, wrapped to syntax */


name            : NAME
                                { $$ = sName(yytext); }
                ;
```

```
literal        : NUMBER
                              { $$ = sNumber(yytext); }
               ;



pragma         : PRAGMA
                              { $$ = Text(yytext); }
               ;



refined        : REFINED
                              { $$ = Text(skip_white(yytext)); }
               ;

property       : PROPERTY
                              { $$ = Text(skip_white(yytext)); }
               ;

end_property   : END_PROPERTY
                              { $$ = Text(skip_white(yytext)); }
               ;

/* Patch for ambiguity of > */



begseq         : LT
                              { begin_sequence(_sequence); }
               ;


endseq         : ENDSEQ
                              { end_sequence(_sequence); }
               ;


/* Trivial lists of items */

anys           : ranys
                              { $$ = reverse($1); }
               ;

ranys          : any
                              { $$ = cons($1, SyntaxList()); }
               | ranys COMMA any
                              { $$ = cons($3, $1); }
               ;
```

```
exprs           : rexprs
                        { $$ = reverse($1); }
                ;

rexprs          : expr
                        { $$ = cons($1, SyntaxList()); }
                | rexprs COMMA expr
                        { $$ = cons($3, $1); }
                ;

exprs0          :
                        { $$ = SyntaxList(); }
                | exprs
                        { $$ = $1; }
                ;

types           : type
                        { $$ = cons($1, SyntaxList()); }
                | type COMMA types
                        { $$ = cons($1, $3); }
                ;

fields          : field
                        { $$ = cons($1, FieldList()); }
                | field fields
                        { $$ = cons($1, $2); }
                ;

gens            : gen
                        { $$ = cons($1, GenerateList()); }
                | gen COMMA gens
                        { $$ = cons($1, $3); }
                ;

optgens         :
                        { $$ = GenerateList(); }
                | PIPE gens
                        { $$ = $2; }
                ;

names           : name
                        { $$ = cons($1, SyntaxList()); }
                | name COMMA names
                        { $$ = cons($1, $3); }
                ;

newlines        : NEWLINE newlines0
                ;

newlines0       :
                | newlines
```

```
              ;

pairs         : pair
                              { $$ = cons($1, SyntaxList()); }
              | pair COMMA pairs
                              { $$ = cons($1, $3); }
              ;

pairs0        :
                              { $$ = SyntaxList(); }
              | pairs
                              { $$ = $1; }
              ;

ties          : tie
                              { $$ = cons($1, SyntaxList()); }
              | tie COMMA ties
                              { $$ = cons($1, $3); }
              ;
```

Bibliography

[1] High-level Petri Nets – Concepts, Definitions and Graphical Notation. Final Draft International Standard ISO/IEC 15909 Version 4.7.1, ISO/IEC, 2000.

[2] Rajeev Alur. Timed automata. In *Computer Aided Verification*, pages 8–22, 1999.

[3] Peter Amthor. *Structural Decomposition of Hybrid Systems*. PhD thesis, University of Bremen, 1999.

[4] Henrik Reif Andersen. Lecture notes for 49285 advanced algorithms e97. Technical report, Department of Information Technology, Technical University of Denmark, October 1997.

[5] S.D. Brookes. *A mode, for communicating sequential processes*. PhD thesis, Oxford University, 1983.

[6] Randal E. Bryant. Graph-based algorithms for Boolean function manipulation. *ieeetc*, C-35(8):677–691, 1986.

[7] Randal E. Bryant. Symbolic boolean manipulation with ordered binary decision diagrams. *ACM Computing Surveys*, 24(3):293–318, 1992.

[8] Randal E. Bryant. Binary decision diagrams and beyond: Enabling technologies for formal verification. In *IEEE/ACM International Conference on Computer Aided Design, ICCAD, San Jose/CA*, pages 236–243. IEEE CS Press, Los Alamitos, 1995.

[9] Bwolen Yang, Randal E. Bryant, David R. O'Hallaron, Armin Biere, Olivier Coudert, Geert Janssen, Rajeev K. Ranjan, and Fabio Somenzi. A performance study of BDD-based model checking. In *Formal Methods in Computer-Aided Design*, pages 255–289, 1998.

[10] Rachel Cardell-Oliver. Conformance tests for real-time systems with timed automata specifications. *Formal Aspects of Computing*, 12(5):350–371, 2000.

[11] Rachel Cardell-Oliver and Tim Glover. A practical and complete algorithm for testing real-time systems. In *FTRTFT*, pages 251–261, 1998.

[12] Eleftherios Koutsofios and Stephen C. North. *Drawing graphs with dot.* AT&T Bell Laboratories, Murray Hill, NJ, November 1996.

[13] Formal Systems (Europe) Ltd, Oxford, England. *Failures-Divergence Refinement*, May 1997.

[14] H.j. Genrich. Predicate/Transition Nets. *Lecture Notes in Computer Science, Springer-Verlag*, Vol. 254:207–247, 1987.

[15] Matthew Hennessy. *Algebraic Theory of Processes*. MIT Press Series in the Foundation of Computing. MIT Press, 1988.

[16] Thomas A. Henzinger. The theory of hybrid automata. In *11th Annual IEEE Symposium on Logic in Computer Science (LICS 96)*, pages 278–292, 1996.

[17] Charles A. R. Hoare. *Communicating Sequential Processes*. Prentice Hall, 1985.

[18] Jacques Loeckx and Kurt Sieber. *The Foundations of Program Verification*. B.G. Teubner, Stuttgart, 2nd edition edition, 1987.

[19] Jan Peleska and Cornelia Zahlten. *RT-Tester 4.1 User Manual*. Verified Systems International GmbH, April 2002.

[20] Jan Peleska, Peter Amthor, Sabine Dick, Oliver Meyer, Michael Siegel, and Cornelia Zahlten. Testing reactive real-time systems. Technical report, University of Bremen, AG Betriebssysteme, Verteilte Systeme, 1998.

[21] K. Jensen. *Coloured Petri Nets, Volume 1: Basic Concepts, Second Edition*. Springer-Verlag, 1997.

[22] Markus Dahlweid and Uwe Schulze. Symbolic execution of csp specifications – csp interpreter applying the operational semantics. Master's thesis, University of Bremen, Department of Computer Science, 1998.

[23] Oliver Meyer. *Structural Decomposition of Timed CSP and its Application in Real–Time Testing*. PhD thesis, University of Bremen, 2001.

[24] Robin Milner. *A Calculus of Communicating Systems*. Springer LNCS 92, 1980.

[25] Robin Milner. *Communication and Concurrency*. Prentice Hall Series in Computer Science. Prentice Hall, 1989.

[26] Brian Nielsen. *Specification and Test of Real-Time Systems*. PhD thesis, Aalborg University, Department of Computer Science, April 2000.

[27] Jan Peleska. Formal methods and the developement of dependable systems. Habilitationsschrift Bericht Nr. 9612, Christian-Albrechts-Universität Kiel, Institut für Informatik und praktische Mathematik, December 1996.

[28] G. D. Plotkin. A structural approach to operational semantics. Technical Report DAIMI FN-19, University of Aarhus, 1981.

[29] Rajeev Alur and David L. Dill. A theory of timed automata. *Theoretical Computer Science*, 126(2):183–235, 1994.

[30] A. W. Roscoe. *The Theory and Practice of Concurrency*. Prentice Hall Series in Computer Science. Prentice Hall, 1998.

[31] A.W. Roscoe. *A Classical Mind - Essays in Honour of C.A.R. Hoare*. Prentice Hall, 1994.

[32] A.W. Roscoe. *Theory and Practice of Concurrency*. Prentice Hall, 1997.

[33] RTCA/DO-178B. *Software Considerations in Airborne Systems and Equipment Certification*, December 1992.

[34] Bryan Scattergood. *A Parser for CSP*, December 1992.

[35] Bryan Scattergood. *Tools for CSP and Timed CSP*. PhD thesis, University of Oxford, 1995.

[36] Bryan Scattergood. *The Semantics and Implementation of Machine-Readable CSP*. PhD thesis, University of Oxford, 1998.

[37] Bernd-Holger Schlingloff. Partial state space analysis of safety-critical systems. Habilitationsschrift, University of Bremen, June 2001.

[38] Steve Schneider. An operational semantics for timed csp. http://www.comlab.ox.ac.uk/oucl/publications/tr/TR-1-91.html.

[39] Steve Schneider. *Concurrent and Real-time Systems – The CSP Approach*. John Wiley & Sons, Ltd, 2000.

[40] Neil Storey. *Safety-Critical Computer Systems*. Addison Wesley Longman Limited, 1996.

[41] Andrew S. Tanenbaum. *Modern Operating Systems*. Prentice Hall, 2nd edition edition, 2001.

[42] Thomas H. Cormen, Charles E. Leiserson, Ronald L. Rivest, and Clifford Stein. *Introduction to Algorithms*. MIT Press, 2nd edition edition, 2001.